Remains of the Everyday

Remains of the Everyday

A Century of Recycling in Beijing

———

Joshua Goldstein

UNIVERSITY OF CALIFORNIA PRESS

University of California Press
Oakland, California

Library of Congress Cataloging-in-Publication Data

Names: Goldstein, Joshua, 1965– author.
Title: Remains of the everyday : a century of recycling in Beijing / Joshua
  Goldstein.
Description: Oakland, California : University of California Press, [2021] |
  Includes bibliographical references and index. | Description based on
  print version record and CIP data provided by publisher; resource not
  viewed.
Identifiers: LCCN 2020021298 (print) | LCCN 2020021299 (ebook)
  | ISBN 9780520971394 (epub) | ISBN 9780520299801 (cloth)
  | ISBN 9780520299818 (paperback)
Subjects: LCSH: Refuse and refuse disposal—China—Beijing—
  20th century. | Recycling (Waste, etc.)—China—Beijing—20th century.
  | Recycled products—China—Beijing—20th century. | Recycled
  products—Government policy—China—Beijing—20th century.
  | Beijing (China)—Social conditions—20th century.
Classification: LCC HD9975.C63 (ebook) | LCC HD9975.C63 G65 2021
  (print) | DDC 363.72/820951156—dc23
LC record available at https://lccn.loc.gov/2020021298
LC record available at https://lccn.loc.gov/2020021299

Manufactured in the United States of America

30   29   28   27   26   25   24   23   22   21
10   9   8   7   6   5   4   3   2   1

CONTENTS

ILLUSTRATIONS

FIGURES

MAPS

TABLES

ACKNOWLEDGMENTS

Acknowledgments are to books like externalities are to industrial economies: they register the air, water, soil, microbial fertilizing goodness, everything uncountable and boundless that makes production possible at all, let alone meaningful. And hopefully in this case (unlike in the case of our current economy), the product's delivery has not resulted in such wonton pillaging of the externalities that enabled it that it has destroyed the goodness that made it possible. In other words, I owe a lot of thanks and gratitude to a lot of people.

I started working on trying to understand the world of Beijing's migrant recyclers back around 1999, and the more I have learned over the years, the more I realize how indispensable my first guides in this research were. Tang Can, a marvelous scholar at the Chinese Academy of Social Sciences, shared her work with me and introduced me to several uniquely insightful advisers, including Boss Lu, an ambitious entrepreneur from Gushi, and Fu Hongjun, a brilliant old hand in the state recycling sector and a generous guide to archival sources who gave me a photocopy of the handwritten memoir that serves as the single most valuable written source for this project. From our first meeting in the early 2000s, Peking University professor Tong Xin gave me helpful advice and support and since then has been a vital provider of critique and insight. She also introduced me to a young scholar named Han Ling, who connected me to the tremendously generous managers of Haidian's recycling company, and to a wonderful research assistant, Chen Tianming, who from 2004 to 2007 helped get me through interviews with officials when I became lost, tongue-tied, or awkward. Professor Mao Baohong was always supportive and encouraging and linked me up with several scholar activists who would become my greatest inspiration and collaborators. It was through him I met

Mao Da, a discard studies scholar and leading voice for waste reduction in China. And through Mao Da I met Chen Liwen. Liwen is one of a kind. Her ethical idealism and ferocious honestly are an endless source of inspiration; she has helped me beyond measure to understand what is really happening on the streets and in the daily lives of recyclers—no one has taught me more. Liwen also brought together a core of volunteers at Green Beagle who made me feel welcome, and out of care for the environment and respect for the humanity of Beijing's migrant recyclers, spent a week in the winter cold with Liwen and me collecting social surveys. Chen Liwen also introduced me to many other supportive and insightful folks over the years, not least her parents and family, who took me in over Chinese New Year.

In arranging fieldwork my superhero was Shi Yaojiang, not just for his skills as a fixer and networker who could open doors in notoriously unwelcoming places, but also for his impassioned acumen as a social scientist and advocate of rural folks. Kao Shih-yang shared his photos and his intellectual spark in both writing and conversation; he introduced me to the fascinating world of construction waste as well as to amazing Pakistani food at Chungking Mansions. Adam Minter has been a font of wisdom; no one knows the workings of our "junkyard planet" more comprehensively. Adam was the first one to urge me to come in off the street and experience the international scrap conference scene, and thanks to Kent Keiser for making it more affordable to attend those conferences. Josh Lepawsky has involved me in his work on discarded electronics, which has been invaluable to my understanding of that aspect of the scrap world; he is a model and meticulous researcher and unbelievably generous with his ideas and resources. Yvan Schulz is another wonderful researcher, whose work informs many of the ideas in part 3 of this book. Madeleine Yue Dong has been a friend in need and scholarly adviser since I started down this path.

Many others have shared their stories, their ideas, their time, and their kindness with me as I've pursued this project over the years. Wang Shude, whom I only met very late in this project, walked me through the day-to-day workings of the Mao-era BRC; I would not have been able to write part 2 of this book without his help. I am grateful to Wan Jing, Ye Wa, and Wang Shaomin for sharing their stories of Mao-era recycling with me. Xu Yijie helped me at the archive and schooled me in the policy discourse on industrial pollution in the 1970s. Wang Jiuliang and Wang Jing have both generously allowed me to use their art here; I cannot come close to doing justice to their work and hope readers will seek it out. Virginia Moore clued me in on the global shipping business while her family were so welcoming, *heimisch* in the very best way. Victor Ho offered more than a room of my own whenever I was in Beijing; he's been a constant companion in trying to make sense of China and of life for over thirty years. Zhang Qin has become a lifelong friend; back in the previous century she first tried to explain Zhu Rongji's tax reforms to me, and two decades later she was still taking time out from work to help me figure things out—in the meantime she raised a lovely son. And I am forever grateful to the scrap collectors, traders, and processors who invited me into their stalls, trucks, and factories over the years. My understanding of their trade does not hold a candle to their expertise; but none that I came to know well wished to be named in these pages.

Researching is one thing, writing another. There are several folks without whom the writing simply would not have gotten done, foremost among them Brett Sheehan. Thanks also to the rock-solid folks at University of Southern California's East Asian Studies Center program (especially Grace Ryu and Alex Eloriaga); Janet Chen, who provided great scholarly input and a needed kick in the head; Zsuzsa Gille for her wonderful critiques and encouragement (all failures to follow advice signal only my lack of creative ability to do so); Sigrid Schmalzer for catching many screwups and suggesting many fixes; an anonymous reviewer who provided great advice; Archna Patel, who was incredibly patient guiding me through the editing process; Reed Malcolm for his support; Sharon Langworthy for excellent copyediting; and Bill Nelson for designing maps.

Thanks also to colleagues over the years who have read and commented on work related to this book or clued me into useful ideas or sources, including (in the hodgepodge disorder of un-standardize-able treasures): Nick Bartlett, Kyung Moon Huang, Deborah Davis, Jen Altehenger, Robin Ingenthron, Ben Steuer, Michael Chang, Susan Fernsebner, Karl Gerth, Jack Wills, Alana Boland, Du Huanzheng, Sonya Lee, Paul Lerner, Adam Liebman, Victor Shih, Dorothy Solinger, and Charlotte Furth. I am especially grateful to Keisha Brown, Liu Haiwei, and Wang Luman, among the many PhD and MA students who, over the years, have endured this grumpy and befuddled guy who keeps blaming his disorganization and incoherence on some never-finished manuscript. It also was hugely helpful to be surrounded in my day-to-day work by supportive colleagues, from Franklin & Marshall College to USC and places in between, including the USC History Department faculty one and all, Lori Rogers, Sandra Hopwood, Simone Bessant, Clay Dube, Karen Seat, Sharon Moran, Doug Anthony, Kevin Martin, Abby Schrader, Maria Mitchell, Richard Mack, Jim Cook, and Justin Hantz. In these pages all errors, inconsistencies, and failures to make adequate sense are my own.

I am grateful to various organizations for the funding and support I received over the years to pursue this research. I spent eight months in Beijing affiliated with Peking University with funding and support from the American Council of Learned Societies and Social Science Research Council. Over the years USC funded a few summertime trips for research and provided a Zumberge Fellowship to work on formulating this project; and the Social Sciences and Humanities Research Council of Canada helped underwrite some of the fieldwork for chapter 7. Along the way I wrote several papers; snippets and the occasional paragraph from one article in *Modern China* and from two different edited volumes (*Everyday Modernity in*

China [University of Washington Press, 2007]; and *Polarized Cities: Portraits of Rich and Poor in Urban China*, edited by Dorothy Solinger [Rowman and Littlefield, 2019]) can be found woven into chapters 6 and 7 of this book.

Thanks to Grandma and Buppa, Bella, and Papajack for always coming to the rescue, braving the interminable traffic to collect Abe and Dal from aftercare and then figuring out how to feed two picky children who have no dietary preferences in common (except for ice cream, and, as of 2020, mapo tofu!). You four have been our rock. Thanks also to Clem, Alexa, Sharon Lee, and Dajana (and your families) for always being there, especially when I would take off for months to do research.

My version of emotional pseudo-stability would have been impossible without Jennifer, Bob, Dina, Tiny, Neil, Jeff, Sharon, Sue, Pops, Dawn and Lali, Cheryl, Eva, Sam, Dan, Merlin, Owen, Julia, Gwen, Billy, Miche, the Altverse Gang (especially Danny and Edrick), and Eng, amazing USC Daycare and Franklin Elementary teachers, and many others too, some long out of touch, some no longer here.

Abram and Dalya, thank you for taking care of each other (most of the time), for growing into such amazing people (all of the time), and for the sweet nudges and noodges of encouragement you gave this grumbling crank. And Cyn, words just fail. I could catalog your weekly feats of solo parenting over the last decade, or your genius holiday trip plans, or your knack for getting me through panic attacks, but it would never sum up. Finally, I can start paying you back; it will take me a lifetime, and I can't wait.

ABBREVIATIONS

BAN   Basel Action Network
BRC   Beijing Recycling Company (1965–2000)
BSC   Beijing Scrap Company (1957–64)
CCP   Chinese Communist Party
CEIP   circular economy industry park
CMRA   China Non-Ferrous Metal Recycling Association
CR   Cultural Revolution (1966–76)
CRRA   Chinese Resource Recycling Company
CSPA   China Scrap Plastic Association
DEEE   discarded electrical and electronic equipment
EPIP   environmental protection industry park
EPR   extended producer responsibility
GLF   Great Leap Forward (1958–61)
MEE   Ministry of Ecology and Environment
MRF   municipal recycling facility or materials recovery facility
NDRC   National Development and Reform Commission
O2O   online to offline
OCC   old corrugated cardboard
OECD   Organisation for Economic Co-operation and Development
OEM   original equipment manufacturer
PBDE   polybrominated diphenyl ether
PET   polyethylene terephthalate
PLA   People's Liberation Army
PPP   public private partnership

PVC	polyvinyl chloride
RCUB	resource circular use base
SMC	All-China Federation of Supply and Marketing Cooperatives
SOE	state-owned enterprise
VAT	value-added tax
WDEPIP	Wenan Dongdu EPIP
WEEE	waste electrical and electronic equipment
WtE	waste to energy (incineration)
ZEPIP	Ziya EPIP

Introduction

Chances are you are reading this sentence thinking, "OK, this book might be interesting in an obscure, geeky kind of way. But why should I care about the history of recycling in Beijing, when I don't really know that much about the history of recycling anywhere?" If you had asked that question in 2017, this paragraph would have answered: "Because odds are that the plastic yogurt container you just threw into your recycling bin at home is going to end up in China, probably in a village where processing it will contribute to some peasant family's livelihood while simultaneously polluting their village water and soil. This book will help explain to you how and why that happens." But if you are reading this sentence now (around 2020 or so), and I have to assume you are, then the answer is because this author currently has no idea where your plastic containers or used cardboard boxes are going. They very possibly are not being recycled at all but rather are heading to a landfill or incinerator in your area. And China is the reason the fate of your recycling is now so precarious. China, the uncontested world capital for almost every form of recyclable waste (plastic, paper, copper, aluminum, etc.) for the last twenty years, abruptly closed its ports to "foreign trash" in 2018, and today urban waste managers throughout the world are still scrambling to figure out what to do with your yogurt container. And it is my hope that by relocating your yogurt container's fate in the context of Chinese urban history, you will come to regard both in a different light.

This is a book about wastes—mainly, but not exclusively, postconsumer wastes—and their reuses as mapped out across a city over a century of change. It is motivated by the urge to highlight the contributions of neglected populations (waste workers, recyclers, scavengers) to the material processes that make urban life possible. Over

MAP 1. Google map compiled by artist and filmmaker Wang Jiuliang. Each numbered "pin drop" designates an illegal waste-dumping site he discovered while exploring the Beijing area ca. 2010. He eventually documented more than 450 individual waste dump sites. For a larger reproduction of the image, and many more images related to this book, visit the Scalar site Remains of the Everyday, Kipple Yard, https://scalar.usc.edu/works /remains-of-the -everyday-kipple -yard/. Image used with permission.

the century under study here, Beijing underwent an urban metabolic sea change, from being a city of declining prestige where every conceivable material resource was reused, repurposed, or repaired and little was discarded—indeed where very little was even thought of as "garbage" or "waste"—to becoming a megalopolis so overwhelmed by practices of disposability that it is perceived, based on some pretty compelling evidence, as 垃圾围城 (laji weicheng)—a city besieged by garbage (see Map 1).

As niche as a history of recycling in a single city might seem, this is not simply a "micro" history focused on a handful of people. A hundred years ago, reuse and recycling work (antique hunters, wastepaper pickers, night soil collectors, used clothes dealers, etc.) combined into arguably the most pervasive economic sector in Beijing, employing far more workers than either the government or industrial factories. A century later, recycling remained a huge area of employment, with an estimated 150,000–300,000 recyclers in Beijing, while nationally the recycling sector employed 3.3–5.6 million, not including a million or two more working in processing.[1] Traversing this century of political and economic revolutions, the dogged persistence of recyclers in finding value and a means of survival through what others rejected speaks to their creativity and hard work, while at the same time their cagey relationship with municipal authorities raises a host of political, ethical, and in recent years, environmental policy dilemmas.

This study attempts to map the circulation of postconsumer materials, following how they have been discarded or sold, transported or dumped, and then disposed of or processed. Building from this material history and geography, other variables shaping these circulations arise: What kinds of materials are being consumed, by whom, and for what purpose? Who performs the labor of collecting, sorting, sanitizing, disposing of, and reprocessing these wastes, used goods, and scrap, and what are the political-economic relationships between consumers, waste workers, and the state that does or does not intervene in their interactions? How do these processes affect the environments in which they occur, helping constitute the dichotomous and shifting status of urban and rural? What values, economic and otherwise, are realized through these processes? How do these processes and values affect, and how are they affected by, a larger context of national and international resource and financial flows?

Over the last century waste recovery and secondhand goods markets have been integral to Beijing's economic functioning and cultural identity, and acts of recycling have figured prominently in the ideological imagination of what constitutes modernity and modern citizenship, as well as the lack thereof. On the one hand, the Chinese state has repeatedly promoted voluntary recycling as an expression of exemplary citizenship—from the patriotic scrap drives to help China "surpass Britain and overtake America" in steel production during the Great Leap Forward (GLF; 1958–60), to the residential recycling campaigns that helped Beijing secure its bid to host a "green" Olympics in 2008. On the other hand, informal

recyclers—from the destitute junk traders of the Republican era (1912–49) hus-
tling cast-offs and counterfeits on the street, to the migrant recyclers salvaging
bottles, cans, and cardboard in Beijing's neighborhoods today—have been pinned
as intractably unmodern, undisciplined, unsanitary. One famous figure, night soil
collector turned model labor hero Shi Chuanxiang (1915–75), arguably China's
most famous recycler of the twentieth century (night soil was recycled into fertilizer by composting), managed in his lifetime to embody both extremes on this
citizenship spectrum. He went from being the denigrated lackey of a night soil
"lord" during the Republican era, to being a lionized model of socialist sanitation in the late 1950s, to being vilified as a traitor during the Cultural Revolution
(CR; 1966–76). Shi Chuanxiang's main rival for the title of most famous Chinese
recycler would probably be Zhang Yin, the CEO of Nine Dragons Paper company,
who in 2006 was the first woman to top the list of the richest people in China.

The city of Beijing today is a towering megacity that marries high-rise architecture with urban sprawl to accommodate over twenty-one million residents. Aside
from the palace complex of the Forbidden City in the eye of this construction
hurricane, little remains of the city's trademark alleys (hutong) or city walls of a
century ago. Yet throughout the last century of economic and political revolutions, the recycling and scrap trades present a consistent reality: the vast majority
of recycling workers toiled at the bottom of the urban socioeconomic hierarchy,
even in the most radical moments of the Mao Zedong era. It might seem axiomatic that waste work should be low valued or even denigrated; the materials
scrappers handle are, after all, generally lower in value than "goods" or "new"
raw materials. Yet the waste and scrap trades also provide services (removing
unwanted matter) as well as yield products (secondhand goods, manufacturing
inputs), so rating their relative economic valuation as low is not necessarily logical
or inevitable. Yet their undervaluing persists. For instance, as discussed in chapter
1, when the Beiping city government under the Nationalists attempted to take
over the night soil/fertilizer industry, it offered only 50 yuan per "shit route" even
though the average market value for a collection route averaged six times that
sum. Later, when the Chinese Communist Party (CCP; the Party) rose to power
through a revolution that proclaimed the ideal of liberating and bringing dignity
to the exploited peasant and laboring classes, it promulgated policies, discourses,
and political spectacles intended to manifest appreciation of waste/scrap workers. Yet throughout the Mao period the labor associated with scrap and waste
remained undervalued and, if not despised, certainly unembraced, as scrap and
waste work units found it nearly impossible to recruit employees. Predictably,
the Maoist government's response to finding few young workers willing to enter
the waste sector was to blame the denigration of the trades on "backward" thinking from the "old feudal society," but as we will see, the persistent undervaluing
of waste- and scrap-related labor was embedded in the structures of the planned

economy. Entering the twenty-first century, as China plunged into reform era prosperity and postconsumer recycling became a booming, multi-billion-dollar business, state media representations of urban migrant scrap collectors typically painted them as uneducated and unethical polluters who disrupted urban order and appearance, and most city policies directed at the sector now aim to prohibit or eliminate them. This is true despite obvious evidence that for the last thirty years informal recyclers have made great contributions to China's cities, diverting 15–30 percent of China's municipal solid wastes from landfills and incinerators, not just keeping the city cleaner but saving city governments millions every year in waste management expenses.

This book unfolds less as narrative than as exploration. I hope, as the reader moves through these pages, that what seem like negligible differences in words or processes—reuse versus recycle, "waste good" (废品 feiwu) versus "waste material" (废旧物资 feijiu wuzi)—unfold to reveal layers of significance connected with larger social processes, economic systems, or "waste regimes."[2] Attending to wastes can reveal how the micro and macro economies and ecologies of daily life intertwine, hopefully nudging readers to notice the myriad ways in which our own small acts of disposal (leaving that old calculator in a drawer for ten years; tossing the apple core in the green bin; saving the newspaper for a papier-mâché project; posting an old bike on Craig's List) relate to the larger systems we inhabit. Like others working in the emerging field of discard studies, I believe that understanding our waste practices in these larger contexts is essential if we are to address the environmental crisis we are currently facing.

THEORIES OF WASTE

One might well ask, "Why bandy about theories of waste? Why not just collect the data and analyze them?" Statistics can surely be important in analyzing the political economy of wastes. For instance, Josh Lepawsky shows that just a single North American facility smelting copper for electronics manufacturing generates 902,792 tons of waste acid each year, 1.8 times the total weight of all electronic wastes (e-waste) exported from the United States annually (estimated at 489,840 tons). Those statistics are crucial for Lepawsky to make a reality-based argument that in the electronics sector the biggest problem environmentally clearly lies in manufacturing, not disposal.[3]

But statistics also have their limits, particularly when it comes to waste. In part this is because data on waste are so scarce. Historical statistics on waste trades are thin, accounts are largely anecdotal, and waste workers in most societies have little voice and leave few records of their lives. Contemporary wastes generate more data, but huge swaths are statistical blanks. In *Secondhand: Travels in the New Global Garage Sale*, Adam Minter shows that the contemporary trade in secondhand goods—books, furniture, child car seats, appliances, clothing, and cell phones—is a huge global business, but it is conducted in cash and barter, almost always off book and outside the domain of gross domestic product (GDP) measurement.[4] Data on what is easily the biggest and most polluting realm of contemporary waste, industrial waste, are politically sensitive, and most corporations as a rule guard waste data from public scrutiny unless legally required to divulge the information.

But lack of data is not the only obstacle; just as important is that data and measurements do not necessarily bring clarity to waste problems. As Brian Wynne argues in his groundbreaking analysis of hazardous waste policy, chasing after scientific precision can prove detrimental or distracting because wastes are exceptionally heterogeneous and indeterminate. By indeterminate Wynne means that even if we know what is in a physical aggregation of wastes, we typically know very little about how these substances degrade, react with each other, or affect living things; we use thousands of chemicals in manufacturing but have only researched the environmental and health effects of a fraction of them.[5] And even when we have information, it is often not convertible or comparable across contexts. Incinerators emit cancerous dioxin, while landfills leak climate-warming methane; how can we compare and choose between them? While there are many references to statistics in the pages ahead, one argument that emerges from this history is that efforts to "know" wastes (discern what they are, categorize, and measure them) are fraught processes that themselves are often central to the puzzle of waste's political-economic construction. Hence the need for a little theory.

I begin, as so many have, with anthropologist Mary Douglas's cogent insight that dirt "is matter out of place. . . . [It is] the by-product of a systematic ordering and classification of matter, in so far as ordering involves rejecting inappropriate elements."[6] In defining dirt as "matter out of place," Douglas asserts that dirt indicates the existence of a system or taxonomy from which it is ejected. Accordingly, what we categorize as dirt/waste will vary over time, culture, and political-economic system. These changes are quite evident in this history; we will frequently find particular kinds of "matter" moving in and out of the "waste" pile (human feces, for instance, will change from valued fertilizer to worthless refuse). Douglas's crucial point is that what we consider to be dirt/waste are objects that disturb the categories, systems, and spatial schematics by which we organize our societies and economies. Her fundamentally spatial framing is also apropos: waste is rarely where we want it to be. Controlling the placement of wastes is thus a central element of how we handle and define them. Think of all the tools we use in the effort to gather wastes and move them elsewhere—dustpans, baskets, diapers, carts, sealed trucks, pipes—all means to take the waste "away." But of course there is no "away," no "permanent sink" where wastes disappear or are quarantined from our biosphere. In reality, we invariably shift wastes (when they do not evade us) into marginal or liminal spaces, siting landfills, incinerators, and toxic waste dumps at the outer edges of cities or in impoverished and racially marginalized communities.

Waste's liminality is not just apparent spatially but also conceptually. Recycling in particular is distinctly liminal in relation to value, straddling the threshold between negative and positive valuations at once. We may agree with Zsuzsa Gille and K. A.Gourlay in defining waste as "material we failed to use," but the past tense of that phrase is an important proviso, particularly when it comes to recycling and scrap picking, in which one person's trash becomes another one's treasure.[7] Risa Whitson, in her work on urban scavenging in Buenos Aires, finds—not surprisingly—that whether one values waste or not often correlates to one's class position; "Defining and categorizing material as waste not only creates waste, but functions to constitute social identities, places, and boundaries as well. . . . [T]he fact that material may simultaneously be both valueless and valuable is an expression of social inequality."[8] Josh Lepawsky and Kate Parizeau nicely condense several dimensions of waste's liminality:

> The uncertain nature of waste is apparent in the multiple positions it holds in the urban sphere in any given moment: it is a negative good whose removal costs money, and whose absence is economically valued; it is a potential economic resource, and thereby subject to contestable property rights; and it is a source of symbolic meaning (as an indicator of anti-social behaviour, as a material linkage between citizen and service provider, etc.). In this way, it can be said that waste has liminal status in society: it is both valued and worthless, legitimate yet unrecognized, absent and present.[9]

I add that recycling/reuse practices articulate waste's liminality and disrupt many of our organizing categories in particular ways:

- *Production/consumption:* Recycling stands assumptions about production and consumption on their head. By taking the waste produced by consumption and turning it into an input for production, recycling reverses the assumed relationship between these processes, demonstrating that in fact consumption is also a form of production. Our economic models generally are linear ones, moving from production through distribution and consumption and supposedly ending in disposal, but recycling shows this assumed linearity is often far from a sufficient description of our economic processes.
- *Public and private property:* Wastes consistently blur or complicate laws, customs, and spaces of ownership. Who has the rights and responsibilities over wastes is a highly contested issue, particularly in municipal administration.
- *Knowledge and risk:* Waste is destabilizing in that it is often illegible. Part of what makes objects "wastes" as opposed to "goods" is that they are deemed of little worth, which from a regulatory standpoint means not worth a large outlay of resources and expenses. Compare the logistics of getting groceries

into your home (each good you purchase has been packaged, priced, taxed, and often, in this era of online purchasing, has had its path of production and distribution followed in great detail) with those dedicated to picking up your trash. Thus, in many respects our knowledge of wastes is fuzzy and limited, introducing a number of risk factors, both environmentally (toxics in the trash) and economically. It is not an accident that the waste trades are often sites for shady dealing; the opacity of waste lends itself to such possibilities. Hence the waste/recycling trades evince a persistent tension not just with regulatory systems, but also with market idealizations based on transparency of information flows.

Finally, wastes are simultaneously socioeconomic and discursive constructs and physical substances, and both discursive and material processes shape and constrain how any particular waste functions in a given time and place.

The question, then, is within this field of tensions and possibilities, how do various forces of agency—political (government regulations), economic (cost-benefit analysis), social (identities vis-à-vis labor), and material (physical qualities of the waste/scrap itself)—shape the meanings and dispositions of wastes and recycling? How do these forces determine on what side of various liminal divides specific wastes will fall at specific times and places in history? If that all sounds too abstract, the questions can be put more concretely: Should a used TV be deemed an internationally tradeable good or a prohibited hazardous waste, and what historical and geopolitical forces will decide how this question is answered, thereby shaping who wins or loses in managing used TVs? Is a bottle picked out of a curbside recycling bin by a waste picker hers to trade for a refund, or property she stole from the state? Zsuzsa Gille offers the term "waste regimes" as an analytical lattice to characterize how sets of social, political, representational, and economic conditions interact to shape these processes and dispositions in particular times and places. I, like many others, have borrowed Gille's term and refer to the idea of waste regime, though often with less analytical precision than the term might properly command.[10]

There are many differences between the histories of recycling and reuse in China and the United States, but comparisons are still fruitful to explore. One idea I use comes from Susan Strasser's *Waste and Want*, a wonderful history of postconsumer waste practices in the United States in which she describes an ensemble of practices she calls "the stewardship of objects."[11] Imagine it is 1890 and a Pennsylvanian family's scorched tin kettle is leaking. A tin peddler comes by on his horse-drawn cart and, in return for a sack of duck feathers given him by the matron of the house, patches the kettle with scrap from a crushed tin cup he got in trade down the road. The crushed tin cup's fate is constrained by the socioeconomic systems (handicraft labor, resource scarcity), cultural practices (an ethic of thrift), and the material potentials of tin. Strasser dubs these practices of repair, reuse, preservation, and frugality "stewardship of objects." Into the twentieth century, and especially after World War II in the United States, such practices of stewardship gradually declined. As industrial production pumps out unprecedented quantities of consumer goods, discarding potentially useable goods or materials from the home went from being frowned upon as profligate to being encouraged as properly hygienic, modern, fashionable, and economically rational—indeed, economically stimulating. Repairing a broken tin kettle or cup was hardly even possible, let alone economically sensible by the 1970s, so such kettles were tossed into the trash bin, to be landfilled or perhaps "recycled," meaning melted down into commodity tin for some industrial process. The form and function of the tin kettle may have changed little over a century, but the infrastructures of its production, collection, repair, and disposal became radically different.

By the middle of the twentieth century the United States was becoming dominated by consumer practices of disposability. Strasser sketches these developments too, but analysis of these practices goes back before her work, with some of the most influential earlier critiques credited to Vance Packard's *The Waste Makers* of 1960.[12] Packard argued that the flood of trash in the twentieth-century United States (what Joshua Reno would refer to as "mass waste") did not just spontaneously emerge because consumers felt like throwing out more stuff.[13] Habits of increased disposal did not just appear; they needed to be taught. The consumption practices that generate mass waste are the creation of capitalist industries working to maximize profit through techniques of design and marketing that compel increased disposal and accelerated consumption. What Packard called "planned obsolescence"—the designing of consumer goods to break, become outmoded, or become undesirable in a short period of time—is just one set of techniques obliging a shift to disposability by consumers. Other methods include creating fashion cycles, changing technologies to make older goods incompatible with newer products, and of course all kinds of advertising to drive consumer demand and hence the production of waste. Once infrastructures for handling mass wastes become naturalized parts of urban life and disposal a habit, industry then designs products premised on the assumption of disposal, inventing an array of products for convenient wasting: water bottles, disposable shavers, single-use products, and so forth.

The historical path sketched in the preceding paragraphs—shifting from an economy built around the stewardship of objects to one based on disposability—has, for better or worse, become what is generally referred to as "development." J. B. R. Whitney provides a similar overview of this trajectory, but rather than focusing on the social habits of material consumption, he sketches this historical process in terms of urban metabolism by describing the changing disposition of wastes, or as he calls them, "unused outputs" (UOs):

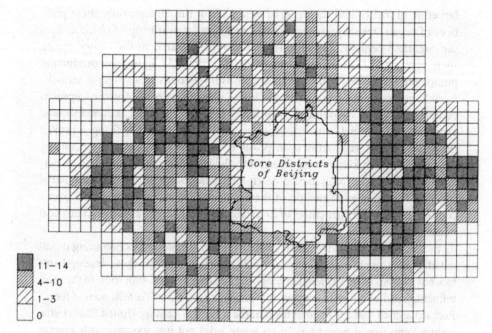

MAP 2. Waste sites surrounding Beijing, based on Landsat images produced in the mid-1980s. The darker the square, the more waste dumps in that area. From J. B. R. Whitney, "The Waste Economy and the Dispersed Metropolis in China," based on an unpublished Beijing Municipality Environmental Protection Agency report, 1985.

When the price of labor is cheap relative to the price of goods, whether manufactured or not, the cost of collecting, sorting and reprocessing UOs is low compared to the value of the material itself, [then] a great majority of UOs will be recycled and reused in the economy. Under such conditions, UOs become internalized and are part of the economy itself. As incomes rise and labor costs become relatively higher than material costs, the price of raw materials and manufactured goods declines. There are fewer incentives to recycle and reuse UOs; and because they are no longer internalized they become divorced from the economic system and become externalities whose costs are borne by the environment and by society as a whole.[14]

As part 1 describes, Republican-era Beijing did indeed internalize its UOs, with human excrement internalized as fertilizer in the ring of farms proximate to the city, and other material UOs intensively reused and recycled, mostly inside the city proper. Very little waste/trash was generated. And though the economic logic and mechanics under the Mao era planned economy will not correspond perfectly to the previously mentioned assumptions, those decades did see the steady increase of UOs becoming externalities, as became apparent in 1983 when satellite images of the city revealed it was ringed by waste dumps. Wang Jiuliang's similar aerial view thirty years later reveals that these externalized UOs only kept growing in immensity (see Map 2).

This book toggles between the micro/social frame of daily acts of material use and disposal (stewardship or disposability) and the macro/spatial frame of urban and rural material flows (cycling of materials as resources or dumping them as wastes) and attempts to sketch how they are connected and disconnected. Moving between the macro and micro levels are the workers, entrepreneurs, and skilled specialists of the waste and reuse trades, turning the millions of daily micro acts into the macro processes that shape the material history of Beijing.

SOME CLARIFICATIONS ABOUT COMMON WORDS AND A PIZZA BOX

Today we tend to treat *garbage* and *recycling* as conjoined twins; chances are your recycling receptacle sits next to your garbage can. But contemporary recycling's historical precursors are usually more closely related to practices of handicraft (mending, tinkering, smelting) than to sanitation. In fact, in the long century covered in this history, it was only in 2017 that the Chinese state started to merge the bureaucratic management of recycling and garbage; prior to that, both the Republican and the People's Republic of China (PRC) states managed garbage through sanitation bureaus, while recycling was overseen by bureaus of commerce and industry. Both were forms of solid waste and both were collected, at times sorted, reused, or disposed of, and so forth, but the agencies responsible for managing these activities were completely distinct.

I use the words *trash* and *garbage* interchangeably, and generally that is how I translate 垃圾 (*laji*). Garbage is composed of objects and materials the identities and physical integrity of which we no longer seek to maintain and so muddle together and amass for removal, say, weekly on garbage pickup day. The things in the trash or garbage are treated as if they have lost their identities as discrete objects, at least in the eye of the disposer (the picker might well remove them from their trashy milieu and treat them differently, turning them into "recyclables").

In contrast, *junk* (how I typically translate 破烂 [*polan*, lit. "broken rotted"] and sometimes also 废品 [*feipin*, lit. "waste good"]) is items and materials that, even if we no longer find them useful, retain a certain identity and integrity. Perhaps we see them as still potentially salvageable, emotionally or economically valuable, but for whatever reason junk ends up retaining some of its identity despite being ejected from our spheres of use. At times I use *junk* very broadly, to capture an array of items from highly valuable antiques to rusty metal cans, but what connects such hugely different items is that they are approached as items with identities (even if badly damaged) that can be (more or less accurately) appraised for distinct use and exchange value, whereas items of garbage/trash, unless somehow otherwise organized and processed, have lost their identities and cannot be so used/appraised.

We might imagine *recyclables* (废旧物资 *feijiu wuzi*, lit. "waste material") as occupying a position between trash and junk: bits of materials—paper, metal, glass, wood—that are no longer seen as retaining their identity as objects but are seen as having identities as kinds of material. The noun recyclable of course arises from the verb "to recycle," so the object is being defined by the process for which it will be used.[15] For my purposes here, recycling is often contrasted to reuse: in recycling the old goods/scraps are melted, shredded, or otherwise processed to the point that their previous identity as an object is lost and they function only as a kind of material, whereas in reuse the good is mended, repaired, or repurposed so that it retains some of its past identity. Sometimes the lines between reuse and recycling are quite clear (will this used shirt be mended to be worn again or shredded into fiber to make paper?), but especially in economies dominated by the stewardship of objects and handicrafts the lines can be quite blurry (this used shirt will be cut into swaths and used to make a mop or patch a coat). In fact, there is a whole realm of tinkering skills and acts of creative repurposing blurring the line between "recycling" and "reuse," which is often where the most economically dynamic and creatively vivid practices occur.

Finally, I use *scrap* as something of a catchall term indicating materials and items that are typically not of much use to the producer but are seen as having a value for reuse, handicraft, or recycling processes. Junk and recyclables are both forms of scrap, though it is worth noting that the word *scrap* emphasizes valuing the material from which an item is made often above the identity of the item itself. Of course, the lines between these terms are fuzzy and at times overlapping (garbage pickers salvage scrap and junk from the trash, and highly valuable junk can, when contaminated, decayed, or misplaced, turn into garbage), so at times I let them be rather vague, and in other instances I try to highlight distinctions. Perhaps at this point a short contemporary example of looking at recycling through these various questions and ideas might help make these generalization a bit more concrete.

Let's say I live in Los Angeles in 2020 and I want to discard a pizza box that has some melted cheese stuck to it. Los Angeles has single-stream recycling, so I can just toss it into the recycling bin, and in theory it should end up being turned into material for another cardboard box, thereby saving some forest, water, and energy resources. But if my pizza box is too cheesy (or too wet, greasy, or saucy), then it might get rejected at the municipal recycling facility (MRF) and will be landfilled (it might turn from recycling into trash). If my cheesy box does make it all the way to the paper mill, the people at the mill will be unhappy—it will either increase their environmental management costs (upping their levels of polluted water and wastes that need handling) or damage the quality of their product. And if by chance a piece of broken glass got into that pizza box while it was in the recycling truck on the way to the MRF (a common problem in single-stream recycling systems), it might end up wrecking some of the paper factory's equipment to boot.

Perhaps I am engaging in aspirational recycling (misidentifying trash as recycling), and my road to recycling hell will be paved with cheesy pizza boxes. Still, I will probably never suffer any worldly consequences from my virtuous-minded sins; as long as the city of Los Angeles can find a buyer who does not balk at buying and processing the city's old corrugated cardboard (OCC) stream, I can effectively remove the cheesy pizza box from my physical and memory space. And from about 2000 to 2017, that is what most Angelenos did, in large part because Chinese paper brokers and processors were willing buyers. But when the Chinese government decided to crack down on the quality of imported OCC in 2018, my LA MRF lost its dirty pizza box buyers, and it suddenly became an LA problem. Maybe the MRF owner will find a Vietnamese or Malaysian processor who buys OCC full of cheesy boxes, and we can let them deal with the risks? If not, my pizza box might have nowhere to go but a landfill. So, everyone should just clean every pizza box and yogurt container, and then processors would buy them? But that is both inefficient (having each household wash out each of their yogurt containers uses lots of water) and unlikely (mobilizing and educating everyone in a city to take the time to clean all their recyclables, then making sure no recycling trucks shatter glass into their paper scrap, etc., would be administrative miracles).

What is the solution now for my cheesy pizza box? There is no simple one, because the problem is not simple. We think about recycling as if it were mainly an act of a resident throwing items in a container, but that is only a small piece of it. Recycling is a process of matching a waste resource with a use, and in contemporary systems almost always an industrial use; without an end user/buyer there are no environmental savings from replacing virgin inputs with recycled ones. Recycling in industrial capitalism is actually a series of relationships between companies and industries in which they use your free social labor as a link in their commodity chain. Only a small part of completing that chain efficiently is contingent on the consumer's act of disposal; product design, manufacturing and shipping processes, and a panoply of consumer habits shaped by infrastructures and marketing histories play at least as big a role as the detail of how a consumer takes out the trash. So, what we experience as simple (behavioral) questions—Should I categorize this pizza box as trash or recycling? Should I clean out the cheesy bit?— are actually infrastructure system questions involving an array of industrial and municipal government calculations and processes, in which our specific disposal behaviors play a small part.

My hope is that by analyzing how such small links function in larger waste and recycling economies across Beijing history, we will see how everyday material use and disposal practices reveal aspects of the historical context we might not otherwise notice. While my description was mainly a kind of economic analysis, one could just as easily use the pizza box as a tool of social analysis. What if, instead of using single-stream recycling, a person came to my house and bought my recyclables, sorting and weighing each kind of material? This is more or less how recycling has worked in Beijing for decades. I would put the pizza box aside as something to sell, and the collector might look at my cheesy box and either clean it out before she weighs it (she does not want to pay me for my cheese, just for the box) or possibly refuse to take it. Or maybe I just give her all my recyclables for free because I know she'll make more money that way, and I appreciate her work. Or maybe I'll clean out the cheese myself before I sell it to her because she scolded me about this last week. In any event, the social process of disposal is now quite different. When I dropped my box into a bin on the curb, I could feel virtuous for having recycled while avoiding the reality that waste management involves labor and often rather stark socioeconomic inequities; but I cannot avoid a social encounter with an independent collector. Indeed, the collector might wear a uniform and do other things to try to lessen my sense of these inequities if she perceives them as making her customers uncomfortable to the detriment of her business. Or as Mihn T. N Nguyen found was often the case in Vietnam, she might explicitly talk about how little money she can make from a cheesy box and emphasize her vulnerability as a business tactic to get me to sell my recyclables at a lower price.[16] As becomes clear throughout this book, the politics of how waste workers are perceived by publics and governments has always been pivotal to how policies governing urban metabolic processes have unfolded over the last century.

OVERVIEW OF THE BOOK

Part 1 sketches Republican Beijing's postconsumer waste and recycling flows, dividing that portrait into two chapters. The first focuses on materials of concern to the city's newly established Sanitation Bureau, namely garbage and night soil, while chapter 2 provides an overview of the city's multifaceted economic engagement with recycling and reuse. Sources for these chapters include gazetteers, documents from the Beijing Municipal Archives, oral histories and memoirs as well as the work of historians Ruth Rogaski, Shi Mingzheng, Du Lihong, and Madeleine Yue Dong. There are several recurring themes: how recycling lays claim to spaces in defiance of urban planning and property laws; the distress expressed by elites and the state at laborers' seeming refusal to embrace the behaviors of sanitary citizenship; and a description of an economy profoundly engaged in reusing discards and recycling wastes to the point that very few material flows were actually treated or disposed of as wastes. My hope is that the reader comes to sense that the practices of repair, mending, repurposing, and salvage—which were so central to the economic survival and vibrancy of the city—do not fit comfortably with and are arguably conceptually disruptive of the categories we tend to use to analyze economic activity today, namely *production, consumption,* and *disposal/waste.* My hope, in sum, is to denaturalize those dominant economic categories and to raise the possibility that perhaps other practices (repair, maintenance, tinkering, etc.) might be frames worth using in evaluating economies, not just past but present as well.

Part 2 focuses on the Mao era and is based primarily on archival documents, propaganda posters, newspaper articles, and oral histories and is informed by several studies of Mao-era urban and economic administration, above all Dorothy Solinger's *Chinese Business under Socialism.*[17] Chapter 3, "The Rural Exile of Urban Wastes," describes that portion of the urban waste/recycling system—night soil and trash collection—that fell under the management of the Environmental Sanitation Bureau. The CCP successfully took over and rationalized these networks, a feat earlier municipal governments had failed to accomplish, removing hundreds of thousands of tons of accumulated trash from the city, mechanizing trash collection, and taking state control over the night soil sector that had been in the hands of rapacious "shit lords." But in the process tensions emerged between the government's intentions to turn wastes into useful resources on the one hand and the sanitary regime of urban management, which attempted to exile wastes from the city as quickly as possible, on the other, tensions that eventually ruptured the metabolic cycle and turned once-useful night soil into unused sewage.

The Mao-era state's acquisition and reorganization of the scrap and reuse trades, covered in chapters 4 and 5, was remarkably successful in achieving its main goals: absorbing the myriad small businesses into a regulated supply and marketing network and directing valued scrap materials—copper, ferrous, paper fiber, glass, rubber—toward industrial uses. The recycling sector was consolidated into and became the responsibility of the Beijing Recycling Company (BRC), which operated not under the Sanitation Bureau but under commercial organs, including the All-China Federation of Supply and Marketing Cooperatives (SMC), the Ministry of Commerce, and the Ministry of Materials. In part, the successful transformation of Republican Beijing's recycling world into a state-owned system was grounded in the promotion of postconsumer recycling as an exemplary patriotic socialist activity, captured through campaigns and statistics demonstrating the huge collective gains the nation could achieve if all citizens did their small bit of thrifty recycling. But it also did not hurt that the BRC paid residents a little cash for their scrap and trade-ins, just as scrap collectors had done for decades during the Republican era. Of course the new order had its profound problems, from the disastrous backyard steel-smelting campaign of the Great Leap Forward to unmanaged industrial pollution into the 1970s. But there is also no doubt that scrap played a pivotal role in keeping China's industry operating despite the country being almost completely cut off from international trade flows of crucial industrial resources like copper, paper pulp, and rubber for much of the Mao era.

The field of Mao-era environmental history is fairly new, and at best this book makes only a fragmentary contribution to that field. But in looking to engage that field, I was struck by how much of it clashes with the general historical trajectory I lay out here. While my evaluation could be summed up as ambivalent edging toward critical, many landmark authors in the field (Vaclav Smil, Elizabeth Economy, Judith Shapiro) are flatly condemnatory. This is not to say that the Mao-era state was a leading light of environmental protection. It was not, and very little of how economic development was imagined or undertaken weighed environmental concerns at all. Rampant wasting of resources during the GLF, waves of deforestation during the CR, uncontrolled industrial emissions, and denials that industrial pollution even existed—these are undeniable phenomena, some of which can even be linked to Mao's pronouncements. Based on these legacies, Judith Shapiro has summed up the era's environmental legacy as *Mao's war against Nature*, while Elizabeth Economy in *The River Runs Black* points to Mao's "The foolish old man who moved mountains" essay as evidence of mass mobilization figuring nature as the enemy.[18] But this depiction strikes me as selective. The sketches of recycling and urban waste management I trace are much more in line with what Sigrid Schmalzer finds in *Red Revolution, Green Revolution* and her more recent studies of local campaigns for terrace farming in the Mao era. She finds that engaging the public, especially when it also involved mobilizing local knowledge, actually meant working within environmental conditions rather than trying to obliterate them.[19] I am not arguing that the Maoist state was environmentally friendly or highly self-conscious, but the Mao-era policies related to urban waste and scrap—night soil collection for fertilizer, municipal solid waste (MSW) separation schemes for composting and brick making, an extensive propaganda and administrative infrastructure for industrial and consumer recycling and reuse—were explicitly aimed to conserve resources and were not implacable in the face of local suggestions and insights. Were all the mass campaigns to recycle scrap or separate urban trash to make bricks and compost successful? Certainly not. Were the ubiquitous calls to reduce waste and conserve resources effective in reducing environmental destruction? That depends: compared to what? Looking just at the picture of urban waste arisings, the limited form of consumerism promoted by the Mao-era state and its promotion of habits to conserve, reuse, and recycle household items produced far less waste than we find in today's economy of disposability. Mao-era policies certainly left a cumulative legacy of environmental damage, but standing in 2020 looking back over the last century, it seems indisputable that in the reform era industry has wrought environmental destruction and damage on the collective health of communities on a scale that dwarfs the despoiling of the Mao era.

This brings us to part 3, in which source materials go from a relative trickle to a deluge. Beginning in the 1980s, several Chinese government ministries began publishing policy and technical journals on waste and scrap resource management, with titles like *Scrap Ferrous*, *Resource Recycling and Reuse*, and *Solid Waste Resourcification*. The last forty years also offer a galaxy of journalistic and newspaper accounts, scholarly articles in both Chinese and English, international trade reports and statistics, and most recently, blogs. Also, from 1999 to 2018 I spent more than two years in the field (between one and two months nearly every summer from 1999 to 2007, seven months in 2008 on a generous grant from the American Council of Learned Societies, and three- to seven-week stints in 2010, 2013, 2018) visiting recycling markets, interviewing and observing informal recyclers, traveling to reprocessing villages outside Beijing (in Wenan, Baoding, Jinghai), meeting with local and national level officials and experts in Beijing's state-run recycling sector, and conducting surveys of Beijing informal recyclers in 2010.

Chapter 6, "A Tale of Two Cities (1980–2003)," describes how market reforms ended up creating two separate systems of urban recycling, one state owned, the other informal. The state-owned network grew out of the Mao-era BRC infrastructure, but throughout the 1980s and 1990s the system underwent a series of reforms that gradually allowed for free trading between units, market pricing, wage differentials and incentives, outside contracting, and so forth. Although the late 1980s seemed like a golden age, with the BRC turning a healthy profit, the good times were short lived. By the mid-1990s an informal network of migrant recyclers was outcompeting the BRC, and by the end of that decade the BRC's network was effectively bankrupt and vestigial (and this was true not just for Beijing but for nearly every city in China). All the while, Beijing's waste stream was aflood with postconsumer and construction scrap; by 2000 recycling in Beijing was generating well over $1 billion in annual profits and gainfully employing 100,000 migrants, who effectively and efficiently monopolized the recycling trades despite state efforts to ban their markets, stop their neighborhood collection, and deport them from the capital. The chapter closes around 2003, when state offices seemed to reach a consensus that the battle against the "guerrilla army" (游击队 *youjidui*) of migrant recyclers was hopeless and instead began to turn a relatively blind eye to their activities, save during particularly important national or international events, such as the Beijing Olympics.

Chapter 7, "Top of the Heap," centers on the 2008 Olympics to sketch the decade (2003–13) during which China's recycling sector exploded from domestic gold rush to global juggernaut. After China's accession to the World Trade Organization (WTO) in 2000, domestic waste resource streams were supplemented by a huge surge in scrap imports, all going to feed China's insatiable manufacturing expansion. From 2001 through 2017 China was the number one destination for almost every form of scrap commodity traded on the international market, accounting for an over 50 percent global market share for scrap paper, copper, and aluminum and over 80 percent of the world scrap plastics trade. In 2003 China imported $5 billion in scrap ferrous, copper, aluminum, paper, and plastic; that total peaked at over $37 billion in 2011. The chapter sketches the stories of people and places that rose to the top of the trash heap in those boom years. But globalization has its up(turn)s and down(turn)s. A few months after the Olympics the global financial crisis struck, followed by a series of other economic setbacks. Equally important, environmental problems were increasingly garnering serious attention from the Chinese government, and some of the most visible and devastating examples involved pollution caused by informal recycling processors. The chapter ends with two examples of falling from the top of the heap: the 2011 crackdown on scrap plastic processing in Wenan county—North China's "waste plastic capital"—and the 2013 demolition of Dongxiaokou market, Beijing's largest recycling market.

Chapter 8 takes us up to the present moment, in which we are all extras in the global-scale environmental drama kicked off by China's definitive ban on the importation of "foreign trash" (洋垃圾 yang laji). After decades of policies that generally encouraged the import of waste resources as integral to its economic development, China's government now sees the toll of this trade on its environment as simply too high. The ban has radically shaken recycling markets across the globe, throwing the recycling systems of Organisation for Economic Co-operation and Development (OECD) countries that relied on Chinese buyers and processors into an economic tailspin and pushing scrap shipments into ports across South East Asian countries unequipped to handle them in such huge quantities. But while China's import ban has gotten extraordinary attention in the international press, there is an equally momentous story going on in China's domestic waste management world that is in many ways the real cause driving the ban, a story that makes a fitting culmination to this one-hundred-year history. The ban is bookended by a domestic policy called "the merging of two networks" (两网融合 liang wang ronghe). President Xi himself has called for the creation of an integrated system of recycling and trash sorting for the entire nation; for the first time since the PRC's founding in 1949, the sanitation and recycling bureaucracies—the two bureaucracies explored in detail in this book, whose bifurcation had served as the organizing spine of these sectors since 1949—are to be merged into one unified system. After a century of modern urban waste management policies, recycling is coming to be explicitly defined by the state as a form of waste, and a new "waste regime" is in the making. The "merge" is arguably far more economically massive than the ban, entailing half a trillion yuan (about US$75 billion) of investments in waste and recycling infrastructure and conglomerates. Chapter 8 explores both the international and domestic consequences of China's recent whipsaw change in waste policy.

Finally, obvious as these may be, I feel it important to highlight some of this study's limitations, not just in scope but in significance. First, though this book is focused on postconsumer wastes, I argue that if we wish to "solve" the dire waste and pollution problems created by neoliberal globalized consumer capitalism, we need to look elsewhere than the realm of "postconsumer" or "tailpipe" wastes. Our waste problems today originate at the site of production and in the financing, economic, and regulatory structures that govern production.[20] Tailpipe solutions—what we do with wastes once they have already been produced—are inevitably weak levers for solving waste problems. There are several reasons for this. First, the vast majority of solid waste generated—Samantha MacBride, while acknowledging the confounding lack of data, guesstimates around 97 percent in the United States—is production, not postconsumer, waste.[21] The destruction of habitats by resource extraction, mining, and deforestation and the massive outflows of pollution emissions by manufacturing industries create far graver ecological damage than postconsumer pollution. Second, the decisions that shape the worst postconsumer pollution outcomes—decisions to include toxic substances or unrecoverable materials in the production process or to build a business model on disposability—all occur at the production end. These problems are exacerbated by the current hegemony of neoliberal governance that enshrines corporate rights to deny public access to information regarding production processes. Activism around waste issues swarms around recycling, landfills, pollution accidents, and incinerators largely because these are the spaces in which waste becomes a visible and knowable problem; the underlying processes that make these visible eruptions inevitable occurrences are often so well hidden and legally walled off that they are difficult to notice, let alone organize around or research. Handling a waste problem after the waste has been made is at best a remedy, not a cure. Effective solutions for reducing postconsumer waste in today's economy must happen at the level of production and distribution; changing consumer habits and choices can have some, but limited, effect. It does not take a rocket scientist or a political radical to realize that the logic of capitalist production is in contradiction to the aim of minimizing waste. Yes, for-profit enterprises have powerful incentives to be efficient and not waste time, money, or inputs in their production processes, but there is no capitalist incentive to sell fewer widgets, and every widget, sooner or later (and preferably sooner from the capitalist's perspective), becomes waste.

It also bears repeating that this book falls well short of providing a comprehensive exploration of all forms of material wastes that have circulated in Beijing's recent history (its second limitation). Indeed, it would take pages just to list what is missing here: sewage treatment, automobile scrap, post-reform secondhand furniture and clothing, the handling of everyday urban toxic and hazardous wastes (light bulbs, batteries, medical wastes), construction wastes, restaurant food wastes, and so forth.[22] This book is only a first attempt to explore the rich worlds and evocative complexities of how waste and recycling have unfolded in Beijing society, and there are many aspects that would reward deeper consideration. As just one example, the reader will catch several glimpses of the gendered aspects of waste regimes; the association of males with handling metal scrap and women with cloth, divisions of household labor that put family waste management on the shoulders of women, and the gendering of informal sector labor are worth much more exploration. I cannot claim that how I chose to limit the scope of this project was always logically consistent, and perhaps the fairest way to frame it would be to say that this is a self-consciously teleological history: it is what happened when I took the contemporary idea of "recycling" and projected it back over one hundred years, then tried to use what I found to look anew at the present society in which we, for the moment, are still managing to subsist.

This book also has a companion at a Scalar website (Remains of the Everyday, Kipple-yard; https://scalar.usc.edu/works/remains-of-the-everyday-kipple-yard /index) with hundreds of images; threads regarding topics underexplored in these pages; links to related research by other scholars that would greatly reward exploration; and regular updates on relevant events, policies, and research.

PART ONE

The Republican Era
(1912–1949)

Recycling of a Different Sort

In February 2008, while roaming around the fourth and fifth ring roads of Beijing checking out scrap markets, I dropped in on an illegal/unregistered market of about thirty stalls, wedged under the high-power-lines near Shashichang road in Haidian district (the market was demolished in 2010). I was chatting with the boss of a wastepaper stall, who was supervising a front-end loader heaping cardboard onto a five-ton truck. Chinese New Year had just passed, so his stall was strewn with colorful wrapping paper and burned-out fireworks launchers—charred cardboard packs full of chemical dust. As the loader scraped the last scoops from the unpaved ground, lifting more dirt, soot, and plastic than paper, I asked the boss a question that I also asked of a lot of paper-stall bosses over the next few weeks, until I finally realized how stupid it was: "Is it really OK to ship that? Won't your buyer complain about all the dirt and trash in there?" The answer I got was always something like: "No problem." I should have realized that, of course, these guys know what they can ship to their buyers; obviously many small Hebei paper factories were taking this kind of mangy load, even though the material had hardly been cleaned or sorted.

The "sort" is a key stage in any recycling process; a lot of value can be created by doing it properly, and even more can be lost by messing it up. Metal alloys and plastics are particularly tricky to sort, requiring skill and experience if not a few testing gadgets or techniques. Beijing collectors, like those in most cities these days, sort their paper into a few rough categories (newspaper, cardboard, office paper, and mixed paper), selling it in rough heaps. In Republican Beijing, however, wastepaper picking was of an entirely different "sort":

When my father [a drum beater] roamed the street collecting scrap, it was mainly book paper and newsprint. At night he'd sort it [*fenlei shoushi*]. He'd smooth each sheet of newspaper and tie it into neat stacks to sell as packaging paper—the small shops and stalls selling sundries like candy, beans, melon-seeds, all used newspaper the way we use plastic bags today. Unprinted paper he'd sort by width; those between 10 and 20 centimeters, small book makers would cut to size and make into books [*ding benzi*] for notes, drafts and homework for students—they were a lot cheaper than buying a notebook. . . . What he couldn't sell became [raw material] for paper-makers.[1]

Sorting sheet by sheet, Republican-era pickers preened their paper for reuse. Only the irredeemable bits went to be pulped and recycled (traveling, interestingly, to some of the same counties near Baoding, Hebei, where paper scrap still goes today).

A comparison of sorting methods reveals a lot about the changing and abiding logics of recycling regimes. In Republican Beijing, reuse outweighed recycling (both in value and volume), and the patchwork crafts and ingenuities of repurposing were central to the city's daily economy and commoner subsistence. Today secondhand and reused goods are a small fraction of Beijing's gargantuan postconsumer waste recycling stream. Still, the economic logic that reuse almost always yields more value per pound than recycling remains true today, with "e-waste" (discarded electronics) being a prime example: an appliance or computer that can be repaired and refurbished for reuse and resale is far more valuable than that same unit after being dismantled or shredded into so much metal, plastic, and other materials.

The snack wrappers and copybooks made from the drumbeater's newssheets were made in the neighborhood, with the paper traveling a few miles at most before being repurposed and resold. Today's used cardboard or newspaper is trucked in compressed one-ton blocks across hundreds of miles for pulping and processing and then often overseas for resale. But lest we wax nostalgic for the quaint local culture of Republican Beijing, I should note that the newspaper sheets the drumbeater painstakingly smoothed were almost certainly imported from the United States or Japan. Republican Beijing had no mills capable of making newsprint, so it was all imported from abroad. Aspects of global trade, economic and technical inequality, and resource scarcity underlie both scrap paper stories, though in profoundly different configurations.

The following two chapters offer a composite sketch of postconsumer waste management and usage in the first half of the twentieth century, ranging over a hodgepodge of flotsam and jetsam and straddling several historical watersheds. Chapter 1 describes the handling of materials addressed by the city government as sanitation concerns: human excrement, coal dust, and street trash. Chapter 2 sketches the trades in disused paper, handicraft materials, used clothes, metal scrap, antiques, and other materials, trades that taken separately were too small in scale to attract great attention from the city government aside from attempts to tidy up the city's appearance and deter the trafficking of stolen goods. Taken collectively, however, these trades can be seen as a sector of reuse/recycling that added together were of great significance to the city's material metabolism, economy, and culture. My excuse for lumping this array of scrap, crap, and effluvia together is that all constitute postconsumer wastes that one way or another were products of Beijing people's daily lives. They are loosely commingled in an inextricable tangle of hygienic, economic, logistical, and ideological relations. The narrative here describes an inconsistent but discernible pressure from city governments to open these trades to state-legitimated managerial intervention. While Beijing governments prior to 1949 made some limited headway in getting a handle on the city's panoply of wastes, the PRC government would bring urban wastes and scrap to unprecedented heights of legibility and government control, levels that proved impossible to attain before or since.

1

Dreams of a Hygienic Infrastructure Deferred

Shit, coal ash, food waste, scrap materials (wastepaper, rags, scrap metal), and secondhand goods (pawned clothing, used books, antiques): in terms of material mass, that was more or less the ranked order of postconsumer waste and goods generated in Beijing across the first fifty years of the twentieth century.[1] Approaching the urban system metabolically, the bulk of the city's material inputs (food and coal) issued from North China's rural and mountain regions. Those inputs were transformed (into ash and excrement) by residents, who consumed them and then sought to eject the remnants from their immediate space. The processes of ejecting and (when beneficial/ profitable) processing these wastes posed headaches for Beijing's underfunded municipal governments, which increasingly were charged with the mission of modernizing and sanitizing urban life. This chapter explores the management of materials and services that would come to be subsumed under the heading "urban sanitation." It begins with the infrastructural backdrop of sewer systems, street cleaning, and sanitation codes, systems aimed at maintaining thoroughfares and public spaces, thereby shaping how waste materials could move and where they were or were not allowed to accumulate. I then focus on what was by far Beijing's largest waste recycling industry: the collection of night soil for fertilizer production.

BELOW AND ABOVE THE STREETS

Beijing's stone and brick sewer system dates from the late thirteenth century, and its expansion during the Ming dynasty (1368–1644) made it one of the most comprehensive sewer networks in the world at the time. By the mid-1800s there were over eighty kilometers of large sewer mains and three hundred kilometers of smaller ones, mostly dedicated to the imperial palace and Inner City, where high-ranking Manchu officials lived. The Outer City's network was less extensive and was expanded haphazardly to meet the needs of merchants and commoners.[2] As in most cities before the late nineteenth century, these sewers were intended primarily for rain runoff and flood prevention rather than waste removal. Beijing's primary system for handling human excrement up through the 1950s was night soil porters, who collected human waste to be made into fertilizer cakes, similar to the *poudrette* of Paris. In other words, far into the twentieth century, human excrement was a valued commodity in Beijing's regional agricultural system and functioned as "waste" in fairly limited contexts, such as when it disrupted the city's drainage system.

As was the case in pretty much every city where sewers were built, many Beijing residents used them to dispose of their effluvia, despite prohibitions against doing so.[3] Residents who lacked privies typically dumped their chamber pots early each morning into the streets' sewers and gutters. Accumulations of garbage and feces in the sewers were a chronic headache, making regular and emergency cleaning necessary to prevent clogging and flooding, a job that in addition to being foul was dangerous; suffocating from sewer gas was a distinct possibility.[4] In Beijing the annual sewer cleaning became a customary rite of spring, coinciding with the arrival of scholars to sit for the imperial exams.[5] The spring cleaning was the inspiration for a few ditties like this one:

> Down along the avenues the gutters run,
> One misstep and their depths you'll plumb.
> Muck heaps up and blocks the stream
> Opened once each spring to repair and clean.
> From the murky black depths evil airs arise
> And one sewer man after another dies.
> Pestilent gases spread, sewer fumes bring infirmity
> Attacking people's health with seasonal regularity.[6]

By the nineteenth century it had become customary for pedestrians to carry "perfumed rosaries" during this season to fend off the odors.[7]

These spring cleanings were hardly adequate to unclog an infrastructure that had served the city for centuries. In 1916 a comprehensive survey of the system revealed that 85 percent of the city's sewers were clogged or in a state of partial or complete collapse. Neither municipal nor national governments could afford the comprehensive reconstruction—such as replacing rectangular stone channels with relatively self-cleansing, rounded concrete culverts—of more than three hundred kilometers of sewer. And even if self-cleansing sewers were built, they would still require substantial water flows to function properly, something Beijing was sorely lacking. The Beijing Waterworks Company, which in 1910 began supplementing the city's limited well-water supply, grew sluggishly at best because most Beijing households could not afford its services.[8] A sewer system that would use such a valuable resource to flush away human waste was far beyond the city's economic and natural endowments.

The city's second line of waste-handling infrastructure, the phalanxes of street cleaners, sanitation patrols, and garbage collectors responsible for keeping city streets clear of garbage and manure, was of newer vintage than the sewers. Street cleaners were Beijing's first state-managed sanitation workers, formed in 1906 under the Metropolitan Police Board. The affiliation of sanitation with policing in China's capital was largely modeled after similar reforms undertaken in 1902 in the treaty port city Tianjin under the leadership of Yuan Shikai. Tianjin had been under the control of the Tianjin Provisional Government, an occupying regime of foreign imperialist powers that had seized control of the Chinese part of the city in 1900 during the Boxer uprising. Ruth Rogaski argues that Yuan developed Tianjin's public health offices, the first municipal public health department in the country, in large part to persuade the powers to return that part of the city back to Chinese control: "Without the ability to administer hygienic modernity, the Qing would not be allowed to administer Tianjin, nor, potentially, the empire."[9] "Hygienic modernity" is Rogaski's translation of the term weisheng (卫生) as it came to be used in twentieth-century policy discourse. As she elucidates:

> Weisheng suggests a harmony of interests between public space and private behavior, presided over by an enlightened and effective government. A weisheng city is free of odors, dust, and harmful bacteria; its streets are ordered and lined with greenery. City residents who practice weisheng do not excrete or expectorate in public places, refrain from littering, and maintain a healthy distance between themselves and other individuals. With its complex allusions to science, order, and government authority, weisheng may best be translated as "hygienic modernity," a major cornerstone of the twentieth-century urban ideal.[10]

The city's low-paid sanitation workers and street sweepers, who were mobilized, sometimes by force, as the front line in the battle to conquer urban refuse and filth, hardly lived or worked in conditions that enabled them to experience or embody these ideals; nevertheless, the shining vision of modern sanitary urbanism would fuel the genesis of many of the reforms described in this and subsequent chapters.

Beijing's first street cleaners, numbering around one hundred, were waterers (shui fu), tasked mainly with sprinkling roadways around the imperial palace with water to damp down the city's notorious dust and dirt and ensure the Qing (1644–1911) court's immediate surroundings were attractive and salubrious. Following the fall of the Qing, such cleaning was extended beyond the palace area; workers were renamed street cleaners (qing dao fu), and their ranks expanded to cover both the Inner and Outer Cities. In 1928, when the Guomingdang (GMD; the Nationalist Party) reorganized Beijing into the Beiping Special Municipality, these cleaning teams (*qingjie dui*) included fifteen street-cleaning brigades and one brigade of sprinkling trucks. Briefly placed under the separate Sanitation Office, then shifted back under the police due to lack of funding, then back again to the expanded Sanitation Bureau, these brigades were batted to and fro by municipal bureaus several more times prior to the CCP's victory in 1949.

These brigades were responsible primarily for the upkeep of the city's major thoroughfares; the alleyways of most residential areas did not enjoy the caress of their municipally supplied brooms. Instead, city bylaws gave residents responsibility for cleaning the street around their doorways. Regarding the cleaning of sewer grates, which were something like metal cages that caught large bits of rubbish borne by street runoff, Sydney Gamble recorded that emptying these boxes and carting off the refuse was a service paid for by local residents and performed mostly by the "inmates of poorhouses."[11] As Janet Chen describes, Republican-era police frequently incarcerated beggars and vagrants and pressed them into "productive labor," including working in gangs hauling water and cleaning sewer boxes.[12] In examining the scientific and political discourses that justified subjecting the indigent to forced labor, Chen finds that nationalism often figured prominently: "'Lazy vagabonds are the vermin (*maozei*) of the nation and the people,' declared Sun Yatsen. 'The government should force them by law to work to transform them into sacred laborers (*shensheng de laogong*), worthy to share the rights and privileges of citizens.'"[13] Suffice it to note that the street sweeps, rubbish haulers, and night soil carriers mentioned in this chapter were often hardly distinguishable from the vagrants and beggars from whose ranks they came.

By all accounts street cleaning was best managed from 1934 to 1937, when the Sanitation Bureau's 2,170 street cleaners were generally paid on a regular basis, about seven yuan a month. Poor rural migrant males vied to get on the waiting list for this job. The living conditions for which they strived were hardly glamorous:

> Street cleaning corps, street cleaning corps!
> Work outside, sleep on the shrine floor.
> In the winter biting lice,
> In the summer mosquitoes and flies.
> A brick for a pillow, a sack for a quilt.
> Four seasons a year, all working full tilt.[14]

Getting a registered slot on the payroll often meant putting in months of unpaid work, and it was common for people higher up on the waiting list to sell their names to those at the bottom. For example, the first vice chairman of the city's Xicheng District Environmental Sanitation Bureau under the CCP had adopted his uncle's name in 1939 to get onto the waiting list and continued to be known by that name for the rest of his life.[15] A street cleaner's job description included keeping down the dust; filling in holes and ruts in the streets; and collecting street rubbish, including animal manure and household garbage. In some neighborhoods household waste was to be left neatly outside residents' doorways; in others sweepers rang a bell on their routes through neighborhoods and residents came out with their rubbish—mainly ash and some food waste. Collected rubbish was hauled by human- or animal-pulled carts for dumping. There were a few experiments with small-scale incinerators in the mid-1930s, but none proved successful, though they did add to local air pollution. In 1928 the city purchased two trucks to haul garbage to landfills outside the city; the fleet had grown to fifty-one by 1949, though reportedly only three trucks were in working order when the People's Liberation Army (PLA) took the city.[16] The upshot was that up through 1949, large quantities of Beijing's rubbish were still hauled by man or beast and disposed of in open dumps either outside or beside the city walls (see Map 3).

But physically hauling garbage was probably not as exhausting as waging the never-ending battle with the city's dust. A good half of street cleaners' days was typically spent drawing water from wells and spigots, lugging it to their turf, sprinkling it over the dusty byways, tamping dirt into ruts, and generally bestirring the dust into mounds and clouds. Some of this dust had traveled from the Gobi in the region's famous sandstorms, but the sweepers were mainly in gritty combat with one of Beijing's major waste streams; 80–90 percent of Beijing's "rubbish" was the ash and dirt from hundreds of thousands of coal-burning stoves and furnaces. Into the 1950s most Beijingers burned briquettes (coal balls, *mei qiu*) made from a slurry of coal (75%) and mud (25%) to heat their homes and cook.[17] Quite literally, Beijing's streets were paved with briquette dust. In many neighborhoods streets were several inches, even as much as a few feet, above the house foundations due to centuries of accumulated dirt and ash. Li Jianxin, a sixty-seven-year-old grandfather who began working in municipal waste management as a street cleaner, recalled, "In the early days after liberation, street cleaners were employed under the Public Security Bureau. They gave us uniforms pretty much the same as the cops, and except for a small badge, no one could tell by looking at your clothes what your job was.... [W]e started sweeping the streets at twelve midnight, but when I say 'sweep the street' I really should say 'sweep dust.'"[18] There was a seasonal flow to residential waste, with the stream of coal ash and dust rising in the winter months and subsiding somewhat under a surge of vegetable waste and melon rinds in the summer.

It is not difficult to understand why, even during the relative stability of the mid-1930s, sanitation workers may have lacked a vigorous esprit de corps. First, there was the seeming futility of taming the dust; "they count carrying their broom across the street as a thorough sweeping," read one bureau report.[19] Threats of fines and firing did little to induce greater effort, for inspectors and supervisors were too few, often too lazy (they tended not to walk the whole lengths of streets), and at times too corrupt; many filled worker slots with "dummy" names and pocketed the wages, a practice called eating vacancies (*chi kongque*). Conditions further deteriorated under the Japanese (1937–45), when cash wages were partially replaced by food rations; by the 1940s workers were often paid in unmilled corn and received no cash at all. Street cleaners resorted to begging for tips on New Year, Qingming festival, people's wedding days, and other special occasions. Many depended on scavenging: unburned bits of coal for heating, food scraps for meals, and wastepaper and glass to trade for spare change. Though numbering around eighteen hundred on the municipality's books at any given time, the actual number of workers on the job was probably less than half that, as "eating vacancies" became endemic in the late 1940s.[20] In many areas, particularly poorer neighborhoods, trash was not hauled and streets were not swept. One of the first major sanitation feats of the CCP in Beijing in 1949 would be a clearing of over 300,000 tons of garbage heaped about the city (see chapter 3).

Municipally provided sanitation relies on a public that complies with its rules and mechanisms, cooperation that is all the more crucial when the reach of those services is extremely limited and underfunded. Lacking the resources to finance a full-scale sanitation infrastructure, Beijing's administrators repeatedly tried to lay a path toward "hygienic modernity" with behavioral and labor regulations. The city's first regulations enforcing the sanitary handling of waste in relation to an explicit public health agenda, "sanitary regulations to prevent epidemics," were issued in 1906 soon after the Metropolitan Police Board was established. The bylaws banned dumping of feces or garbage on the streets during epidemics, ordered residents to keep their doorways clear of trash, asserted the intention to have sanitation officers make regular inspections, and advised that all stinking sewer openings be fumigated with chlorine and sprinkled with lime. Night soil carriers were ordered to repair their carts to make them leak proof, perform regular collections, never allow cesspits to overflow, disinfect pits with lime, establish night soil drying yards only where designated by the patrol office, and not dally in the streets.[21] Needless to say, with no funds to enable the enforcement of these codes (subsidize the repair of more than two thousand night soil carts, provide residents with trash and wastewater receptacles, finance the massive real estate transaction of relocating the city's four hundred night soil drying yards, etc.), these rules amounted to an expression of aspirations that would go largely unmet for the next few decades.

Residents seem to have been as unfazed as the street cleaners by regulations threatening penalties for unsanitary behavior. The 1906 Draft Code of Offenses and Crimes for Beijing Area Police (*Zhuo ni Jingshi difang wei jing zui zhuan ze*) claimed that members of households spilling urine or wastewater buckets or dumping stove ash in the streets could be arrested for three to ten days or fined from one to two yuan.[22] In 1928 the city cautioned that children and adults urinating or defecating on the street would be fined.[23] The 1930 Regulations on Eliminating Solid and Liquid Waste insisted:

> Each residence must prepare a basket for waste-earth and a bucket for wastewater for the daily collection by public waste carts or to be carried themselves to neighborhood temporary waste collection ponds. It is forbidden to dump them in the streets or gutters.
>
> Every household should sweep up the area in front of their doorway and ensure its cleanliness; when wastes accumulate in these gutters or streets residents should remove it. . . . If residents find someone dumping garbage or urine near their door, they should bring them to the police to be fined.[24]

A similar list of rules in 1934 went into greater detail: buckets should not leak; shit and piss should not be put in trash baskets.[25]

There were also attempts to compel a more expansive sense of public responsibility for urban cleanliness and appearance by offering carrots instead of sticks. In the early 1930s the city began holding sanitation conferences and in 1934 began convening annual Sanitation Campaign Assemblies for one week each summer. Assembly activities included sending battalions of sanitation workers out to perform extraordinary service in neighborhoods that needed more attention. Other events were directed at raising public participation and awareness, such as exhibitions on disease prevention, mother and infant health, and daily hygiene habits, as well as a "fly extermination day" in 1936 that reportedly mobilized 2,780 students to annihilate 1,719,665 flies.[26] The Japanese regime continued these summer cleanup festivals at first, but they fell out of use and were only revived by the GMD in 1946. But such flurries of citizen activity and propaganda could not renovate the city's sanitation infrastructure and at best could only temporarily paper over the shortfall. When it comes to shaping daily regimens of waste disposal, material infrastructure tends to have far more persuasive power than barrages of banners and public lectures.

This summary of aspirations unrealized, legal codes ignored, and bureaus unable to staff or motivate their employees, of Beijing's municipal workers and residents falling short of hygienic modernity, should not be read as a claim that Beijingers lacked a suitably modern mentality, though many contemporary commentators saw cause for precisely such nationalistic self-flagellating. Governments might hope the governed will expend unstinting effort to handle things as unpleasant as garbage and excrement in ways that can make up for infrastructural shortcomings, but the governed can hardly be blamed when the results are uneven.

I fear that my repeatedly pointing to the city's incomplete infrastructure may create the misimpression that the city itself was somehow physically stagnating; change on this account was also highly uneven. Amid decades of dramatic and traumatic

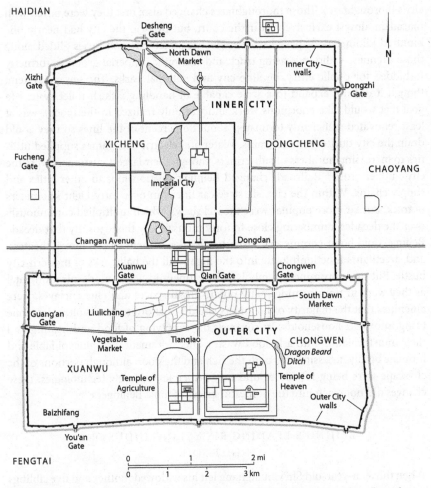

HAIDIAN

Desheng Gate

North Dawn Market

Inner City walls

Xizhi Gate

Dongzhi Gate

INNER CITY

XICHENG

DONGCHENG

Fucheng Gate

CHAOYANG

Imperial City

Changan Avenue

Dongdan

Xuanwu Gate

Qian Gate

Chongwen Gate

South Dawn Market

Guang'an Gate

Liulichang

OUTER CITY

CHONGWEN

Vegetable Market

Tianqiao

Dragon Beard Ditch

XUANWU

Temple of Agriculture

Temple of Heaven

Outer City walls

Baizhifang

You'an Gate

FENGTAI

| 0 | | 1 | | 2 mi |
| 0 | 1 | | 2 | 3 km |

N

MAP 3. Republican-era Beijing with points of interest, including informal used goods markets. Map by Bill Nelson.

political change (the fall of the Qing, warlord battles, GMD rule, Japanese invasion and occupation), Beijing also underwent tremendous material changes that could surely be termed modern improvements. I cannot do justice to their variety and importance here, but I can summarize a few of the most significant changes to the cityscape.[27] For one thing, the shift from empire to nation-state markedly changed the scope of the "public" behind the concept of public space and its management; this is evident in how street sweepers from 1906 to 1911 mainly circled the palace, then after 1911 expanded to cover greater and greater extents of the city's thoroughfares. Those thoroughfares changed also; first they were paved with macadam almost exclusively near the court, but by 1930 the city had nearly one hundred kilometers of paved streets. Electric street cars and buses glided along those avenues, as did increasing truck and car traffic. Imperial grounds, formerly forbidden for public entry, became city and national parks. The sewage system, though it did not expand to a scale capable of handling a flush toilet system (a goal that would take enormous work and was only realized in the 1990s), was at least renovated sufficiently to unstop about 80 percent of the lines so they could drain the city during summer rains. Water and electric companies supplied utilities to increasing numbers of subscribers, though their largest customers were the city's upper crust.[28] Railroads changed Beijing's relationships to other cities and supply chains. Within the city, six streetcar lines ran over forty-eight kilometers of track, but far more popular were the rickshaws, which multiplied continuously over the decades, numbering close to forty thousand by the 1930s. By that decade Beijing could boast commercial districts with department stores, movie theaters, and streetlights functioning late into the night—all the hallmarks of modern-city bustle. But these prominent symbols of investment in urban modernization, vital as they were in transforming many public urban spaces and elite enclaves, were amenities that the majority of Beijingers could not afford to access often, let alone bring into their households. In contrast, the supplying of food and heating and their transformation into ash, food wastes, and excrement were unavoidable and intimate bodily necessities for both the rich and the poor; although portions of the cityscape were being rebuilt around new principles and new technologies, these changes did not reach into the domestic spaces of most Beijingers.

BEIJING'S LEADING RECYCLING INDUSTRY: NIGHT SOIL

When thirteen-year-old Shi Chuanxiang left his widowed mother and five siblings behind to scrounge for work in Beiping in 1928, he could never have imagined the historical journey upon which he was about to embark. His life story would resonate decades beyond his death, resulting in the building of not one but two memorial museums in his honor. As a young man seeking employment, Chuanxiang had one thing going for him, although many would argue that it was not an asset: he was from Shandong. Shandong migrants had a veritable monopoly on some of the hardest, dirtiest work in Beijing, including water carrying and privy cleaning. Chuanxiang was taken in by a night soil merchant. He would eventually rise to great fame, fall into abused infamy, and finally settle into posthumous sainthood as one of China's labor heroes, often pictured shouldering the totems of his trade: a wooden barrel full of excrement strapped on his back and a pole-handled ladle for scooping out cesspits in his hand (see figure 1).

FIGURE 1. Painting by Zhou Peichun (fl. late Qing) of a Beijing
night soil collector carrying the totemic tools of the trade: a long,
wooden-handled scoop and a wooden barrel slung over the back,
as well as a lantern for working at night. From Wiki Commons,
Wellcomeimages.org/indexplus/image/L0008547.html.

It is believed that Beijing's shit became a problem of urban management
requiring a dedicated solution sometime around the Jiajing reign (mid-sixteenth
century). Up until then, Beijing had only been partially walled off from the surrounding suburbs, so residents could rather easily dump their crap into street
gutters or outlying fields. The completion of the city walls not only brought added
security and a population boom; it also limited ingress and egress and made trucking crap to the fields a time-consuming ordeal that threatened to induce a bout of
metropolitan-scale constipation. The business of poor migrants collecting urban
manure for sale to nearby peasants started soon thereafter. Drying yards, where
the semiliquid night soil was sunbaked into fertilizer cakes, became key nodes in
the trade. In the 1900s there were about four hundred drying yards clustered just

beyond each of the city's eleven outer gates. The night soil carriers working for these yards often bunked there and worked evenings making fertilizer.

Beijing was not unique in having a substantial night soil economy; nearly every sizable city (population of 100,000 or more) across China developed economic networks processing urban human wastes into nutrient-rich fertilizer for nearby farms. Over the centuries this created a notable ecological effect, whereby "the fertility of soil around the major cities became greater than that at greater distances, and the yields of crops were greater in proximity to urban centers than farther from them."[29] The intensive economic interactions between urban centers and their adjacent agricultural lands were reflected in the imperial bureaucracy's lack of administrative distinctions between city and countryside. Qing dynasty Beijing, for instance, was roughly split down the middle into two counties, Wanping for the west half, Daxing for the east, with both counties administering both urban and rural lands. The night soil cycle was thus a sustained feature of China's urban-rural ecology that contributed to shaping enduring economic networks and the administrative structures governing them.

By the late Qing, Shandong migrants had cornered Beijing's night soil trade, though how they won their monopoly is a mystery. Oral tradition among Shandong collectors had it that their forefathers, after decades of street brawling with rival collectors from Shanxi and Hebei—during which, along with fists and sticks, the shit truly did fly as those long-handled ladles also served as handheld catapults— emerged victorious. The Qing historian Qiu Zhonglin guesses that the Manchu Banners' habit of hiring Shandong natives as porters during their military conquest naturally evolved during peacetime into their carrying water and night soil.[30] In any event, by the Republican era most of the four thousand workers responsible for emptying Beijing's privies hailed, like Shi Chuanxiang, from Shandong.

As putrid and exhausting as the work was, biographical accounts of Shi Chuanxiang stress that the greatest indignity he endured was not the filthy nature of the job but the degrading treatment he and his fellows experienced:

> One day Shi Chuanxiang was scooping crap for a rich family in Liubukou. The butler was keeping an eye on him and wouldn't let him inside for fear he'd dirty the house. When he had finished the job, Shi Chuanxiang, his back dripping from sweat, asked for a sip of water. . . . The butler handed Shi the bowl used to feed the cat. It had a little brackish water in it, a dead fly floating on top. Shi Chuanxiang shook with rage, but knowing he couldn't afford to offend him, turned and left.[31]

Similar stories of everyday discrimination are common in the oral histories collected after 1949. Yet these daily injustices were minor compared to the abuses night soil collectors might suffer from the shit lords (fenfa) and shit hegemons (fenba) for whom they toiled. The night soil trade was hierarchical and contentious. Near the top were night soil merchants (fenshang), the most powerful of whom were dubbed lords and hegemons. There were about four hundred night soil merchants in Beijing.[32] They held various portfolios of excrement-related assets, mainly of three kinds: public toilets (including access to usage fees and the night soil there collected), composting/drying yards (where night soil was processed into fertilizer), and shit routes (*fendao*). Ownership of a shit route was a form of customary property right. A shit route could cover a dozen cesspits or nearly a hundred, blanket an entire street, or be peppered among a neighborhood's privies and public toilets. The average route was plied by from one to five night soil men (*fenfu*), laborers who collected and carried the waste. Many shit merchants had rights to only a few routes, but the wealthier ones had extensive routes and commanded scores of underlings. Hegemon Liu Chunjiang was in the sixth generation of his family to work in night soil. He owned four homes, had two concubines, had routes covering over one hundred privies, and owned a large drying yard. Liu also owned about a dozen public toilets. Public toilets in Beijing date back to at least the late Qing, but during that period there were very few (the number repeatedly cited is eight), all of which were located near the imperial court. After the Qing fell, public toilets quickly appeared in other parts of the city, in step with the public hygiene trends common in treaty ports. Some Beijing public toilets (there were over five hundred in the Inner City alone by the 1920s) were government owned, but most were built by shit lords, who in addition to having exclusive rights to their toilets' night soil also made money by charging usage fees (one fen per customer).[33]

The average night soil man was far from prosperous. There were anywhere from fifteen hundred to four thousand *fenfu* depending on the condition of the urban economy and one's definition of the term. For my purposes, a night soil man/collector/porter was someone with recognized customary rights to ply a shit route, whether he owned it himself (several hundred owned their own modest routes, typically selling their night soil to yard-owning merchants or directly to farmers) or worked it for a boss or lord. Reports from the 1930s claim that shit lords typically paid their underlings from four to seven yuan a month and provided crude sleeping quarters. Night soil men might supplement this pay with the tips they collected (some would say extorted). In his detailed portrait of the trade written in the early 1930s, Zhao Wanyi (himself a night soil lord) claimed that collectors were paid about seven yuan a month by their bosses, though if they collected more than ten yuan in tips, that base pay often dropped as low as two or three yuan.[34] Many collectors regularly sent some of this money home to their families. All in all, this would put night soil workers about on a par with rickshaw pullers, servants, and other occupations filled by Beijing's "bare sticks," bachelor males too poor to marry. Post-1949 oral histories contain many personal accounts of night soil men claiming their bosses withheld pay, beat them regularly, and threw workers into the street when they became ill.

The shit route was the fundamental economic unit of the night soil trade, and its market value varied based on the quantity and quality of the ordure in question. The Western Inner City, where the wealthiest nobles lived, had the "fattest" night soil, and the resultant fertilizer fetched the highest price.[35] There were also various kinds of routes that could be economically ranked. Dry routes (*han dao*) were the most common and involved scooping out cesspits and household privies. A water route (*shui dao*) involved cleaning chamber pots for a fee and was worth about half the value of a dry route. Often these chamber pot cleaners had a follower route (*gen tiao dao*) accompanying them, someone who collected the watery swill from the chamber pots—literally the cheapest shit—and sold it to farmers or yard merchants for income. There were also a few hundred "pirate collectors" (*pao hai fenfu*) who scavenged for whatever excrement they could glean off the streets (ox and horse manure was also a valued ingredient for fertilizer making) or steal from other's routes and public toilets—a risky business in which getting busted typically resulted in a fine or a beating.[36]

By the late Qing, a comprehensive night soil recycling system was in place, and by most accounts, all too firmly. Late Qing and Republican-era reformers had little luck dislodging or reshaping it. Many accounts claim that for most of the Qing, night soil men charged the households they serviced nothing and even brought their patrons gifts from the Shandong countryside, like tea or bean-thread noodles, to express their gratitude; it seems that in those good old days the profit from selling night soil and fertilizer cake was sufficient reward. But gradually these polite menials realized they had their clients over a very unsavory barrel, and they started down a path of merciless extortion: a New Year's tip, a mid-autumn "gift," tips on sweltering dog days, and wine money when it rained or snowed. The public, at least as represented in newspaper articles and editorials with titles like "Outlaw the Night Soil Carriers," was fed up and disgusted:

> On a sparkling clean avenue, a few so-called "stinking crap carts" are dragged along, now and then spilling shit-juice and spreading a stench that stops pedestrians in their tracks; how can this not inspire people to curse and complain! . . . For anyone sojourning or living in Beiping, attending to cleanliness and sanitation—in dress, food, housing, and other forms—these are all manageable, all can be dealt with. It is only the unavoidable biological imperative of relieving oneself after eating and drinking that is simply impossible! You might know how to shit, and can explain how to shit, but it is impossible to do so. Maybe you've got a chamber pot or outhouse and you want them cleaned; the night soil man won't heed your directions. If perhaps you express a tad of displeasure or raise a question, the night soil man will rudely give a brusque response. Next comes perhaps some cursing match (*dui ma*) and then a face-off (*shuang da*). Otherwise you get the disappearance act—idleness. Your shit pot or pit is soon brimming full, stink wafting in all four directions, disturbing your home. There is fairly no one who has lived in Beiping for a time that has not borne

this kind of painful experience.... Complaining residents still complain endlessly [to the sanitation bureau], rude night soil men are still unfailingly rude. I have long lived in Beiping and heartbroken by what I have seen, I have taken a long-view and have written this essay on the history of stink.[37]

Beijing was not the only capital in history to be decried as a city of stink; London's Great Stink in 1858 drove Parliament from its chambers, and Paris was besieged by a month-long stink in 1880. The bourgeois ideology of sanitation, described in Alain Corbin's *The Foul and the Fragrant*, announced its arrival on the historical stage with the discovery of overpowering stench, a sensation deemed all the more threatening due to the miasmic theories of contagion that dominated public health discourse for most of the nineteenth century. In the twentieth-century context, this stink signaled to Beijing's modern-minded residents a shameful absence of modernity in infrastructure and customs: roofless and dirt-floored cesspits; and the night soil carriers' shit-crusted ladles, open-topped barrels, and single-wheeled carts, which dripped and sloshed. Sanitation reached a nadir during the rainy summer months, when drying yards stopped taking in excrement, so carters tipped their loads into whatever fields or gullies they could find.[38] But most vexing of all, the impertinent and filthy night soil man seemed proud to flaunt modern standards of hygienic practice and reveled in his despotic power over the individual resident in matters scatological. Newspapers frequently ran letters to the editor fuming that the whole profession should be abolished, "Sanitary/unsanitary (*weisheng/ bu weisheng*), they have no conception of this in their minds, but they sure can tell when their 'wine money' has not been added to their monthly wage."[39]

Night soil men exercised their social power to use filth not just individually but also collectively. The Beijing city government appears to have been no match for them. This was not due to any particular weakness in the municipal government; Tianjin's night soil and water carters, known as "dark drifters" (*hunhun'r*), were widely reputed for extorting and bullying residents (and one another) and proved equally impervious to regulation. Even Tianjin's foreign concession governments had little luck loosening the dark drifters' hold; the Japanese Concession Resident's Association of Tianjin finally conceded formal recognition of their monopoly over excrement in order to gain some supervisory power over the timing and discharge of collection.[40] Thirty years of regulatory failure would lead Beiping's government to settle for a similar compromise.[41]

Beijing's night soil merchants and carriers organized as a guild for the first time in 1906, not surprisingly in reaction to the creation of a bureaucracy aimed at policing sanitation. The Fertilizer Industry Guild expanded to encompass portions of Beiping beyond the city walls in 1928 and in 1932 was renamed the Beiping Municipal Occupational Guild of Night Soil Collectors (Fenfu zhiye gonghui). But the title was misleading: "In order to dodge commercial taxes, the business-owning shit merchants did not organize their own guild, but instead joined the labor-er's Occupational Guild of Night Soil Collectors. Claiming to be a unification of capital and labor, it is like a moat-protected rampart and is unique among all the occupations in Beiping."[42] Dominated by the owners of drying yards, with carriers only informally affiliated through their ties to their bosses, the guild proved nearly impregnable to outside political forces. When it "was not defending its communal interests it was wracked by internal disputes." The guild's presidency, always in the hands of a yard owner, changed eleven times between 1918 and 1925, and the power struggles could get ugly. In 1924, guild vice president Nue's suggestion to exact a forty-copper fee from all carriers resulted in outrage from the rank and file. Repudiation of Nue's proposal by other guild officers failed to satisfy many carriers, who demanded Nue resign. The situation devolved into a massive street brawl between the enraged carriers and Nue's loyal underlings, spurring the guild leadership to expel Nue from the organization. In response, Nue had the newly installed guild chairman, who had called for his ouster, killed.[43]

As fractious as it was internally, the night soil business hardly budged in response to external pressures. The government sought to reform almost every aspect of the profession. Aspirations for public hygiene and olfactory modernity demanded night soil collectors abide by regulated collection times, set transport routes, and minimize the leakage and stench from their carts and implements. Rational management required collectors be registered, collection fees be set, workers be disciplined, demands for tips be halted, and excess workers be elimi-nated. Such reforms were met with protests followed by strikes. In 1912 and again in 1918, attempts to press collectors to adopt lidded barrels and leak-proof carts failed.[44] A 1925 government order to move drying yards to less-populated areas was canceled after a three-day strike.[45] The 1929 law applying strict licensing stan-dards to public toilets was toothless; a 1934 survey found only 5 of the 627 licensed toilets up to par.[46] Attempts in 1931 to regulate collection times and fees met with mass demonstrations and came to naught.[47]

For the Beijing government, the crux of the problem was the shit route. It pre-sented a bedeviling form of customary property right, with night soil men having sole control over the sale, rental, or inheritance of routes, and neither property-owning residents nor the government having any say in the matter. In 1928 the Nanjing national government, in the name of public health, declared management of household pollutants within the government's purview, and high court deci-sions in the early 1930s found that shit routes had no legal standing as property rights. Based on these changes, and drawing a lesson from decades of piecemeal regulatory failure, in 1935 Beiping mayor Yuan Liang proposed a truly compre-hensive reform: the night soil trade would become government run (guanban), with the city buying out all claims to shit routes at 50 yuan a share, a "generous" price given that according to national law night soil merchants had no ownership rights at all. But Yuan had drawn the wrong historical lesson; worse than utterly failing, his reforms proved politically disastrous. "Looking extremely respectful, each with a shit ladle in their right hand and shit barrel on their backs, solemn as if in full battle gear," the night soil carriers marched to the gate, not of Yuan's office, but of a political rival, Song Zheyuan, commander of the Ping-Jin Garrison, and pleaded with him to annul Yuan's plan.[48] Yuan resigned his post two days later.

Aside from the regulatory standards Yuan's proposal sought to impose on night soil collectors' pay, routes, hours, and so forth, the 50 yuan offer was deemed ridiculously low and unacceptable to the shit lords. Legal standing be damned; market prices for shit routes ran 600–800 yuan for premium routes and 100–300 for the least lucrative water and pole-following routes. Yuan's plan allotted only 200,000 yuan for the routes, though a study published by the city's Social Bureau estimated the total value of the sector's infrastructure at 1 million yuan (960,000 yuan for routes, 40,000 yuan for drying yards), about one-fifth of the city's annual tax revenue.[49] This disjuncture occurs repeatedly in the history of urban recycling and waste management: governments wishing to regulate the system balk at acknowledging anything approaching the actual market value (much less the environmental or social value) of handling wastes. In general, the urban public also drastically undervalue these services, viewing the profits generated from wastes as akin to extortion.

Following Mayor Yuan's failure, Beiping's new mayor, Qin Dechun, took a different tack; rather than pursuing the expensive plan of eliminating the shit lords by buying them out so as to strip them of ownership over their routes, the state would fully legitimize them through an officially-managed merchant-run (*guan du shang ban*) solution. In summer 1936, the Office for Handling Night Soil Affairs, made up of ten Beijing sanitation officials and nine leading shit lords, many of whom were Night Soil Guild leaders, fashioned the plan. The city would regulate the working hours, fees, and sanitary conditions of the carriers. Every carrier was required to register with the city and pay a registration fee of 6 percent of the value of his route, followed thereafter by a monthly fee of no more than 5 percent of his monthly pay, to be used to pay for equipment upgrades and other improvements. The procedure for calculating the values of shit routes proved fairly accurate, if highly elaborate; number of privies, chamber pot washing fees, market prices, and even travel times were all part of the calculus. Carrots and sticks were used: registration gave full legal recognition of route ownership; to continue collecting without a registration card resulted in warnings, then fines, and even arrest; those too poor to pay the registration fee all at once could put down 10 percent and receive a loan from the Beiping City Bank at .8 percent monthly interest to cover the rest (220 carriers signed up for loans). The registration deadlines had to be extended five times to finally register 1,868 routes, and even then, only one-third of those registered had paid their fees. Over the next several months, as registration cards and new buckets and barrels were issued, fee collection increased.

For the leading shit lords, this was a winning compromise. Registration, regulations, and fees were applied to carriers, not shit lords, and drying yards and public toilets were not subject to extra taxation. Shit lords received full legal authorization of their customary monopoly. For the carriers, the burden was far greater, and several hundred "shit pirates" and small-time independent carriers tried to organize in opposition, but it was an uphill struggle. With the Night Soil Guild firmly in the hands of yard-owning lords, these lesser independent carriers had to organize secretly, dodging government spies and risking arrest. On three different occasions organized groups of two hundred to three hundred demonstrated and petitioned against the reforms, accusing the director of the Night Soil Affairs Office, the shit lord Yu Deshun, of "deceiving officials and exploiting his fellows." The government at first turned a deaf ear to these protests, but in spring 1937 it cracked down hard, arresting eighteen participants in the third protest and threatening to ban all unregistered carriers from plying their trade. It is fair to say that by the summer of 1937, the plan was a success from the government's and shit lords' points of view. The vast majority of collectors were registered, and reforms were underway, with hundreds of new carts, barrels, and ladles being distributed. How effective and enforceable these reforms might have been is difficult to know; the Japanese took over the city a few months later, and though they continued with ostensibly the same system in place, commitments of attention and money to reforming the system slackened. Still, by choosing to accommodate the night soil industry's existing ownership structure and hierarchy, the city had managed to formalize (register, regulate, and even partially reform) a vital part of the urban infrastructure and an unruly trade that had been notoriously resistant to state management.

The director of the Night Soil Affairs Office, Yu Deshen, retained his comfortable and respected status throughout the Japanese and later GMD regimes, but under the CCP he was one of several shit hegemons executed in 1951 for his alleged brutal abuse of common workers. During the Mao era, the CCP's history of the night soil trade spoke with the voice of the aggrieved. Indeed, it is hard to square the Republican-era accounts of night soil men as bathroom bullies with later Communist era portrayals of Shi Chuanxiang and his long-suffering comrades:

An old comrade in our department's night soil disposal team, Liu Changfa, was once scooping shit at a villa in Houmachang, and asked the master for a bowl of water to drink. When he had finished drinking the fellow took the bowl and threw it in the ash heap.[50]

The shit lord made over 100 silver dollars a month just in collection fees, but those of us who scooped out toilets never even laid our hands on our three-yuan monthly wage. The lord lived in a tile-roofed home; we slept in a mule shed. The shit lord wore fox fur pants and a leather coat; we wore tattered cotton-padded pants with layer upon layer of scrap cloth pulled from the garbage patched together as a top.[51]

Sanitation worker Wang Jiyun, native of Changping, when he was over 40 took ill but could not pay for the hospital, and died in the dormitory the next month. Worker Wang Jinchi, from the Houhunwa dorm, in his twenties, got sick from eating spoiled food and the squad head not only didn't get him treated, he threw him into the street. Wang's older brother found him, got him into a room, but he died soon after.[52]

Stories like these start to feel formulaic, and in certain respects they were, becoming litanies during the Mao era, but they were doubtless usually true. That night soil workers were abused was likely just as historically factual and pervasive as were their savvy cesspit shakedowns of patrons, but it is striking how starkly representations of the night soil trade differ across the 1949 divide. Such warring representations are common when it comes to subaltern groups; lacking much of a historically recorded voice, the complexity of subaltern communities becomes pancaked into monodimensional images that support an author's argument. Arguably such contrasts are even more caricatured when it comes to representing waste workers, as the strong association of their professions with filth/purification and shame/redemption serves to further exaggerate this schizoid split in historical accounts. The waste worker is either a devil (able to subhumanly thrive in the muck that paralyzes common citizens, he uses filth as a weapon of extortion) or a saint (he suffers to cleanse us of our daily sins and offenses). While the post-1949 images of night soil men as self-effacing victims are saccharine, they raise to greater visibility class tensions within a trade that, by every account, bristled with fierce resentments and strong loyalties.

CONCLUSION

The night soil trade was a metabolic system that reconnected urban bodies to the agricultural lands that nourished them. In 1949, a CCP survey estimated that more than seventeen hundred carriers handled about 84,000 tons of night soil per year in Beijing, also noting that the sector was devastated after years of war and had reportedly been twice as large in the 1920s and 30s (a claim that fits with Sidney Gamble's finding that carriers in 1919 numbered close to five thousand).[53] A survey done in 1950, when the economy was recovering and the urban center population was projected at 1.8 million, estimated that 125,000 tons of watery night soil, or 83,900 tons after drying, were handled in Beijing, though of course that dried ordure would be mixed with 20–80 percent ash and organic wastes to make fertilizer.[54] However the numbers are crunched, the night soil cycle was vital in replenishing soils in the region and keeping the city fed. Ridding the city of wastes, sustaining regional farming, and providing for the livelihoods of a few thousand workers, the sector was of indisputable benefit to the city and the surrounding countryside. It was also a recurring headache for municipal officials, resisting outside management and assaulting orderly and olfactory sensibilities. Nor was this cycling of soil nutrients a miracle of healthful waste treatment; the night soil business also provided intestinal parasites with free round trips in and out of Beijing residents' innards, to the extent that roundworm was endemic to the city.

Lacking sufficient funds to transform the city's physical infrastructure, Republican-era governments were forced to negotiate with the night soil trade, which despite its limited governability performed a crucial function. In the city's residential neighborhoods, with their narrow, unpaved alleys, crowded housing, and cramped toilets, the only way feces got out was by being hoisted by a human body. The night soil man with the barrel on his back would be necessary until the city's housing stock and sewer system were transformed. The architectural/spatial limitations not only forced night soil workers to keep shouldering that heavy shit bucket; they also condemned the workers to shoulder the outsized burden of embodying sanitary consciousness in their daily labor. The lack of infrastructure focused all the more pressure on the night soil worker as symbol and scapegoat in the hygiene crusade.

The night soil business, over a period of centuries interfacing with the city's changing built environment and demographics, developed into a system built around the enforced customary ownership of shit routes. Though I have found no work on the status of shit routes in the Qing legal code, in Republican-era law the shit route became contentious and disruptively liminal. Neither public nor private property, shit routes were eventually determined by the GMD state to have no legal standing as property at all. Yet the Night Soil Guild and the workers it mobilized claimed those routes as property whether the law agreed or not, and they compelled the government to confirm their claim. This happens repeatedly in the history depicted in this book: under regimes of modern urban governance, the transition point of waste disposal—the spaces or activities whereby disavowed waste materials move from private (domestic or corporate) possession into the public realm—is a complicated and conflicted zone.

The Beiping city government's solution to the problem under Mayor Qin—giving credence to a set of property rights that national legal authorities claimed did not exist—added another layer of messiness to the already messy bodies of waste workers. This formation recurs as well: precisely because waste workers labor in liminal spaces wherein property rights tend to be unclear, and precisely because their labor moves materials across categories in ways that are often illegible to the state, the work they perform, which is already materially messy, acquires added layers of political, legalistic, and economic messiness. What is materially dirty is seen as ethically tainted as well, simply by virtue of the liminal and illegible nature of the spaces within which it is handled and transacted. Ironically, the economic and legalistic categories modern states create to sanitize waste handling and bring regulated legibility to commerce end up submerging the waste trades in clouds of moral suspicion that reinforce the impression that the lucre they make is particularly filthy.

2

From Imperial Capital to Secondhand Emporium

The concept of recycling makes it possible to view the city as a whole.
—MADELEINE YUE DONG, *REPUBLICAN BEIJING, THE CITY AND ITS HISTORIES*

In *Republican Beijing, the City and Its Histories,* Madeleine Yue Dong rummages into the city's daily material economies, social structures, and cultural and literary representations and finds that recycling refracted kaleidoscopically through nearly every facet of Republican Beijing life. Though all cities metabolize materials for reuse, Republican Beijing's unique historical position put these processes front and center. As the imperial seat of the Qing, the largest empire in Chinese history, the city had been a magnet for elite culture and consumption. When the Qing fell, and Beijing with it, the city's status fell to that of a titular capital of a likewise titular Republic, and in 1928 it forfeited even that distinction when Nanjing became the seat of the Nationalist (GMD) government. Globalizing currents of production, shipment, and consumption were not absent from Beijing, but many flows bypassed the city in preference for Tianjin and other treaty ports. Industrial manufacturing steadily grew in China's treaty ports throughout the Republican era but hardly at all in Beijing, which in 1930 had little modern industry aside from a match factory, an electric company, and a few printing plants. So Beijing fell to cannibalizing its greatest resource, its own majestic past:

> The city's economy was no longer focused on trade in luxury goods, as it had been during imperial times. During the Republican period, it was trade in secondhand goods that most affected the city's daily economic life and was a practice necessary for the survival of the city and its people. Modern urban planning, commerce, and transport radically transformed the city, but the material past, from old books to imperial kiln bricks, was still needed in a declining and war-ravaged economy. Nothing in Republican Beijing surpassed the grandeur of the imperial period. The bricks

of the city walls were sold to pay off Republican government employees, were used to repair other imperial architecture, or ended up in people's houses.[1]

In addition to tourist sites that "recycled" Beijing's imperial legacy for modern cultural consumption, the city's most famous markets—the antique shops of Liulichang and the open-air stalls of Tianqiao—specialized in secondhand books, curios, used clothes, and tinkered goods. "Recycling penetrated every population in the whole city. The labor-intensive material practice of recycling ranged from restoring antiques for sale to wealthy foreigners to the remaking of rags into shoe soles for the poor"; there was a guild of "cloth-pasters" with over 150 members who specialized in mixing rags and glues to make stuffing for insulating shoes and caps.[2] The uneven patchwork of Beijing—geographically (from alleyways to boulevards), socially (from the wealthy to the destitute), and materially (from antique vases to cigarette butts)—was woven together in a web of recycling:

> At the heart of the recycling process was the tension not only between the old and the new, but more fundamentally between agency and its lack. The recycling potential of the old commodities themselves was limited by the histories etched into them. Their past could be partly erased, mended, torn, or elaborated, but never eliminated—a product of recycling could only masquerade as new, and rarely convincingly.[3]

These process of reuse and recycling bear a strong kinship to what Susan Strasser describes in the US historical context as "the stewardship of objects." While today we might refer to these objects as "waste materials" (feipin 废品 or feiwu 废物), they were rarely called that at the time. The catchall word most commonly used for such things was 破烂 polan which I usually translate as junk or, at the lowest end, rubbish. Junk was not so much "garbage" but rather objects or scraps that were no longer useful to their owners that might be possible to salvage, repair, modify, or trade. For the purposes of drawing this distinction I often call these processes reuse rather than recycling. Only the most hopeless rubbish that could not be refurbished or repurposed was finally reduced to raw materials (paper pulp, copper ingots), in a process akin to what today we call recycling.

COLLECTION

Estimating how many households directly depended on the reuse/ recycling economy is a shot in the dark, but there were surely several tens of thousands, with the overall numbers rising considerably from 1911 to 1949. In what is by far the most precious source I have for the history of Beijing recycling, an unpublished memoir of a manager from the Xuanwu branch of the Beijing Recycling Company (BRC) in the early 1950s, this motley sector might best be diagrammed by cataloging the various types of collectors and the wide range of buyers to whom they sold their gleanings. Though collectors often directly repurposed or consumed the scrap they collected themselves—at times keeping food, unburned bits of coal, and discarded clothes for their personal use—most of the scrap they collected they sold or bartered through markets to craftspeople, peddlers, and shop owners, who added their own labor and then resold them. Used goods and scrap changed hands via "dawn markets," "night markets," pawnshops (which sold expired tickets, primarily clothing, in lots), and "hanging goods shops" (described later in the chapter).

As is typical in almost every recycling or reuse system, even the most automated, the largest number of laborers worked at the collection stage in these chains (see figure 2). Most were so poor that their scavenging and trade went unmarked by the taxman. Meandering the city's labyrinths of hutongs, collectors were often designated by the tools of their trade. "Net carriers" toted large woven nets and mainly collected paper, which they speared up from the streets or collected from shops and homes. "Shoulder-pole carriers," better known as *dagu'r* or drumbeaters (balancing a pole with one hand and rattling a small drum with the other), were generally men who bought a variety of scrap materials, calling out phrases like, "I buy scrap copper, rusty iron! Rags and bottles, I buy!" Elderly or infirm collectors who lacked the strength to carry their loads were "plank-cart pullers." "Big-basket toters" were often older women who could more readily transact with female residents. Often too frail to balance a shoulder pole, they hoisted their loads of rags and old clothes in baskets on their backs. Heading out before dawn, when housewives (typically the first up) wanted matches to light their cook fires, basket toters threaded the alleys, calling, "I trade matches for junk and rags!"[4] Indeed, scrap collectors seem to have bartered for scrap more than to have bought it with cash. There were women who traded soap for rags. Others bartered small reed flutes or hair combs, and mud molders made cute little clay figurines that were very popular gifts for children.[5]

Of these collectors, the largest group was the drumbeaters, who could be divided into small and big or, in the parlance of the trade, hard and soft. Big/soft drumbeaters, more numerous but less well documented, collected all forms of scrap materials. Small/hard drumbeaters, the elite of the junk collectors, traded in more valuable items, including furs, jewelry, watches, and jades. Hard times were good times for this trade; one industry insider estimated that upwards of two thousand hard drumbeaters scoured Beijing in the run-up to 1949.[6] Dressed in long robes, they were discreet, even secretive, about their work; unlike other collectors, they never called out a chant, only sounded their distinctly high-pitched drums. The profession had its own slang. It was even claimed that each district's drumbeaters had a different set of code words for the numbers one to ten so they could talk prices without fear of customers eavesdropping, though for greatest secrecy they would grip their hands in the long sleeves of their robes and transmit

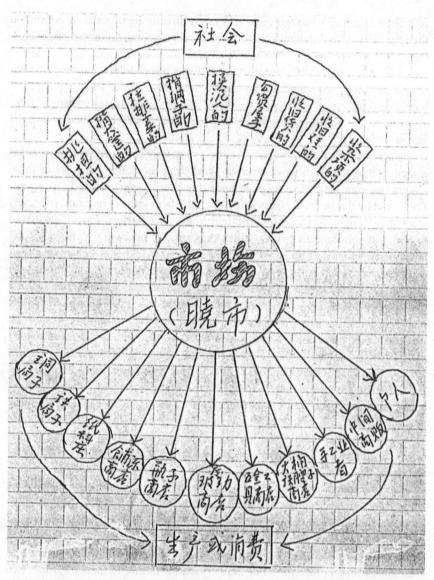

FIGURE 2. Diagram of Republican-era Beiping's used and waste goods sector, by an anonymous BRC manager. Top: Society. Next layer, left to right: pole carriers, large basket toters, flat-cart pullers, net carriers, mud-figure makers, hanging goods shops, used goods collector, used shoes collector, miscellaneous items. Center: MARKET, Dawn Market. Next layer, left to right: copper shop, ferrous shop, paper materials shop, miscellany shop, bottle shop, waste glass shop, hardware shop, barrel and iron band shop, handicraft enterprises, middleman peddlers, individuals. Bottom: Production or consumption

numbers through hand signs. Groups of small drumbeaters usually frequented a particular place such as a teahouse, and these gathering places were known in the trade as *zan'r shang* (攢兒上). In the absence of anything like an organized guild, *zan'r shang* were important forums for sharing information, seeking the advice of expert colleagues, and concocting business schemes. To be successful at the luxury end of the trade, a small drumbeater needed a discerning eye, business savvy, and sensitivity to the frailties of his clients. On their daily peregrinations, these drumbeaters were often invited inside to do their business in private, particularly if the items being traded were valuable. Collectors came to know their down-at-the-heels customers quite well and took care to protect their clients' face, for the neighbors all knew that a visit from a drumbeater meant a household had fallen on hard times.[7] If a piece of merchandise proved too expensive, several drumbeaters might chip in together for shares to buy it. They might also conspire to boost their profits. Say, for instance, a customer needing cash wished to sell a fur coat and mentioned this to a drumbeater, who in a glance realized it was worth about 150 yuan (a good drumbeater was quite skilled at knowing markets and evaluating goods). The drumbeater then might advise the seller to consult a few other collectors to get the best price and the next day send two friends over, who would make offers, each lower than the one before it (say 80 yuan, then 70). The original trusted drumbeater would return and offer 90. The seller, convinced his friend was offering the best price, would sell for 90, and the threesome would in turn resell it for 150, with the drumbeaters pocketing a profit of 20 yuan apiece.[8] If a customer remained steadfast in asking too high a price, word could be put out to area drumbeaters to boycott the seller until he backed down.[9]

While a successful drumbeater might slowly ascend the junk world's business ladder, perhaps eventually opening his own antique shop, the living conditions and prospects for most junk and scrap collectors were dismal. Their working hours made getting rest nearly impossible. A typical day meant leaving home at dawn and collecting junk until dusk; sleeping a few hours and then waking around 2:00 a.m. to sort the day's haul and head to the dawn market to sell it all; then rushing home for a quick breakfast before heading out to collect again. Our Xuanwu district recycling depot manager recalled doing the rounds during Chinese New Year in 1956 to distribute five yuan of charitable "dumpling money" to over one hundred households of destitute collectors. He found that many of these households, even after six years of CCP rule, owned nothing but what they had gleaned from the streets and trash heaps; many families still lacked sufficient clothing to dress all household members at the same time.[10] A report from the city's recycling bureau that same year estimated that there were still more than two thousand garbage pickers in the city, and doubtless their ranks were considerably greater in the Republican era.[11] And of course, in addition to such full-time collectors, many other populations were veteran part-timer pickers: beggars, refugees, street urchins, street cleaners, etc. Venturing a ballpark estimate would be scholarly hubris, but no doubt many thousands depended to some degree on scavenging and scrap for income.

MARKETS

The collection stage of any recycling system is naturally geographically dispersed. The next stage, the market nexus at which materials move from collectors to middlemen, processors, or resellers, occurs at nodes that are more concentrated and so, at least in theory, easier to locate and quantify. However, in the junk trades these nodes are often shrouded in the intentional fog of gray market dealings and further obscured by historical neglect.

The primary nexus at which junk moved from the hands of collectors to those of peddlers, crafts workers, shop owners, and brokers was the dawn markets (*xiaoshi*) or ghost markets (*guishi*).[12] These date back to at least the late Qing, when this ditty of homely advice was recorded:

> At night at the 5th drum, before the crows call
> The dawn market teams with people, tangled like jute.
> Resist the tempting bargains, shun the stolen goods all
> For you'll end up in the yamen when you're mixed up with that loot.[13]

Vendors at dawn markets included all sorts of collectors, from rather established drumbeaters to destitute scavengers, but there were also handfuls of declining Manchu and scholarly families (clandestinely hawking their valuables in the dark to save face), as well as thieves and their fences.

The timing and placement of these tenebrous gatherings harmonized a variety of necessities. Forming in the wee hours and dispersing around dawn, these bazaars squeezed snugly into the daily work cycles of the participants; by dawn craftsmen needed to be back at their shops and collectors back on their beats.[14] The darkness was conducive to trading in stolen, counterfeit, and shoddy merchandise, and informal markets were especially prone to sprout up along the edges of ponds or ditches, into which stolen items could be quickly ejected if the police came nosing about. As attempts to tax or regulate dawn markets proved futile, the authorities generally turned a blind eye to them, allowing a few to become well established:

> Dawn markets congregate around 3 a.m. and disperse at dawn, the peddlers of each occupation gathering, doing their business and dispersing in a few short hours. One type of dawn market, called an "Odds and Ends Market," has two locations, one at Inner Desheng Gate, one at Chongwai Tangxibo Street. The peddlers call them "North Market" and "South Market." From large items, like wood furniture and bolts of cloth, to small ones like staples and sheets of newsprint, from valuables like gold, pearls and jade pieces, to the cheapest rusty iron and copper scraps, all kinds of

edibles, there is nothing they don't have. It all centers around the drum-beaters who collect scattered old goods from every corner of the city. Every day, at the crack of dawn, the city's merchants and peddlers come seeking goods, like ants swarming to the smell of mutton. Buyers hope to get a low price and sellers all harbor the goal of making some profit.[15]

Whether one went to North or South Market was largely a function of proximity, though South Market was said to do a livelier business. Several other locales also offered predawn trading, including at Inner Guangan Gate, the Vegetable Market at Outer Xuanwu Gate, and the Pearl Market at Qian Gate. No one seems to have bothered tallying the number of "stalls" (often no more than a blanket laid out on the ground), but according to our BRC cadre's memoir, the number shot up from a few hundred in the 1930s to nearly one thousand in the late 1940s—yet another indication that the reuse/recycling sector flourished most during troubled times. Scrap and secondhand goods also moved at night markets (wanshi), periodic markets that typically gathered from about 5:00 to 9:00 at night on a rotating ten-day cycle.[16] "Peddlers with goods from the odds and ends markets, in addition to their business from the day, hurry here with the hope of earning a bit more income. Most of the goods here are old things made new. They are cheap and unreliable."[17]

Nocturnal markets were ecosystems of ingeniously adapted foragers and predators. One fellow could assay the purity of metals by the tone they made when struck; another could discern that a dingy, lidless teapot was actually made of antique porcelain and knew where to scrounge up a matching antique lid (or an expertly crafted fake) that would cap it as a valuable piece of merchandise. Each genus of goods—books, jades, clothes, furs, brass locks, religious curios, glasses, watches, paintings—had its expert hunters. Counterfeit goods lurked everywhere: forged Han bronzes; pipes of fake ivory; shoes that smell, shine, and feel like polished leather but are made from pressed cardboard, which begins to fray and disintegrate after a few days' wear. The markets' pace was surprisingly fast; sellers relied on a rapid daily turnover so they would have cash in their pockets for their next days' purchases, and the peddlers and brokers whose businesses sourced from dawn markets came early to get their pick of the best goods. Common folk, who strolled the market hunting for discarded treasures or bargain goods for their own personal use, typically showed up a couple of hours later, just before dawn, but by this time most of the best merchandise had been sold off; hence stroller's goods (guangshihuo) was the junk trade lingo for scraggly items that did not sell quickly. Despite all the cautionary tales, people of all stripes, including many cultural elites, could not resist the allure of discovering an undetected treasure; perhaps that heap of wastepaper selling for a few cents a pound was actually the lost letters of a famous scholar? And of course there were snack stalls: tofu (stinky and sweet), tea stalls, skewered mutton and donkey meat, breakfast buns, and crullers.

The geography of used goods markets was in constant flux during the Republican era as the city was being reimagined and reconstructed in relation to national and international transformations and technological change. The East Dawn market that gathered in empty lots near the Medicine God Temple outside Chongwen Gate was forced to shift as housing was built, winding up in alleys near Fahu Temple by the 1940s.[18] Major events also reshaped the market landscape; markets appeared, disappeared, and gradually shifted location depending on construction projects and policing regimes.[19]

By far the biggest and most famous used goods market in all Beijing was Tianqiao, home to hundreds of stalls, traders, entertainers, and snack sellers. Tianqiao was not a dawn market but a daytime market, and its location was more or less fixed. A sprawling open-air used goods emporium, Tianqiao catered to the vast and diverse clientele of Beijingers who could hardly afford to purchase anything new, but also to residents and tourists looking for novelties and entertainment. If dawn markets were where scrap collectors sold flotsam for various merchants and craftworkers to fix, polish, and gussy up—transforming broken and scrap items into saleable used goods—then Tianqiao was where much of that gussied-up flotsam was sold to consumers. And though Tianqiao was often portrayed, even in some Republican-era tourist guides, as an "ancient" site, its origins were actually thoroughly rooted in post-Qing urban transformations. Many of the earliest businesses and performers relocated to the Tianqiao area after their own venues were demolished in Republican-era urban renewal projects, leading Madeleine Yue Dong to characterize it as a "concentration of elements expelled from the reordered Republican Beijing."[20] Also crucial to Tianqiao's phenomenal expansion and popularity was the building of rail and streetcar routes, which made it an accessible attraction not just for south-city locals, but also for residents from all across Beijing and even tourists. In addition to all sorts of snacks, Tianqiao was perhaps best known as a free-for-all, open-air performing ground for wrestlers, drum singers (*Jingyun dagu*), storytellers (*Pingshu*), and martial arts performers cum patent medicine sellers. And all this was centered on its overflowing market stalls:

> The volume of goods and the level of excitement at Tianqiao made it something more than a market satisfying people's daily needs. The low prices not only allowed but also lured shoppers to buy. The commercial mechanism at work in the newly developed department stores was not totally absent at Tianqiao. In a sense, Tianqiao was a new market for old goods and a training ground for consumers in a modernizing city.[21]

Unlike the department stores, however, Tianqiao posted no price tags. Every purchase was a negotiation, a potential heist, a step into the "tiger's mouth," as many of the used clothing stalls were known.

But not all scrap and secondhand goods transactions happened in the streets and outdoor markets. Often relatively valuable materials and curios bypassed such street markets and went directly from collectors to a range of junk shops. Some drumbeaters and net carriers developed close relationships with what were called hanging goods shops (*guahuo pu*). These shops, mostly clustered in neighborhoods like Tianqiao, Liulichang, and the Qian Gate market area, emerged in the last decades of the nineteenth century as many Qing elites slipped from opulence to penury:

> In the 1870s it had been stylish to travel in customized carriages drawn by well-decorated horses. When these decorations for carts and horses became too soiled, they were collected for sale at shops that hung them at the door, hence the name. Later these stalls grew into secondhand goods stores dealing in every conceivable item. . . . These shops had close ties to the drum beaters and antique shops. If the hard-drum beaters had items beyond the marketing ability of the hanging-goods stalls, they contacted antique shops, who often paid a commission. Alternatively, hanging-goods stall owners might pool their capital to purchase pieces to sell to antique shops. The best items went to antique shops; utterly bedraggled items went to the used-goods booths at Tianqiao, which proffered an entire spectrum of the lowest-quality secondhand goods and items most closely related to the daily lives of Beijing's residents.[22]

Lying somewhere on the spectrum between the more respected antique shops (*guwan pu*) and the cruder old goods shops (*jiuhuo dian*), the hodgepodge of the hanging-goods stalls was dizzying: jade pendants, porcelains, carpets, iron farm tools, horse reins, saddle bags, Mongolian leather boots, Tibetan Buddhas (a few shops specialized in Mongolian and Tibetan products), old knives, cricket cages, fans, water pipes, lanterns. Some drumbeaters sourced exclusively to a particular hanging-goods stall were said to *gui hang* (归行).

As one might imagine, just as there was an economic hierarchy of used goods shops, there was a ladder of success in the junk trades, with drumbeaters and shop apprentices hoping to make good and open their own stalls, and hanging-goods stall owners dreaming of becoming antique sellers.[23] He Baotang, a gangly, illiterate youth from rural Hebei, realized this dream. In 1929, after spending more than fifteen years scouring the dawn markets for porcelains to sell to antique and hanging-goods shops, he had become so expert in the field that the Muslim owners of the Derunxing antique store asked him to become their manager so that they could finally enter the antique shop guild. (Muslims were banned from the guild, supposedly to prevent the guild from descending into internal conflict.)[24] A similar story of rising from poverty in the trade is that of Han Yiquan, who started out by buying calligraphy at dawn markets, cleaning them up and mounting them nicely and reselling them on the street, gradually schooling himself in the fine points of calligraphy and appraising until he was a renowned expert. The hanging-goods business thrived in the wake of the looting of the Boxer uprising in 1900, and again when the Qing's fall tossed thousands of Manchu households into poverty. In the 1930s hanging-goods shops numbered around three hundred, with perhaps one thousand employees. In a rough schematic of the recycling trade, one could say that antique shops were retailers, while hanging-goods shops played the roles of both retailer and transactor, both buying and selling used goods to other junk-handling businesses.

A final important way goods entered the recycling loop was via pawnshops. Beijing's Chamber of Commerce listed eighty-eight pawnshops in 1927, and Sidney Gamble's survey estimated employees and owners totaled more than sixteen hundred.[25] Since the Ming (1368–1644), pawnshops had played a role in the finances of Beijing commoners, helping them through rough spots with small sums of cash in exchange for personal items to be redeemed in better times. In the late Qing, the Manchu court invested in pawnshops because they offered fairly high interest on their deposits, and this investment boosted the number of pawnshops in the capital to more than two hundred. But Beijing's pawnshops were looted in the Boxer turmoil; the number recovered to only around one hundred and hovered there throughout the Republican era.[26] While they would hold just about anything of value (jewelry, rickshaws, furniture, watches, musical instruments), pawnshops' largest-volume trade by far was in clothing. It was a highly seasonal business; for example, residents pawned heavy winter clothes in spring for redemption in autumn. But customers often lacked the cash to redeem their goods. Shops were required to charge limited interest (3% up to 1929 and 2.5% thereafter) and to hold goods for a designated term (two years, shortened to eighteen months in 1929). When the redemption period expired, shops auctioned off the "dead number" items in lots to secondhand clothes dealers. The volume of these sales was considerable:

> The old clothes business (guyi ye) put simply is the sale of pawned clothing the tickets for which have expired. . . . This business flourished most in the first years of the Republic, with businessmen from the three Northeastern provinces [Manchuria] and Shanghai passing through Beijing in an endless stream, buying and shipping wholesale in great quantities. But in 1929 the price of goods shipped to Manchuria collapsed due to the unsettled political situation, and Beijing businesses took considerable losses and couldn't claim their debts. In 1930 Beijing's businesses sent out their own shipments, but then the Chinese-Russian relations issue arose, prohibiting their sale and they were sold at a big loss. . . . Shipments to Shanghai are [now, in 1932,] slim. . . . Only in the Northern Hebei and Inner Mongolia (Suiyuan) region are the old-style clothes of Beijing still in fashion, so today's old clothes shops are all battling to find new outlets.[27]

For the first few decades of the twentieth century, Beijing's old-clothes trade regularly exported merchandise throughout the country. But by 1930, Beijing's Manchu-inflected fashions, once highly popular even in Shanghai, had lost favor with all but northern country folk, leaving Beijing's local markets bursting at the seams with used clothes. Tianqiao, Beijing's raucous marketplace and folk carnival, packed into its alleys at peak seasons as many as five hundred used clothing dealers (ranging from itinerants selling old clothes from a sack to established shopfronts). The Beijing Old Clothes Guild registered 220 shops and more than two thousand members.

The eventual disposition of cloth scrap and clothing items wove through a broad range of crafts and peddlers. Some silks and furs were resold as luxury items. Garments that were worse for wear underwent a variety of cosmetic surgeries, dye jobs, and alterations, reemerging in stalls masquerading as younger and healthier than they actually were. Cloth by the ton was cut into swaths and sold in batches for use in making other cloth products (three or four dozen stalls in the city dealt primarily in such scrap bundles). Cotton bunting was refluffed and restuffed, though it was well known to be nearly worthless as insulation. Threadbare scraps might be mixed with paste to be made into insulating material for caps and shoes, tied into mop heads, or sold to make paper. But this is already slipping into the portion of the recycling chain involved in the repair, handicraft, and (re)sale of scrap to consumers.

REMAKING AND RESELLING

Businesses that reworked scrap or sold used or refurbished goods to consumers were, predictably, the most specialized link in the recycling chain and the most liable to be rooted in permanent shops. The majority of used goods and junk shops were located in neighborhoods around the Chongwen and Xuanwu Gates. They had set addresses, were usually registered with the city government, and had some assets and capital, though many were in nearly constant debt.

Like used clothing and fabric, wastepaper was a material traded in considerable quantities and met with a wide variety of fates on its path to reincarnation. A tiny but noteworthy portion was rescued from the waste pile by gentlemen historians, the city's turmoil on occasion impelling people or even government offices in need of quick money to sell off archives, letters, and other documents as wastepaper. The famed dramaturge Qi Rushan rescued many palace records pertaining to court-performed dramas from the wastepaper dealer.

Paper that was relatively clean and intact could be sold for binding into small notebooks, to wrap merchandise, or for papering over windows and walls as insulation. Collectors themselves might keep such paper and make these items at home to sell for extra cash. In terms of quantity, wastepaper probably ranked second to used cloths as the largest scrap sector, employing thousands of collectors and hundreds of small intermediary sorting, trading, and processing shops, almost all of them household businesses with almost no capital or mechanization. The bulk of collected paper went to the city's few dozen scrap paper shops, which served as brokers, sorting, aggregating, and the selling bundled paper and fiber for various uses. Rougher scrap often headed out to paper mills in nearby Dingxing and Xushui counties near Baoding. There it was made into various kinds of (generally lower quality) paper, but chiefly *maotou* paper, a soft, slightly furry brownish paper used mainly to pane windows and wrap goods.[28] (Interestingly, in the late 1990s these same areas became centers for processing Beijing's lower quality wastepaper scrap in small-scale, often highly polluting factories.) Waste paper shops sourced not just from street collectors but from other city businesses, handling trimmings from printing shops, empty cement bags from building sites, and (especially after 1949) defunct paper currency. Somewhat ironically, these larger wastepaper brokers became even more dominant in the industry after 1949, when Beijing was reborn as China's political capital, and hence also as the capital of the CCP's enormous propaganda printing industry, a major by-product of which was trimmed paper scrap. In the 1950s perhaps one hundred new shops blossomed in an area known today as Baizhifang (White Paper Workshop) to fight for the best bits. Big printing outfits, particularly the government's most prestigious press, Xinhua, were wined, dined, and wooed by ardent wastepaper traders, a handful of whom parleyed these warm friendships into a veritable monopoly by orchestrating large advance payments to the company for its scrap paper.[29] After the state takeover of private businesses (*gongsi heying*) in 1956, these shops became the core of the city's state-run paper-material enterprises.

There were a few hundred scrap metal shops in Republican-era Beijing, though very few had more than one or two employees outside the immediate family. Beijing's "Copper King" had a grand retinue of two paid employees and around 30,000 yuan in capital. While shops typically specialized in one metal and its alloys, they collectively formed a guild under the name copper, iron, and tin shops. Copper was the dominant commodity in this group; relatively high in value, it was used to mint coins as well as to make various luxury items (statues, incense burners, fancy wash basins, and the occasional fake antique ritual vessel). Shops purchased their metal scrap mainly from local collectors, but they also imported some from outside the city; a report from the Chongwen Gate customs office notes five tons of scrap copper and sixty-five tons of scrap iron entered the city in 1929.[30] The proprietors of Beijing's two hundred or so ferrous scrap shops mostly hailed from Hebei's Zaoqiang county. Too small to supply major industries or railroads (who got their materials via Tianjin), they mainly provided iron and steel to local blacksmiths and toolmakers or hardware shops. Many shops could produce ingots and simple materials like wire and brads used in handicrafts. A plethora of handicraft trades—decorative brass fittings, brass statue making, locks, glasses frames, pots and pans, tinware, and so forth—relied in large part on metal scrap shops for materials, and there were also hundreds of tinkers who specialized in repairs of all sorts of items and also needed scrap. The tinkers' guild (called the Clever Stove Guild [Qiao lu hui] because their main implements were a portable stove and diamond-tipped gimlet) claimed 380 members who could "mend articles made of porcelain, brass, iron and certain other metals. . . . [They] are perhaps best known for their skill in joining together securely broken pieces of china, by both gluing the pieces together and fastening them firmly by brads melted into tiny holes which they have bored in the porcelain."[31] Hardware shops often had a sideline in repairs, buying used or damaged tools and fittings at night markets and restoring them to serviceable quality. There were also several shops that sorted and brokered broken glass to be sold to glass factories, and a few dozen shops that specialized, some with an extraordinary level of precision, in the reuse of bottles. These shops would not only wash and disinfect bottles but would also carefully sort bottles that might be used by specific retailers, as well as provide special services like making lids and stoppers to order.

Antique shops were at the pinnacle of the used goods trade. Cultural treasures of all sorts populated the dusty tableaus of Liulichang. Initially a book market that thrived during the Qianlong emperor's Four Treasuries project (1772–83), the area began attracting the sale of antiques as well in the nineteenth century, with its first antique shop, Boguzhai, opening in the 1830s. By the late Qing, Liulichang claimed over 130 stalls crammed into a single eight-hundred-meter lane, and in the Republican era the vendors were overflowing into the nearby fire-god temple neighborhood.[32] Many items that passed through the hands of small drumbeaters found their way here. Hidden among the shiny tchotchkes and curios, cunning facsimiles of Han bronzes and bogus Ming paintings were indeed some truly precious finds for the cognoscenti.

CONCLUSION

Habits suited to an economy of disposability are not innate; they are acquired. They involve unlearning attitudes of thrift and stewardship, unlearning habits of mending and repair and learning new habits of consumption and disposal, and adopting a new economic calculus that makes such behaviors seem reasonable and preferable. While there is an individual consciousness aspect to these behaviors (Strasser, for instance, describes how US housekeeping magazines in the early twentieth century chided "modern" housewives to prioritize hygiene and/or fashion over thrift), these habits are profoundly informed and enabled by infrastructures of production, distribution, and disposal (waste removal).[33] Disposability is unthinkable without the annihilation of space brought by mechanization—industrial systems that can produce streams of items and rapidly deliver them within our reach and then whisk them away after we have sucked them of their transient vitality. Certainly in other historical eras there were the rich and powerful few who could experience the luxury of disposability prior to the rise of hydrocarbon-impelled capital, but they could only do so conspicuously surrounded by a mass of servants who produced, procured, served, and removed objects of consumption. Fossil-fuel-impelled infrastructures that enabled such consumption for a more common populace emerged unevenly in the nineteenth and twentieth centuries, but Beijing was only partially linked into such infrastructures and far from suffused by them until the late twentieth century.

When looking at Beijing households' practices of reuse, mending, and repair and the elaborate web of junk trades and handicrafts in the city's alleys and markets, we can see ways of (re)making and managing goods that do not easily conform to the three dominant economic categories—production, consumption, and disposal—that have become naturalized in industrial capitalism. Many of the trades discussed in this chapter could be seen as extensions into the public/remunerative sphere of domestic labor (mending clothes and shoes, fixing broken housewares and tools, etc.) that is neither production or consumption. And in the other direction, many handicraft industries extended into household spaces (making paper flowers, matchboxes, etc., from paper scrap; making clothes, shoes, and toys from waste cloth and bunting), in this way accessing cheaper female and child labor. Part of what could be described as the liminality of the scrap/recycling sector is the blur between domestic and public economies involved in many of the trades discussed here, a blur that occurs on multiple levels: stores being also homes, scavenging for personal use and for sale, and so forth.

We still repair, clean, and creatively repurpose our possessions today, but in Republican-era Beijing these activities constituted a broad sector of economic activity and were of far greater economic significance to most of the population than modern industrial "production." Madeleine Yue Dong's claim that "the concept of recycling makes it possible to view [Beijing] as a whole" points to the failure of our typical economic categories to map the material and economic processes by which Beijing functioned. To group together practices of scrap collection, reuse, recycling, scavenging, handicrafts, and antiques is to interpret the history of Beijing in a particular way; this is not an unmediated representation of an economic truth nor the reconstruction of a commonsense categorization of urban life at the time. What brings these goods, materials, acts of commerce, and tinkering together is that they all clearly disrupt the simplified production-consumption binary into which we typically lump economic processes. In recycling, acts of disposal become the preliminary stages of production; production inputs originate as consumption outputs, by-products, or wastes. Refashioning and tinkering reinvigorate or reinvent goods that are losing their useful identities. It is precisely because these processes are so varied and pervasive that the marketplace in which they occur functions along quite different rules and assumptions (there are no set prices, buyer beware, etc.) than those governing markets in which the policed bifurcation of production and consumption (virtual though it in fact is) sets the rules (every instance of each item uniformly priced, of uniform quality, etc.).

To put this another way: the production-consumption binary of industrial consumer culture is enabled by the foreclosure of the uses and reuses of wastes; it is only because after consumption comes disposal that we can imagine economic processes as linear, and that linearity underwrites the standardization of products sold on the market. As Josh Reno explains, the certainty that disposal follows consumption is vital to enabling the mass consumption of virtual permanence, the confidence that every time I consume a product it will be indistinguishable from the previous time: the potato chips just as crunchy, the feel of the T shirt cloth just as smooth.[34] An exploration of the scrap trades in Republican-era Beijing serves to remind us that the categories *production*, *consumption*, and *disposal* do not offer a complete or accurate portrayal of human economic interactions with goods and materials. We might see our own contemporary economy in a different light if we introduced mending, repair, cleaning, and maintenance as important economic measures (and several discard studies scholars have expressed far-reaching insights along these lines).[35] It seems irrefutable that our current bias to measure sales volumes and GDP has led us to valorize economies that are patently unsustainable, and we might indeed benefit from rethinking not just the kinds of energy and materials we use in our economies, but how we measure their performance.

Modernity of a Different Sort

If the modernity of an infrastructure were evaluated through the kinds of materials mobilized, sources of energy used for production and transport, or the legibility of planned design and management, then Republican Beijing's recycling infrastructure (wooden ladles and hemp bags, foot power transport, informal markets, and customary night soil routes) would appear clearly premodern (or preindustrial). But in fact, through recycling practices Beijingers were intimately engaging with modernity. Matters modern permeate everything discussed in the preceding two chapters. Regarding night soil, for example, we should not confuse Beijing's poverty and lack of industrialization (which made visions of flush toilets and a comprehensive sewer system unattainable) for lack of modernity; from 1906 onward the sector was constantly under pressure from city governments trying to enact a modern hygienic vision, and the Fertilizer Guild only emerged in response to those pressures. Wastepaper traders placed premium value on newsprint and other foreign imported paper products, and many of the poorest collectors bartered matches (a product of industrial chemistry) for scrap. At the top of the used goods hierarchy, the antique and trinket shops of Liulichang paid special attention to attracting foreign collectors and tourists. And by far the largest, most raucous, and most famous used goods and recycling market in the city, Tianqiao, only became a center of cheap amusements due to large-scale relocation and trolley construction, which were part of Beijing's modern urban planning.

Rather than premodern holdovers, recycling and reuse practices were strategies that enabled many of Beijing's poor to survive the dislocation of their city from its privileged position and to cope with its incorporation into an economic system increasingly shaped by foreign imperialism and industrial capitalism.

Beijing's recyclers were not lagging behind; they were coping with the modern present by mobilizing the resources available from the material past (from yesterday's newspaper, to last week's shit, to last year's coat, to last century's vase, to last dynasty's bricks) to survive the stressful, accelerating economic cycles of the twentieth century. The world of recycling and reuse in Republican-era Beijing entailed a fundamentally modern encounter with society and the nation. Its rhythms of production moved as much to the daily pace of modern urban markets, as to the cyclical rhythm of China's rural marketing system. Experiences of consumption in places like Tianqiao were imbued with a distinctly urban and alienating lack of trust and familiarity; the social reflection that the world of recycling and urban poverty inspired in elite observers and sociologists engaged distinctly modern ideas of what proper Republican citizenship should entail.

Activities of recycling and reuse in Republican Beijing were social and rarely aspired to the virtual anonymity associated with mass consumer culture. Bartering scrap to a drumbeater and purchasing secondhand goods at a street stall were personalized acts of economic exchange, and not always in a friendly and trusting way. There were no price tags, quality guarantees, or receipts. Whereas industrial commodities are purposely designed to be interchangeable, to bear no fingerprints, and to display no obvious evidence of individual labor (imperfections), the reused goods of the Republican era could not help but display the scuffmarks, bruises, and mended scars of exchange, wear, and craft labor.

The scrap trades could generally be characterized as allergic to state attention and regulation. Whether a poor picker afraid of being incarcerated for indigence, a peddler avoiding registering and tax collection, or a used goods trader who preferred not to know if the goods she was selling had been stolen, those engaged in the scrap trades generally derived few advantages from attracting the police's interest. Though the authorities could be abusive and arbitrary, the state was not terribly interested in the scrap traders. Street sweepers and night soil collectors were subjected to practices of governmentality, however uneven and half-hearted; the state expended money and effort not just to be punitive but to support these trades, paying street cleaners wages and funding the restructuring of the night soil system. But the scrap trades were not fostered or shepherded, only restricted and harassed. Aside from hoping to keep scrappers from clogging important thoroughfares or trafficking in stolen goods or munitions, the municipal government saw little worthy of its attention, either punitive or nurturing. The experiences of Republican-era informal scrap markets serve as an apt expression of the power relations between the state and recyclers. Junk traders found unclaimed spaces, not in the middle of high-visibility avenues and districts, but close enough to share in the hubbub and activity. Dawn markets might start tentatively, but they would gradually become more established over time. A few eventually turned neighborhoods into nightly bazaars, crowding the road space with their "stalls" (blankets on the ground) until there was hardly room to walk. Urban renewal projects reorganized the checkerboard of regulated and less-regulated spaces but did not sweep it clean.

Though the peddler/recycler wrestling match with Republican-era municipal authorities over access to urban spaces was something of a stalemate, those plying the scrap trades could never breathe easy. They often formed protective communities and cultures to shield themselves, developing their own shared secret jargons and practices of apprenticeship and community self-regulation. This is not to say that somehow the trades themselves were harmonious communities of dependable mutual aid; as many informal businessmen like to joke, nobody cheats you worse than your own colleague. The upshot of these complex, opaque, often desperate commercial relations was a raucous urban marketing experience offering an encyclopedic array of goods that were never above suspicion. The recycling sector was vital to the survival not just of the tens of thousands of collectors, traders, and peddlers, but also to their countless low-income customers, yet it created public spaces and public attitudes that were profoundly different from the kinds of citizenship that regimes like the GMD hoped to instill in the public.

Nobody needed to scold and educate Republican Beijingers to conserve or recycle materials for the national interest; thrift was for survival, not for the nation or to help develop industry. No motivation or agenda shaped recycling and reuse practices more powerfully than the desire of every actor in the system to make a profit; nationalism, hygiene, environmentalism, legal codes, and concerns for social welfare all made scant impression on these behaviors. As obvious as this seems, it is worth noting, because the PRC state was profoundly committed to trying to reframe the individualistic profit-motive mindset that was the fundamental mechanism energizing Beijing's recycling infrastructure.

PART TWO

The Mao Era
(1949–1980)

Recycling According to Plan

Almost everyone I have met who grew up in the Mao era waxes nostalgic about recycling in those days. Most tell stories about how much they looked forward to trading some old newspapers or an empty toothpaste tube to a shabby but kindly collector for small candy figurines or a few cents to buy a popsicle. Such stories convey how special it felt in the tightly planned Mao-era economy to have a little pocket money and indulge in a small, guiltless pleasure. Some tell more elaborate stories. Wang Shaomin positively glowed when I told him about my interest in Mao-era scrap. Wang had been a high school senior when the Cultural Revolution (CR) swept him out of the classroom and into the streets, where he had a rewarding stint masquerading as a recycler. The junk heap offers those who explore it many opportunities to role-play: the adventurer sifts the detritus of daily wastes for lost treasures, and the detective sorts the befouled archive for incriminating evidence, which disposers wish to cleanse from their identity. During the CR, treasures and incriminating evidence were often one and the same object, and Wang played both adventurer and detective. With the campaign to destroy the Four Olds (customs, culture, habits, and ideas) at its height, Wang's teachers (and many intellectuals throughout Beijing) were panicking over what to do with many of the cultural items contaminating their homes. A book lover himself, Wang came up with a fun and helpful way to spend his revolutionary school vacation. Through a friend who worked at a Beijing Recycling Company (BRC) depot, Wang borrowed a three-wheeled bike cart and a scale and hung out around the residential compounds of teachers and writers, offering to buy their books as wastepaper. One of Wang's favorite memories was buying a full set of Lu Xun's collected works at 10 cents a kilo and then mailing it piecemeal to a friend "making revolution" on the Soviet border (his friend became an academic after the CR). Some books he kept, some he gave to friends, and most he sold to the recycling office by weight for cash. After becoming friendly with the depot boss, Wang also got access to the depot paper warehouse, where he scavenged and smuggled out any banned foreign pictorials he could find. Under the ideological cover of the Mao-era craze for scrap collecting, Wang dabbled in a brief career as a book profiteer and smuggler of contraband publications. The liminal messiness of the scrap world, even in the Mao era, proved fertile ground for opportunistic creativity.[1]

Wang's story touches on many aspects of Mao-era recycling, but I start with the masquerade itself. What had changed since "liberation" that Wang, not a poor peasant but a relatively privileged high-school bookworm, would want to play at being a scrap collector? More to the point, the very idea of "registered recyclers"— that Beijing in 1966 now had a recycling bureaucracy of authorized collectors whose trademark identifier was their company-issued three-wheeled carts—and that Wang, in order to deal in used books, found it fruitful to impersonate one, tells us that the scrap sector's relationship to state and society had undergone some fairly profound changes since 1949. On the other hand, an itinerant collector roaming a neighborhood with a bike cart buying used paper would have hardly seemed out of place a generation earlier. If the BRC looked like a state-run, formalized version of the junk collectors of a slightly earlier time, that is largely because it was. As we will see, the state created the BRC mainly by gathering and organizing the myriad strands of the city's scrappers; even the capital and assets to build the BRC came largely from them.

Domestic habits of conserving and preserving material objects changed only gradually with the development of socialist industrialization, but how practices of the "stewardship of objects" interfaced with the larger economic system was fundamentally altered. There were still roaming collectors, but these state-licensed employees no longer bartered with residents or participated in intricate and illicit webs of trading transactions; the netherworld of dawn markets with their patched, pawned, and picked objects that gathered nightly had been swept from the streets. Instead of anticipating that one's scrap bits would be used to patch some clothes or make some tin trinkets, one was instead meant to envision her bits of used material joining with similar bits to form great resource streams that would feed and drive the nation's steel and glass furnaces and copper and rubber refineries. To trade with the BRC collector was to participate in the great collective project of socialist industrialization. The small change the BRC gave people for their used "resources" was a valuable treat in a money-scarce economy. Mao-era China underwent industrialization without consumerism, or, if one wishes to quibble over that last term—for there definitely was brand consciousness about bikes, cigarettes, liquor, and watches—industrialization without disposability.

When the CCP took over, it did not immediately demolish the intricate, market-based web of resourceful recycling and reuse practices upon which millions of Chinese urban dwellers depended. Rather, the state carefully surveyed, analyzed, and reorganized the recycling/reuse sector until it had enough control over the sector's personnel and materials to regulate and reshape it to meet the government's priorities of industrial production and urban sanitation. This is not to argue that the story of the Mao-era takeover of the sector was gentle; CCP reform of the sector was in many ways a sorting process, rewarding cooperation and discouraging recalcitrance. Along with the provision of welfare and unsolicited acts of "education," there were plenty of confiscations, incidents of state-directed violence, inadvertent economic disasters, failed experiments, and policy betrayals. By the 1960s, the state had effected fundamental discursive and systemic transformations. The market trading networks, the circulation systems of the recycling/reuse sector, were eliminated and replaced by administrative channels. At the same time, what had been a dizzying hodgepodge of materials and goods had been tamed into flows of standardized commodities: six grades of copper, thirteen subcategories of rubber, and so forth. Together these changes, two sides of the same reform process, formed the seemingly contradictory process of commoditization through market elimination. But the historical processes of building the state system also made for several unmistakable continuities: most BRC recycling workers had worked in the sector before 1949; habits of frugality, mending, and reuse were still prized; and the main method by which recyclers obtained scrap from residents was by purchasing it, making recycling a social rather than an anonymous act.

This domestic, often very local, story was also very much shaped by a global economic and political context. China's international trade in the Mao era was extremely constrained, putting great pressure on conserving resource endowments and making scrap recycling an indispensable part of economic policy. The country's supplies of copper, rubber, and paper fiber had long relied on import markets. The US embargo cut US-China trade to almost zero in the 1950s, and the governments of Western Europe and Japan felt compelled to follow suit. China's trade with the Soviet Union accounted for over half of its total foreign trade in the 1950s, and the Soviet Older Brother usually got more goods than it gave. The 1960s brought little relief, for just as US allies broke ranks on the embargo and hesitantly revived their trade, the Sino-Soviet split severed the bulk of China's trade with the socialist bloc.[2] Still, over the three decades of the Mao era, Beijing's per capita consumption gradually increased, with municipal solid waste collection nearly doubling and scrap collection quadrupling between 1958 and 1977. Despite what appears to have at times been the suffocatingly inefficient bureaucratization of a sector of generally low-value goods, there is no question that the Mao-era recycling system assisted in circulating crucial resources and making them available for China's industrial development.

3

The Rural Exile of Urban Wastes

THE CCP SWEEPS IN AND SWEEPS UP

Sanitation was a high priority for Beiping's new Communist municipal government in the winter of 1949, and for good reason. War crushes infrastructures, including urban sanitation, leaving cities dangerously vulnerable to epidemics from cholera to plague. Over decades of urban mismanagement, untold tons of trash had mounted to form permanent heaps hunched against the city's walls and canal banks. Removing these massifs of refuse would be one of the new city government's first marquee campaigns. It was still freezing cold when Beiping was "peacefully liberated" in February, but soon the waste heaps would thaw, breeding swarms of vermin and disease vectors. Time was of the essence. By coincidence, some Nationalist officials had just been prosecuted for embezzling USAID supplies that had been earmarked for a citywide cleanup, helping set up a narrative in which the CCP would not only be cleaning up decades of accumulated garbage but also sweeping away the moral rot of the previous regime.[1]

The big cleanup began in earnest on March 8 with a planning meeting of representatives from city government, sanitation, public works, the 41st Army, the Beiping student union, the police, workers' pickets, the chamber of commerce, and more. The fledgling city government lacked the resources to remove the estimated 180,000–300,000 tons of garbage from the city in short order and would need the military and the masses to help. Civil engineers hashed out the overall plan. The Sanitation Bureau would employ about twenty-five hundred workers to collect trash and clean streets on a regular basis—about one for every one hundred households. These workers would support the cleanup, but their main role was maintaining regular sanitation; otherwise new wastes would just keep piling up. Students, shop owners, pickets, and the army all vowed to deliver the bulk of the muscle for the massive garbage removal campaign. Transportation resources, however, were in tight supply. The 41st Army pledged sixty to eighty horse-drawn carts; they also offered the use of about forty trucks, but they had no gas to fuel them. A sense of excitement comes across in the meeting minutes, with everyone eagerly volunteering their services. Several civil engineers cannot seem to help sharing their visions of the city's future. The public works representative, whose main practical input was scouting dump sites, notes that the costs and complexities of waste hauling and dumping will be hugely reduced when Beiping's households shift their mode of heating from coal-briquette-burning furnaces to modern gas or electric heaters. Fan Yuying from Sanitation responds that if food and coal wastes are separated, they can be used to make compost and cinderblock, respectively, making trash dumps virtually unnecessary. Mostly the discussion stayed focused on practical and immediate goals, and within days of the meeting the campaign was in full swing. Documents report that somewhere from 200,000 to 400,000 tons of old garbage were removed from the city that spring.[2]

In November an outbreak of rat-borne plague in nearby Chahar prompted a second sanitation blitzkrieg. In response to the Epidemic Prevention Committee's appeal, Beijing residents reportedly organized into a gobsmacking 12,645 neighborhood "people's sanitation small groups."[3] These squads shoveled out another thirty-one thousand tons of detritus from the city, this time mainly from residential hutongs and household courtyards. While the statistics are likely overblown, the sanitation groups formed during this campaign and over the following months would serve in future years as Beijing's hygiene infantry, doing battle regularly to tidy the city for national holidays or to lead the charge in the many maggot, mosquito, and rat elimination campaigns over the years to come. These committees were typically led by neighborhood retirees and housewives, paid in part by the city and in part by neighborhood sanitation fees.[4]

Mass cleanups were conducted in fits and starts, but effective urban sanitation is fundamentally a systematic practice grounded in daily routinized rhythms, clear spatial divisions, and the rationalized allocation of resources for collection and transport. In January 1950, the newly established Sanitation Engineering Bureau (Beijing shi weisheng gongcheng ju) took charge of city street cleaning crews (formerly under the police), moved a few hundred old and disabled street cleaners to retirement, and then registered and unionized 1,826 able-bodied workers at pay reported to be 172 jin (about 1.1 pounds) of grain per month (about as much as a party cadre mid-level ration).[5] Equipment was in sad shape; garbage crews had only six hundred usable handcarts and a fleet of fifty-seven trucks, of which only three worked.[6]

The city would rapidly devolve back into a hive of dumps unless both sanitation workers (notorious for their shirking and begging) and city residents (also known for a host of hygiene sins, including allowing their children to piss and shit at will in public) were more disciplined, so the state put them to work monitoring each another. Residents were urged to report any street cleaner seeking bribes or begging to the police; street cleaners in turn admonished residents through the *People's Daily*: "We ring our bells when it's time for residents to dump their trash (*dao tu*, literally "dump their dirt"), but they don't come out; after we leave they dump it on the street. . . . We now have enough equipment [the police allocated one thousand handcarts and thirty trucks] and team members' enthusiasm for work is high, we just need the broad mass of city residents to start cooperating with us."[7] Like previous regimes, the new city government posted regulations threatening residents who dumped excrement in the streets or let their kids relieve themselves in public with "education and fines." But as a civil engineer noted in a letter to the *People's Daily*, these bad customs were not just due to ignorance; they were the result of the city's limited infrastructure:

> To protect public health, the municipal government has established a clean-up campaign committee and mobilized a campaign. This was done many times in the old society too, but after a brief success conditions would soon become filthy. To avoid walking this same path again, I humbly submit these two points for public consultation: 1) Aside from a few major streets with covered gutters most have no drainage infrastructure, but many residents dump all their piss and sewage in the street. When the district government recently banned this, these residents shifted to dumping at night. 2) Children's shit: Because most residents' sanitation facilities are old-style shit pits, people want to avoid the danger [of their children falling in or having accidents] so they let their kids poop on streets, at the base of walls and in corners.[8]

Bad infrastructure spawned bad habits. Despite filling in scores of crudely dug pits, leveling 150 night soil yards, and replacing them with 80 approved cesspits, many residents still did not have a proper place to dispose of their excrement in the winter of 1949–50, and street and gutter dumping remained an issue; the city government asked residents to be patient and have faith that cadres were working hard to provide everyone a proper place for their ordure.[9]

A comprehensive overhaul of city infrastructure would take decades, but the city government had a clear awareness that certain hygiene hot spots needed immediate attention. Dragon Beard Ditch (Longxugou) was such a site, a low-lying, open canal along the northwest edge of the Temple of Heaven that clogged under meters of refuse of every imaginable kind and swelled into a putrid swamp whenever it rained. The city quickly dredged and covered a series of canals in the area, and by 1951 it had piped in water for residents and built a small, pleasant park, nationally publicizing the makeover (Lao She wrote a play about the neighborhood and its renovation) as epitomizing the new regime's commitment to bringing urban amenities to the destitute and neglected.

Infrastructure challenges confronted garbage collection as well. There were no specialized trash transfer stations or networks of trash containers, and there was limited trucking. For the first few years trash collectors, like peddlers, announced their presence to residents by ringing a bell, inviting them to empty household trash into their carts. This mode of collection was both labor intensive and dependent on residents being home. In 1953 the city switched to having residents dump their trash at dusk at designated roadside trash piles, which were shoveled up overnight by cleaning crews. This was more convenient for all the city's residents, including its rat population, eventually prompting a return to the previous method of daytime household pickups. Each method had its drawbacks, but it is worth noting that provision of standardized, sealed waste containers citywide was off the table as an extravagance that even the nation's capital simply could not afford, and this remained the case until the late 1970s.[10]

Trash hauling, on the other hand, became progressively more efficient. Beijing had 75 motorized trash trucks by 1952, and by the summer of 1955 a fleet of 130 trucks had completely replaced animal carts for trash hauling in Beijing's central districts.[11] Outlying districts made the upgrade somewhat later: Chaoyang in 1958, Fengtai in 1964, and so forth.[12] Some of the collected trash was hauled to composting yards, where it was mixed with night soil to make fertilizer; most was dumped at ten open-air suburban dumping grounds. There, pickers (between one and two thousand basket toters, etc., still roamed the dumps up to 1956) retrieved whatever scrap they could, and the remaining mixed garbage (80%–85% dust and dirt) was largely used as landfill in open pits and gullies.

Sanitation workers could only do so much. If urban hygiene was to become a reality, residents would have to do their share. Public hygiene campaigns had been annual summer events of limited effect under the GMD, but the PRC state made them into national seasonal events in which every work unit, school, and neighborhood was expected to participate. The first national Patriotic Sanitation Campaign, launched in 1952, aimed the state's entire arsenal of public mobilization weapons at fighting dirt and disease: broadcasts, community cleanups, vaccination campaigns, and vermin and vector annihilation. Dragon Beard Ditch residents made the national press a few times, expressing their gratitude to the state by sweeping every alley of trash, emptying and sprinkling lime in their toilets daily, and conducting inspections three times a week with a set schedule for spraying of hexachlorocyclohexane (commonly known in China as "666").[13] The 1952 campaign set the norm for how hygiene campaigns were to be conducted for the next decades. Each campaign had an appropriate seasonal focus. Spring campaigns emphasized cleaning out canals and ditches as the spring thaw began. The fall campaign was a lead-in to National Day, so urban appearance, especially in Beijing, was a priority; extra effort was made to see that Tianqiao's food stalls had glass covers and screens to protect the offerings from flies in preparation for the crowds of vacationing workers.[14] Summer campaigns targeted insects, with the goal that "everyone should develop the habit of exterminating mosquitos—swat them as soon as you see them—and also regularly clear away trash and any standing water where mosquitoes can breed."[15]

By the mid-1950s the city had shoveled out from under decades of garbage, and a reliable routine of rubbish collection, semimotorized hauling, and disposal was in place. Though the occasional toddler in split-bottom pants might be spied taking a poop in the gutter, countless Beijingers regularly pitched in to keep the city clean, participating in the ritual tidying-up of the city for national holidays and pursuing various sanitation certificates, like the "Three Nones" (households with no mosquitos indoors, no trash in their courtyard, and no maggots in their privy), "Three Cleans" (clean rooms, clean courtyards, clean streets), and "Sanitation Red Flag Unit."[16] The new municipal government had made great strides in regularizing trash removal from the city center, even if this mainly meant dumping it in an organized manner several miles out in the suburbs.

NIGHT SOIL REFORM

Night soil was no less urgent a public health concern than trash, and its significance went well beyond public hygiene. No other form of urban waste was as inevitable and pervasive, affecting every resident, employing thousands of workers, providing crucial inputs to rural livelihoods, occupying hundreds of plots of land, and always threatening to make a stink. The fertilizer-making process was far from antiseptic, and intestinal parasites were so common as to be nearly universal in the Beijing region.

Three months after taking Beiping, the new government undertook a comprehensive survey of the night soil sector.[17] The city had about 85,000 household privies and 510 public toilets tended by 1,162 night soil men. An estimated 80 percent of those night soil men, like Shi Chuanxiang, hailed from northern Shandong, and some families, by virtue of the customary ownership of shit routes, had been in the profession for generations (their wives and children typically remained in Shandong). Ownership of the city's 1,630 shit routes and hundreds of night soil drying yards was highly stratified. Most night soil collectors (892) owned just one route; 179 owned two routes, four powerful shit lords claimed control of about ten routes each, and one owned nineteen. Of the city's 694 night soil merchants with yards, nearly half (293) handled fewer than ten cartloads of crap per day, whereas forty-eight owned large yards that took in about thirty loads daily. The report confirmed that the Night Soil Guild had long been a hollow sham under shit lord control, but the Night Soil Affairs Office established during the 1936 reforms was even worse, serving as a tool for its leader, Yu Deshun, and his cronies to squeeze the average night soil man. Yu's abuses included enriching himself on fees, pocketing loans meant to aid indigent night soil men, and extending extortionate loans to desperate underlings as a means to get leverage over their routes.

After sketching out these economic and class dynamics, the survey analyzed the mechanics of the trade and its link to the seasonality of regional agriculture. While the city, machine-like, emitted a steady output of excrement, that constant flow had to be modulated to meet the seasonal conditions that ruled both agriculture and the night soil fermenting process itself. Winter turned night soil piles into glacial mounds, while the summer months were subject to losses from flooding rains and insect infestations that could ruin fertilizer quality. This left spring and fall the best months for making fertilizer. The processing involved recipes that mixed human and animal excrement with ash in different ratios to produce different kinds and qualities of fertilizer. Sales boomed in March and August, but farmers often delayed delivering payment, usually in bushels of corn, until after the harvest. The merchants then paid out the corn to the collectors, typically in monthly quantities ranging from 80 to 200 jin. In light of this seasonality, extensions of credit by shit lords to farmers and long delays in paying night soil collectors were commonplace, and the accumulation of customary debt arrangements gave shit lords tremendous paternalistic leverage over collectors.

In 1949 this whole system was in crisis. Night soil collection was alarmingly low. Experience dictated that Beiping should produce about 12.8 million jin of night soil per month, but collections were down to 3.8 million, 30 percent of normal. The use of flush toilets in a handful of wealthy neighborhoods could hardly account for this massive shortfall. More significant was an aggressive wave of "shit pirates" (*pao hai*) running amok, stealing excrement from public toilets and others' routes. But as alarming as a 70 percent dip in night soil collection seemed, undersupply was not the real problem; in fact, yards were brimming with unsold fertilizer. The real crisis was that for several seasons farmers had not been buying fertilizer, leaving even the biggest night soil merchants on the verge of bankruptcy. Collectors were not delivering night soil because the merchants had run out of money or grain to pay them. Hobbled by years of military predation, the sector was now paralyzed by uncertainty due to land reform. Rich peasants were reluctant to pay to fertilize fields they might no longer own, while the poor could not afford fertilizer at all. Lack of demand, the researchers concluded, was the root of the crisis, and they proposed that the Federation of Supply and Marketing Cooperatives (SMC) should stimulate consumption by buying and distributing the city's languishing stock of fertilizer. These recommendations were followed, and local farm production soon revived.

But this short-term remedy did not solve the sector's fundamental long-term issues: the desperate poverty of most night soil men; the abusive power of shit lords; erratic collection made worse by an epidemic of piracy; and the stain,

stench, and health hazards resulting from shoddy infrastructure. Reviving the sector was hardly the ultimate goal; it needed thorough reform. But how to proceed?

> So-called shit routes, simply speaking, are a means of production, just like land is a
> means of production, only the former is abstract and the latter is concrete. Peasants
> without land cannot produce crops; similarly, night soil men without shit routes can-
> not produce shit, so those who want to produce shit first need to get a shit route. It fol-
> lows from this that shit routes become private property that can be bought and sold,
> and just as in the case of land, this leads to the concentration of ownership, resulting
> in producing shit bosses and unemployed workers. "Stealing shit" [or "shit piracy"]
> is thus effectively an act of class struggle by the unemployed against the shit bosses.[18]

Shit pirates, though a sanitary menace, were not villains but victims of dispossis-
sion. The land reform analogy also prescribed the correct path for reform: equal-
ize the distribution of routes and yards, strip the shit lords of their excess wealth,
and share it out among the struggling night soil men and "pirates." Following
this redistribution, the city should gradually abolish private ownership of routes
altogether and replace it with state ownership and rational public management.[19]

That would be the plan, but not yet. Night soil men, the report warned, lacked
political consciousness. Many were closely tied to shit lords, who would incite
them to sabotage policies of property redistribution. Instead of tackling redistribution, the Party spent 1949 brokering a standard contract between night soil
collectors and merchants/yard owners that provided an agreed-upon living wage
of between 150 and 200 jin of corn monthly. Many collectors were eager to sign
on, particularly those who had been earning as little as 80 jin per month, but
those with routes in wealthy neighborhoods complained they could make more
on tips.[20] Contracts included fees for medical care and family welfare, a bonus for
the customary bimonthly summer wheat noodles, and provisions regarding sick
leave and firing. Bosses complained that it was they who now ate wowotou (crude
corn dumplings eaten by the poor in North China) while serving their workers
noodles, but most complied. The city also created a new trade union under the
Party's thumb. But some shit lords apparently were not cowed. In October 1950,
when contracts were up for renewal, night soil merchant Yang Cunzhi, boasting
he could mobilize one thousand workers, tried to stir up a movement to resist the
contracts, boycott the new union, and oppose government annexation of public
bathrooms, but to little effect.[21] In November 1951, after the second round of contracts expired, Yu Deshun and twenty-two other shit lords were arrested; Yu and
four others were executed a few months later.

Yet even deadly retribution and the government's appropriation of 1,165 shit
routes (more than two-thirds of the city's total) in early 1952 did not bring the
sector completely to heel.[22] Later that year a night soil unit near Fucheng Gate
was gripped by several months of infighting. The trouble began with the arrival of

Liu Changhai, a newcomer to the unit. Liu reportedly made a habit of invading the women's dorms and slopping his food around the cafeteria, bellowing things like, "This kitchen's no better than a toilet. The plates are worse than urinals. How does this count as raising up the workers? Being assigned to this shop is like going to prison." Liu's shenanigans incited cadre Wu to attempt his removal, but Wu was blocked by the head of the unit's workers' union, an old sworn brother of Liu's named Dou. The stalemate resulted in a supervisor, Yu, being brought in from outside to manage the unit. Upon taking charge, Yu attempted to discipline a cadre named Zhang, who was notoriously lazy. But cadre Zhang and cadre Wu were sworn brothers, and Wu was miffed that Yu had been brought in as his superior, so Wu allowed Zhang, Dou, and Liu to orchestrate a call for Yu's removal, tactics that included a "strike" by unit workers. Eventually an even higher level supervisor was brought in, cadre Wu was disciplined, and Liu and Dou were fired. The official report concluded that the fact that night soil workers would engage in collective action against a Party official, though not technically a "political incident," was a sign of political backwardness and evidence that the workers mistakenly "looked upon cadres as capitalists."[23]

On the other side of the political education spectrum stood night soil men like Shi Chuanxiang, who eagerly broadcast his appreciation for the new regime through word and deed. Shi joined the municipal Night Soil Cleaning Squad in 1952. His turf in the central district of Xuanwu was one of the first neighborhoods with motorized trucks. But Xuanwu was not a modernizing paradise for sanitation work; the district's narrow hutongs and enclosed privies were too cramped even for wheelbarrow access, forcing collectors to shoulder the city's iconic shit barrels on their backs, filling and then emptying them into those new modern trucks around fifty times each day. Shi brainstormed a way to reorganize truck pickups that enabled Xuanwu collectors to up their rate from fifty to eighty barrels per day, an innovation for which his superiors knighted him a "vanguard of production" model worker, starting him down the path to becoming a member of the CCP in 1956.[24]

By early 1954 the city was ready to compel the last remaining holdouts, around three hundred collectors, to relinquish their privately owned shit routes.[25] Dorm housing, carts, draft animals (including sheds and fodder), and tools were readied for these remaining workers; funds for the retirement of those too weak or old to continue working had been set aside; and a plan for matching manpower with trucks and carts for more efficient collection—with the best equipment dedicated to the city center or course—was readied. Municipal fertilizer yards stopped accepting any night soil from private collectors, leaving them few options but to relinquish their routes to the Sanitation Bureau. By late 1954, night soil collection and storage were fully under municipal authority, and a visitor to Beijing might even catch sight of one of the city's two sealed tanker trucks cruising a downtown street or emptying the catch of a public toilet with its motorized vacuum pump hose.[26] Still, hundreds of collectors kitted with bucket and scoop remained indispensable for extracting night soil from the city's many tight spots.

In the process of changing the property rights and management over shit, shit itself changed. Beijing's night soil had been enmeshed in highly differentiated chains of production and marketing, with rich people's excrement making for expensive routes and higher value fertilizer, while chamber-pot washers lived on tips because their watery night soil lacked nutrient content. Now Beijing's night soil was standardized; one shit fit all at one standard price, set in 1952 at 34 fen a barrel. But standardizing night soil was not so easy. The city had to drop its price in 1955 to 28 fen, and again in 1956 to 22, but even then farmers complained the price was too high because the night soil was too watery. Inspection showed the farmers were right; the renovation of thousands of public toilets had replaced dirt pits with concrete-lined chambers and this, along with shifting to a routine of daily collection, meant that urine had time to neither evaporate nor seep out from the excrement, making for a watered-down product.[27]

With all the city's night soil under state ownership, where was it all to go for storage and processing? By 1953 all private yards in the city had been shut down, replaced by six designated suburban night soil yards at locations that today would place them between Beijing's third and fourth ring roads. There, night soil was converted into fertilizer using the "mud-sealed garbage/night soil composting method." A replacement for the purportedly "unscientific" methods of drying used by the city's traditional merchants, the mud-sealed method involved mixing three parts garbage with one part night soil and letting the mixture ferment in large heaps for a thirty- to sixty-day period (depending on the season).[28] Done properly, the compost was said to reach sustained temperatures of 50–70 degrees Celsius, resulting in excellent fertilizer while simultaneously killing most larvae and pests, thereby helping impede the cyclical reintroduction of intestinal parasites that had been rife for decades if not centuries.[29]

These large open-air composting yards proved short-lived; by 1957 all six had been shut down due to complaints about the relentless smell and pollution.[30] They were replaced by underground, covered, concrete three hundred- to five hundred-ton capacity cesspits clustered at twenty-four suburban locations. These facilities ranged in size, the largest ones being situated in areas outside the city gates. These cesspits' sole purpose was to serve as holding tanks for the city's excrement until such time as it was needed for making fertilizer; unlike the previous drying yards, they performed no composting function.

These changes fundamentally restructured the administrative and labor processes governing night soil. From 1957 on, the city's Night Soil Cleaning Squad workers were tasked only with collecting night soil from households and trucking it to these storage facilities, and they were now completely divorced from the fertilizer-making process. All the shit work after that—hauling the night soil by horse-drawn carts and trucks to rural units and transforming it into fertilizer—was now relegated to laborers from rural units. Night soil processing was now split between two distinct bureaucracies: city sanitation workers were only responsible for efficiently removing human wastes from the city, and rural units had the labor-intensive task of turning it into useful fertilizer. This administrative division of labor exiled organic wastes away from the bodies, senses, and daily lives of city dwellers and shunted it to rural spaces and residents; night soil was becoming a marker inscribing urban and rural difference.

Urban excrement collection rose rapidly throughout the 1950s, leveling off in the early 1960s at around 680,000 tons a year.[31] About 80 percent of it was hauled (increasingly by truck) to suburban installations of concrete cesspits; the remaining 20 percent was held in septic tanks throughout the city. The yearly late summer campaigns to empty those septic tanks provide a glimpse into the administrative complexity of decentralized night soil management. The Sanitation Bureau choreographed the many intricacies of the annual undertaking, which involved (to use 1962 as an example) about twelve hundred temporary laborers from over 120 different agricultural units and suburban communes, each removing its allotment of sludge from assigned tanks, for a total of eighty-nine thousand tons of excrement conveyed out to the countryside on more than seven hundred horse-drawn carts and twenty trucks between mid-July and late October.[32] The laborers' wages, bonuses, and means for hauling the night soil were all paid for and managed by their agricultural brigades. City Sanitation trained any new recruits (though in 1962 a group almost died of asphyxiation in one tank) and coordinated access to pumps, protective clothing, and other supplies. This annual coordination of urban bureaucratic planning and rural elbow grease shifted the burdens of physical labor onto rural units: "In order to improve fertilizer quality, this year's emptying sceptic tanks of fertilizer will proceed by the method adopted in past years, "scoop it yourself, ship it yourself", no city vehicles leave the city, no [urban] cleanup blitz."[33]

THE GREAT GARBAGE SORT: 1956–1962

During the late 1950s, the high point of Mao-era collectivization, the Party exerted a will to socialist transformation that aspired to encompass every socioeconomic realm, and the rubbish pile was no exception. If an idealized capitalism is a universe of profit maximizers, an idealized socialism is one of use-value maximizers. In the Mao-era socialist ideal, there is no such thing as garbage; rather, garbage is actually just "misplaced resources" (*laji jiushi fangcuo de ziyuan*), and socialism, according to the Mao-era maxim, "changes the useless into the useful" (*wuyong bian youyong*). In the first half of the decade, Beijing's garbage production had nearly doubled, from 550,000 to 940,000 tons (see Table 1), testimony to the city's economic recovery, indeed, to its budding prosperity. But in the eyes of the use-value-maximization faithful, this meant that nearly a million tons of potential resources were going unused. Having brought Beijing's garbage and feces fully under the government's management, city officials and engineers began mapping a reorganization of material flows intended to move Beijing's wastes toward more perfect usefulness. The aspirations were not merely for Beijing but national. Other cities, from Shijiazhuang (population around half a million at the time) to Shanghai, experimented with similar programs.

Though the quantity of Beijing's MSW had nearly doubled, its composition was much as it had been in the Republican era: 52 percent ash, 28 percent dirt, 12 percent organics, and about 7 percent recyclable scrap of all kinds. In short, the residue from coal burning made up a whopping 80 percent of the city's MSW, making reducing coal waste an obvious priority. Most Beijing households and work units were heated by coal stoves that burned "coal balls" made from a slurry with a 25 percent dirt content. While some larger buildings and work units could be converted to central heating, short of major renovations in Beijing's building stock, the city would be wedded to small indoor furnaces for the foreseeable future. Fortunately, a technical fix existed: beehive coal briquettes. Beehive coal had a low dirt content and generated half the residue of coal balls. The furnaces were small and simple to produce; in fact, about 5 percent of Beijing households already used them by 1956. The universal adoption of beehive coal alone would slash Beijing's MSW (and its dumping and transport fees) by 40 percent. But even if the city could magically convert to beehive coal overnight, there would still be hundreds of thousands of tons of cinders needing disposal. Turning those cinders into cinderblock bricks was not a technical problem; it was a mass mobilization problem on a household level. Residents needed to be trained to dispose of their cinders separately rather than mixing all their trash together in a commingled jumble.[34]

Waste commingling was judged the enemy of utility maximization on multiple fronts: "For several years, we've used mixed garbage to fill in suburban pits, but in the summer they swarm with flies and maggots, pollute the air, and residents complain terribly. Also, it is not possible to erect any structures where organic waste is part of the landfill."[35] If urban residents could be trained to practice the "three separates" (keeping their organic food waste, cinders, and recyclables for separate collection and handling), a whole interconnected set of problems would be solved: rural dumps would no longer pose pollution and health problems, ash and dirt could be used for construction to make bricks or as (actually stable) landfill, food waste could go for pig feed and composting, and an estimated 180 tons of recyclables could be recovered annually for handicraft shops. In addition to putting a million tons of materials to good use, more than nine hundred scavengers (basket toters and the like), who in 1956 still survived by picking recyclable scrap from urban dumps, would be spared from such unhealthy work; the state would help the sick and elderly with retirement and the young and fit with employment in handicraft production co-ops (HPC), helping sort and process scrap for craft production (see chapter 4).

This plan would require coordination among multiple bureaus and mass participation. Sanitation and recycling organs handled the education campaigns and designed touring exhibits to teach the "three separates" throughout the city's residential neighborhoods. The HPCs would handle the collection of recyclable scrap, sending workers into neighborhoods for door-to-door collection (another avenue of employment for displaced dump pickers). Organic food waste would be trucked to rural composting yards. Coal residue collection could be handled as a reverse logistics operation in tandem with the Beijing coal company. Residents would drop off their cinders when picking up new briquettes at company coal stores, and those cinders would be loaded onto the company's coal delivery trucks and shipped back out of town—an elegant solution to what had often been an empty backhaul.[36]

A trash-sorting pilot launched in Xuanwu district in 1956 went well but not perfectly. The first few months saw 80–90 percent effective sorting, but that dipped to 50 percent when the rains came that summer. The Sanitation Bureau sent despairing managers on a pilgrimage to Shijiazhuang—a source-separation mecca that claimed 100 percent participation in its citywide system—and they returned with more confidence and several practical fixes, like alternate day pickups for ash and organics (to prevent commingling) and using "big public trash cans" managed by neighborhood committee members, who made sure wastes were separately dumped. By early 1957 Xuanwu boasted a 99.6 percent participation rate, having spent only an additional 5,600 yuan on extra receptacles and 1,400 yuan on educational materials.[37]

In 1958 all of central Beijing rolled up its collective sleeves and set to work on a great garbage sorting. The timing, the beginning of the Great Leap Forward (GLF), was not accidental; the "three separates" campaign was just one of many collective mobilizations aimed at realizing a utopian vision of a collective economy. There were several GLF campaigns involving waste and/or scrap. The campaign to make steel in backyard furnaces from household scrap is today the most infamous, but the "Fight for Fertilizer," marvelously described in an article by Andrew Morris, was also flogged with utopian gusto:

> "Fight for Fertilizer" streamed down the left side of the February 1, 1959 issue of Renmin Ribao, while the horizontal headline read "North and south jubilantly fly the flag of fertilizer collection." Updates were given on seven different battle fronts. In Yunnan, "one million people of every race fought bravely" to collect manure and build toilets. In Hubei "ten thousand people entered the battle like flying horses to collect manure and march side by side." . . . The 25 billion jin of (12.5 billion kg) of manure that the cities hoped to produce every year was calculated to be enough to spread over 1,300,000 mu (214,00 acres) of land, which would produce 760,000 tons

of grain, which in turn would be able to feed 2,500,000 people for a whole year. Several writers performed this kind of numerical hocus-pocus, using the power of statistics to illustrate just how valuable the substance really was.[38]

In the GLF imaginary, wastes—scrap metals, garbage, shit—were sources of unlimited potential that, when liberated for full utilization, would fire the rockets of socialism's miraculous growth.

Despite the enormous enthusiasm for unleashing the revolutionary power of waste, problems soon emerged. Coal cinders proved unexpectedly unaccommodating. Bricks made of them were too crumbly for construction, but they were just as problematic in fertilizer making. Though in some sticky or acidic soils cinders can be a helpful amendment, their sharp edges are particularly damaging to the roots of sprouting plants, and because they take years to break down, adding them to the soil year after year greatly compounds the damage. Even before the sorting experiment, farmers had been noticing diminishing returns. Also, few composting yards practiced the mud-sealed technique assiduously, often using too little night soil in their mix or squeezing the two-month process into two weeks, nullifying its sanitizing intent.[39] All of this was made harder to manage because the city's waste profile was naturally inconsistent. Garbage inescapably reflects consumption patterns, and Beijing consumption had its seasons: melon rinds in summer, ash in winter. In the winter of 1960 organic waste fell to 10 percent of MSW; in 1961 it fell again, to 1.4 percent, an almost unimaginably low figure exposing the dire scarcity of edible matter, even in the nation's capital, at the height of the famine years. Though organics rose to 25 percent by the spring of 1962, by then household sorting had gotten so lax that cinders and organics were hopelessly intermixed. By 1963 Beijing's waste sorting experiment had completely unraveled; the city reverted to mixed disposal; and the quantities of trash continued their slow climb, topping 1.1 million tons by 1965.[40] Beijing was not unique in its failure. Cities across China attempted source separation, and not one was successful. Shanghai's efforts collapsed even more rapidly; collectors grumbled that it was too labor intensive, households complained that managing separate containers took up too much space and time, and the wastes residents worked hard to separate often got remixed when loaded onto trash boats, undercutting the enthusiasm of those who witnessed this.[41] Source separation seems simple, but in fact it is extremely difficult to implement. It relies on efficiently linking millions of behavioral choices across dispersed infrastructures, making enforcement terribly difficult. Failure anywhere in the chain disrupts the whole process, and most participants see no direct practical or remunerative benefit from the extra effort they put in.

The matter of remunerative benefit helps explain the one aspect of the "three separates" program that was tremendously popular: the segregation and sale of recyclable scrap. The next chapter takes a deeper dive into this aspect of Mao-era waste management, but as just one example, a Xicheng neighborhood report in 1960 noted that scrap recycling rose 57 percent in the wake of the three separates:

> Scrap collection workers collect door to door, providing a great convenience and adding to residents' incomes. For instance, a resident at Fusuijing #3 reflected: "In the past I just tossed recyclables with the garbage, but now I sell it and with that money I've bought my courtyard a vat, 2 brooms, and a dust pan, improving hygiene, doing a public service, and providing resources to industry."[42]

Even in the rush of GLF volunteerism, the masses were most taken with the part of civic cleanup and socialist construction that also happened to pay a little cash on the side. Managing the remaining 93 percent of the MWS was a less-rewarding household chore and remained an administrative challenge.

The Sanitation Bureau also faced recurring headaches with night soil. Having relinquished responsibility for fertilizer making to rural units, the bureau only had hands-on control over night soil collection and storage; it lacked direct authority over what transpired from there. Predictably, rural-bound shit did not always follow urban managers' directions:

> Lately Shunyi, Sanhe, Xincheng etc. county peasant production teams and cooperatives, carrying their village approved documents are coming into Beijing to collect night soil, then proceeding to dry it on the spot, violating our city's night soil management and rules banning shit drying. . . . Our office has repeatedly explained to these people and urged them to return home, to no avail.[43]

Such incidents became even more common in the famine years of the early 1960s as food shortages prompted urban work units to barter with rural units for access to food. In late 1962 the city cracked down on scores of cases of urban units (construction companies, factories, schools) trading night soil outside the plan directly with agricultural communes in Haidian, Fengtai, and as far away as Tianjin and Hebei, for access to land or food. Residents secretly housed rural relatives and farmers when they came to the city to collect the illicit night soil, but they typically had their cover blown when the farmers started turning Beijing's roadsides into shit-drying yards.[44]

Three years later, rural demand for night soil continued to outstrip supply, and rural populations still chafed against regulations on its management. When the city attempted to strictly enforce a ban on informal night soil drying yards between the second and third ring roads in 1965, a partial survey found hundreds of violations of municipal regulations, including 7 large and 292 small unpermitted yards, 303 dirt cesspits, and 128 rural households stealing shit. Few of these were cases of hard-nosed criminality: some brigades lacked money for bricks to line their night soil pits; most rural night soil thieves returned to their homes when confronted by authorities; and composting yards tended to face NIMBY opposition no matter where they were put. Still, the 1965 ban marked yet another step in hardening administrative boundaries regarding urban and rural inter-actions with human waste, explicitly emphasizing that areas inside the third ring road were higher priority than those outside it.[45]

While authorities pushed the stink of excrement farther out into the suburbs, in the city center the number of sealed, vacuum pump trucks providing urban neighborhoods with relatively pristine night soil removal had risen from two in 1955 to ninety-eight by 1965.[46] Trash collection protocols spotlighted areas like Tiananmen Square, foreign embassies, exhibition halls, and major thoroughfares as needing extra attention and fastidious trash removal.[47] The city was subject to strict protocols enhanced by technologies that effectively hid filth and sealed it off for removal, increasingly deodorizing the spaces of urban experience and con-sumption—all of which required significant expenditure and labor. Rural areas saw little such investment and were increasingly cast as the recipients of urban waste and stink, though at least up through the 1960s most rural units remained grateful, if not for the mixed garbage, at least for the life-giving night soil.

SHIT AS HISTORY

In fall of 1959 Shi Chuanxiang attended the weeklong National Conference of Heroes, giving a celebrated speech (published in the *People's Daily*) and sharing an ill-fated handshake with then head of state Liu Shaoqi (see figure 3). When Shi bragged to Chairman Liu about his work team's growing literacy, Liu spontane-ously handed Shi his fountain pen, urged him to keep up his studies, and told Shi to write him before the year was out. It was a friendly if paternalistic ges-ture, confirming Shi's cultural competence and his liberation from the illiterate and degraded role that had been the night soil carrier's lot in the "old society." This encounter catapulted Shi to new heights. For the next several years, Beijing environmental sanitation workers aspired to Shi's model and credo: "Better one person gets dirty so 10,000 families can be clean." A seemingly endless stream of officials and revolutionary aspirants made the pilgrimage to Xuanwu to strap a shit barrel to their backs for a day of studying with Shi Chuanxiang.

But while the public glorified sanitation workers as the epitome of socialist consciousness, and officials vied with one another for a chance to shovel night soil by Shi Chuanxiang's side, sanitation workers had a different opinion of their own work. In 1962 the central government offered urban residents a chance to strengthen the agricultural "front line" by volunteering to move to the country-side. The policy was meant to extol those willing to sacrifice the great (and from the state's perspective very expensive) privileges of urban residence for the much harder life in the countryside. Apparently Beijing's waste workers were excep-tionally revolutionary, for they displayed a fervid desire to give up their cushy

FIGURE 3. Shi Chuanxiang shaking hands with Liu Shaoqi at the National Conference of Heroes, October 26, 1959. From Beijing Environmental Sanitation Engineering Group, www.besg.com.cn/content /details25_4597.html.

urban existence. In just three months, more than 150 Beijing sanitation workers moved "back" to the countryside, and another 150 were awaiting approval for their applications.[48] This, the Sanitation Bureau reported, was posing a major problem, particularly in night soil collection, which for several years had had no new recruits. "The Dongcheng district cleaning team, through introductions from the City Labor Office, brought in 23 workers from Shijiazhuang Steel plant, some very capable labor power. They had the work persuasively explained to them, but as soon as they heard it was shit work, not one was willing." If all those workers leaving for the countryside were not replaced, "the capital's sanitary conditions" would face major problems. But the Sanitation Bureau was in no position to block its employees from volunteering for rural reassignment; it was a national-level policy, and volunteers were to be praised, not hindered. Aside from pleading for some assistance in finding replacement workers, the bureau ended its request by asking for a small favor for its remaining 583 shit workers: while grain was still in short supply (the year was 1962), perhaps the city could allocate a greater allowance of supplemental foods (soy milk, fish, meat) as well as two pounds of white liquor (*baijiu*) every month to help chase away the "stink" of a day's work.[49]

By 1964 the night soil personnel crisis had only deepened, so the Sanitation Bureau sought comrade Shi's help and placed him in charge of educating a newly created "youth team" of workers. Months later the *People's Daily* ran a twelve-thousand-character-long feature in which Shi Chuanxiang shared his revolutionary spirit, not just with those youths but the entire nation.[50]

His lecture affirmed the Maoist memes of the time: never forget class struggle, serve the people, study Lei Feng. It also spotlighted the political ritual of those years: speaking bitterness, a practice of recounting the nightmares of the preliberation past so as to place the sweet present in proper historical perspective. Shi recounted numerous vignettes of how he educated young night soil workers, and in every case history was the key to transforming them into dedicated workers. In one case, a trainee slipped and spilled a barrelful of excrement all over someone's floor. When the mother of the house sympathized that "it's not easy for a school boy to put down a backpack and pick up a shit barrel," Shi took the opportunity to describe how a similar offense in the bad old days of his youth wound up with him getting hauled to the cops and beaten. When another young worker dripping sweat was offered a bowl of water by a friendly citizen, Shi recounted his famous story about a resident, replying to Shi's request for a drink, offering him water from a filthy catfood dish. Postliberation shit work might be exhausting, embarrassing, and filthy, but in the past it was even shittier because the worker was treated like the object with which he worked. Shi explained: "Do you know in the old society what the head cook in a kitchen was called? 'Oily rat' (*youhaozi*). . . . Workers who made coal balls were called 'Coal Blackie (*meiheizi*).'" Needless to say, sanitation workers were called things like Dung Beetle (*shikelang*). The Party had changed all this; night soil workers' dehumanizing identification with the object of labor was shattered, the old taunts silenced. Shi used history to remind these youths that though they hauled shit every day, shit no longer defined them.

This logic deepened in Shi's vignette about Little Qi, who worked with his cap pulled low to prevent his old classmates from recognizing him. Eventually one spotted him: "How did you end up doing this, it's like using a front door for a coffin lid—what a waste!" Dejected, Qi vowed to quit. A few days later, an old lady asked Qi to rinse out her chamber pot after he had emptied it; when he refused, she complained and Qi was reprimanded. On Qi's next visit he made a point of emptying her crap into his barrel while standing in the middle of her courtyard, making the whole house stink. Qi's path to reform began when Old Shi told Qi's dad, a retired night soil worker, about his son's antics. Shi had to convince Qi's dad not to beat or curse his son but instead to share stories of his preliberation life (beaten by his boss, too poor to save two of his children from dying of illness). Soon Little Qi was instructing his cohort:

> We are all dirty and tired, but we provide millions of people with a good healthy environment, so the more dirty and exhausted the more glorious. Whoever wants to dig out shit, first needs to dig out their own stinking thoughts influenced by the old ideology. . . . Precisely because we were the most looked down upon in the past, today [we] must be more willing to work hard to serve the people, be the vanguard of improving customs, and completely dig out society's stinky ideas, make it spic and span.[51]

The past wasn't just shitty; handling shit provided a model for handling history itself. Like shit, history must be dug out daily, removed, and confronted. If left to pile up, it rots, stinks, and contaminates, but fully unearthed and correctly applied, it spurs inexhaustible growth and renewal. The revolutionary masters history as the night soil worker does shit, tirelessly and personally digging it out and turning it over to create a generative future.

Every young night soil worker described in Shi's account either had inherited the job from his father or was an orphan; nobody willingly became a night soil worker. Nothing was more politically fashionable than a day slinging night soil, and nothing less desirable than a lifetime spent doing it. Night soil workers were no longer taunted as "shit-eggs," but as Andrew Morris argues, the political praise heaped upon them for their willing self-sacrifice buried them as deeply as ever in associations with human feces, reinforcing the lowliness of the job in an urban society striving for sanitary modernity. Shi Chuanxiang's generation of night soil collectors had been illiterate, landless men with few if any options, but this new generation of urban literate youth—the future of the new China—saw no future (and no future wives) coming down this particular career path. No longer enchained to their roles by shit hegemons and explicit discrimination, these youths were enchained by the arbitrary reality of their personal histories as children of night soil workers or orphans. Liu Shaoqi's gesture of handing Shi a pen had been a symbolic affirmation that in the "new society" workers in low and denigrated trades were no longer to be treated as outcasts; shit workers were no longer just defined by shit, they could have culture too, could be writers and model workers. But the state's employment structure dictated the opposite: once a night soil carrier, always a night soil carrier. Socialism might have brought night soil workers liberation from a collective history of class exploitation, but it failed to liberate them from, indeed largely enchained them to, their personal family histories.

Fortunately, their dead-end jobs were coming to a dead end as well. After taking his obligatory fieldtrip to visit Shi Chuanxiang and strapping on a shit barrel for a day in 1965, Vice Mayor Wan Li proclaimed that the city was committed to "liberating" the night soil man from his bucket and scoop and putting an end to these icons of feudal backwardness and oppression once and for all. The city undertook an accelerated plan to replace all household privies with street-accessible public bathrooms, a project that began in earnest, predictably, in the city's central districts. When it was finally completed in 1974, the city had eliminated around 85,000 household privies and replaced them with 2,879 public bathrooms accessible to pump trucks.[52]

FROM USE TO DISPOSAL

It was easier for Shi Chuanxiang to wash away the stink of night soil than to wash off the stain of his handshake with Liu Shaoqi. In late 1966, at the height of the Cultural Revolution, Jiang Qing publicly slandered Shi Chuanxiang as a sell-out traitor, hurling him as bait into the anti-Liu feeding frenzy. Over the next year Shi was paraded through the streets, bullied before stadium-sized crowds, and subjected to repeated beatings that left him brain damaged.[53] Red Guards accused him of hiding a secret preliberation past as a shit hegemon who liked to dress in scholarly robes.

The upheaval of 1967 was followed by the Environmental Sanitation Bureau's elimination in 1968. Management of trash and night soil collection (as well as street cleaning and the care of public restrooms) was transferred to the Beijing Bureau of Public Utilities, which received guidance from the city's Revolutionary Committee. Much of the day-to-day functioning, including the recording of statistics, seems to have been disrupted; I have found no statistics for municipal trash or night soil collection between 1966 and 1971, and when figures reappear in 1972 they are markedly lower than when they left off in 1965. Still, the handful of accounts and archival documents available shed some light on these years.

The #1 Sanitation Truck Yard Annals contains a 1972 "Circular Regarding Implementing the Beijing Municipal Public Utility Bureau's Leadership Small Group's Labor Allocation and Work Quality Standards for Trash Removal, Night Soil, Street Cleaning and Public Bathroom Sanitation." It holds few surprises. Regarding trash, for example, routes, schedules, and assigned staffing for trucks should be strictly followed; trucks should be sealed properly to avoid leaks and spills; and trash truck safety for both collectors and residents is emphasized. Workers are told that if "entering households to remove trash/dirt (ru hu qu tu) take good care of the trash receptacles, do not toss or bump them, lift and replace them lightly. . . . Build good relations with the masses." Excrement removal was to occur every other day; collectors using buckets to empty household privies should "empty the cesspit clean; wipe the pit's outside clean; cover your bucket whenever moving between stops; clean the area where the truck stops; be polite; [and] do not smear feces on walls or drip on doorways." Night soil truck drivers were told to avoid stopping in front of restaurants, shops, or areas where people congregate.[54] In short, the rules promote the timely elimination of any traces of excrement and trash from the urban experience. Similarly, a 1974 notice about emptying septic tanks recommends that in active areas like Wang Fujing, Qian Gate, the People's Hall, and near restaurants, tanks should be emptied at night.[55] And a 1977 report from the Public Utilities Office, "On the Elimination of Cesspits from Urban Districts and Their Construction outside the Third Ring Road" explains that the process of moving the last of the city's night soil storage facilities into the hands of rural units, begun in 1976, was approaching successful completion. Rural communes in Haidian, Chaoyang, Shunyi, and elsewhere constructed seventeen storage tanks with a total holding capacity of 5,890 tons, entirely using (with the exception of Haidian) their own resources and labor. Though the relocations meant that the city's night soil trucks would on average have to drive 5.9 kilometers farther to empty their holds, it also completely transferred responsibility for night soil storage from the city to rural units. The Sanitation Bureau's old cesspits had been "too near the city, especially the Dongzhi Gate cesspit which was very close to the North Embassy District and had a big effect on the city's environmental hygiene. Especially in summer, even with the almost daily application of pesticide it was still difficult to prevent mosquitos from breeding."[56]

But by the 1970s it was not just the city that was rejecting trash and shit; agricultural units increasingly complained that the city's refuse was of no help to them either. Despite the fact that documents from as early as 1962 show that officials knew the city's ashy wastes were damaging local soils, the city continued using commune compost yards as trash disposal sites well into the 1970s. But by the mid-1970s many suburban farmers started refusing the city's trash; Chaoyang apparently kept accepting "mixed trash," but Fengtai and Haidian refused it.[57] While the nearby countryside was becoming an extended dumpsite, urban districts were experimenting with subterranean garbage platforms as a way to more effectively quarantine urban waste from urban experience. Collected trash was consolidated in these underground holds during the day, then raised to street level for truck loading at night. But this solution to nighttime trash piles was still deemed too sloppy, so the city finally began adopting the use of trash containerization in 1979. As usual, the central districts were given priority, Xuanwu becoming the first to fully containerize its trash in 1985, at which time the suburban district of Chaoyang was still only one-third containerized.[58]

There is no decisive turning point in the Mao era when the city's garbage and human wastes changed from a stinky and germy but valuable productive rural input into waste streams deemed worthless, but there is no question that the process accelerated dramatically in the reform years of the late 1970s and early 1980s. Between night soil and garbage, it was garbage that was rejected the most decisively. As the #1 Sanitation Truck Team yearbook puts it: "Before 1985, there was a portion of trash that could be sold, bought by [agriculture] production teams. After 1985, you could try to sell it but no one would buy it, our unit even had to pay others to dump the trash—in reality we went from selling trash to paying for dump sites."[59] A 1983 aerial survey around Beijing (see Map 2 in the introduction) revealed that what just thirty years earlier had been the region's most prosperous farmland (precisely because it had been sustainably maintained by a nutrient cycle with the city) had become a ring of thousands of garbage dumps; Beijing was turning from a city ringed by rich agricultural lands into a city surrounded by trash.

Farmers had long been more favorably disposed to using the city's night soil than to composting its garbage, but by the late 1970s night soil too was losing its allure due to the increasing availability of chemical fertilizer. Chemical fertilizer had long been popular with farmers, as it was generally less labor intensive than the alternatives (composting, pig manure, night soil), but it had been hard to come by. This changed in 1973 when China contracted with a group of

US, Japanese, and Dutch firms to build ten ammonia factories for production of nitrogenous fertilizer.[60] By the late 1970s Beijing area farmers were switching from night soil to chemical fertilizer. The city, struggling to hold onto its outlet for human waste, tried slashing its price in 1978 from 3.5 to 2 yuan per ton.[61] The final death knell for large-scale use of night soil fertilizer came with the dissolution of communes and the shift to the household responsibility system in the mid-1980s. By the late 1970s commune brigades had become fully responsible for both night soil storage and composting; when those brigades parceled out land to households and relinquished control over farmers' labor, they effectively dismantled both the land and human resources needed to manage, store, and treat large quantities of night soil. Some individual farmers continued to use night soil from their own household or local privies, but the city no longer had an outlet for the excrement of millions of urban residents; that metabolic loop was severed. Beijing was not unique; the same breakdown occurred throughout the country. In Shanghai, for example, after communes were dismantled farmers refused to unload the city's trash and refuse barges without being paid, and even then, they just left the wastes in open dumps lining the roads.[62]

CONCLUSION

By the end of the Mao era, the sanitary waste regime, according to which shit and garbage had been reorganized, had reconfigured the handling of these organically volatile and potentially valuable postconsumer material flows. Urban development and prosperity had doubled Beijing's MSW stream even as the proportion of ash in that stream fell from 80 to 55 percent by the early 1980s. (Ash continued to make up around half the city's MSW until the 1990s, when its share began falling precipitously as massive waves of creative destruction replaced coal-furnace-heated, single-story housing with centrally heated apartment buildings.) By the early1980s Beijing's trash was disposed of by residents into trash hoppers or enclosed collection stations and then hauled by motorized trucks for dumping in rural suburban areas ever farther from the city center. In theory, this garbage—increasingly rich in food waste—could have been even more useful as compost than it had been in the 1950s, yet ironically trash composting grew increasingly rare. One key reason for this was the growing availability of chemical fertilizers, which were highly effective and required much less labor than either trash composting or applying night soil. Another reason trash composting was being abandoned was that the city's trash contained increasingly large quantities of substances such as plastics, metals, and broken glass that damaged soil and young plants.

The city's prodigious flow of night soil, by far the most important source of fertilizer for regional farms when the Mao era began, was also all but eliminated from agricultural use by the mid-1980s. The reconfiguring of Beijing's shit economy in the name of hygienic modernity turned night soil from a complex commercial sector into unused waste. In the Republican era, the night soil business had carefully differentiated night soil products based on a range of variables. A shit route's value was linked to the nutritive richness of the excrement, which in turn reflected the wealth and diets of those who produced it; composting processes varied across seasons; and so forth. But under central economic planning, night soil was reduced to a single commodity, treated as a uniform substance and sold at a uniform price. A bureaucratic division of labor separated urban waste removal work from the rural work of waste transformation and application, contributing to a rupture in the metabolic cycle of nutrients that had connected city and country for centuries. The sanitary regime of routinizing and deodorizing urban night soil collection proved incompatible with the metabolic loop, not just conceptually but materially; the infrastructures adopted to whisk the city's night soil to the "away" of the countryside physically reconfigured night soil so that it was less worth reusing. Whether it was night soil's being too watery to have nutritive value or its being mixed with highly alkaline ash or with garbage too full of debris and contaminants, the outcome was increasingly the same: Beijing's night soil was not worth shit. The city was compelled to develop a sewage treatment infrastructure to replace what had once been a productive, if highly contentious and infectious, sector of labor and trade.

This regime of urban sanitation contributed to reconfiguring the geography of value between urban and rural space. Urban night soil had been part of a cycle that had for centuries contributed to the significantly higher productivity of farmlands that ringed large cities throughout China. That ring of suburban farmland was a zone of metabolic exchange in which urban and rural activities, rhythms, and values commingled and transformed (shit to fertilizer, fertilizer to food, food to shit). The Mao era saw that ring gradually transformed from a space of productive metabolic exchange into a dumping ground, a border line demarcating where regulatory enforcement of sanitary standards was no longer deemed cost effective. Making the city a modern, sanitary, socialist space required creating a rural "away"—the unavoidable real-world manifestation of the fantasized no-place, an "away" where we wish our wastes would disappear; the Beijing countryside became the "away" where the city's night soil and garbage would go.[63] Where the modern sanitary zone ended and the "away" began was determined by administrative maps and cost calculations; wastes were to be trucked and dumped just beyond urban administrative boundaries. This is not very different from how the locations of urban waste sites are determined in capitalist land markets, wherein waste, having no market value and being a nuisance and obstruction to the exchange and movement of other valued goods and services, is pushed to wherever it can be most cheaply put. To go beyond the ring where land prices fall low enough for dumping would be to waste money and time on unnecessary transport. Waste gravitates to this zone, this suburban ring where everything one wishes to exile from the city can be most affordably and conveniently dumped. Ironically, this dumping zone was approximately the same space that had once been so fertile due to its access to urban night soil.

In sum, the sanitary waste regime begins by turning shit and garbage from useful inputs in a cyclical economy into useless wastes; by severing the metabolic cycle of give and take, it results in redefining the economic logics of land valuation itself. Spaces that once had value in a system of economic and nutritive mutuality become dumping zones valued on a one-way trajectory—the farther from the city center, the dirtier, the cheaper, and the less valued they are—and this in turn is underwritten by using that land precisely in ways that reinforce their devaluation: the making of suburban wastelands.

4

Standardizing Chaos

Rationalizing the Junk Trades in the 1950s

In early spring of 1949, the *People's Daily* ran the following update:

> After just a month of work since [Beiping's] liberation, the Dongdan Training Ground—that place where American imperialism humiliated Chinese schoolgirls and where Nationalists squandered the hard labor of thousands of citizens and destroyed scores of common people's homes and shops to build an airport so they could flee the country—has emerged anew as a peoples' market. The market includes 1500 peddler shops and stalls, small and large. In terms of businesses, there are four general types: wood work, second-hand clothes, food and drinks and miscellany— over 30 wood workers, 260 used clothes, 200 food, and 1000 odds and ends. The goods in these shops are mostly collected by petty urbanites, small drum beaters and Beiping residents.[1]

The opening of the Dongdan People's Market was in fact a reopening; prior to being turned into a military training ground and air field by the GMD, the area had been a popular open-air peddler market, known as Dongdan Big Trading Ground (Dongdan da di). In short, the article told readers that life in Beiping was returning to normal—the norm being a bustling, largely impoverished populace eking out survival through scavenging and petty trade. Still, the article managed to imbue the old economic grind with a touch of progressive, anti-imperialist sentiment:

> Business these days is pretty good. A three-person snack stall takes in over 2000 yuan for about 400 yuan in profit a day. A second-hand clothes seller says, "We average about 200 plus yuan a day." If anyone's business is doing the worst, it's sellers of Western-style clothes. One who has been in the Western clothes business for four years said, "I haven't made a cent in three days. Western clothes are really out of

fashion this year. We're getting ready to remake the Western suits into uniforms, that should work."[2]

Changes in fashion consciousness (and consciousness fashion) aside, the tempo, geography, and goods of Beiping's recycling metabolism pumped along much as before, as was generally true in cities throughout China in the years following World War II:

> When we came back to Shanghai [in 1946] we moved into some Japanese people's house, a very new one. We didn't bring anything back with us from Fujian, nothing. We needed to buy everything; we bought old furniture, simple and cheap from an old goods market . . . but there was nobody collecting recycling then. . . . As people started to get back, cooking meals, life started to get more lively, and by about a year or so later there were a lot of junk collectors. In those days [our household] sold everything. There was nothing we didn't use. Toothpaste tubes, toothbrushes, broken combs, broken glass, bottles, waste paper, torn cloth (there was no synthetic cloth then, it was all cotton). Some we sold, some we traded. There were a lot of collectors. This one gave you more, this one less, but it was all around the same. For broken glass, they traded sweet fermented rice. They had a shoulder pole and baskets and they'd come down the alley chanting: "Fermented rice trade this, trade that, trade the other." Sometimes they wouldn't chant, they'd drum. My mom never bought sweets, she didn't eat sweets, so I always traded for sweet fermented rice. If we could trade for it, we were really happy. We also gave any left-overs to beggars. And we put peelings and food scraps in a big tin outside our door. They'd collect that to feed pigs. My grandmother managed it mostly. Everything had a use.[3]

TRADING SPACES: FROM STREET
PEDDLERS TO STORE VENDORS

The revived bustle of a peddler economy also meant the resurgence of petty scams, adulteration of goods and measures, and chaotic markets that spilled into the streets, all detrimental to urban order and appearance. But the CCP apparently learned something the GMD authorities never did: that cracking down on common folks who engage in unlicensed peddling just to scrape by—as the GMD did in Shanghai in November 1946, inciting a massive peddler riot, and again months later in Taiwan, where the beating of an old woman peddling cigarettes sparked the 2.28 Incident—is bad for regime stability.[4] As Janet Chen notes, the CCP adopted a strategy of management, not prohibition, to handle Beiping's estimated fifty thousand peddlers. In May 1949 Mayor Ye Jianying held an open meeting attended by more than one hundred peddlers, the kind of barrier-shattering gesture involving a high official reaching out to the lowest members of society that was a hallmark of CCP political performance. Ye asked for his audiences' advice, praised their "legitimate business," and explained that the government would not ban but rather register them to facilitate their businesses by sorting out law-abiding sellers from shysters. He quipped, "We are not just doing this for the sake of the city's 'appearance' (*shirong* 市容). Whenever peddlers see the two charac-ters '*shirong*' they say, 'Our stomachs have no *neirong* (contents 内容), what is there to say about *shirong*?'"[5]

The scrap trades wove skeins of interdependence among beggars, pickers, handicraft laborers, and peddlers, overlapping social strata whose survival dan-gled from a shifting web of minuscule market transactions. Bo Yibo and other architects of the 1950s economic reforms understood that "the economy of inde-pendent handicrafts is a small business economy; its existence is inseparable from the market, from material supplies and sales, and cannot have its connections to other economies and consumers severed. Cut off supply and sales and pro-duction cannot proceed."[6] Of course CCP leaders envisioned a future in which small-scale handicrafts would be replaced by modern industrialization, but as Liu Shaoqi insisted at the July 1950 National Cooperative Worker Conference, such changes would have to wait: "We must insure that the original [handicraft] pro-duction processes do not change, and absolutely not allow adoption of industrial methods."[7] As Bo Yibo reflected, if in the early 1950s the government had "relied on big industry to resolve the employment problem, every worker absorbed would have cost the state about 10,000 yuan of investment. By comparison, the expense of absorbing the employment of a worker into most handicrafts was far less."[8] Until the state had more industrial and financial capacity, handicrafts and their market habitat were to be tolerated, even encouraged.

It was no secret that the Party's long-term vision would eventually leave little room for private business. Getting to that goal would clearly take years; precisely how many years or which policy path would lead to that goal was far less clear. How to go about building socialism—how quickly to absorb businesses into state ownership, and based upon what model (one of centralized state capitalism as in the Soviet Union? or along a relatively decentralized plan that would be associ-ated with radicalism, à la the GLF or the CR?)—was a key question over which debates raged and factional battles were waged. Dorothy Solinger, Lynn T. Whyte, and others have analyzed the twists, turns, and U-turns of these policies with regard to China's petty retail trades. Compared to sectors like industry and large wholesale businesses, small retail was among the last sectors absorbed by the state. Industrial factories and wholesalers held strategic fixed assets, and their owners, even if sympathetic to the CCP, were clearly identified as capitalists. By contrast, small retailers, craftspeople, and peddlers were too crucial to the everyday func-tioning of the urban economy to be eliminated, too dispersed and mobile to be easily managed, and too vulnerable to strip of their meager subsistence. Unlike larger capitalists, small retailers had a highly ambivalent class status; compris-ing a blurry spectrum from petty capitalist to virtually property-less laborers, at different political moments peddlers were characterized as pernicious, tolerable, or even beneficial to socialist development. As a result, it was in the peddler/small retailer/*getihu* (individual/independent business) sector that market activity was allowed to linger the longest, and it was often the first sphere where markets were opened up when economic stimulus was deemed necessary. Such stimulus was deemed crucial on the eve of liberation.

In spring 1949 thirteen authorized day markets for peddlers were designated, and by October the city had registered 2,470 peddlers, half trading in daily staples (foodstuffs, coal, etc.) and the other half trading mainly in used goods and small crafts, including cigarette rolling (95), soap making (93), and metal working (62).[9] The objective of registration was less to gather taxes (though a small monthly fee was required) than to help separate vagrants, thieves, and AWOL soldiers from honest urbanites.[10] Registration was also meant to help interdict the most volatile and valuable contraband from the market. In the wartime wreckage, public goods like train rails and telegraph wire went missing, pilfered for sale as scrap by ne'er-do-wells. Grenades, ammunition, and military-issued items regularly found their way into junk shops and night markets. As these newly government-authorized markets gave residents and peddlers approved spaces to trade in the light of day, night markets atrophied. Registration undertaken by the Market Management Office helped authorities detect and deter less savory activities.[11] The process was far from foolproof, and many peddlers still flitted between sites, preferring to dodge the registries and taxes. Shop owners, on the other hand, having permanent addresses, had little choice but to comply; as in the Republican era, used goods shops had to keep records of every item bought and sold, and any failure to cooperate with police investigations could be punished.

But such punishments were quite rare. Rather than attempt to induce order by forcibly cracking down on the grubby jumble of the scrap sector, the CCP instead set about gathering data to make the sector legible. Surveys, unprecedented in their detail before or since, aimed at a comprehensive head count and painstaking understanding of the sector's mechanics. Registration invariably entailed enrollment in new or reconstituted trade unions, gradually bringing scrap workers under Party supervision. For peddlers, registering came with trade-offs; legitimacy with the authorities brought stability and respectability but also fees, regulations, union dues, and meetings. Under previous governments, few peddlers had found this deal worth making, but the CCP was more persuasive. Indeed, by early 1951 a group of over one hundred wastepaper traders were practically begging the government to recognize their union:

> We profoundly understand that our trade is backward and that we must anxiously catch up to the more progressive trades, unite as one, exert our effort and organize our union to advance our profession's development to bring our understanding in

line with the government's. . . . We request the prompt recognition of our union so we can resolve the current difficulties listed here: 1) The city of Beijing has no less than 10 garbage dumps each with scores of old, young, female and feeble [persons] who pick waste paper to survive which we collect. Without our trade, these would all be jobless; this concerns the people's livelihood. 2) The government is enacting a waste materials use plan. Waste paper is a waste material, and our trade collects it, selling it to paper making factories to make good paper. Due to market conditions, there is a paper shortage. Though we use waste paper, we help make it into good paper and can supplement the government's shortfall; this concerns the national plan. 3) Ever since the country has enacted a tax policy, trades have had to ask for licenses to be permitted to do business, but up to now our trade hasn't received business licenses. . . . Over 100 of our businesses have asked to register, but the Bureau of Commerce and Industry won't issue a license to a business unless it can prove it is in a trade union, so, for over 100 households, business has ground to a halt. It's hard to survive. Please promptly approve of our trade union.[12]

Though ably lip-synching state rhetoric, the paper traders actually had their backs to the wall. They could not sell up to factories without the Ministry of Commerce and Industry's approval, and that required having an officially recognized (Party-supervised) trade organization. Rather than round up and beat up street hawkers and tax-evading brokers, the CCP applied pressure from the top down as gate-keepers to factories and large work units. For peddlers whose trade depended on selling up to industrial buyers, this strategy helped herd them toward the political fold. But such top-down pressure had little effect on the thousands of pickers/collectors who sold their daily harvest to small junk and craft shops or at day markets. Compelling these elements of the recirculating economy to accept state management required a different set of strategies.

The story of the Dongdan Big Trading Ground illustrates how the city gradually formalized used goods peddlers. Dongdan Big Trading Ground sprang up when Beijing's Japanese occupiers fled at the end of World War II, abandoning troves of personal goods. Occupying an area of open lots and adjacent streets east of the Forbidden City, the market thrived through civil war chaos until another fleeing regime, the GMD, cleared the area to use it as a temporary airport for evacuating goods and personnel. When the CCP revived the market in early 1949, the Market Management Office designated daytime hours, roughly organized stalls and food vending areas, and gave the market the official sounding name Dongdan People's Market. As the economy picked up, business did too, quite literally, as many vendors went from spreading out blankets to displaying their wares on stands and tables, even adding stall partitions like small rooms.[13] Commerce Bureau cadres encouraged traders to list prices clearly and fostered the creation of representative bodies through which trade groups could be organized, community leadership recruited, and proactive participation in market management encouraged.

Receptiveness to such political work was mixed, of course, but many peddlers were eager to garner respect and authority by leading groups charged with market sanitation, fire prevention, public safety, or dispute resolution.

City planners never intended to make ad hoc markets like Dongdan into permanent fixtures of the cityscape; rather, they deftly took advantage of market relocation as a mechanism of peddler management. The land Dongdan Market occupied was earmarked for the Bureau of Foreign Trade, so in 1951 construction began on a facility to house the market near the Longfu temple. Dubbed the Dongsi People's Market, the new site's construction would run about 4 million yuan, half to be footed by the Bureau of Foreign Trade, another million coming from the Bureau of Trade and Industry (aka Commerce), and the last million kicked in by those peddlers who chose to make the move; about three-quarters of Dongdan peddlers did so, recouping their shares within two years. At Dongsi stalls were sorted into zones according to trade group; small business loans were made available for the move and business upgrades. Of the one thousand businesses that moved into Dongsi (some peddlers were relocated from other street markets), about half dealt in old and used goods; the other half sold food items or new goods for everyday use. The new market, crude but still far grander than anything the peddlers had known, was comprised of four large, roofed structures that by 1955 had acquired doors, windows, and concrete flooring. And so, in a matter of a few years, the junk vendors of Dongdan had transformed from hustlers squatting in murky dirt lots into respectable members of trade unions who kept regular hours running tax-paying businesses in one of the city's greatest indoor markets.

Several smaller outdoor day markets were kept open as outlets for residents who might occasionally have to sell their personal items for cash and for peddlers who could not afford (or were not willing to comply with) relocation. Another option for peddlers was to join a co-op scrap shop under the management of the Supply and Marketing Cooperative (SMC, discussed in greater depth below). Wang Shude chose this second option. In 1947, at the age of twelve, Wang had come to Beijing from Rongcheng county, Hebei, with his father and uncle, peddling whatever junk they could find from their "stall" (a blanket on the ground) at the Zhaodengyu Road market near Fucheng Gate. When the market was moved for road repairs the young Wang, with nothing much worth selling and no defined skills, chose to become an apprentice in an SMC used furniture co-op (*muqi hezuo shangdian*) in Desheng Gate along with about forty others. After learning a bit about woodworking and repair, he was transferred, in 1957, to a general scrap-processing warehouse in Xizhi Gate, then in 1958 to the district recycling company in the Western suburb of Mentougou.[14] By the end of this process, Wang had risen from a destitute peasant youth scrounging up junk to make ends meet to a fully legitimate state employee and member of an established work unit on the government's payroll.

While considerable street peddling and waste-heap picking continued late into the 1950s, thousands of Beijing's used-goods peddlers were amenable to these acts of spatial reorganization, which also served as steps toward imposing order on the city's errant scrap menagerie. In the Republican era, Beijing's bustling dawn and night markets had doubled as sites of both consumer trade (the selling of used goods [jiuhuo] to residents) and trade for production (the sale of inputs for handicraft manufacturing). Vagrant peddlers like the young Wang Shude had offered a hodgepodge of used furniture, cloth scraps, chipped ceramics, and copper knickknacks to passersby—some destined for household (re)use, others to become inputs in local handicraft shops or factories. Through the new government's processes of relocation and reorganization, that hash of economic transactions was being sorted and rerouted into two related but distinct streams, one flowing toward "consumers" and the other toward "producers." Dongsi Market was not just tidier than the Dongdan Big Trade Ground had been; it was also more purely a site of, indeed something of a working-class palace dedicated to, consumption. Scrap destined as inputs for industry and handicraft was not sold there. While this gradual formalization of peddler markets brought legibility to used goods headed for consumers, quite different forms of control would prove necessary for the state to get leverage over the scrap materials that headed toward production, and this project in many respects was far more important to the regime given its aspirations for firing up industrial development.

1950–1955: THE STATE HARDLY GETS A SCRAP

Scrap had long been the lifeblood of Beijing's handicrafts shops, but CCP planners were determined to see the nation's scrap, particularly its metals and rubber, redirected toward industrialization. The degree to which specific industrial processes depend on scrap varies, but in general scrap's importance and value rise when primary material supplies are tight. And tight they were in the Mao era, with foreign trade strangled by a US-led embargo in the 1950s and then slashed again in the 1960s and 1970s by the rift with the Soviet bloc.[15] So the incessant Mao-era rhetoric and campaigns promoting thrifty (qinjian jieyue) industrialization were not just driven by an anti-capitalist/imperialist ideology of national self-reliance, but also by the hard realities of a stifled foreign trade.

While all forms of scrap were to be prized, they were not all prized equally, certainly not from the state's perspective. By far the highest priority on the eve of liberation was copper, a crucial industrial, military, and electrical input and the first form of scrap material placed under state management. In 1951 the government initially assigned control over scrap copper nationally to the China National Native Industry Company (Zhongguo tuchan gongsi), but it transferred the task in 1952 to the All-China Federation of Supply and Marketing Cooperatives (SMC;

Zhonghua quanguo gongxiao hezuo she).[16] In this chapter swarming with bureaucracies, the SMC played a leading role. The CCP had long supported the creation of co-ops of all sorts (trade, credit, consumer, and handicraft) as a means for poor peasant, worker, and peddler households to develop economic opportunities. In 1950 the SMC was formed as the national-level state organ providing guidance to the tens of thousands of co-ops in cities, towns, and villages throughout China. The SMC was to foster the development of co-ops, guide them toward socialism, and align them with state policy.

In the scrap sector, the SMC's work promoting the creation of trade and handicraft co-ops was intended to go hand in hand with increasing state access to industrially useful materials. The new regime understood that it could not simply upend the peddler sector and confiscate its materials, so "shrinking the proportion of recycling trade going to the free market" became one of the SMC's explicit missions.[17] The idea was that giving peddlers and traders who became SMC affiliates exclusive access to state contracts would entice them to join up, and the free market share would shrink. But things did not pan out quite as planned.

One reason most peddlers were reluctant to join SMC co-ops was that SMC units were forbidden to engage in profiteering, at least when it came to materials the state coveted, like copper. The 1952 regulations charged SMC co-ops with kicking any copper they collected up to central planners, instructing them to "uphold the interests of the nation and the masses, eschew pure market motives" and dutifully transfer scrap copper to the Ministry of Materials Management (Wuzi guanli zongju).[18] SMC's and the Materials Ministry's responsibilities broke down roughly as follows: local collection (purchasing of scrap materials from households and small independent shops, sorting, and local transport) was handled by the extensive network of SMC co-ops while purchases and transfers from state-owned industrial units, national-level planning, extra-local shipping, storage, and allocation were handled by the Ministry of Materials Management (in accord with central planning and pricing commission guidelines).

This arrangement for copper was among the least confusing scrap management regulations of the Mao era, but note that even here scrap required the coordination of two discrete bureaucracies. Indeed, one theme of this chapter is that building a regulatory system to collect and allocate scrap was unaccountably confusing. Managing scrap was impossible without the coordination of multiple government bureaus; this is nearly axiomatic because scrap, by its very identification *as* scrap, is liminal. Placed into a bureaucratized geography, scrap's out-of-placeness emerges in clear relief as the incessant crossing or blurring of organizational boundaries. Moreover, scrap is scattered across space and *kinds of spaces*—industrial, rural, domestic—so just collecting it typically requires engaging an array of social and economic units. It then needs to be sorted, transported, stored, processed, and reallocated for reuse. (Note: the steps are not always taken in that order, and the processes for each type of material are often extremely different.)

A more typical example of a scrap-related order is a four-page notice from 1953 for handling ferrous scrap:

> In principle, cities should keep ferrous scrap for local use because it is heavy and inefficient to transport. But at present Beijing units should ramp up collection to provide ferrous scrap to the North China region [Hebei, Inner Mongolia, Shanxi, Beijing and Tianjin] because ferrous across the region is highly dispersed and difficult to collect. The SMC will purchase the scrap, while the Heavy Industry Department will be in charge of collecting and shipping; they should meet to draft contracts. For large scrap, if Heavy Industry has trouble transporting it, supplying units should try to help by smashing it; if that is not possible receiving units will get a 10% fee for handling scrap processing. Supplying units located far from rail lines are encouraged to use their scrap themselves; if they cannot do so Heavy Industry will collect their scrap, but without payment. Though as a rule scrap can only be shipped outside Beijing after passing through SMC units, given the urgency, Beijing factories can sell directly to North China factories, though they must inform the SMC when they do so.[19]

And so, it would appear, our osteological investigation into that extinct economic behemoth, the state scrap sector, has begun. Why, one might ask, should anyone care about the arcane anatomy of this socialist relic? My hope is that this excavation can provide understanding of how that fabled colossus, the Chinese planned economy, functioned on an everyday level. Like other great beasts that have vanished from the earth, this bureaucratic dinosaur has left behind fossilized remains and passed on genetic material, remnants that still calcify, complicate, and enliven China's waste and recycling system to this day (see appendix).

By 1953, Beijing SMC units were charged with purchasing several types of material for state needs, including rubber to send to the China Chemical company, wastepaper for processing in North China mills, and bones for a host of uses (handicrafts, fertilizer, glue). A national shortage of lead spurred a campaign to recycle soft-lead toothpaste tubes, with state-managed retail shops and department stores giving discounts to consumers who returned empties, which were then passed to the SMC.[20] The geographies and methods of collecting, sorting, processing, and reallocating each of these materials were completely different. It was precisely this jumble of locations, specialized labor, and logistics that had animated the Republican-era urban bazaar and its maze of niche trades and intricate supply chains. Shoehorning the scrap sector's kaleidoscope of materials, geographies, and skills into a coherent bureaucratic structure pushed administrative rationality to the brink of futility. Still, there was no question that the goal was to bring all scrap materials under state control; in late 1954 all government units were instructed that they could no longer trade any forms of scrap copper, rubber, lead, oil, ferrous, cotton, paper, glass, or wood on the open market; they could only go to SMC or other specifically designated state units.[21]

Despite all this, the government had only captured a fraction of Beijing's scrap materials markets by 1954. It was most successful with materials that moved through state work units or that relied on large factories (already under tighter state control) for processing. Scrap paper in particular fit that bill. Having reclaimed its status as the nation's capital, Beijing was now home to hundreds of government offices that released floods of printing orders. Scrap paper dealers enjoyed a brief golden age, pitching banquet battles to win government contracts.[22] But rubber scrap, waste oil, and almost every form of metal remained dominated by small private businesses.[23]

In its 1954 midyear report, Beijing's SMC reported collecting only seventy-nine of its there-hundred-ton copper quota. There was copper out there—residents and private businesses were selling it to roaming drumbeaters at 60 percent above the SMC price, and a steady supply of around forty tons of copper coursed through Beijing's private shops each month, some shipped from as far away as Shanghai—but it was not going to the state. State agents were directed to pressure politically vulnerable elements: "Temples and shrines have many copper and iron bells, vessels and Buddhas, which, as long as they have no preservation value and are not under state cultural or religious protection, fall in the scope of recycling collection."[24] Some former landlords also had copper troves, though internal circulars warned "that landlords and rich peasants who sell their stashed copper cash and wares need to be treated appropriately and still need to receive payment; using confiscation or similar methods is not allowed."[25] Beijing's SMC experimented with burning used insulated wire to extract the copper—a highly toxic practice praised as a sign of technological progress in 1954 but that today is synonymous with the worst forms of "primitive" informal e-waste "dumping."[26] Despite all these methods, it was clear that Beijing would never make its copper quota without cracking the market, so the SMC gave in and greenlit its 138 collectors to purchase copper from residents at market prices. Control over other metals was no better. Of the city's 233 registered ferrous shop, a few approached the SMC for supplies, but most coped just fine on market flows of used oil drums and horseshoes. Beijing's 267 privately owned mixed metals shops profitably accessed several tons of aluminum, tin, and lead through the free market.

Overall, the 1954 report conceded, little had changed since liberation, with about sixty-five hundred private businesses supplied largely by two to three thousand impoverished waste pickers/collectors (often mothers, children, and elderly) doing a total of approximately 1 million yuan in business each month. Moreover, these pettiest of petty bourgeois entrepreneurs exhibited a cutthroat drive for individual profit, jacking up prices when demand peaked and threatening pickers with starvation-level prices when it slumped. Consolidating the sector under the state, the report argued, would better serve both Chinese industry and indigent pickers, but absorbing it had to proceed gingerly so as not to crush the sector's economic vitality, which depended on peddlers' diverse skills and their agile negotiation of constantly shifting supply chains and market conditions.

MOBILIZING THE MASSES

The state may have been frustrated in its attempts to access secondary materials through scrap traders, but there was another angle it could try: urban residents. The state experimented with campaigns and media messages that forged links, both ideological and tangible, between individual acts of recycling and the national realization of thrifty industrialization. The 3-Antis and 5-Antis campaigns of 1951 and 1952 directly associated wastefulness with the evils of official corruption and unrepentant capitalism. Citizens everywhere were encouraged to stay vigilant and to expose cases of profligate waste to the authorities and state media, and though both campaigns ended by 1953, the representation of wastefulness as antirevolutionary never dissipated. In one high-profile case in 1954, several peasants reported gross wastefulness at the nation's premier Angang steel factory to their local newspaper. This lead to an exposé by a team of investigative journalists which revealed that waste heaps outside the factory gates were loaded with so much scrap iron, steel, and copper that some peasants in the area "had stopped working hard [in the fields] and made picking their 'part time job.'"[27]

The fight against waste could also take on a more positive tone, in the form of volunteer efforts to bring in the scrap. Stories of such efforts soon became a staple of media coverage. In Shanghai, for example, 240 cadres from various units teamed up in fifteen squads, each focused on a particular material (copper, coal, tobacco, rubber, cloth, etc.), that fanned out across the city looking for opportunities to conserve resources.[28] A favorite target for antiwaste mobilization was students; in Beijing dozens of frugal youth squads (qingnian jieyue dui) literally swept through the city's factories and work units, gathering any scrap in their wake.[29] Even elementary school students could make spirited contributions. At a national Young Pioneers conference a fifth-grade boy insisted even kids could make significant contributions to help the country reach the lofty goals set by the first five-year plan, vowing to "plant one sunflower or castor oil plant every year, plant trees if conditions permitted, and collect scrap ferrous, copper and paper, used ink bottles, toothpaste tubes, apricot pits and rubber shoe soles."[30] The People's Daily invited readers to write in with suggestions to free up strategic materials for higher priority uses; sports shoe factories responded by vowing to replace the copper eyes on their tennis shoes with aluminum or steel ones.[31] Scrap drives, like hygiene-forward cleanup campaigns, became a reliable widget in the toolkit of mass activities around National Day and Spring Festival.

FIGURE 4. One of four panels of a set of posters encouraging recycling, each representing a season, printed in Hebei. This poster represents winter and some of the festivities and activities of Chinese New Year. Writing at the top reads (taking liberties to preserve the rhyme): "On holidays sweep out the scrap that's piled up, Sell it and serve the people as you clean up!" Used with permission of the International Institute of Social History, Amsterdam.

As productive as frenetic bursts of mass recycling could be, the key to an effective scrap infrastructure lay in tapping into residents' daily life habits, making scrap collection a routine part of the daily functioning of every household and work unit. To this end, one approach was far more publicly persuasive than any other: trading trash for cash. Beijing residents, like urbanites throughout China, had been bartering and selling their recyclables to peddlers for decades; the state allowed roaming scrap collectors to continue their trade, all the while coaxing and prodding them into the SMC. Many collectors bartered small trinkets for scrap, which was particularly appealing to kids. Most people who grew up in Beijing in the 1950s fondly recall the scrap collectors, who exchanged things like figurines made of candy or dough for scrap. The state's call for children to contribute scrap to build the new China also added a layer of seriousness to these small acts of frugality; one interviewee recalled that as a young girl she had a showdown with her nanny, trying to convince her to hand over her favorite cooking spatula for the GLF steel drive.[32]

The theme of everyone contributing their little part all adding up to create monumental national change was such a prominent trope in Mao-era education and campaign propaganda that I feel compelled to apologize to readers for dwelling on it. Still, it is worth pointing out that this trope, epitomized in Mao's "Foolish Old Man Who Moved Mountains" speech, was particularly well matched to the project of recycling. Public participation in recycling with SMC collectors (see figure 4) served as a tangible expression of this vision of how small acts, repeated across China's hundreds of millions, could make real contributions to the economy.[33]

TURF BATTLES AT HIGH TIDE

The verb *excavate* (*wajue*) appears often in recycling circulars. Often it is a metaphor for summoning up idle resources or energy, but in some cases, it was literal. Copper cash foundries had been common around Beijing in the Qing era, and many had left behind mounds of ash and slag that could potentially yield copper and other alloys. Often such mounds lay within the grounds of factory or military units that were perfectly happy to let SMC agents muck about in the seemingly barren dirt. But when SMC workers started actually carting off valuable scrap, many units changed their tune and barred their gates. Apparently these units saw their grounds as their property, and so the scrap was theirs as well. The SMC pleaded with the State Council (Guowuyuan) for support, and it was decided that the SMC must be given access to all units but should also pay them the state-set price for any scrap excavated.[34] In other words, the units were granted a kind of property right over their space that extended to things of value found there, while the SMC (though having to pay for the scrap) retained the exclusive right to excavate it. This was just one iteration of a set of questions that dogged scrap management: who specifically should have ownership rights, trading rights, and/ or use rights to scrap, those all being potentially different things.

Late 1955 and 1956 saw the "Socialist High Tide," in which agriculture rapidly collectivized and urban commerce transitioned to joint public/private partnerships (*gongsi heying*), a management form that more or less consigned private businesses to state control. To design the blueprint for Beijing's scrap sector's transition to state control, SMC cadres were brought together with political education, planning, and tax officials to form the Beijing Scrap Management Office (Beijing feipin jingying chu).[35] Office personnel compiled detailed surveys mapping out and quantifying the city's overall solid waste profile and the entirety of its scrap and used goods trades and evaluated peddlers' and pickers' household assets, incomes, and productive potential and proposed frameworks for their reorganization. Hundreds of these households were old, sickly, and/or terribly destitute. The Xuanwu manager whose memoir chronicled the sector's transition worked for the Scrap Office and recalled that many pickers broke into tears of gratitude when he delivered them 5 yuan in dumpling money for Spring Festival.[36]

Also responding to the socialist wave, the Beijing Handicraft Production Cooperative (HPC; Beijing shi shougongye shengchan hezuoshe), made up of over one hundred handicraft co-op workshops, formed its own central office, the similarly named Beijing Used Goods Management Office (Beijing feiqi pin jingli bu). Perhaps municipal planners did not quite grasp that the Scrap Office and the Used Goods Office—which in the abstract seem clearly differentiated, with the SMC focused on scrap collection and trade and the HPC on craft production—in reality were overlapping networks claiming control over the same materials. Soon accusing fingers were pointing from both sides. The HPC said SMC purchasing agents were paying scandalously high prices to snatch up scrap that rightfully belonged to the HPC. In one case an SMC agent allegedly visited an HPC workshop and asked to look at the shop's cloth scrap. The shop manager balked at the SMC agent's request because the HPC obviously had undisputed authority to allocate scrap within and among its subsidiary units, and this scrap was contracted to another HPC shop at .35 yuan per pound. But the SMC agent offered an apparently irresistible .52 per pound and waltzed out with the entire load. Such unfair competition over materials, cried the HPC, threatened to starve craft shops of their supplies and handicraft workers of their livelihoods.[37]

By the spring of 1956 cases of SMC and HPC agents furiously brandishing their credentials, racing each other to arrive first at factories, butting heads at loading docks, and trading charges of capitalist exploitation were daily affairs. The SMC accused HPC agents of falsifying credentials and masquerading as SMC representatives in order to make off with scrap. If the SMC was to be believed, HPC agents regularly paid markups of 50–100 percent on state prices for copper and iron, turning the socialist transition into cutthroat capitalism and causing the SMC to fall seriously short of quota. But the SMC's most damning accusation was that although the state had given the HPC access to scrap so craft shops could use it for *production*, instead the HPC—by accessing scrap improperly; paying (black) market prices when it wanted; and selling scrap for profit to factories in

Beijing, Shandong, and Tianjin—was using it for *trade*. But trade (meaning the state-condoned purchasing, selling, and supplying of scrap) was the sole responsibility and prerogative of the SMC, which followed strict rules regarding prices, fees, planning quotas, and reporting protocols. The HPC was banned from any such activities based on the accusation that its horizontal trading spree threatened chaos and undermined socialism.[38]

Adding bureaucratic insult to economic injury, the Sanitation Bureau was just rolling out its visionary new MSW management plan, called the "three separates." The plan (see chapter 3) required all Beijing residents to sort their household garbage into three categories (ash, food waste, and recyclable scrap) so that it could be used in production (ash for bricks, food waste for compost, and scrap for handicraft and industrial inputs). The extensive planning documents for the three separates snubbed the SMC, not even mentioning them, and funneled all recyclables directly to HPC units.[39] Doubtless from the Sanitation Bureau's point of view, collaboration with the HPC seemed perfectly natural. Sanitation staff was surely aware that the pickers who scavenged the city's dumps sold most of what they picked to handicraft workshops, with the SMC playing no role whatsoever, so directly plugging waste-stream scrap into the HPC seemed rational and efficient. But the SMC was incensed; those 955 waste-picking and -trading households that scoured the city's dumps were neither Sanitation Bureau employees nor HPC handicraft workers but fell firmly in the SMC's bailiwick—indeed, the SMC had conducted the very surveys that counted them![40] Again, the right to "trade" scrap supposedly belonged exclusively to the SMC (just as in the slag mounds case previously discussed), so any scrap transferred horizontally between bureaus (from Sanitation to the HPC, for instance) must in principle pass through the SMC.

After months of dander-raising memos, the City Planning Commission resolved the stalemate. It placed about half the employable scavengers into HPC shops and the other half into SMC units, then merged the SMC's Scrap Management Office and HPC's Used Goods Office to form the Beijing Scrap Company (BSC Beijing shi feipin gongsi). The BSC was now the municipal-level authority over the entire scrap sector. Vertical lines of authority parked the BSC under the SMC, and all BSC subunits were SMC affiliated. But the BSC was also directly under the supervision of the Beijing Materials Bureau. Basically, recycling collected from neighborhoods, known in the parlance of the sector as "society" (*shehui*) recycling, was SMC managed, whereas collection and trade between state-owned industrial units and extra-local allocation were under Materials Bureau management. Through this dual oversight, planners framed scrap as dual in nature, at once fundamentally embedded in "society"—household consumption and commerce, the realm of peddlers and pickers whom the SMC now oversaw—and industry—the realm of allocated provisioning of and trade between industries, overseen by the Materials Bureau.

Despite its short and bureaucratically brutish existence, the Beijing Scrap Management Office laid the groundwork for the state's absorption of the scrap sector during 1956. In addition to managing hundreds of peddlers who had joined SMC co-ops already, the Scrap Office took charge of managing around three thousand independent collectors, peddlers, and scrap traders and their families and employees (a total of about eleven thousand people). Most were poor, even destitute; on average the "capital" (including tools, carts, etc.) owned by a recycling business totaled around 50 yuan. During rainy and snowy spells, many families, unable to go out to work, became penniless. On the more comfortable end of the spectrum were 111 businesses (about 3% of the independent scrap sector) that averaged about 2,000 yuan in capital. These, along with businesses with two or more employees, were labeled capitalists and were given little choice but to sign over their businesses to the state in a joint public-private arrangement.[41] Over half were in the metals trade and had done well through the economic recovery of the early 1950s, but since the Socialist High Tide they had been facing a shrinking and ever more proscribed free market. Now they were completely barred from selling outside state channels and from jiggering with prices. Instead, they received payment from the SMC on a fee-for-service basis (an incentive to maximize throughput). Within months their incomes fell from 150–200 yuan to 40–70 yuan per month.

For the other 97 percent of the scrap sector, 851 shops and 2,133 street peddlers, the medicine was not as bitter. They were compelled to merge into small teams on a largely voluntary basis, their options ranging from pooling inventory and equally sharing their profits (liangou lianxi; about 38% chose this route) to forming mutual aid small groups (huzhu xiaozu) in which each trader remained essentially economically independent (about 59% went this route). So aside from a bit more state supervision and being placed into groups, the business structure of about 60 percent of Beijing's scrap retailers, even after the 1956 Socialist High Tide, had changed little.

The tide also swept into the "old goods" retail business realm. First, to ferret out any unregistered vendors, Commerce Bureau inspectors teamed up with city police to implement daily registration (as opposed to monthly) at the city's remaining open-air day markets. Individuals were allowed to sell their own possessions, but anyone who showed up repeatedly was suspected of being an unregistered peddler, questioned, and even escorted home to confirm they were actually selling their own belongings and not peddling without a license.[42] It was an onerous process, but after a month inspectors felt confident that anyone still evading registration was a malefactor. The authorities then shifted to inspecting formalized markets like Dongsi People's Market, compelling vendors to reorganize. Businesses that made on average between 50 and 100 yuan a month were converted to partnerships, and stall owners became wage-earning "bosses" making 35 yuan a month, while their assistants were paid 15 yuan. Officials took over the management of these shops' supply chains. To soften the financial blow, officials scrambled to narrow the boss/assistant pay gap, created a bonus system, and considered giving loans to households to weather the transition. But the Commerce Bureau soon decided to reverse these reforms specifically for stalls specializing in used goods because their businesses involved so many complex markets and craft skills that officials were incapable of running them effectively. To avoid looking like they had failed to implement socialist reforms and also to prevent used goods businesses from being painted as politically backward, the Commerce Bureau let them keep the *gongsi heying* shingle on their stalls even though they were still functioning as essentially independent businesses.[43]

And so, despite all the political pressure, many used goods retailers and scrap recyclers came out of the *gongsi heying* movement still retaining most of their business independence. But this would not last long; larger economic trends were now severely affecting them. By the fall of 1956, hundreds of scrap-peddling households had been pushed into even graver poverty due to increased state control over markets:

> [B]oth state and jointly-owned (gongsi heying) factories have been incorporated into the recycling system, cutting off the market from some of its original multiplicity of sources. Especially for the nationally recycled materials copper, tin and lead the black market price is over twice the state price, and this is affecting small businesses with a serious supply problem. Waste paper and junk collectors (big basket-toters and drum-beaters) lack funds, are typically elderly, especially old ladies with little earning capacity. Some household heads have been arrested for selling stolen goods, a total of 31 people, directly influencing their households' incomes and making subsistence difficult.

Some 447 households (1,164 persons) were facing serious financial difficulties, with 135 families living on less than 4 yuan per person per month.[44] A raft of measures was taken to address the difficulties: "breaking through the old specialization" and getting nonferrous metals shops to expand into iron/steel where scrap was more plentiful; merging cash-rich/labor-poor households into teams with their opposites so as to fill one another's gaps; shifting families lacking able-bodied laborers to government relief; and extending loans to about 260 cash-poor businesses. These might have been helpful measures, but the underlying cause of these problems was that market space was shrinking as state-managed units were coming to dominate the entire economy. Though the process of state takeover sputtered a bit throughout 1956, by the end of that year it was clear the situation had flipped, with the state-managed sector of the economy so dominant that independent recyclers could hardly access any materials and being squeezed out of viability; or, as Lynn T. White describes, "it took constant checking to caulk the leaks in this system," but state control over retail had been normalized.[45]

THE BSC AND THE STANDARDIZATION
OF THE SCRAP MENAGERIE

When the BSC rose from the ashes of the Scrap Office in 1957, there was still plenty of organizing to do. The BSC was charged with rationalizing about seven thousand workers with widely ranging job conditions. Of these, about five thousand were jammed into the alleys of Chongwen, Xuanwu, and Qianmen districts, which since Qing times had been the buzzing commercial core of Beijing, where peddlers and craft trades hived. Now they needed to be dispersed across the city as the state transformed Beijing from a city of consumption into a managed metropolis of socialist production. Hundreds of scrap workers were relocated to other districts or placed at large industrial units like Capital Steel (Shougang). Wang Shude, for example, was transferred first from Chongwen to a depot in Xicheng district and a year later again to a new depot in the distant suburb of Mentougou, near Capital Steel.

The urban scrap-space was to be strictly rationalized: collectors were instructed to cover assigned routes that conformed to administrative boundaries, across which they were not allowed to tread or trade. Authorized collectors were issued numbered badges, and residents were warned against selling scrap or used goods to anyone without one. According to the Xuanwu memoirist, the government did not spend "even once cent" on forming the BSC and its citywide network; its shops, carts, tools, and 2 million yuan of capital all came from the holdings of those consolidated into the company, with everyone, in theory, holding shares relative to their investment.[46] This seems to have been common; Fuzhou's 638 shoulder-pole-toting junk traders similarly built their city's scrap company on pooled resources.[47] Scores of new BSC collection sites were quickly erected on small barren plots throughout the city, and some BSC administrative offices were crammed into corners in other bureau's offices, markets or department stores. As BSC sites established a more substantial geographical footprint over the years, the company handled its own facilities upgrades; the Xuanwu cadre's memoir notes with pride that many BSC workers became excellent carpenters and mechanics.[48]

State recycling companies convened an ensemble of technicians, traders, and pickers around a buffet of manufacturing by-products, residential flotsam, metallic bits, chemical wastes, and daily discards worthy of a Hieronymus Bosch painting. In January 1957 the People's Daily boasted: "The SMC, thinking from every angle, unearthing potential, penetrating city and country, has expanded types [of goods they purchase/sell] from 120 to over 500. Some provinces and cities, like Liaoning, Beijing, Shanghai handle over 10,000 types."[49] Shanghai units, for example, excelled in collecting fish scales—more than ninety thousand pounds of them (uncommonly versatile, they could make film emulsion, matches, medicines, and industrial textiles). A single barber from Fujian collected twenty-seven hundred pounds of human hair on a rural haircutting tour.[50] The BSC ran a shop that offered a candy-box assortment of used gizmos and machine parts, attracting mechanics from far and wide hunting for hardware both mundane and exotic.[51] Used oil, discarded film stock (from which silver was extracted), bitumen and rare-earth metal scrap, waste plastics, used feathers, old leather goods, frayed hemp rope, and burlap—the list of goods and materials was enormous.

But all those materials were at the sector's fringe. The heart of the endeavor was the staple scrap materials that engaged national planners. Regarding those, a seventy-page *Recycling Handbook* was distributed to SMC recycling shops throughout the nation, outlining the uses, handling, and quality specifications (specs) for evaluating seven key materials: copper, tin, lead, bone, rubber, cloth, and cotton fiber. Here are a few representative snippets:

> Copper is divided into the following 6 types: 1. Waste electrical wire and waste purple copper: includes waste copper wire, waste purple copper sheet, purple copper pipes, tubing, rods, plating etc. 2. Purple copper cash: includes purple and red copper cash; 3. Typical purple copper utensils, machine parts, chunks: includes pots, kettles, basins, bolts, chunks . . .
>
> Tin: Because the names for different kinds of tin and tin alloys are so numerous, and even differ by region, we will just discuss the proportion of tin [in goods] but cannot provide immutable specifications. . . .
>
> Bones: When purchasing wet bones deduct for water content as appropriate. Also, mixed bones (*za gu*) can be divided into fresh and cooked. . . . Material bones (*liao gu*) are rather big pieces like oxen leg bones that craft workers can make into tooth brushes or other utensils [nine types of "material bone" are then listed, followed by three categories of water buffalo horn, etc.]. . . .
>
> The Problem of Waste Rubber Categories and Specifications: There are many types of waste rubber, specs are complicated, qualities differ. In the past specs were very inconsistent across regions, some places had 30-40 categories, making purchasing, pricing and processing very difficult. . . .To take a first step at unifying our trade at present, below are 3 categories [tire rubber, shoe rubber, miscellaneous] divided into 13 types.[52]

Specs were also provided for seventeen kinds of old cloth and twenty-one types of used cotton fiber. More than just evidence of the complexities of categorizing scrap, the handbook marks a fundamental transformation in the junk world's workforce: the dissolution of the hodgepodge of discrete trade and handicraft specializations into a bureaucracy that aimed to produce generalists. Of course, many old specialists were still hard at work under the BSC's orchestration, but they were now stationed at collection points and depots that collected and sorted the entire spectrum of scrap from every community and work unit in the capital. Every BSC collector now had to know how to evaluate every kind of scrap, at least well enough to classify it, sort it, and pay the right price for it. The handbook is meant to compile and pass on those skills, but that was not always easy. The chapter on copper, which opens with a seven-page subsection on how to evaluate copper goods and alloys "based on sensory evidence" (color, weight, resonance), begins reassuringly: "These methods are not 'mysteries beyond comprehension,' they can be learned." But a few pages on, a reader starts to wonder, particularly in the section on using sound to evaluate an alloy (striking a piece of metal and listening to its tone), which boils down to, "This evaluation method largely depends on experience."[53] Wang Shude received extensive training in how to evaluate and sort different materials, but he recalled that whenever he, or anyone else at the Mentougou depot, came across tricky metal alloy scrap, they would seek out the other Mr. Wang, a Shanxi native and old hand in the metals business, for help.[54] The handbook's chapter on copper also includes twenty-six pictures of bronze cultural relics—mirrors, ancient currency, ritual vessels, spear points—with directions to send such items to the city's cultural bureau for appraisal. Given the SMC workforce's limited literacy, those pictures were likely more useful than the text. Some marvelous research by Di Yinlu describes the enormous quantities of historical artifacts recovered through the scrap sector in Shanghai under the leadership of a group of scrap archaeologists. Selected in 1951 from among specialists at the most reputable old bookstores and antique shops—essentially the experts at the top of the Republican recycling world hierarchy—salvage archaeologists were sent to factory sites and scrap depots to retrieve finds of possible historical worth. By 1957 Shanghai's salvage archaeologists had helped retrieve more than 500,000 ancient texts and 27,000 bronze artifacts—and that was before the manic activity of the GLF.[55]

The handbook signals a profound change in how knowledge and training were to be transmitted between generations. Specialized trade skills had been passed privately from masters to apprentices; skills and business contacts had been prized and guarded, as much because they were hard won as because they afforded specialists an edge in their trade. The *Recycling Handbook* documents a process of simultaneous deskilling and reskilling, a pedagogical shift from apprenticeships to booklets, department meetings, and group training.[56]

The handbook and the specs within it are discursive objects with profound material consequences marking the consolidation of a new socialist "waste regime."[57] The handbook, with its definitions and terminology, marks not merely a shift in trade lingo but a transformation in how scrap would be defined and handled across the national economy; these were changes in terminology that would in many ways reshape waste materials themselves. The 1960s–80s were awash with circulars regarding prices, regulations, and processing protocols, none of which could be implemented without first having a set of definitions describing the scrap objects and materials being so managed. This Mao-era process of standardization differs little from similar historical processes of commoditization in capitalist industrial economies. Specs enable traders to transform particular goods (e.g., a specific harvest of wheat from a specific farm, or a specific load of steel from a specific forge) into abstracted commodities (wheat from any farm that has kernels of a certain size; steel from any forge with so much manganese, etc.) and thereby facilitate trade while effacing particularistic aspects of sourcing. Historically, such processes of commoditization and standardization often incur resistance, both human (individual producers struggling to keep their products distinct from the generic flow of similar goods) and nonhuman (not all goods easily conform to measurable market standardization) in any sector. But in the world of scrap, the resistance of "the object" to standardization can be particularly acute. Indeed, one way to understand the fabulous jargon of the US scrap industry (the 2006 *Scrap Specifications Circular* lists and defines forty-two different forms of copper scrap with names that include Barley, Berry, Birch, Candy, Cobra, Dream, Drink, Druid, Elias, Honey, Lady, Maize, Melon, Naggy, Nomad, Pales) is as an inspired attempt to wrestle these wayward objects into the commodity straitjacket. That wrestling act has material consequences in shaping the objects so defined; goods and materials are processed to meet the specs (What size should this metal scrap or bone be cut to?) and then become relied upon inputs in production processes. In some industries, this standardization can increase efficiency, but in finicky manufacturing processes it can undermine quality. Moreover, when sourcing from multiple and unclear sources—for instance, if one tried to smelt steel from a wide mix of used iron goods like pots and pans—if specs are not applied consistently throughout the supply chain, one might end up with a very poor product in the end (see the GLF backyard steel furnace debacle described later in the chapter).

Organizing thousands of workers, standardizing thousands of materials; if the BSC's mission was not challenging enough, the company also had to fit all that within a Byzantine and ever-shifting regulatory framework, because different materials were regulated at different (and often shifting) levels in the national administrative hierarchy. Briefly, there were three categories of commodity—(1) national, (2) provincial/municipal, and (3) local—each with its own general trade guidelines. In 1957, scrap copper, lead, and rubber were national commodities, meaning their prices, allocation quotas, and the units authorized to trade them were determined by the central government. Scrap ferrous, cotton, and bone were provincial- or municipal-level commodities, managed at that tier in accordance with central planners; all other materials—used rope, oil cloth, broken glass, etc.—were type 3 goods, which in Beijing put them under the authority of the BSC (with Beijing municipal approval).

Amid this baffling complexity, one principle underlying all scrap trade regulations was clear and would remain consistent (in theory) throughout the Mao era. It is stated in the first quoted sentence from a 1957 circular:

Every unit can only trade and move scrap according to state price via the BSC, not to each other, not to units outside Beijing, and not to their higher units. Citizens should not sell any scrap (废品 *feipin*) to anyone lacking the official license to trade them, and these agents all should have an official insignia that they wear on their chests. For production units seeking scrap supplies, all metals and rubber requests are submitted to the City Planning Committee and handled by Materials Supply Office; paper, cloth, broken glass, etc. are supplied by the BSC. Any units from outside Beijing can only trade scrap at five designated scrap markets, not with any other units or markets. Unless presented with proof of approval, transportation units should refuse to ship any important scrap out of the city.[58]

Any scrap traded outside state-mandated channels came increasingly to be treated as "black market" and illegal. But where the lines between permissible and improper trade lay varied from one material to another, as did the relative severity of violating the rules. If a work unit traded fast and loose with broken glass, it was merely violating BSC authority; but trading copper at the wrong price or through the wrong channels was violating national law.

Despite these increasingly high stakes, copper management continued to resemble Swiss cheese. But by 1957 the culprits evading the rules were not private traders but state-managed enterprises. As the BSC remarked, "The tendency of state-run and joint public-private enterprises to free/self-management (*ziyou jingying*) is severe."[59] This was true not just locally, but nationally. The Hunan Provincial Planning Committee, on track to collect only half of its 1957 copper quota, complained that "some metals enterprises are unwilling to sell their copper scrap to the SMC, but instead barter it with other production units for needed materials, or even sell it on the market . . . engaging in trafficking and profiteering."[60] In 1957 north China only met 50 percent of its copper scrap obligations to central planners. Where was it all going? The SMC pointed foremost to the "needless (*bu biyao de*) recovery and expansion of copper and tin handicrafts."[61] The healthy economic growth of the mid-1950s was proving too healthy to rein in; the city of Taiyuan, for example, saw its handicraft collectives grow from 22 to 163 workers and its copper inputs likewise jump from 10 to 140 tons, mostly sourcing through covert trade and sometimes selling copper to shops in Shijiazhuang at 90 percent above state prices. With demand surging, anyone in the supply chain might succumb to the temptations of the black market, from a band of twenty-one Hebei peasants caught smuggling two hundred kilos (441 pounds) of copper out of the province to a group of state-owned Tianjin production units that traded a total of 150 tons of copper on the black market monthly while sending only 20 to the city's recycling company. From the regulatory point of view, a unit "self-managing" its copper scrap and one engaging in black market profiteering were, for all intents and purposes, becoming indistinguishable.

FROM MARKET CHAOS TO MANAGERIAL LEGIBILITY

With the First Five-Year Plan ending and the nation poised on the threshold of the GLF, late 1957 is a good moment to take stock. What a decade before had composed Republican Beijing's unruly bazaar of junk, repair, and picking trades had now been slotted into separate bureaucratic sheds. The BSC managed what we typically think of as recycling: the collection and processing of scrap to supply materials to production, both industrial and handicraft. Its collection scope covered both residential scrap (what might be termed "postconsumer" but in the language of the BSC was termed "society" [*shehui*] scrap) and industrial scrap, with the ratio of residential to industrial running around 30/70. Recycling was in no way administratively linked to the Sanitation Bureau or urban trash collection; it was instead tied to manufacturing and affiliated with the Ministry of Commerce, the SMC, and various industrial bureaus.

As for the reuse sector—the galaxy of discarded "old goods" revived through mending and modification and sold to private consumers—by 1957 it fell within the scope of the city's newly formed Consignment Company (Xintuo gongsi). About one thousand used goods businesses and peddler co-ops were folded into the company's unified management, marking their final loss of managerial and economic independence. In Tianqiao, the city's legendary kingdom where haggling was a blood sport, the price tag now reigned supreme—at least in theory.[62]

In reality, the old profit-oriented habits of the used goods trades died hard. It was not long before a run on used sewing machines became cause for an emergency meeting of consignment shop managers. Agents from Beijing and Hebei communes had been scouring the city's shops for old sewing machines; when they found that prices varied between shops, market manipulations soon ensued. By July 1958 some shops were selling used machines at 22 percent above the state price of new models, while Hebei communes were hoarding machines to drive up the market and then reselling them.[63] An internal investigation of the company's shops found them riddled with similar problems. Luxury goods proved especially prone to manipulation, with leather goods, watches, and fur coats all being turned for a profit either through fees or horizontal trades. While these problems could be contained through strict oversight and ever heavier doses of socialist education, management was stuck in a bind: uniform pricing for used goods is inherently fraught because used goods are, by their very nature, not uniform. Who is to say if this chair, that leather jacket, or those binoculars are 90 percent as good as new or only 50 percent? Regulations often drew a line in the sand, only to erase it a sentence later:

> Scrap and Consignment professionals are forbidden to engage in lateral trading, and used goods cannot be sold to workshops of other retail shops. But, for those goods

that are damaged and need repair to be useable, those can be sold to pertinent work-shops, like damaged leather can be sold to leather shops, or a broken watch to a watch shop, etc.[64]

The bureaucratic state framed commerce (the trade of goods between enterprises) and industry (the manufacturing or transformation of material goods) as distinct processes to be managed by distinct administrative organs and clearly had dif-ficulty accommodating the used goods and recycling sectors, which were a messy amalgam of both functions at once.

Despite the thicket of complications and resistance, the new administrative structure built to enforce uniform pricing unquestionably changed the normative expectations of the used goods trade, which in the Republican era had been one of cheating and price gouging. State media advertised the sector's newfound dedi-cation to serve the people and "correct illegal speculative activity," publicizing anecdotes of customer satisfaction. One Beijing consignment shop received sixty letters of thanks in just one month; in another, a clerk helped a costumer selling a telescope get it repaired first so he could sell it on far better terms.[65] Similar reports of recycling collectors offering immediate payment at fair posted prices conveyed the same message: the used goods and scrap recycling trades had undergone a cultural conversion, from a realm of swindlers to bulwarks of socialist citizenly values.[66]

THE GLF FROM A SCRAP-EYE VIEW

The BSC would oversee scrap management in Beijing from 1957 until 1999, but there would be some bumps on that forty-two-year road. One of the biggest appeared only about one year in, when the municipal-level BSC was eliminated at the height of the GLF.[67] It was not just the municipal BSC that was dissolved, but also its national-level parent, the SMC. In the radiance of the GLF's vision of catapulting China toward communism, co-ops that gave shares based on invested capital and adopted profit-maximizing incentive structures smacked too much of capitalism. With no BSC, Beijing's nine district-level recycling offices were placed under the management of their respective District Planning Committees, and the BSC's processing factories were carved up according to material type: metal processing went to the Beijing Materials Bureau, hides and leather to the city's Animal Products Company, scrap wood to the Lumber Company, and so forth. It was hoped that suspending high-level organs like the SMC and municipal-level BSC would unleash local autonomy and fire up mass-roots economic activity, which it likely did, but what also ensued, as happened across the nation during the GLF, was a dis-coordination of economic management that created crippling inefficiencies. By the summer of 1959 the BSC was being reconstituted. But the lightning restructuring of Beijing's scrap sector did have one very important long-term result, turning about seven thousand co-op members into fully fledged state employees who received government wages and benefits in assigned work units, a momentous change considering that only a decade earlier many had lived a hand-to-mouth existence on the city's streets.

It seems both ironic and predictable that it was precisely in this time of turbulence, with the regular channels of management upended, that scrap had its biggest moment on the modern Chinese historical stage. Scrap rarely gets to star in the drama of history and is usually typecast in supporting roles, supplementing production for this or filling in during a crisis for that. But the GLF was ferrous scrap's big break, and it snagged a lead role in China's Great Backyard Steel Furnace Debacle. The story is well known: chasing the rabbit of doubling national steel output in 1958 to "overtake Britain and catch up to America," communes and work units across China answered Mao's call to "Take Steel as the Key Link" in waves of mass action. Beijing responded with a "support industry" campaign to bring in the scrap from July 26 to 28. After collecting 90 percent of its annual ferrous quota in just three days, Xicheng district was crowned the campaign role model and asked to share its secrets of success at a postcampaign meeting. First, during the three-day lightning assault, all but the most indispensable work ceased so that everyone, including the district party secretary, could focus on scrap collecting. To encourage participation, the scrap drive was linked to other political campaigns and slogans; churches and temples contributed more than three hundred tons of copper statues and iron wares under the motto, "Everyone oppose imperialism and love the nation!," while residents combined scrap collecting with neighborhood sanitation activities, all the while chanting slogans decrying Great Britain's incursions in the Middle East. Industries and businesses evaluated their units for every bit of potential slack: "A shop manager went himself to inspect inventories and discovered 50 large iron pots that were going unused. His comrades were not sure if they might be useful in the future and planned to keep 20 of them, but the leader saw clearly, and knowing leaving just 10 was enough, handed over 40."[68] The scrap went to feed crude smelters that seemed to spring from the soil like mushrooms after a rainstorm; Henan province alone boasted over forty-five thousand of them by September. Throughout September and October the furnaces gorged day and night on the pails, pots, pans, and other housewares of millions of households, who were willing to donate these wares in part because they were promised that meals would be provided by work units and commune canteens. The result was that countless useful housewares were smelted into seven million tons of iron too impure and brittle to use. By December the debacle was all too obvious, and it was time to mop up and rest the troops. The Finance Ministry patched up the smelting drive's enormous financial losses, doling out 300 million yuan, of which 5 million went to Beijing. The capital recalled 10,350 students it had scattered to various rural areas as "techni-cal advisors"—it was time to go back to class.[69]

The scrap-related archival documents I could find from the GLF era in the Bei-jing Municipal Archives point to rather mundane problems that pale in impor-tance next to the tragic events of an era that saw tens of millions perish from a government-created famine. But a few are still worth exploring here to under-stand urban daily life, particularly in the immediate post-GLF years of material scarcity. Copper, again, comes up a lot. Even though ferrous was the hero of the GLF, copper regularly got costar billing in GLF scrap drives. But while ferrous donations were going gangbusters, copper was less forthcoming. And while citi-zens invariably donated ferrous for political glory, it seems that few were willing to part with their copper without monetary compensation. Indeed, the state repeat-edly raised the buying price for copper well into 1959.[70] And while the enormity of the steel drive captivated the state's propaganda apparatus, by contrast, copper was far less quantitatively impressive but pound for pound more critical; the State Council found that a whopping 80 percent of the copper inputs for military and industry needs were sourced from scrap channels.[71] The state piled on incentives. Local units were allowed to keep 20 percent of over-quota copper collection for their own use.[72] To spur households to sell their copper basins, agents were told to pay 20–50 percent over a basin's value by weight, and there was a national-level call to manufacture enamel basins to exchange for copper ones—all this at the same time millions simply gave away their iron woks and pots.[73] And even when copper got into the state's hands, it slipped through its fingers; in November 1958 Jiangxi reported collecting more than 3,000 tons of copper scrap, almost four times its quota, but it only kicked 623 tons of that to the center. Especially under GLF administrative chaos, horizontal trading was hard to tamp down.[74]

In the Republican era, secondhand goods had been an invaluable resource for Beijing's indigent; in the catastrophic wake of the GLF, used goods again proved precious. Consignment Company managers, who had been preoccupied with stamping out profiteering and horizontal trading of luxury items in 1957–58, were swamped by customers looking for much more run-of-the-mill used goods to help weather the crisis just two years later. When in 1961 cotton goods were in extremely short supply and rationing coupons were issued, consumers turned to used goods, for which coupons were not yet necessary: "Since March 1st with the big expansion of requiring distribution coupons for cotton textiles, a portion of consumer demand has turned to old goods, sales have risen and inventories are low. Long lines are now typical at [used good] shops, and there are problems of buying and selling at inflated prices."[75] Many shops were selling used clothes far above the set price and often for more than comparable new items. The problem only worsened that summer as the supply of used goods from other regions flow-ing into the Beijing market fell precipitously, by 87 percent compared to 1960.[76]

One report recommended hiring workers to mend clothes and other goods, noting that those services had been extremely common at used goods markets like Dongsi People's Market just a few years earlier; the sector's consolidation into the state-owned Consignment Company had eliminated these mending and repair services and thereby inadvertently limited the scope of what goods could be reused.[77] Eventually it was decided that the only way to manage the demand for used goods was to ration them also, and in 1962 rationing coupons became required to purchase many forms of used items.[78]

Another item in short supply, predictably, was cooking pots/woks. Back in 1952 the city had had nineteen workshops producing a half million pots yearly, but by 1958 those foundries had all been amalgamated into a wing of one large factory in Zhoukoudian. The factory had a capacity to produce hundreds of thousands of pots, but during the GLF it diverted its energies to other products, casting only nine thousand pots in the second half of 1958. When commune cafeterias across the nation were ordered closed in 1960, millions of families were sent back to their kitchens without a pot to cook in. In Beijing's suburbs, dozens of iron pot workshops were hastily mustered to fill the breach, but the shortage was compounded by quality issues:

> Before 1958 the quality of our city's cooking pots was relatively good, but it declined after 1958, mainly due to the materials. Before '58, Shigang factory used #2 and #3 iron; after the "Great Iron and Steel Smelting campaign" of '58 we shifted to factories like Shahe, Miyun, Yanqing and Xuangang and their "indigenous iron;" those pots' useable life is half of what it used to be. . . . Before '58 Shigang's iron pot . . . wastage rate was 2-5%; . . . now the wastage rate is 10-27%.[79]

Iron and steel factories did their best to avoid using the shoddy GLF "indigenous iron." For years, Beijing's scrap ferrous collection rates exceeded targets by thousands of tons (due in part to the high wastage rates), clogging warehouses because no factory wanted to use it. In late 1963 the People's Bank informed the city government that so much money was tied up in idle and rusting ferrous scrap that it would no longer provide loans for any over-quota collection.[80]

To be fair, overstock would be a recurrent issue across the planned scrap sector, if not the whole planned economy. Gauging aggregate demand trends in the planned economy was a clunky process, because state-set prices "serve[d] more as writs of calculation for planners than as scarcity indicators in the market—that is, they [were] meant to direct physical planning rather than to guide supply to meet demand."[81] Raising the buying price for a certain kind of scrap generally raised collection rates but did not help with getting manufacturing units to purchase and use that scrap; in fact, it just made it more expensive for them to do so. Moreover, the planning mechanisms of assigned production targets and planned allocation generally had the unintended consequence of encouraging wasteful practices across industries and state units, much as Janos Kornai observed and theorized for Soviet planned economies. In *The Cult of Waste*, Zsuzsa Gille describes with analytical lucidity and humor how the planners' determination to make wastes useful induced hypertrophy across the waste/scrap management system. The Hungarian state promoted what Gille dubs a "cult of waste," based on the faith that all wastes can be made useful, that they are "free" resources awaiting the proper unleashing of their useful potential. Her analytical insights fit many aspects of the Mao era:

> [T]he key goal was making sure these wastes were collected and redistributed; reducing them or making sure they were economically reused remained of secondary importance. . . . This discourse on waste, in fact, turned out to be counterproductive. First, because the reuse of waste materials itself required additional raw materials, energy, and labor, which, along with most products, were all in short supply, the already collected wastes were often left to rust and rot and turned into useless materials. . . .Waste delivery quotas, furthermore, encouraged waste-intensive production.[82]

All of these problems were endemic under China's planned economy as well. Throughout the 1960s and 1970s the BSC grappled with the paradoxes and challenges that thwarted its efforts to maximize use values to achieve socialist "thrifty development." The contradictions endemic to the system shaped mass culture, the treatment of waste sector workers, and the bureaucratic culture within the state recycling sector, topics the next chapter explores in greater depth.

5

Effortful Equilibriums
of the State-Managed
Scrap Sector, 1960–1980

A blow-by-blow history of the bureaucratic vicissitudes of the scrap sector over the next two decades would inflict unwanted pain on even the most masochistic reader. Suffice it to say that like every other organ of the PRC state, the BSC was tossed about on shifting policy waves that have been tracked repeatedly by historians: GLF radicalism, early 1960s retrenchment and recovery, CR leftism, and so forth. For all that tumult, there was never a threat that state control would come undone; precisely which bureau or planning office managed Beijing's scrap changed frequently over these decades, often with real economic consequences, but the shifts were always between state organs, not beyond them (see the appendix for a timeline of major bureaucratic shifts). For the average BSC worker, these bureaucratic battles had little effect on their daily work.[1]

Rather than track how each policy struggle rattled the rebar, I approach the scrap sector of the 1960s and 1970s as framed by three fundamental contradictions: between recycling and reuse, between remunerated and voluntary labor, and between regulatory rigidities and expedience. These tensions were embedded in how the planned economy in scrap functioned regardless of which faction was in charge of national policy. The goal of effective scrap management required repeatedly revisiting these unresolvable tensions in the material economy in an attempt to maintain a functional equilibrium between each pair of poles. But before fumbling into these abstractions, a sketch of how everyday scrap management worked is in order.

The largest component of the BSC, its "front line," was collection. This was divided into two distinct channels: residential collection (*shehui shougou*, "collection from society") and industrial collection (*caigou*, "purchasing"). The division between daily-use household scrap and workplace/production scrap was strictly enforced, because one of the easiest ways that scrap might wander off or be embezzled was by employees or managers letting waste materials slip out of the factory to be sold for personal enrichment to neighborhood collectors.

Residential collection accounted for roughly 30 percent of scrap collected in Beijing but was by far the most visible part of the apparatus, with a network that reached into every urban neighborhood and most rural areas as well. There were two modes of residential collection: roving collectors and fixed stands, both of which bought recyclable goods from residents at set prices in cash. Roving collectors, wearing uniforms and/or displaying visible licenses, usually rode three-wheeled bike-carts (with a carrying capacity of a couple of hundred kilos) and were equipped with scales, an account book, price lists, sacks, ropes, and often banners, chalkboards, or other signage. Some collectors traveled overnight routes to remote villages, but most ran routes in urban neighborhoods, returning to the district depot each evening to deposit their haul. There were also fixed collection stations that increased in number over the years, from 59 in 1960 to 444 by 1985. In the early1960s these stations could be quite rudimentary, but by the 1970s they were becoming standardized affairs with strict guidelines. There was a counter where goods were received, weighed, and paid for, and a separate sorting and storage area in back. A collection point always had three workers, not just to divide the work but to police each other and prevent any monkey business: one at the counter, managing the scales and serving customers; one in charge of the money and account books; and a third managing sorting and the storeroom. Community collectors were forbidden to accept any materials that might be industrial, railroad, or military scrap, and at times they were required to collect housing permit information from residents selling metal scrap.

Industrial/production scrap collection was a larger-scale affair, arranged through contracts or phone calls asking for pickups, with materials transferred by truck. Cash exchange was forbidden; scrap loads were weighed on both ends of the transaction, and once the quantity and the quality of materials were verified as conforming to spec, account transfers were made. This node in the scrap network was more contested and more intensely regulated than residential scrap collection. In principle, factories were supposed to avoid producing scrap in the first place, as it was viewed as a sign of inefficient production, and only the SMC and Materials Bureaus (recall that the BSC was under both bureaus, which was true of recycling companies throughout the country) could engage in scrap collection and trade. Unless clearly spelled out by a national-level regulation, the BSC had exclusive rights to collect work unit scrap in Beijing; all other trade in scrap was prohibited unless explicitly arranged and approved by the BSC.

Collected scrap was consolidated at various facilities throughout the city, either at district-level depots that received the whole gamut of scrap types or at more specialized ones that handled specific types of materials (ferrous, wood, bottles). The main challenge for warehouses was that scrap flows could be highly inconsistent; it was either feast or famine. The immediate cause of chronic overstocks and shortages was tensions between the BSC and the production units with which it interacted, but in a more general sense these resource swings were symptoms of structural contradictions intrinsic to the command economy. In *The Economics of Shortage*, Janos Kornai explains how the Soviet planned economy model generates a resource-scarce competitive mentality among production units, creating both scarcity and waste simultaneously. In a climate of taut resource allocation, production units often hoard valued resources to furtively barter with one another to make it through crises, and good-quality scrap was one such highly lucrative, off-the-books resource.[2] In 1963 the BSC started stationing its own employees to work full time in many large factories, supposedly to assist factories in their scrap management, but also as a form of surveillance to discourage such hoarding.[3] The incentive to hoard high-quality scrap and the celebration of putting wastes to use (turn the useless into the useful!) combined to incentivize the substitution of lower-grade materials in production. And this could feed a vicious cycle: using poor-quality scrap materials in production often resulted in making a lot of poor-quality goods that no one could use, and these defective goods might wind up piling up as scrap materials in BSC warehouses, and so forth.

THE NATURE OF THE THINGS: BETWEEN ABSTRACTION AND OBJECT, RECYCLING AND REUSE

At a meeting in Shanghai in June 1965, the nation's leading scrap officials announced that the entire sector would undergo a name change. No longer did they deal in 废品 *feipin*—"waste goods"; from now on they handled 废旧物资 *feijiu wuzi*—"old/disused materials." The word *feipin*, it was felt, "does not sufficiently convey these materials' potential and use value."[4] In this book I have generally (though not rigidly) translated *feipin* as scrap and *feijiu wuzi* as "recycling (n.)," but it is important here to highlight their differences. The word *feipin* is composed of the character 废 *fei*, meaning something like "waste" in English, and 品 *pin*, meaning an item, a good, an object. In contrast, 废旧 *feijiu* adds "old" to "waste," while 物资 *wuzi* is an abstract noun meaning "material(s)" and lacks the discrete object-ness of the character 品. The *wuzi* here is the same word used to designate the Materials Bureau (物资局, Wuzi ju), which handled allocation and distribution of flows of materials used in industry and production (iron, steel, copper, rubber, glass, paper, etc.) and, as part of that mandate, cosupervised the recycling system along with the SMC. So *feiju wuzi* aptly denoted a subset of "materials" under the Materials Bureau's management. After the Shanghai meeting, the BSC (and China's other municipal scrap companies) changed its name from Beijing Scrap Company to the more abstract sounding Beijing Materials Recycling Company (北京市物资回收公司 Beijing shi wuzi huishou gongsi, hereafter BRC).[5] The renaming shifted the imagery of the stuff being named, nudging it away from an image of deteriorating odds and ends for handicraft tinkering and toward the aspirational goal of abstracted industrial material flows.

Not long after the adoption of this new moniker, Beijing SMC cadre Du Jianming made a small splash as a nationally celebrated model bureaucrat. Du refused to lead from behind a desk. When he decided to solve the puzzle of the SMC's intractably low rural recycling rates, he grabbed a bamboo carrying pole and hiked out to the hillsides to collect rural scrap himself. Just as Chairman Mao would have predicted, in going to the people he made a breakthrough. The problem was not that rural residents had nothing to recycle; it was that they did not really grasp how words like *feijiu wuzi* related to their lives. As soon as Du adopted rural phrases and started shouting "Collecting junk (收破烂, *shou polar*)! Collecting junk! Buying old shoes and rotten socks!" folks came to him in droves.[6]

Cartoonish as it is, this parable of translating bureaucratese into plain talk points to the gaps that often existed between state planning aspirations and the material conditions of communities. These gaps could erupt in mundane but unanticipated ways, as in Beijing's fertilizer bag crisis of 1962. In 1961 the Beijing Experimental Chemical Company had shipped 437,823 bags of chemical fertilizer to area communes, collecting a deposit for each plastic bag in which the fertilizer was packed. A year later, as they readied to bag their annual shipment, the company realized that only 14 percent of its bags had been returned; farmers found the bags made great raincoats, table covers, and fodder bags, and so chose to keep them.[7] It was not just farmers who creatively repurposed industrial packaging materials; the city's Lumber Company sent out a call for concerted help from work units to make sure that customers returned their wooden crates and stopped keeping them for their own uses.[8] The problem for the BRC was not getting folks to see stuff as (re)useful; it was getting them to (re)use stuff on the state's terms.

There was no one-concept-fits-all scrap solution in Mao-era China; the spectrum of scrap's utility ranged from recycling's abstract aggregations to reuse's careful preservation of the integrity of specific objects. For recycling managers, this meant negotiating a complex decision tree that branched into several very different networks. How a specific good was to be handled at the very initial step of collection—tossed into a scrap pile or preserved for reuse—could be determined at nodes far up the tree. In wastepaper collection, for instance, old newspaper was separately sorted and preserved in sheet form, much like in the Republican era. Of the two thousand tons collected in Beijing each year, about a third was repurposed as retail shop wrapping paper and the rest shipped to farms in the Northeast or Shandong to wrap young fruits as protection from infestations. But when insecticides were introduced, the BRC faced a one-thousand-ton overstock and the question of whether or not to continue the laborious processes of preserving newspaper in sheet form; in the event, the BRC chose to sell the sheets locally as paper covering for shed walls and ceiling cracks.[9] The old-for-new toothpaste tube exchange that began in 1954 and was still going strong in the mid-1960s posed similar choices, with BRC circulars advising shops not to mix fully intact tubes (which could be cleaned, refilled, and reused) with damaged ones that could only be used for scrap.[10]

Scrap cloth sorting provides an example of the dense field of choices between recycling and reuse that BRC depot workers navigated daily: "Large pieces were supplied to factories for use to clean/wipe machinery, small scrap to cloth shoe making factories, cloth strips to tie into mops, clean factory cuttings to make buffer wheels or stuff toys, synthetic fibers (after being separately sorted and reconditioned) to make non-woven sheeting, scrap from new sweat cloth shredded to make floss, and other cloth scrap for paper."[11]

The system for enabling the reuse of cardboard boxes is an example of a large-scale process poised between industrial and craft logics, a realm rather unique to Mao-era recycling that we might dub "mass reuse." A poster titled "Conserve Cardboard for the Revolution, Recycle and Reuse Old Paper Boxes" illustrates the steps various individuals should take to conserve cardboard (see figure 5). The captions for the illustrations read: "With cooperation from marketers, we can improve packaging design"; "Adjusting patterns for cutting, we can conserve materials"; "Educating clerks at the counter, we conserve packaging"; "With mending and repair, the old can serve as new"; and "Dismantle carefully, handle properly, and return for reuse." In the middle, in modern industrial imagery is the mathematical abstraction of materials saved for each ton of cardboard boxes reused: 1,700 tons of rice stalks, 570 tons of coal, 350 kilowatts of electricity, 100 cubic meters of water. The bottom half of the poster shows the array of boxes—small, large, even cylindrical—that can be saved. Finally, the poster lists ten factories with their addresses, phone numbers, and the array of products they produce (and reuse). The meticulous detail of this poster, in its representation of the materials, the processes of box design and preservation, and the network of units involved, speaks to how much labor, attention, and administrative coordination was involved in the effort to cope with China's limited industrial and resource endowments in paper manufacture.

Mass reuse schemes such as this evoke an economic logic and material culture quite distinct from the habits of disposal we associate with most industrial modes of production. Rather, these are practices associated with the stewardship of objects, practices of mending and reuse that are being extended to industrially produced goods and packaging materials. This is a stewardship of objects not just for private use but for the national community and economy.

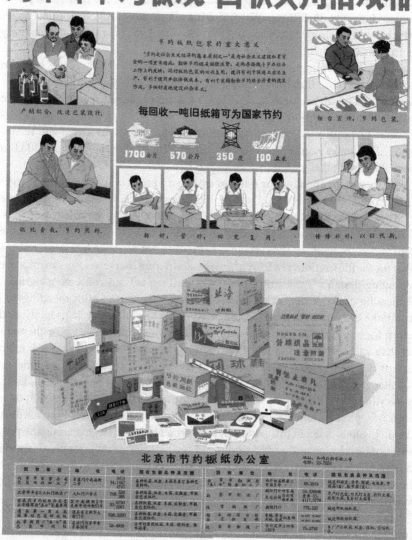

FIGURE 5. Mao-era poster showing how to reuse cardboard boxes by carefully dismantling and returning them to designated enterprises. The poster was specifically for circulation in the Beijing area, as all work units listed for contact were in the Beijing region. From author's collection.

The main foundation of this collective effort was the public's engagement in recycling, and the key to mobilizing that engagement was quite clear: cash. The PRC state, far from stamping out the Republican-era practice of residents bartering and selling scrap, instead internalized, regularized, and promoted it. The state enforced consistent pricing and fair weights and measures, and it worked to strengthen and extend its collection network and public outreach to inform residents about recycling. When certain materials were in short supply, the state raised prices to incentivize households to sort and sell, sometimes doing so even when raising material prices pushed up production costs and squeezed factory profit margins.[12] Indeed, from the government's point of view, money spent to buy recyclables from households (dare we call them "consumers"?) was money well spent, "adding to the masses' incomes."[13] Annual reports regularly broke down figures about such income: "Calculating by population, every person in the country on average recycles one yuan in value. For the three biggest cities, Shanghai is 12 yuan per person, Tianjin is 9 yuan, Beijing 6 yuan. Qinghai, Liaoning, Jilin, Heilongjiang, Inner Mongolia are above one yuan."[14] One might view these differentials as obvious evidence of deep economic inequalities in society; wealthy urban residents obviously were consuming far more stuff than people in less wealthy regions and therefore also received much more money from selling their waste materials. But that was not the frame of analysis used. Instead, such figures were interpreted as indicating a need for specific regional governments to work harder at expanding their collection networks. Cash paid by the state for household scrap was income above reproach.

The wholehearted embrace of recycling was conveyed in pretty much every Mao-era poster and news article about the subject. Recycling was depicted as a community affair and a family affair; in urban domestic settings recycling was almost always depicted as the domain of housewives and children. The homely flotsam that went to recycling was never represented as wasteful remnants from elite consumption, but always as the logical extension of household thrift, the final disposition for goods after a working-class household's exhaustive use. State educational propaganda presented recycling as a boon to a larger socialist economy, a tiny link in an enormous national industrial chain; garbage was simply misplaced resources, and directing scrap to the SMC was to put those materials in their proper and useful place. Posters were a wonderful medium for capturing recycling as a microcosm of socialist economic practice (see figure 6). They effortlessly invoked these linkages by splicing together images, typically pairing an anonymous portrait of a small recycling scene with an image of the great aggregate outcomes that such small acts generated, represented by arrays of shiny new manufactured objects or industrial emojis and boldfaced numbers of resources saved.

Mao-era Beijingers did not imagine they had realized a socialist utopia (even for the Party faithful, that lay in the future), but a visit to the recycling depot imparted

FIGURE 6. Poster depicting a common mode of rural recycling collection in the Mao era. A recycling team visits a village and sets up a stand with educational information on recycling. Large red characters across the center of the poster read: "The uses of scrap cloth, waste hemp, and waste paper are great. The reuse value of recycling is high." The lower half of the poster uses images to quantify specific industrial uses and resources saved. Printed by the Guangdong Native Goods Company, ca. 1970s. From author's collection.

an inkling of what such an ideal economic system might be: an economy in which nothing was wasted and every scrap and gesture of thrift contributed to an ethical national totality, to a technical marvel that converted each voluntary effort into a bit more industry, a bit more production, a bit more surplus, a small reward, a few cents, a sweet. This idealized image of recycling beamed from propaganda posters, but it was also a lived experience. This linking of daily material practice to collective (national) triumph is not so different from how recycling was touted in the United States or Europe during World War II (save scrap for victory!) or as part of environmentalism today (save our planet's forests by recycling paper). But recycling under socialism enacted more than just participation in an efficient collective political economy; it was framed as a momentary inversion of capitalism, turning capitalism and capitalist time on their heads. In capitalism, all consumption is tainted by the sins of exploitative production that produces the goods being consumed. Surplus labor is extracted as capitalist profit; unequal wealth leads to unjust labor relations and inequuities in consumption, the deprivation of the poor on the one hand and decadent, wasteful excessive consumption on the other. In socialism, however, consumption is not tainted in this way, for supposedly there is no longer unjust labor exploitation or gross inequality among citizens. And what better proof, what more convincing fetish of this fundamental systemic difference, than recycling. At the recycling depot consumption actually becomes productive; the material "produced" by the act of consumption is returned to the circle of production. Recycling—*consumption (re)figured as productive contribution*—generates surplus use ("turning the useless into the useful.") Hence, the state, the keeper of the national economy, can provide a small reward, a token of the surplus, a bit of change to buy an extramural sweet, born not from exploitation but from virtuous *surplus use*.

BETWEEN VOLUNTARY AND PAID LABOR

In October 1964, the *Shanghai Liberation Daily* ran an article titled, "Now That the National People's Economic Situation Has Recovered, Do We Still Want to Reuse Old Bottles?" Apparently, this was the Mao-era equivalent of clickbait. The paper received more than three hundred letters in response, and soon other news outlets got into the debate with chatty articles featuring reader feedback. In the original article, the reporter, hearing that used bottles were piling up in warehouses, visited several Shanghai factories that produced bottled products and heard complaints about the hassles of bottle reuse: "They are dirty and *mafan* (麻烦) [a hassle, bothersome] to process, and are easily damaged." One Shanghai recycling worker wrote a response claiming that in his warehouse alone sat fourteen million used bottles going to waste.

Of course, the correct answer to the bottle backlog was never in doubt— get over the *mafan* and reuse the bottles! The ideological stance of putting the national economy before personal comfort was axiomatic, but for readers who needed persuading, one factory manager laid out the math. His factory used standard two-liter bottles supplied by the recycling company, a kind of bottle that was used "everywhere" and therefore often was returned dirty, oily, and otherwise tough to clean. From the enterprise's perspective, even though old bottles took more time and workers groused, the factory saved over 2,000 yuan a month over using new ones; from the national perspective, old bottles were far more valuable than the equivalent in broken glass, and the state would lose 5,000 yuan a month if the bottles were crushed and recycled rather than reused. The proper response to workers' complaining that reusing old bottles was *mafan* was to use this opportunity to further their socialist education.

What *mafan* really meant in this context was: this requires extra labor. Willingness to contribute that labor won praise, but no compensation. By framing extra labor as *mafan*, what was actually a complaint about labor exploitation was turned into a matter of insufficient socialist consciousness. A crew of soldier-worker volunteers summed up the logic with a chant they coined during their "lightning campaign" cleaning out a metals plant warehouse: "To clean up the scrap, first clean up the person; to clean up the person, first clean up the thought (清物先清人, 清人先清思想; *qing wu xian qing ren, qing ren xian qing sixiang*)!"[15] True enough, any waste is potentially useful, with enough labor; the fetishization of use value depended on that labor being disavowed.

The sleight of hand that turned labor extraction into a test of political commitment was common across many Mao-era contexts, but it had outsized importance in shaping the scrap sector for at least two reasons. First, the processes of recycling and reuse were in large part the accumulation of countless scattered acts of extra labor, almost all of which were framed in this way. Second, recycling was often the focus of mass mobilizations of voluntary labor, raising the question of whether recycling labor was a public performance of citizenship or paid work. While I have never found a Mao-era document that directly challenged whether recycling was important to the national economy—precisely the opposite, the propaganda "protests too much" that it was enormously important and noble—this economic context could not help but reinforce a sense that recycling work was low value, perhaps not even fully "work."

I would not blame the reader for finding this assertion confusing; having just read about the cheery hoopla associated with paying households for their small acts of recycling, the claim that scrap work was explicitly not compensated in the workplace might seem contradictory. But workplace and "society" recycling were framed as distinct processes, handled by separate collection channels, and the state took great pains to differentiate them. For an enlightening example, a 1979 newspaper article looking back on the Mao era recounts the experience of workers at the Shanghai Electrical Appliance Factory, who, noticing that their shop received a lot of boxes each month, decided that rather than throw them in the trash, they would collect them to sell to a nearby recycling shop. They used the money to buy things for the work unit like a newspaper subscription, a broom, and a washboard. "Who knew that this act was in line with principle but not with the 'law' (合理而不合'法' *he li er bu he 'fa'*)." The Shanghai Municipal Finance Bureau got wind that these kinds of activities were occurring across the city and issued an order forbidding city recycling shops to buy boxes from any factories, enterprises, or other work units and demanding that the money from any such transactions "always be handed over to the public (一律上缴归公 *yilü shangjiao guigong*)." The Appliance Factory workers went back to throwing out their boxes; it was not worth the effort.[16] Out in "society" recycling was rewarded with a monetary token of appreciation; in the workplace, all recycling belonged to the state, only state entities were rewarded, and it was up to the work unit to determine if scrap work was valued.

Often it was not, or at least not much. In many work units scrap sorting was slated for after work hours with no compensation. Instead of picking and sorting scrap regularly, many factories just swept up their daily dust, shavings, and waste and dumped it in heaps to be picked over later, perhaps during a seasonal cleanup campaign. National-level regulations on scrap repeatedly provided detailed rules regarding who could pick from factory waste piles:

> If the metals industries cannot muster the strength to pick them, people's communes or resident committees near the trash heaps, with the factory or mine's permission, can organize a group of residents to pick, and based on a letter of introduction from the resident committee or commune can sell the picked materials to a recycling station, but not to roaming collectors.[17]

Residents were compensated; workers were not. When workers did embrace scrap work, it was seen as worthy of beatific news coverage. Workers at Capital Steel were praised for regularly "sacrificing their holiday rest to run about to every corner of the factory collecting scrap ferrous."[18] There were also individual labor heroes like Li Zichun of the Shenyang Smelting Factory, who at the age of fifty-two and suffering from a lung ailment, begged to be shifted from his post to the factory sweeping crew (dust be damned!). Once there, he organized the sweepers into an "after-hours materials recycling and saving small group" that managed to deliver a few tons of useable copper scrap back to the smelter every year. From there Li led his crew to sift through the factory's decade-old, three-hundred-ton waste heap, again during off hours and without compensation (also in winter, in the murky cold hours of dawn and dusk, and in Li's case, without gloves because he felt they made his hands less agile.)[19]

Unlike workers in other production units, BRC employees worked at recycling full time, but they too found certain aspects of recycling work especially irksome. Wang Shude became one of Mentougou's most reliable workers, honored almost yearly as a model employee and eventually invited to join the Party and elevated to district management, but even he dreaded certain jobs. Recalling his days in the early 1960s doing neighborhood collection by bike-cart (a step up from the hand-cart he had used in the 1950s), he remembered winter days as particularly hard to bear, and he had been very grateful to find residents who would let him stop at their homes and help him warm up his lunch.[20] BRC internal reports regularly mention having to correct the thinking of employees who valued big-item scrap over small stuff, a behavior also reflected in public complaints that recycling company employees avoided collection runs for small amounts of material or refused to purchase low-value items.[21] Despite the many ways that it attempted to account for values differently, the state-managed economy did not change the logic that wastes, relative to other goods, were lower in value, and thus scrap work was perceived as relatively less worthy of time and effort.

The administrative solution to this was to mobilize work that was relatively cheap, if not essentially free, supplementing routine workplace scrap management with "cleanup assaults." Such campaigns often coincided with national holidays, when folks were conveniently off from work. Collection rates for the 1971 New Year's ferrous scrap assault in Beijing's Fangshan county were reportedly up 29 percent over the previous year, with everyone from old men to housewives to the entire student body of Zhangxingdian elementary school (working only in free hours before and after school) chipping in, coining the chant, "If you've never done some picking then you'd never surmise, but as soon as you start picking you'll jump in surprise! Recycling has not reached its limit. There's still so much potential in it!"[22]

From the BRC's perspective, residential recycling was particularly labor intensive and was rarely the most profitable investment of time and muscle. Postconsumer recyclables were scattered in small quantities across large areas, making collection both time and labor intensive. Especially in an economy of highly circumscribed consumerism like Mao-era China, residential collection could never generate large returns per unit of labor. At the same time, the only way the BRC could keep pace with urban development and the city's steadily growing postconsumer waste stream was by expanding its network of recycling points. The BRC was far from wealthy, and building a new collection point—hiring at least three full-time employees for each point, each with the full package of work unit benefits, fully outfitting them with equipment, and so forth—was a major expense. A 1973 report on the national recycling system laid out the problem: "Following the principle that we will not increase the number of our employees, we need to rationally increase our recycling collection network nodes and through internal reorganization put forces on the frontline of collection to make selling more convenient for the masses."[23] Much cheaper than hiring new workers was having neighborhood committees help find unemployed residents who could serve as collectors in their neighborhoods, to be trained, supervised, and licensed by the state recycling offices as purchasing agents (*daigou yuan*). The BRC made concerted pushes to recruit agents over the years, especially in the early 1960s and again in 1974–75, along these lines:

> Purchasing agent sites (*daigou dian*) are under the joint leadership of the neighborhood committee and the recycling office. The neighborhood revolutionary committee is responsible for agents' allocation of equipment, ideological education, financing expenses, and managing distribution of pay and welfare services. The state recycling office [BRC] is responsible for coordinating with upper levels, implementing and inspecting economic policies, planning and mapping collection points, price management, professional training and helping handle problems that arise in the process of doing business.[24]

Like SMC recyclers in the 1950s, agents bought scrap from residents at state-set prices and turned it over to the state-owned depot, earning fees based on quantities and materials collected. Now, however, neighborhood committees served as the key financing intermediary, fronting seed money for equipment, providing space for collection points, and distributing the fees earned to the workers each month, while pocketing some for themselves. It seems to have been a win-win-win arrangement, with the BRC adding around 220 such collection points between 1974 and 1977.[25] Throughout the rest of the decade, contracted agents collected about sixty to seventy thousand tons of scrap a year in Beijing, and the arrangement "gave 1000 idle people in neighborhoods some proper work. In 1980 the collection sites earned 958,000 yuan in fees, and, aside from what went into workers' pay, about 500,000 accrued to the city's neighborhood committees."[26] The savings from contracting out rather than using state employees made residential recycling affordable for the city.

In sum, to make mobilizing the labor to "transform the useless into the useful" affordable, a variety of schemes were deployed, from ideological pressure, to volunteer brigades, to contracting out. Another means of saving labor costs was simply to pay recycling company workers poorly and stint on their work conditions and benefits, but that was not something that Mao-era newspapers crowed about. State media regularly scolded "some people" for continuing to hold to the "mistaken thinking" from the "old society" that recyclers were "inferior to others," basically depicting the poor treatment of recycling workers as a kind of historical hangover. It was not until a report was issued in 1977 that state authorities began to acknowledge more openly that not all was right in the scrap shop:

> In 1976, the recycling bureaus of four [Beijing] districts (Dongcheng, Xicheng, Chongwen and Xuanwu) planned to hire 154 persons, but because most people were unwilling to enter this line of work, they only hired 25, 16% of their target. . . . A thirty-one-year-old worker in the Haidian district recycling management office has been introduced

many times to girlfriends, but none have worked out because he works in recycling. Recently he found another girlfriend, but she demanded, "I'll marry you only after you get transferred out of the Recycling Bureau, otherwise let's call it quits." This youth repeatedly comes in tears to his supervisors, asking to change jobs.

The Recycling Bureau collects loads of old clothing, rotting socks, waste paper, pus and blood-soaked bandages, matted cotton and animal bones, which are not only full of dust and stench, but often carry all sorts of bacteria and viruses. Many workers responsible for sorting and processing have hepatitis, skin diseases, TB, tracheitis, septicemia, and urinary tract infections.... Of the 45 female workers processing rags and waste paper at the Jianguomen depot in Dongcheng, 43 suffer from contagious urinary and other infections. Especially at some mining, metals and laboratory units, the bottles, barrels, pallets, pipes, bags and other packaging have contained or touched sulfuric acid, potassium cyanide, sodium nitrate, mercury and other poisonous materials. When [recycling] workers come in contact with these things, from a light exposure they might become nauseous and vomit, break out in rashes, turn red in the face; heavy exposures are life threatening. Recently three workers at a depot in Fengtai processing some canisters from a navy yard went dizzy and collapsed, only escaping danger after hospitalization.

Pay is low, benefits and protection little. In this profession, first level workers make 31 yuan, second level workers 36 yuan, it is even less than street cleaners. First level street cleaners make 33.66 yuan, second level 39.05 yuan, and they get a monthly sanitation bonus of 7.65 yuan, and 20 fen daily for food money. Recycling workers receive none of these bonuses. [27]

The contrast with sanitation workers is particularly interesting. Sanitation workers were seen as sacrificing their own bodies, working in close proximity to unhealthful and foul pollutants to safeguard public health, hence the "sanitation bonus." Recyclers, while getting sympathy for doing dirty and grueling work, had not been portrayed as protecting public health. By raising the matter of health risks and associating their work with pollution, it became possible to make their work a public health matter and so compensate them as well. The BRC adopted a bonus system around the time of this 1977 article, with awards of 3, 5, and up to 7 yuan under the banner: "Use spiritual encouragement as the pillar, and material encouragement as the supplement." [28] But why had these issues of disease, toxic chemicals, and pollution not been raised earlier? And why were they finally surfacing in 1977?

Again, a comparison to trash and night soil is helpful. The Sanitation Bureau's primary mission was seen as removing contaminating wastes from the populous urban center; trash dumps and night soil facilities were exiled to rural areas. There was no comparable process of quarantining the scrap sector. Facilities for collecting, sorting, and processing recycling were scattered throughout the city with little concern about their proximity to residential or commercial neighborhoods. This was because for most of the Mao era, industrial processing was not perceived as raising public health problems. Even as the United States and European countries were coming to realize how damaging industrial emissions and wastes could be in the 1950s and 1960s, many socialist bloc governments downplayed industrial pollution as a problem of capitalist industry that socialism would largely avoid. Pollution, after all, can be seen as a kind of unmanaged waste, and while capitalist industries valued only profit and therefore were not averse to producing and dumping waste in pursuing that goal, socialist industry focused on maximizing resources and turning "wastes to treasures." For most of the Mao era, an industrial pollution problem was just a poorly managed industrial waste problem, and industrial wastes were being addressed by calls to minimize or find uses for the "three wastes" (三废 san fei: gas waste, liquid waste, and solid waste).[29]

But in the early 1970s a shift to increased concern over industrial pollution became discernible following a spate of ecological disasters, especially the poisoning of Beijing's Guanting Reservoir, which led to Beijing residents consuming tainted fish; a subsequent investigation traced the problem directly to factory runoff.[30] A few months later, when the first United Nations Conference on the Human Environment was convened in 1972, Zhou Enlai sent a Chinese delegation to attend, and a year later Zhou convened the first National Conference on Environmental Protection. By 1974 words like environmental protection (环境保护 huanjing baohu) and pollution (污染 wuran) begin appearing in BRC-related documents, though it is worth noting that these concepts were often conflated with and hard to distinguish from concerns about urban appearance (市容 shirong). One of the first environmental protection–related policies for the BRC involved preventing recycling from cluttering the street, a directive summed up in the slogan "collect scrap, don't see scrap," which required all new collection points to have storage facilities separate from the publicly visible collection counter.[31]

By the end of the decade, the language of pollution and environmental protection was becoming increasingly common for justifying policy decisions related to recycling, from the need to provide more protections for workers' health to the desire to make the city look more modern and appealing to visitors. By these new lights, the city's recycling system began to appear "backward" and unorganized:

> The city's 53 recycling factories are scattered in every corner of the city districts, mostly in residential neighborhoods and even in the embassy area and scenic sites.[32]
>
> For a long time because recycling work was not sufficiently respected, its features have been backward, conditions poor, funding difficult, the system constantly changing, creating contradictions among factories and residents. This has been manifested in the fact that collection and processing points are scattered in every corner of the city, transportation vehicles are primitive, mechanization is minimal, creating problems in the capital like pollution, noise in residential neighborhoods, and has had a major influence on urban sanitation and social appearance. At every recycling depot, nearby residents complain about these matters, repeatedly writing letters of complaint to the central and municipal government.[33]

In 1980 the central government pressed Beijing municipal offices with a slate of proposals for "making the capital into a beautiful, clean and complete top tier modern city," including relocating all scrap warehouses and processing factories outside the third ring road.[34] The BRC responded enthusiastically. The company envisioned four scrap complexes, one in each compass direction, composed of ten warehouses/factories, each with a specific purpose (a dismantling yard, a baling yard, a technical research facility, etc.) and appointed with modernized equipment: hydraulic balers, five-ton grapplers, and power shredders and shears. Each zone would be serviced by sealed and beautified trucks so "the whole handling center realizes the goal that you see no waste going in and no waste leaks out (进门不见废, 外观不露废; jinmen bujian fei, waiguan bu lu fei)." The first step would be to build one such zone as an experimental site. But for any of this, the BRC would need central and city government support. The city would need to provide the BRC with a chunk of land around two hundred mu (thirty-seven acres) in size. The facility should be located "outside the third ring road, but not too far away, because scrap trading profit margins are too low, and adding too much expense [through long shipping distances] will cut profits or result in a loss." The company estimated total costs at about 8 million yuan; here the central government would have to help. The BRC suggested that instead of providing a loan, the central government could simply forgo collecting tax on the company so it could invest its funds in the project. If the zone processed 100,000–200,000 tons of scrap each year, at a profit of about 2.5 million yuan each year, it would pay for itself in three years.[35]

Though I have found no evidence that this specific plan was funded, throughout the 1980s the relocation of facilities outside the city center was a persistent trend. Once a laudably modern and urban activity, recycling processing was now presented as polluting, unpleasant, and incompatible with the image of salubrious modern urbanism. I should note that recycling was not unique in this regard; industries generally were being moved out of the city following the same logic. The new concern about industrial pollution cut both ways for the scrap sector. It meant that after decades of neglect—low wages, unhealthy work conditions, little or no state investment in modernizing—BRC workers were getting a bit more protection and compensation, and the company might even get facilities upgrades. Yet just at the moment the state claimed to be giving the sector the respect it deserved, it also decided that recycling, like trash, needed to be ejected to the city's lower-value periphery.

MANAGING SCRAP'S INHERENT ILLEGIBILITY: BETWEEN ROUTINE AND EXPEDIENCE

In routine contexts, waste materials are far from the most valued items in circulation. But economies rarely just stick to their routines. Factories hit resource bottlenecks, industries experience technical failures, and predicted markets fail to materialize. Emergencies tend to arise, and when they do, a particular form of scrap can suddenly become precious: a lifesaving patch for a supply gap, the key to making quota and pleasing the boss. In an economy in which resources were limited and allocation was both taut and sluggish, a quick, outside-the-plan scrap fix could be a godsend and worth quite a bit in either cash or barter. But if the state allows enterprises to trade scrap among themselves outside the plan, that will surely destabilize prices and quotas. Even worse, a hole in the fabric of the scrap trade will, like a run in a stocking, quickly widen into a gaping tear in the plan, with all sorts of goods moving in defiance of state plans and prices because pretty much anything can become (or be traded under the sign of) "scrap" or "waste goods." There was nothing new or unique to socialism in this. Scrap markets and junk shops in the Republican era were commonly used to pass stolen goods, and the masquerading of wastes as valuable goods and vice versa is a core problem plaguing the trade in "e-waste" today; the scrap and waste trades have a reputation for being prone to corruption for precisely this reason (though ethnic and racial discrimination often play a major part as well).[36] What this meant in the Mao era (and often means in other contexts) was that the regulatory stakes of recycling were far higher than the actual value of the materials being regulated.

The government's solution was to place exclusive rights to scrap trading with a single body: the state recycling offices, which in the case of Beijing was the BRC. This seems simple enough, except that the incessant reshuffling of the bureaucracy and the frequency with which scrap evaded restrictions compelled the state to repeatedly revisit the regulations, often spelling matters out in great detail. A 1963 State Council circular provides a prototypical iteration, first explaining why yet another clarification of the rules was needed: "In the last few years, several factories and mining enterprises have had repeated incidents of materials theft. The thieving elements have exploited loopholes in waste materials management, weak regulations, collaborating from within and without to carry out illegal activities, with significant loss to our national property."[37] The rules that followed were more than four pages long, but the core points were as follows:

> The SMC is uniformly responsible for the collection of all scrap copper, aluminum and lead from every central, provincial, autonomous region, or municipal enterprise, work unit, construction enterprise, school, collective etc....
>
> Aside from the [Materials Bureau's] Metals Recycling Management Office and the SMC, all other organs are forbidden to trade or allocate non-ferrous scrap.... Scrap metals are not permitted to enter trading markets.... Any cooperation (xiezuo) between enterprises, departments, or areas (diqu) outside of the plan is forbidden.[38]

All this made sense in light of how scrap trading, if not managed closely, could destabilize prices and become a cover for other forms of illicit trade.

But when we recall that in most routine circumstances scrap is low in value, then the principle of essentially demanding that an extra link be inserted into every scrap supply chain—that tons of low-value freight be loaded, shipped, and unloaded one extra time before arriving at its destination—starts to look much less sensible. This paradox—the necessity to ban horizontal trading, coupled with the obvious inefficiency of such complicated arrangements for such cheap materials—was completely understood by recycling bureaucrats, and they experimented with various remedies and work-arounds. One solution was to regularly convene "trade balancing meetings" (*pingheng jiaoliu hui*), which essentially fulfilled the market function of bringing together representatives from factories and work units (on local, provincial, and even national levels) so they could work out who might need what from whom. From such meetings, the recycling companies could adjust their decisions about how to allocate resources and could also give their stamp of approval for work units to hook up directly with each other. Such arrangements could develop into sanctioned exceptions to the principle forbidding direct trade. They could result in direct trade agreements with written contracts between units, approved by the recycling company and confirmed with higher levels of government so that allocation accounting could be properly adjusted. Helpful as such contracts could be, they were rigid one-offs; they removed an unnecessary recycling office link from a specific supply chain but in no way opened up sourcing flexibility. Any unauthorized horizontal trading remained off limits as "black market" trading. In addition, elaborate regulations attempted to list all the goods and materials that recycling companies were forbidden to trade:

> Expensive consumer goods like cameras, binoculars, bikes, sewing machines, watches, radios, furs, embroidery; factory products, semi-finished products, defective products, primary and secondary materials the producing factory could use itself, supplementary materials, equipment; any materials from overseas Chinese or embassies; dangerous, toxic, or medicinal products; communications, irrigation or other technical equipment that might have un-noticed chemical properties; any materials sold by private citizens with no clear source; any undestroyed papers that might relate to national security secrets; coupons; any factory or mining enterprise or national work unit bulk discarded tools/equipment such as metals or electrical materials.[39]

Some of these restrictions were intended to protect public health and others to protect state security; some, like the ban on trading "defective products," were directed at stopping production work units from evading responsibility for shoddy work.

Even when recycling units worked strictly within these delineated trading routes, there was still plenty of room for conflicting interests with other work units. A question that repeatedly arose was what recycling companies like the BRC were permitted to do with the materials they managed. In theory, the answer was simple: collect, sort, and help reallocate them effectively; in short, execute the commerce function of the planned economy. But trading scrap almost always demands some degree of processing—sorting, cleaning, packing, cutting. Of the BRC's employees, 15–25 percent were listed as working in processing (*jiagong*).[40] Where did scrap processing to facilitate the supply chain end and manufacturing begin? Recycling companies already had an exclusive monopoly to access waste materials for trade; if they could also process those materials, they could easily manipulate scrap management for their own self-enrichment.

The BRC was not immune to such temptations. In 1962 the Handicraft Bureau, on behalf of its Clothing Shoe and Hat Company, lodged a complaint with the city Planning Commission demanding the BRC stop processing used tires. The Shoe and Hat Company had been losing money on its popular tire-scrap-soled shoes for over a year. It made 240,000 pairs each quarter but was losing about 1 yuan per pair, and the company blamed the BRC. Over a four-year period the BRC had raised the price of a pair of tire-scrap soles from 1.8 to 3.02 yuan. So the Handicraft Bureau did some homework. It consulted with the shop that cut the tire scrap into shoe soles and learned that the BRC bought tires at .437 yuan per kilo, and after rudimentary processing (separating the sidewall, tread, lining, etc.) sold the scrap for 2.3 per kilo to the sole-making factory, a markup of over five times the tire buying price. The sole manufacturers claimed that if the BRC would just deliver the whole used tires to them, they could supply soles for 1.6 yuan a pair, about half their current price. The Handicraft Bureau therefore requested that the BRC be ordered to get out of the tire-processing business.[41]

This kind of pushback from production units did not occur just on the level of single factories but could happen on a citywide or systemwide scale. The year 1962 was a bad one for the recycling bureaucracy in this regard:

> At this time, under the influence of the thinking that "the Bureau of Commerce should not run industries," and without seriously considering the real needs of the recycling sector, many regions passed recycling processing enterprises over to the industrial branch, dealing a big blow to developing recycling processing. In Shanghai for example, the city decided to transfer 40 of the recycling sector's 108 processing shops to the Handicraft Bureau.[42]

As Dorothy Solinger argues in *Chinese Business under Socialism*, battles like this one between handicraft and recycling interests were symptomatic of a basic structural tension between industry and commerce units, which she describes as "already hostile enough in the 1950s to be described as 'mutual tearing to shreds.'"[43] The conflict was rooted in the structure of the plan. Industrial units were evaluated by how much they produced, incentivizing them to produce large amounts of low-quality goods. Commercial units had to sell whatever industry manufactured; therefore they stressed quality and resented getting stuck with overproduction of shoddy goods. Additionally, commerce units supplied industries with the materials they needed for production and could therefore price what they supplied to potentially usurp profits from industry (as in the tire-scrap sole example). Politically speaking, commerce was often the more vulnerable of the two, for commerce units were directly engaged in sales markets, so when anti-market ideologies gained ascendance, commerce units tended to suffer. During the CR, for example, Liu Shaoqi, the number one "capitalist-roader" scapegoat, was accused of using "the commercial department to rule the production department."[44]

Such bureaucratic infighting can seem arcane and irrelevant today, but oddly this issue reverberated across the state recycling sector long after the planned economy had become a relic of the Maoist past. Indeed, as the plan was dismantled in the reform era and the strictly defined roles, rights, and responsibilities of ministries and work units were unleashed and eroded, the grudge match over controlling interests in scrap materials only intensified. This is foreshadowed in a minor non-incident in which, in 1977, Beijing's Metals Bureau apparently made a play to take over collection of nonferrous scrap from the BRC. The archive seems to have lost the Metals Bureau's proposal, but the BRC's letter in response, "Regarding our disagreement with the Beijing Municipal Metals Bureau taking over unified control of the city's scrap non-ferrous," provides a spirited defense of the BRC. The BRC authors begin by reviewing their great success in raising recycling rates: "In 1957 our city recycled 28,032 tons of materials worth 19,280,000 yuan; in 1977 [it is] 383,351 tons worth 57,410,000 yuan." They then remind everyone just how often the higher ups have entrusted the BRC with exclusive rights over scrap collection:

> 1963 national regulation #642 states "aside from the Metals Recycling Management Office and the SMC, all other organs are forbidden to trade or allocate non-ferrous scrap[";] 1970 Municipal Revolutionary Committee circular #69 placed all non-ferrous scrap trade form the 18 central government work units engaged in metals in the city with our company. 1975 City Planning Commission announcement #606 clarified: the entire city's non-ferrous scrap recycling and all passing of it to upper levels is the responsibility of the BRC. . . . The Metals Bureau is proposing building its own non-ferrous network, which will certainly be redundant with our network of 8000 workers across the city. There are about 4000 units, factories and enterprises spread across the whole city, and the Metals Bureau's suggestion that they simply wait for these to deliver their scrap to them will be very inconvenient to these units.[45]

I cannot say with certainty how the Metals Bureau pitched its takeover to the city, but it is not difficult to guess that it argued that (1) the BRC was simply an extra and inefficient link in the supply chain and (2) Metals Bureau specialists would be better at evaluating, sorting, and preparing metal scrap than the generalists at the BRC. As valid as such claims surely would have been, we know that the BRC's case won the day: for two decades it had delivered scrap to the state and met the center's quotas; despite myriad challenges it had helped keep the state's planning and pricing systems from unraveling into chaos; it had kept the recycling company running, even expanding, with little or no external funding; and as the BRC's rebuttal argued, the BRC actually had a collection system, while the Metals Bureau did not. As we have seen, such systems are expensive, hard to build, and always underestimated by novices that have not yet built them. But the BRC's rebuttal also makes it clear that it was only indispensable so long as the state made it so by renewing its exclusive monopoly over scrap trading. Were the state ever to rescind that monopoly and allow scrap-producing and -consuming units to trade among themselves—or even more radically, allow nonstate players to get into scrap trading—then the BRC might quickly start to seem superfluous.

CONCLUSION

In the summer of 1977, China's recycling world reverberated from what was arguably the most momentous event in its two decades under the planned economy. It was an event that had occurred in Xinhui county, Guangdong, nineteen years earlier. Late on the night of July 7, 1958, while attending an exhibition on recycling, Premier Zhou Enlai, had brush-written the following lines:

> In the glorious light of the Party's general line on Socialist construction, all our nation's commercial bureaus should learn from Xinhui and grasp the key link of utilizing waste and practicing recycling; transform the useless into the useful; expand our processing capacity and change single-use to multiple-uses; through diligence and conservation, turn the broken and old into the brand new. We must unite workers, peasants, merchants (商 *shang*), students, and soldiers into one body and closely cooperate to completely develop this service to production. Through this task we diligently and thriftily build the nation and reform society.[46]

Withheld from public circulation for nineteen years, the note was publicly approved for national release by the State Council in the summer of 1977. Newspapers trumpeted Zhou's words for months, and conferences were held in 1978 celebrating the quote's twentieth anniversary. In 2002, more than forty years after those lines were written, facsimiles of Zhou's brush-written lines graced the front gates of several of Beijing's state-run recycling markets and offices.

I was always puzzled by the cult-like status of this quote full of hackneyed Mao-era clichés, but I believe its potency rested less in its content than in its timing. Zhou had been a powerful political figure in his lifetime, but he was arguably even more so after his apotheosis. For the National Council to emphasize Zhou's personal regard for recycling had great symbolic cachet in 1977. It is also possible that one word in Zhou's quote, "merchants," had outsized importance as well. Most recycling company workers had been labeled peddlers/small merchants, making them ideologically suspect under leftist rule, so even though recycling was celebrated as epitomizing Mao's thrifty industrialization, recycling company workers themselves had been treated as tainted with petty capitalist tendencies. With Mao gone and the Gang of Four deposed, recyclers wrapped themselves in Zhou's brush-written praise and laid claim to a political legitimacy and importance they had been denied during long years of heightened class struggle. Over the next few years, national-level offices issued a series of circulars and reports aimed at improving work conditions for recycling workers—providing health check-ups and safety protections, encouraging city- and provincial-level governments to invest in better facilities and equipment for recycling workers, and implementing a system of worker bonuses—and every report, regulation, and announcement made mention of Zhou's quote.[47]

Wang Shude, who worked his whole adult life in the BRC, remembered the late 1970s well. He said nothing about the political climate or Zhou's quote, but he very clearly recalled that first round of bonuses, from 1 to as much as 7 yuan per month. They would look piddling compared to the 100 yuan bonuses of the 1980s, but in the 1970s a few extra yuan were a welcome boon. When I met Wang in 2018, he was eighty-five years old, living with his wife, who was also retired from the BRC, in a two-room, state-provided flat. Incredibly patient with my questions, Wang was too modest to mention all the awards he had won as a model worker, which I only learned about from his wife as we were leaving. Wang had worked hard for the company, but there was no denying that the company had given him a great deal as well. Under the BRC (and its precursors) he went from a young migrant scavenging for survival to a wood-goods co-op worker, a neighborhood collector, an industrial purchasing agent, and finally a Party member and district manager. He met his wife when she joined the BRC in the 1970s; they had raised two caring and successful children and now were comfortably retired on their pensions.

Not every BRC employee experienced such a smooth transition from hardship to national inclusion, economic stability, and comfortable family life, but Wang was not unique, either. Fu Hongjun, vice secretary of the Chinese Resource Recycling Association (CRRA) in the early 2000s, had been sent to the BRC in the early 1960s as punishment for refusing a job assignment and other nonconformist behavior. Previously a schoolteacher, Fu was first assigned to collecting in the very neighborhood he once had taught in, daily facing the mockery of his former students as he pedaled around on his three-wheeled cart. Yet he spoke of his career in the BRC with affection and described his time as a collector as invaluable in giving him a foundational understanding of the trade. Of the dozen or so former and current BRC employees I met over the years, all spoke proudly of the Mao-era BRC. It was dirty, tiring, and not highly respected work, yet they shared a great sense of accomplishment. They saw themselves as playing a pivotal role in helping China successfully industrialize despite its international isolation. They worked diligently and honestly; underpaying or cheating residents was unheard of, and BRC workers helped crack many cases of stolen materials and goods. Above all, they forged a system that meticulously put material wastes to use. Fu Hongjun ably summed up what many others had expressed:

> I'm not saying the planned economy is better or the market economy is better, but back then we had a complete system. At the time, as part of the plan, we knew how much scrap each factory generated, how many recyclables every household produced, also how much trash. Today [2010] ten-something or twenty-something percent of Beijing's trash is recyclable materials, paper, plastic, cans. Back in the 50s and 60s you wouldn't even find one sheet of paper [in the trash]. . . . These days we talk about environment and resource conservation, but not back then, we didn't have that kind of consciousness. Then it was just diligent national development (*qinjian zhiguo*) and thrift (*jieyue*), but it was exceptionally thorough (*wanzheng*).[48]

Hopefully the last two chapters have produced a set of critiques that enable the reader to at once acknowledge the truth of this description and appreciate the sense of pride and accomplishment shown there while also recognizing that there were many other elements and tensions shaping that story.

As Fu Hongjun's description makes clear, the state system was premised on the necessity of tight control. Everything needed to be accounted for; uncoordinated trading between state units was problematic and market trading was anathema. Deng's market-oriented reforms in the 1980s, therefore, posed a huge challenge to state companies that had to reinvent from scratch networks for market research and communication.

But the nostalgic historical narrative of a well-managed Mao-era recycling system is, as we have seen, also a bit sugary and obfuscating. It presents the recycling company as diligent and honest but utterly naïve about how markets work, hence its rapid demise in the brutal chaos of reform-era market competition. But of course the BRC was part of a larger state system that was not merely naïve about markets; it banned markets, criminalized many forms of scrap trading activity, and treated with suspicion any transactions outside its control. Restrictions on who could collect and trade scrap were only one element of this. Across the last few chapters several other forms of regulatory control have been described that might seem peripheral but in fact were crucial to setting the context for successful control of the scrap sector: the policing of the uses of urban space and containment of peddlers, the insertion of the Party into all scrap-related trade communities and guilds, and the stringent restrictions on rural-to-urban migration. Without these systems in place, the state recycling sector could never have achieved its unifying control. It would have been full of leaks—just as night soil distribution leaked when peasants came to town, and used goods and scrap leaked when out-of-town buyers passed through. These restrictions were not just about preventing smuggling and disruption but also about managing the political-economic divides of the Mao era. One internal report from a BRC manager noted that whenever recycling agents from out of town visited Beijing, they always marveled, "What you throw out and don't use could solve our big problems!" [49] The problem with the nostalgic story of Mao-era recycling is that it disavows the restrictions and inequities that underwrote the system.

As historical disavowals often do, this one returns to haunt the present. Almost as soon as Deng's economic reforms began to take hold in the early 1980s, independent informal recycling reappeared in China's cities. By the late 1990s informal recycling had developed into an enormous sector with millions of workers. Yet as shown in part 3, the state recycling companies and other state agencies that interface with informal recyclers have failed to see informal waste picking as a symptom of larger social, political, or economic inequities that need to be addressed. Rather, like Fu Hongjun, state recycling officials tell a story about a scrap management sector that worked in the Mao era because everyone was honest, hardworking, and thrifty, but which now fails because informal recyclers have degraded the entire system. They describe migrant recyclers as only after a quick buck however they can get it, evading regulations, cheating customers, adulterating goods, and polluting without conscience. Whenever any problems arise in the informal sector—and there have been many serious problems over the years—they are seen as proof that the sector is unethical, polluting, and recalcitrant. In this framing, an idealized version of the Mao era past serves as the basis for interpreting the present. In the Mao era, recycling was under control and the companies that managed it played by the rules; the problem today is that informal recyclers evade regulations and break the rules, and therefore the solution is cracking down on such evaders and imposing control.

It is striking how different this policy approach is from where the CCP started in 1949. At that time, and throughout the 1950s, CCP cadres looked at informal scrap peddlers and asked: What exactly are they doing, why are they doing it, and how, if we wish to have their cooperation, can we create a balance of incentives and prohibitions to get them to work toward our goals? In the 1950s, state agents approached informal recycling as a symptom of much larger socioeconomic inequalities, not as evidence of peddlers' intrinsic ethical and character flaws. Of course, during the 1960s and 1970s the idea that peddlers as a class were inherently untrustworthy did become the state's master narrative—and the recycling world's embrace of Zhou's quote in 1977 shows how quickly the leaders of that sector tried to act to displace that discriminatory version of their identities. And this makes it all the more ironic that when informal recycling emerged again in the reform era, it was nearly impossible to find anyone in the government or the BRC adopting the 1950s approach. What seemed so self-evident to the CCP when it was coming to power—that the first step in dealing with the informal sector is to try to understand it rather than simply crack down on it—seems almost unthinkable among state sector actors in the reform era.

Beijing's Waste-Scape on the Cusp of Market Reform

The Socialist government that took over Beijing in 1949 managed to sort out the city's unruly jumble of reuse and recycling networks and turn those ragged webs into a rationalized, state-managed system. It was an undertaking requiring a great deal of sociological research and what at times looked like Sisyphean administrative effort. In the two separate administrative waste realms—sanitation and scrap/used goods—the state accomplished many of its modernization goals, at the same time also inadvertently rupturing some urban metabolic processes.

In the realm of sanitation, garbage and night soil were efficiently collected and removed from the city, bestowing public health benefits on city residents and certainly making the city more presentable to foreign dignitaries.[1] But the reorganization of night soil management ruptured the metabolic cycle that had supplied fertilizer to local agriculture, while mounting flows of municipal trash turned what had been productive farming fields into trash dumps.

The reorganization of the scrap and used goods trades was more complex, involving tens of thousands of people in dozens of different professions. The most evident accomplishments were the cleaving of the sector into two streams (recycling and used goods retailing), enabling the organizing of used goods to be retailed under state oversight and ownership, and the consolidation of the scrap trades so materials could be directed toward state industry. Handicraft, which had been intimately tied to these trades, was not a favored child of state economic planners but managed to carry on. But there was an element of reuse practices that did get squeezed out during Mao-era rationalization: the multiplicity of small businesses that handled mending, repair, and tinkering.

Historical documents and even memoirs do not always comment on things that go quietly missing. Aside from one of the reports from the Beijing Consignment Company in 1961, which mentioned that the scope of reuse trades had narrowed because mending and repair was no longer part of shop clerks' jobs, I found little mention of this change.[2] But if one steps back, it is fairly obvious. It is well known that retail and service businesses of all kinds contracted dramatically under the planned economy, and this of course included repair. For example, in her recent work on furniture design, Jennifer Altehenger notes that "repair services, a traditional and established service provided by carpenters, declined swiftly" in the Mao era.[3] Not surprisingly, the pent-up demand for repair and maintenance work immediately surfaced with the reforms of the late 1970s and early 1980s, as the state began issuing licenses to small self-employed businesses, or *getihu*. Marcia Yudkin, in a small study from the mid-1980s, provides an overview of China's new small business economy. About half of the entrepreneurs she interviewed ran repair businesses: Hu Dapeng fixed radios in Beijing; Fan Dagui opened a bike shop in Xicheng district; Li Tianlu repaired fountain pens and Yang Chenghua musical instruments; Ma Yulin became a licensed cobbler, and Shi Hui became a tailor.[4]

This is not to say that the stewardship of objects weakened in the Mao era; mending and repair remained a central household ethic. But a key adjective here is *household*. One important difference between Republican- and Mao-era stewardship practices is that in the Republican era practices of repair, mending, cleaning, and so forth occurred both as unremunerated home care and as paid labor integrated into markets for reused goods. Indeed, repair, maintenance, and cleaning labor frequently crossed and blurred lines between work and home, paid and unpaid labor. But in the Mao era, formally seeking remuneration for such skills was discouraged. For a few years between 1962 and 1965, in response to a national wave of state work-unit layoffs, more leeway was allowed for people to take up small, independent businesses like washing and mending clothes for neighbors, but aside from that brief period, extending these skills for pay was discouraged if not prohibited.

Statistics on Beijing's urban waste trends in the Mao era, whether of overall urban trash collection (see Table 1) or the quantities of recyclables collected by the BRC (see Table 2), present a record of economic expansion and increasing waste generation. But the rate of growth in trash volume is hardly steep, and surveys of trash composition from 1976 show only 2 percent of Beijing's trash was composed of recyclable materials, so the general impression that people did not throw away much of value in the Mao era certainly seems to be confirmed by the numbers.[5] And while the statistics on fastidious recycling no doubt reflect citizens' practices of thrift, they certainly also reflect the fact that socialist industrial production

TABLE 1. Beijing's Trash

Year	Annual quantity	Average tons per day
1932	365,000	997
1933	365,000	1,000
1944	589,840	1,612
1951	583,210	1,598
1953	656,950	1,800
1955	815,410	2,234
1958	957,030	2,622
1960	836,968	2,287
1963	1,179,541	3,232
1965	1,115,164	3,055
1972	742,128	2,028
1974	864,453	2,368
1976	925,574	2,529
1978	919,248	2,518
1985	2,140,000	5,863
1987	3,070,000	8,411
1989	2,986,248	8,182
1990	3,307,884	9,063
1998	4,951,000	13,564
2007	6,009,000	16,463
2013	6,717,000	18,403
2017	9,248,000	25,337

NOTE: Quantities for 1963 and 1965 include some nonresidential waste. Data for 1932–90 are from *Beijing Environmental Sanitation Gazetteer*, 2002. Annual data vary by up to 2 million tons depending on methods for measurement and estimation. Figures for the years after 1990 from *Beijing Statistical Yearbook*, 2018.

was decidedly not oriented to encourage practices of disposability. Neither was there much packaging waste, as urban goods distribution was not based on manufacturing presealed, standardized packages. Stores sold most items in bulk, with clerks measuring out things like cookies and sunflower seeds into paper bags; soda and beer bottles had deposit fees and were sent back to bottling plants for cleaning and refilling.

The kinds of materials cycling through Beijing daily life changed in the Mao era, though also fairly gradually. There was a slow and steady decrease in dirt and ash wastes as households went from burning high-dirt-content coal briquettes to beehive coal and then to centralized heating—as always with the city's central districts coming first. Ash and dirt fell from comprising 85 percent of MSW during the 1950s to just above 50 percent by 1990, then declined rapidly to nearly zero in that decade.[6] Plastic, on the other hand, went from a rarity to an everyday substance during the Mao era. The BRC collected about fifty tons of waste plastic in 1957, mainly factory scrap and rural ground cover. Quantities were up to

TABLE 2. Beijing Municipal Recycling Company, Annual Recycling Quantity and Value, 1957–94

Year	Total nonferrous collected	Total ferrous collected	Total all scrap collected	Total value in scrap (in 10,000 RMB)
1957	849	12,792	28,032	
1958	3,444	33,840	65,452	
1959	1,329	75,855	138,958	
1960	889	131,258	277,110	
1961	935	118,176	202,002	
1962	884	47,183	99,943	1,813
1963	1,088	44,389	99,865	1,858
1964	1,163	156,816	211,223	2,052
1965	1,714	224,512	280,733	3,475
1966	1,485	112,045	183,751	2,912
1967	1,045	70,242	127,145	2,613
1968	1,185	128,805	197,200	2,899
1969	1,687	186,353	273,087	3,986
1970	3,176	233,271	308,161	3,286
1971	2,663	196,004	280,498	3,496
1972	2,832	202,614	295,570	4,547
1973	3,261	214,644	319,969	5,082
1974	3,372	234,895	351,586	5,201
1975	3,734	252,889	382,566	5,704
1976	3,799	249,221	383,351	5,742
1977	3,969	265,624	407,987	6,258
1978	4,989	323,726	481,692	7,558
1979	5,535	352,960	520,091	7,562
1980	6,518	384,806	549,660	8,157
1981	5,959	351,599	518,327	9,294
1982	6,190	395,183	564,697	10,845
1983	7,177	321,486	604,115	12,923
1984	6,136	441,093	644,318	17,210
1985	4,565	373,814	569,618	21,215
1986	4,139	343,141	528,552	18,100
1987	4,255	355,233	535,824	26,059
1988	2,731	381,252	524,211	34,641
1989	1,910	360,422	491,408	34,612
1990	2,208	397,298	504,582	32,951
1991	2,331	409,459	514,259	
1992	2,608	418,069	510,345	
1993	1,924	374,814	445,283	
1994	7,31	212,156	246,343	

SOURCE: Statistics on quantities of collected materials are from *BJGXSZ*, 150–51; figures on total value of scrap are from *Beijing zhi, zhonghe jingji guanli juan, wuzi zhi* [Beiiing gazetteer, comprehensive economic management collection, materials gazetteer], ed. Beiing Local Records Compilation Committee (Beijing: Beijing chubanshe, 2004), 201.

Blank cells are due to lack of available data.

fifteen hundred tons by the late 1960s, fifty-six hundred tons by 1979, and eighty-six hundred tons by 1984.[7] Still, from the 1960s into the early 1980s most plastic waste went unused or was sold at low prices to small household contractors.[8] The association of recycling with emerging concerns about industrial pollution in the late 1970s also led to some materials being taken out of recirculation. Waste bone came under particularly intense pressure due to the stink it created in warmer seasons; collection sputtered in 1985, and Beijing's bone-processing plant was shuttered in 1989.[9]

The pace and unevenness of change regarding material reuse picked up rapidly with market reforms. The 1980s saw the end of the BRC's involvement with scrap glass and used bottles; the broken glass had no buyers, and private vendors drove the BRC from the market in empty beer and soda bottles.[10] Paper fiber went through waves of extreme shortage throughout the Mao era, with calls in the mid-1970s for government offices to turn over all nonessential files for pulping; but under Deng's reforms pulp and wastepaper imports soared, rising 163 percent on the year in 1980 to reach $188 million.[11] Many other scrap commodities would enter similar cycles of intense swings of undersupply and oversupply in the 1980s.

Perhaps most fundamentally, the Mao-era economic policy changed the relationship of the waste/scrap sector to the overall economy. A comparison helps illustrate how fundamental this shift was. In Republican Beijing, scrap reuse had been central to the city's functioning and identity in large part because the city was in economic decline. Manchu aristocrats, lacking stipends and income, sold off their valuables to survive. Floods of high-end consumer goods that had once poured into Beijing markets went instead to wealthier treaty-port cities that could attract more trade and industrial investment than Beijing. Rural migrants fleeing war and famine scavenged and hawked junk to get by. In sum, when times were tough in the Republican era, the processes of collecting, mending, repairing, reusing, and extending the useful lives of every object and good were all the more crucial. But once scrap is shifted away from being mainly used for handicraft/mending/reuse, once it is primarily a material destined for recycling as an industrial input, then the relationship between scrap markets and the economy shifts. In an industrially dominated system, scrap markets thrive precisely when industry thrives, and recycling lulls and prices for recycled materials nosedive when the economy slumps. When the market is hot, demand for inputs goes up, competition for resources stiffens, and even manufacturers that do not usually use secondary materials often start doing so. Demand for scrap rises, and so do scrap prices. Conversely, an economic downturn typically hits scrap the hardest; prices of virgin materials drop, so why would a factory buy secondary raw materials if primary materials are cheap?

While these logics of supply and demand do not play out in precisely this manner in the planned economy, from the high perch of overall statistics, it is quite clear how recycling trends parallel the overall economy. The BRC's sales stats for the Mao era plot neatly with overall economic trends: general growth in the early 1960s, chaos at the outset of the CR, stagnation for a few years, a return to steady growth in the 1970s, and accelerating tremendously in the 1980s. On the other hand, the glimpses presented here into the Mao-era, state-owned, used goods business present a very different picture. While I have been unable to gather as much evidence as I would like regarding this sector, we did get a glimpse of these shops during the catastrophic economic crisis of in the post-GLF famine years of 1960–1962 and saw how that downturn led to a rush to buy the used goods sold by the state-owned consignment shops. But during the following decade of generally stable growth, the consignment shops dealt less and less in the buying and selling of everyday used goods. In the early years of the CR (1966–69), Beijing's consignment shops processed a surge of valuable used goods, either confiscated from victims raided by Red Guards or cheaply sold off by citizens attempting to stave off the violence of such raids, but by 1970 "goods confiscations were winding down." Several shops closed, and sales revenues at many stores fell by as much as one-half. By 1972 Beijing's consignment shops were becoming primarily a conduit for overstock and unpopular or defective manufactured goods, which by then made up over 50 percent of their trade.[12] Unlike scrap recycling, which grew when industrial production grew and shrank when industry stalled, the market for used goods in Beijing experienced the most intense activity and consumer demand when the economy was in crisis, but contracted when industrial production held strong.

What this tells us about how the economics of the waste reuse sector interacts with the larger economy is worth noting. Recycling is often portrayed as being about reducing waste, as a kind of pushback or resistance to industrial profligacy and material waste, but in fact, recycling for industry creates a common interest between the recyclers—even if they are from marginalized groups—and the interests of industrial production. More industrial production means more demand for material inputs, more postproduction by-product scrap, and more goods being consumed and discarded. As far as recyclers interfacing with an industrial system are concerned, the more waste the better. Mao-era industrialization served to forge this common interest between recyclers and industry. But the command economy of the era also imposed an inherent limit on this kind of growth, in that it promoted a system that idealized resource reuse, sanctified, as Zsuzsa Gille found in socialist Hungary, "a cult of waste," and constructed a system of industrialization without disposability. As shown in part 3, once the shift to embrace forms of consumerism based on disposability was made, the wealth to be made through the expansion of waste making and recycling surged as never before.

PART THREE

The Reform Era
(1980–Present)

Fighting over the Scraps

Aside from the Forbidden City, some historical monuments and a few gems of socialist state architecture, Beijing has been veritably demolished and rebuilt several times in the last four decades. The shockwaves of creative destruction have splashed ever outward, submerging the once rural suburbs out to the third ring road (completed 1993), the fourth (completed 2001), the fifth (2003), the sixth (2009), and beyond.[1] In reform-era China (1978–present), migrant garbage gleaners and collectors of recyclables have reemerged, again mapping China's city through their labor, sorting and consolidating the haphazardly dispersed slough of urban consumption. What they collect—plastic bottles and cardboard boxes tattooed with foreign and domestic corporate logos—tells a story of changing consumption patterns. Who they are tells a story of continuing divisions of labor and unequal citizenship rights. And where they go to collect and sell their goods, their bureaucratic and geographic steeplechase over the last four decades, makes legible a story of changing urban land uses, skyrocketing land rents, and shifting policies of urban management.

The titanic transformation of Beijing's physical environment has been both a product of and an impetus for radical shifts in the rhythms and patterns of urban daily life. The ways in which residents experience and manage both space and time have been transformed. During the Mao years, people typically lived and worked within the relatively contained spaces of their work units. Transportation was primarily by bus, by bicycle, or on foot, and people's daily schedules rarely took them far afield. Prices were lower, and the economy was less monetized. Staple goods such as food grains, oil, and cloth were part of subsidized rationing systems; health-care costs, school fees, and housing rents were minimal;

employment and migration were state managed; and neither real estate nor businesses could be privately owned or rented. All these sectors have now entered the market. Alongside these economic changes, the trickle of migration into the cities that began in the mid-1980s surged into a torrent in the 1990s and up through the present, forcing the old housing registration system (*hukou*) to adapt, at times loosening and bending but never breaking; *hukou* continues today to determine many life-shaping decisions for migrant workers, recyclers among them.

These changes have had an enormous impact on habits of urban consumption. As the choreography of daily life quickens, "convenient" consumption becomes alluring, if not imperative: lightweight, transportable, sealed, serving-sized commodities are tailor made for Taylorized consumption in a high-velocity service economy. Convenience, by another name, is disposability. The city's waste streams overfloweth; Beijing's MSW nearly quadrupled between 1978 and 1990 and since then has grown at around the same rate as China's GDP, rising at around 8–10 percent a year.[2] Most recently, the triumphs of online shopping (*kuaidi*) and meal delivery (*waimai*) have fired off like twin booster rockets, accelerating the generation of urban trash. Both managing the removal and disposal of these wastes and picking recyclable materials out of them have become billion dollar businesses. The following chapters explore the battles over control of these wastes: where they go, how they are handled, and who profits from them.

No one has done more to raise public awareness of the environmental damage wrought by China's flood of postconsumer waste than the artist and filmmaker Wang Jiuliang. Wang's documentary *Beijing: City Besieged by Waste* (2012), equal parts dogged investigative journalism and heartbreaking landscape photography, delivers a gut-punching anti-capitalist critique by holding up a brutal and meditative mirror to the ecologies and communities that are being sacrificed in the service of Beijing's gluttonous consumption. Between 2007 and 2011 Wang photographed more than five hundred illegal waste-dumping sites on the outskirts of Beijing, then "pinned" each of the locations on Google Maps, revealing a city ringed by unmanaged dumps (see figure 1 in the introduction).[3]

Several of the dumps in the film serve not just as picking sites for human scavengers, but also as feed lots for herds of cows, pigs, and goats (see figure 7). As we know, this cyclical story of urban wastes returning to the countryside for reuse in agriculture has a history; the metabolic circle of life continues. This cycle has never been trouble free. In the Republican era, the price of the metabolic cycle (the use of night soil fertilizer) had been the endemic presence of intestinal roundworms in Beijing residents; in the Mao era, increased applications of city garbage made Beijing's fertilizer more harmful than amending of rural soils.[4] Today Beijing's garbage is no longer imaginable as fertilizer; its plastics suffocate any water or plant life buried beneath it. But it can be an inexpensive feedstock to grow meat and milk for urban consumers. This new cycle speaks of continuities

FIGURE 7. Dairy cows grazing in a field of garbage full of plastic in the Beijing suburbs, ca. 2009. Photo taken by artist Wang Jiuliang while making *City Besieged by Waste* (2010–11). Used with permission.

that persist—the wealthy city's wastes remain the poorer countryside's valued resource—and of changes in what is being metabolized and its environmental effects and side effects: today's garbage helps satiate the increasingly meaty diets of urban consumers while destroying land fertility and knotting plastic through the bodies of herd animals.

As the urban metabolism has changed, the sources of Beijing's urban solid waste arisings have shifted. Industrial scrap, which had accounted for 70 percent of the BRC's collected materials in the Mao era, rapidly declined in the 1980s as manufacturing—increasingly deemed polluting, unattractive, and incompatible with global elite expectations of top-tier cities as centers of sanitized consumption—was relocated outside the city. Instead, the capital's waste came to be dominated by postconsumer trash and demolition wastes as the city convulsed in waves of creative destruction. The chapters that follow focus mostly on Beijing's postconsumer recyclables and the forty-year tussle between state-owned and informal recycling networks to control them. But recyclables are only one current within the city's overall waste stream, so before diving into the details of postconsumer recycling, a sketch of the larger waste stream provides an important context.

As independent businesses catering to consumers blossomed under Deng's reforms, new forms of waste proliferated while others declined. The transformation was already evident by 1984. Recyclables, which only made up 2 percent of Beijing's garbage in 1976, were up to 7.3 percent by 1984, amounting to an estimated 200,000 tons of materials worth 30 million yuan. Quantities of plastic, paper, and glass had quadrupled. Equally significant, the proportions of the two main components of the waste stream—coal ash and food wastes—flipped, with food wastes (mainly vegetables and fruit matter) rising from 17 to over 50 percent, while coal ash fell from 80 to 40 percent, due largely to the adoption of central heating.[5]

Those who "got rich first" led the way in setting new consumption patterns. In 1991, paper, plastic, metal (cans), and glass already made up more than 70 percent of the waste generated in wealthier residential areas but was still less than 11 percent of the waste in lower-income, single-story neighborhoods.[6] But the changes soon became increasingly universal in urban districts; from 1990 to 1998, the proportion of paper in Beijing's waste stream reached 18 percent, and plastic and glass both doubled, to 10 percent each.[7] This occurred as total MSW collected ballooned from under one million tons in 1978 to over three million in 1990. In 2015 that figure reached 7.9 million tons (see Table 1 in the conclusion to part 2).

In the 1980s, when this trend started, the timing could not have been much worse for Beijing's sanitation managers, as the city's waste stream surged in volume just as rural units were refusing to accept trash shipments. By 1981 the People's Daily reported that the city's Number Two Sanitation Truck Fleet was openly admitting to dumping wastes haphazardly throughout the suburbs and was petitioning the city to set up permanent dump sites, but that did not happen—in part because the city had not yet owned up to that responsibility.[8] Recall that under the Mao-era waste management system, the Sanitation Bureau only took responsibility for sanitizing the city, meaning it only handled night soil and garbage collection and removal, not disposal. Once these wastes were expelled from the city, all responsibilities for handling them fell upon rural administrative units. Complicating matters, the early 1980s saw the government experimenting with contracting systems with the goal of incentivizing efficiency and proactive management. In 1985 each city district was left to solve its own trash disposal problem through contracting out, and with "no place to put it, they just dumped it on roads, streams, canal banks, fields and remote spots (See Map 2 in the Introduction)."[9] It is hard to blame the district haulers for being so irresponsible because as late as 1984, the Beijing Urban Appearance and Environmental Sanitation Management Regulations provided details for keeping urban areas free of animal droppings, vermin, and spit and specified in great detail how and when trash should be collected, but in no way touched on how collected trash should be disposed of.[10] In the 1990s, Beijing finally came to acknowledge that disposing of its waste was its responsibility and applied for a World Bank loan to build the city's first modern sanitary landfill, completed in 1994.[11]

Yet two decades later, and despite the building of several massive sanitary land-fills and incinerators, Wang Jiuliang's film revealed that Beijing's "Great Wall of Garbage" had only gotten greater. Why has Beijing been so ineffective at finding methods to reduce or contain its flood of postconsumer and demolition wastes for nearly four decades? It is not just that the city government has had trouble keeping pace with the torrents of wastes; more important, it has been unable to contain/define those wastes *as wastes*, as trash lacking use and value. The dumps flourish not because there is too much waste, but because there is too much valuable mate-rial in the waste to stop dumping and picking. In part, this phenomenon has roots in how urban waste was administratively constituted in the Mao era. That system framed recycling and garbage as separate matters under separate bureaucracies, even though in everyday life there was considerable blurring and commingling of these materials. In the mid-1980s, the city's Sanitation Research Office looked into the possibility of removing the recyclable fraction from Beijing's garbage but found that "the newspaper, glass bottles, etc. recyclables in residential waste are already being recycled [by the BRC]. As for the recyclables in the mixed garbage, if we used human and machine labor to pick it out, the cost would be very high." Even more expensive would be mobilizing the public to undertake comprehensive waste sorting. Given Sanitation's limited funding (about .5% of the city budget), landfilling was seen as the best, cheapest option.[12] So the sanitation bureaucracy chose to stay out of the recycling business.

But if the city government found Beijing's trash not profitable enough to pick, suburban farmers calculated differently. Beijing's trash made terrible compost, but what it lacked in fertility it made up for with other valuable resources. As dumpsites grew in extent and richness, dump picking became not just common-place but organized. A retired cadre wrote a letter to the *People's Daily* describing a landfill near his home in the Beijing suburbs in 1989:

A trash dump is a treasure chest. Don't mind that the dump is dirty and smelly, it is still a place with considerable appeal [*xiyinli*]. . . . After visiting repeatedly to soak up the excitement [*kan re'nao*], I joined in the picking. My "colleagues" were other retirees, old workers, elderly housewives, and some younger women. . . . I've inter-viewed over a dozen folks who pick food to raise pigs. Most are from the Beijing suburbs, farming and raising pigs on the side, some five, some ten, even thirty pigs, and the trash dump is their feed lot. . . . [In less than two months] I collected over 250 pairs of shoes. . . . These days most nuclear families [*xiaojiating*] only have one child, the past practice of mending the older child's shoes and passing them down to the next one and so on are over. Now, when the kid's feet get big, the shoes are tossed. Most of the shoes I collected were 70 or 80% new, no obvious defects. . . . I've seen a lot of arguments at the dump, but I've never seen anyone who was arguing stop their picking and start fighting. The old saying "the gentleman acts with his words, not his hands," is fitting and could be considered a trademark quality of the trash dump as a field of "healthy competition."[13]

For suburban farmers and migrants, dumpsites were resources over which to compete, but for the city government—hosting the 1990 Asian Games as a possible dress rehearsal for an Olympic bid—the dumps were embarrassments demanding modern management. The city sought international consultants and funding to build sealed-off sanitary landfills, but these too were soon hosting waste-picking communities. At one supposedly sanitary landfill I visited in south Beijing in 1999, pickers had opened their own extra "gate" in the brick wall encircling the facility. By the 2008 Olympics, the city had successfully booted pickers from its facilities, but Wang Jiuliang's 2011 film showed that informal dumping and scavenging continued unabated (See Map 1 in the Introduction). Unfortunate as these dumps may have been for the local environment, they persisted because, across an array of often contradictory and liminal (simultaneously under- and overvalued) uses, they created their own economies of colluding beneficiaries: waste truckers and construction businesses looking for low-cost dumpsites; village and town governments looking for a quick way to make cash; old empty quarries seeking cheap landfill; and communities of local and migrant scavengers extracting lost riches.

While all this was transpiring at dumpsites, there was another even larger contingent of migrant recyclers accessing recyclables through a different means. By the late 1990s a network of about 100,000 informal migrant collectors had put the BRC out of business at its own game, usurping its role in neighborhood and street recycling collection, right down to using the BRC's signature vehicle, the three-wheeled bike-cart. Less scavengers than small traders, these recyclers worked from dawn to dusk buying recyclables from neighborhood residents and shops, then secured their cartloads of scrap (often well over one hundred kilos) and biked several kilometers (the distances growing longer each year as the city sprawled) out to clusters of informal markets at the edge of town, where the materials were sorted, aggregated, and shipped to regional factories for processing. The following chapters focus on these informal migrant recyclers, the economic networks they have built, and the vicissitudes they have confronted over the last four decades.

6

A Tale of Two Cities,
1980–2003

It is an honored custom in state socialist journalism to pack as many big numbers as possible into an article. A short *People's Daily* article published in 1992, "'Junk Kings' Pick a 'Gold Mountain,'" followed in this venerable tradition:

> What in the old days we called "Junk Kings" (*polan wang*) . . . today takes the form of our waste materials collection, processing, and comprehensive reuse system. 1992 will see our national recycling resource industry recycle an estimated 220 million tons of scrap . . . for a total value of 14 billion yuan, 8.3 times that of 1978 . . . with 26,000 companies at the county level and above, 110,000 collection nodes, 658,000 employees, over 1500 processing plants. . . . China's resource recycling industry is developing rapidly.[1]

In this same vein, the BRC was no slouch. Throughout the 1980s its twenty companies, more than four hundred collection points, and thirteen thousand employees collected about eight hundred different kinds of scrap totaling 500,000 tons and 84 million yuan in profit annually.[2] State enterprise reforms of the 1980s, especially the contracting out system (*chengbao jingying*) that incentivized productivity by having companies bid to fulfill state contracts and retain their profits for their own investment (including for employee bonuses), catalyzed SMC recycling company growth.

But what a difference a few years can make. From the lofty historical height of 2002, a Chaoyang district BRC manager looked back over the 1990s and sighed at the "unimaginable changes. . . . By 1996 [the BRC's] recycling volume had fallen to 140,000 tons, handling just five or six types [of scrap] with less than 3000 employees actually working." By 1998 the BRC was bankrupt and had been disbanded, and its district-level offices scrambled to restructure as shareholding companies in hopes of reinventing themselves under new names and new models.

How, in less than a decade, did the state recycling system go from flourishing to bankrupt? Seen through the lens of policy reforms, it is a complex story involving enterprise restructuring, new forms of taxation, the triangular debt crisis, the two track system, and other factors. Yet it is also a much simpler story: the state recycling system collapsed because migrant recyclers utterly outcompeted them. When I asked manager Wang Shude how the Mentougou district company dealt with the rise of rural migrant recyclers in the 1990s, he replied, "What did we do? There was nothing to do. It was all over."[3] The outcome seemed inevitable, or in academic jargon, overdetermined. Or rather, the "inevitability" story is not so much "simpler" as it is a view from a wider angle that takes in a much broader context of structural urban-rural metabolic and political-economic reconfigurations. Exploring how specific reforms and events internal to the recycling bureaucracy reshaped the sector is informative but insufficient. The context of China's rapid urbanization, its massive waves of construction (or more aptly for our purposes, "creative destruction"), the opening of countless new commercial spaces, the concerted promotion of consumerism, skyrocketing real estate markets, resurgent economic inequality, and the largest rural to urban migration in human history are all crucial to understanding the sea change in China's recycling system in the last decades of the twentieth century. It is through this wider, admittedly sometimes fuzzy lens that it becomes clear that the story of recycling in Beijing in these decades is not just a tale of two competing networks, but of two cities.

THE STATE SECTOR: GOING BROKE IN THE GOLDEN AGE

The 80s and 90s, for the recycling company was the best period. There was money, we built apartments for workers and office buildings. Bonuses were higher, prices went up and so did bonuses. Not just three, five and seven bucks, but tens or hundreds of bucks.

—WANG SHUDE, LIFETIME BRC EMPLOYEE AND DISTRICT COMPANY MANAGER, INTERVIEW WITH AUTHOR, JULY 2018

The 1980s was something of a golden age for the state's recycling companies. As BRC Haidian district company manager Li recalled:

Under the planned economy, even if you wanted to develop you couldn't, it was entirely the planned economy. The recycling company under the planned economy system did not produce profit, all profit was given upward.... Then around '85, it changed to collective contracting (*jiti chengbao*). That contracting structure really invigorated the recycling company, because before you made, 30, 40 yuan [a month] and 5–10 yuan bonus, basically that level. Recycling in society is rather looked down on, nobody really wants to do it, but in '85 and '86 a lot of people, some from government offices, were very willing to come to the BRC. Why? I remember very clearly, our [Haidian] company had six depots, the lowest compensated worker at one of those depots could make 1900 yuan [per year]. At the time, the average annual pay in Beijing was around 600 yuan.[4]

The BRC was not unique; the contracting out system was an economic steroid shot for many recycling state-owned enterprises (SOEs). In 1984 Zhang Yujin, an upstart recycling company manager in Benxi, Liaoning Province, defiantly unseated his old-school superiors, outbidding them for the city's recycling contract by promising to deliver twice the scrap in half the time, and he did so. He succeeded in part due to a generous bonus system and by promoting dozens of low-level employees whom he knew to be hands-on materials experts into management. It took a few years before the higher echelons blessed Zhang's management methods as reform kosher; from then on the state press crowned him "Junk King."

Zhang's fame peaked in 1990 with an eponymous nine-episode miniseries on Chinese state TV. *Junk King* celebrated the transformative power of two unstoppable forces: romantic love and the contracting out system in SOEs. Of course, being a miniseries, it included a romantic subplot about Junk King Zhang's daughter (played by the actress Liu Bei), who, thrown out of her dream job in a drama troupe by a vindictive cultural cadre because she refused his lurid advances, lands back home in the trash heaps of Benxi. At first she can only break down in tears when she has to use her lovely singing voice to call out "Buying Junk! Cash for Trash!," but by the end of the miniseries she has found both a husband and pride in her work, exemplifying her father's motto, "There are only waste materials, not waste people" (*zhiyou feiwu, meiyou feiren*). This message is also conveyed through the show's images of recycling company workers. Benxi is much poorer than Beijing, and the first episode introduces us to the workers' lives a few days before Zhang makes his bid to become boss, still living in shanties on the edge of town and behaving in a scandalously uncivilized manner. Episode one features a wedding turned brawl, a seamy extramarital affair, and a drunken man and woman having a stripping contest in the middle of the street. By the last episode, Zhang has triumphed: Benxi's Party secretary confirms Zhang as a model worker, renews him as company head, and shames his opponents; the SMC recyclers rejoice as their shantytown is bulldozed for new housing; and the woman who was having the shameful affair has told her partner that now that she has been promoted to depot manager, she has found her self-respect and can no longer countenance cheating on her husband. The message is clear and not so different from that of BRC manager Li: it is hard to have self-respect when you are poor and marginalized; the contracting reform brought state recycling companies prosperity, and with money comes self-respect.

But the reform era was not simply a smooth march toward free market trading and rapid growth. Between 1977 and 1984 BRC scrap volume rose by over 50 percent, and its value nearly tripled, but from 1984 on, though profits kept climbing, throughput hit a wall and then began to decline. There were many reasons for BRC volume to level off. In the 1980s many factories were relocated outside the city since industrial plants—with their unsightly smoke, noise, odors—were seen as insalubrious for urban living. The reforms also allowed other state units to bypass the BRC and trade materials with one another, eroding the BRC's monopoly over scrap commerce. Still, with demand high and profits growing, many branches of the BRC kept expanding even as throughput stalled; Fengtai district's recycling company went from 150 employees in 1983 to 900 in 1989.[5]

The BRC also faced difficulties maintaining its urban collection network. Even in the Mao era, opening new collection sites had been very expensive, leading the BRC to contract neighborhood collection out to small collective shops (xiao jiti) under the management of neighborhood committees. By 1981, more than 200 of the city's 297 collection sites were contracted in this manner. But the economic reforms were opening up a panoply of new small business opportunities, many of which were clearly more attractive to neighborhood residents than running a recycling stand. Soon the BRC was pleading its case to city officials:

> Since 1979, in the name of providing work for youth, not only have recycling sites not received much support, but on the contrary, some have been put to other uses, mainly for businesses seen as making big profits. This has led to a stream of conflicts and contradictions. For example, at Inner Desheng Gate in Xicheng district a collection site is now a grocery; a site near Dongsi People's Market is now a general store; the depot at Guangnei in Xuanwu district is now a shop.[6]
>
> New construction is underway throughout the city so we will need more recycling collection sites, but recently not only are we finding no way to expand the network of recycling nodes, but nodes are getting squeezed, taken over or dispersed. Recently we have lost 15 collection sites. Please quickly issue an order to prevent more sites from being pushed out.[7]

Note that this was 1980, when new construction was still moving at a relative snail's pace; in the construction tsunami of the 1990s and 2000s, for the BRC's recycling network to survive would have been something of a miracle.

The mid-1980s saw industry hungry for more materials, compelling the BRC to expand its collection network, just as looser trading regulations made controlling where collection nodes were located, who managed them, and what they could and could not collect all increasingly challenging. For example, in 1985, in order to get more ferrous scrap, Beijing opened ferrous collection to independent (geti)

collectors (ones licensed individually rather than through the authority of a neighborhood committee). But government "oversight could not keep up [with the rush
of new independent collectors]. Unlicensed businesses, speculative trading, rule
violations, unreported buying and selling, and even internal conspiracies" quickly
became rampant; a year later independents were stripped of their licenses.[8]

In order to try to prevent these kinds of problems, one principle that
remained sacrosanct throughout the 1980s was the strict division of industrial
and residential/society scrap collection. Industry scrap was to be traded by BRC
district-level offices only; neighborhood collection nodes were forbidden to accept
any industrial scrap. But profiteering schemes that passed off industrial materials
as residential scrap had always been difficult to combat, and the jumble of deregulation and reregulation in the reform era made policing the line even harder. The
recycling company's new bonus systems did not help either. By linking workers'
rewards directly to how much they collected, bonuses made fudging the lines
between industrial and residential scrap for personal gain all the more enticing. A
People's Daily exposé in 1979 described an extreme case at an oil company town
in Jilin where investigators alleged there were more than 650 incidents of scrap
metal smuggling worth over 550,000 yuan. Oil company workers regularly used
company tractors to haul off loads of pipe and machinery at night for illicit barter,
and a brigade leader accepted bribes from local residents who gleaned any metal
parts left lying in the oil fields to sell as scrap to residential SMC shops. The residential SMC recycling shops accepted everything that came their way; rather than
facing rebuke from their bosses, they were showered with rewards and plaques for
exceeding quotas. Several anecdotes involved SMC shop clerks telling customers
trying to pass off undamaged equipment as scrap, "I can't accept objects intact like
this; you need to go smash them first."[9] The Jilin case might have been extreme,
but it was not isolated. From 1981 to 1987 the People's Daily ran more than twenty
articles describing cases in which public goods—utility wire, railroad equipment,
iron manhole covers—were laundered through recycling shops; in particular,
independently contracted recycling shops were represented as dens of thieves.

The reforms also radically changed how recycling SOEs were managed, forcing them to adopt a whole new set of business strategies and essentially build a
national market. To succeed in a commercial environment in which trade channels
were no longer dictated, territorial restrictions were being erased, and prices and
supplies fluctuated, BRC managers needed the equivalent of market information—
something they had not needed or been provided with for decades. In the first
half of the 1980s three scrap trade journals appeared, and in the second half of the
decade, ten more.[10] In addition to offering market information, articles provided
management advice for the reform age, often a seemingly contradictory mix praising pro-market strategies while fiercely guarding elements of the state's monopoly,
as in these pronouncements from a Tianjin Planning Committee member:

In line with the continued deepening of the economic reforms, the government has been eliminating the command system of ferrous and non-ferrous scrap allocation and gradually building an orderly and directed scrap metals market. But lately, in many regions, peddlers and groups (*lianhe ti*) have taken advantage of the reforms and engage in vigorous speculative activities, buying up everything, pushing up prices to get rich in the scrap trade. Our [Tianjin] metals management bureau has given the police over 600 leads on materials with uncertain origins. . . . It must be emphasized, recycling enterprises are the main channel for scrap ferrous, no other enterprises are permitted to expand into this business; unlicensed peddlers must be eliminated; licensed independent and group enterprises can only collect residential scrap and cannot enter business units for trade, nor are businesses allowed to trade with them. . . . Also we have to firmly implant a big market, big transport, big trade strategic mentality. Our Tianjin is a large city and based on that scale we must break through the old administrative boundaries (*tiaokuai*) and orient towards all of North China, the whole nation... We should strengthen our horizontal economic connections, build communications networks with other big cities, build relationships for agents to buy and sell.[11]

Independent/informal recyclers were not the only competition. Old rivalries within the state scrap sector continued to boil just beneath the surface. A 1991 State Council circular claimed the sector's biggest problem was not the plague of unlicensed agents but a decades-old sibling squabble: "The two Bureaus of Materials and of Commerce need to negotiate and cooperate in practical operations, and stop squeezing each other out and competing over acquisitions."[12]

Competition from within and without, the erosion of its monopoly over trade, pressures squeezing its collection network, inconsistent regulations, factory relocations, and a marked increase in illegality—the 1980s were treacherous waters, yet the BRC still managed to prosper. But then a series of economic shocks in the early 1990s decimated them.

In the early 1990s the state loosened credit, stoking inflation especially in the industrial sector. Fixed asset investment in 1992 grew by 43 percent, and steel prices rose by 80 percent.[13] Zhu Rongji attacked the problem, tightening credit in 1993 and reforming the tax structure in 1994. Haidian's manager Li recalled:

Ferrous was in the process of shifting from the planned economy to the market, it was the time of two-tracks. I would be allocated a ton of steel for 800 yuan, but by market prices I could sell it for 1300. At the time, mid '92, scrap steel was really cheap, 300+ bucks a ton, but by the end of the year it was 800 a ton. At the peak in May '93 scrap steel had risen to 1750 per ton, construction steel was 3700 a ton, prices were soaring. Then in June the price crashed. No one was willing to sell at so low a price, we had huge losses. We were a grassroots level unit, I remember we bought over 1000 tons of Russian rebar, we brought it in at that time at what price? 3700 per ton. It sat so long it turned to dross, just sat there. Finally we sold it for 700 a ton.

No relief came in 1994:

> In January '94, the tax reform started, the value added tax (VAT). Before, why were the recycling company's profits so high? Our commercial tax...at the time was called "price-difference tax" (*chajia shui*), it was 2.5% [of the difference between buying and selling price]. But the VAT was 17% [of sales minus purchases]. And if you did not have receipts . . . this put a huge tax burden on recycling companies. . . . This was one reason why collection rates fell.[14]

The VAT, particularly that bit about receipts, was to be one of the biggest policy obstacles affecting the recycling sector for the next two decades, so it is worth getting into the weeds here. The VAT was essentially calculated as 17 percent of an enterprise's total sales receipts minus its total purchasing receipts. But of course urban residents could not provide any receipts when the BRC purchased recyclables from them, and neither could the informal/independent collectors who were increasingly taking over residential, commercial, and nonstate industry scrap collection by the 1990s. With no purchasing receipts to subtract from their sales totals, BRC companies were stuck paying a VAT of 17 percent on their total sales—a huge sum of money that often all but nullified any profit. Under these conditions, many low-value materials were no longer worth collecting at all, so, as manager Li notes, collection rates fell. That the VAT devoured the BRC's healthy profit margins, and indeed those of state recycling companies throughout China, was not the end of it; well into the 2000s the VAT was among the biggest deterrents preventing independent recyclers from registering their businesses with the government; for many recyclers, the moment they registered they would essentially also go bankrupt. Well into the 2010s it made more sense for most recycling entrepreneurs to remain informal, pay bribes, and dodge inspectors rather than register and pay the VAT.

Still, the VAT was not the final nail in the BRC's coffin. The late 1980s and early 1990s had seen a nationwide wave of overinvestment in poorly planned capital construction projects, resulting in chains of bad debt between interrelated SOEs, a syndrome dubbed triangular debt (*sanjiaozhai*):

> Triangular debt was the worst. Our company in 1994 was in what kind of shape? After two decades of just accumulating [profits], in 1994 it became accounts receivable. . . . I was basically running every day to a different factory. If I had pretty good connections with them (*guanxi gao de bucuo*) then if they had some cash they'd give me a bit. Scrap ferrous was important stuff, we gave it all to Capital Steel, they owed us 30 million yuan at the worst point. . . . Down to today [2008] our company has a dead account of 17 million yuan.[15]

Though the triangular debt crisis subsided, the BRC kept losing money; losses in 1998 came to 8.7 million yuan. Of 8,074 BRC employees on the books, fewer than 2,000 were still actually working. The company's residential collection network had disintegrated, with just six sites remaining inside the city's third ring road.[16] The municipal-level office of the BRC passed into oblivion in 1998.

Certainly all the managerial crises of the 1990s took their toll, but an autopsy would have found the BRC died of starvation; in the end it simply could not get its hands on any scrap to trade. The painful irony was that the state recycling system starved in the midst of the biggest deluge of scrap the Chinese economy had ever seen. The market reforms celebrated consumerism as a symbol and engine of economic development. Especially in megacities like Beijing, thousands of independently owned businesses—restaurants, shops, convenience stores, supermarkets, hotels, shopping malls—were generating a deluge of wastes and recyclables and fueling new habits of disposability. In addition there was the demolition waste goldrush; Beijing's countless construction sites were aboveground ore deposits to be mined. If supplies of scrap were robust, demand for them was even healthier; township-village enterprises were going gangbusters in the 1990s, and demand for cheap inputs seemed bottomless.

Yet the BRC could not lay its hands on any of it. Beijing's new businesses were part of a shifting economic geography, new patterns of commerce and consumption that the BRC had no relationship to or monopoly over. Instead, this newly developing cityscape was being mapped as quickly as it emerged by an industrious phalanx of rural migrant recyclers who laid claim to the profitable waste streams of an increasingly commercial Beijing, even as they were in many ways both socially and administratively excluded from it.

THE MIGRANTS' BEIJING: MAKING A LIVING
WHERE YOU ARE NOT ALLOWED TO LIVE

In August 2001 the *Southern Capital News* ran a story titled "Suspecting His Junk Has Been Stolen, [Man] Brutally Beats His Fellow Traveler." It began: "While on a passenger train, Mr. Jia beat and critically injured his colleague (*tonghang*) Mr. Luo in a struggle over a single empty plastic spring-water bottle."[17] According to the article, two "trash hicks" (*laji lao*) clambered through the cabin windows of a train at a station in Hunan and soon came to blows over a few recyclables. The mocking tone of this slapstick tale was typical of how informal recyclers were described in state media at the time; it would seem the main point of such articles was to confirm that rural migrants were "low quality" (*suzhi di*) brutes apt to run amok if not taken in hand.

The article is not just evidence of the normality of anti-migrant bias in the national press in those days (a bias that recurs in many texts cited here); it can also be used to broach what has arguably been the core political-economic contest over recycling from the 1980s to today. The issue at stake in Luo and Jia's fight was not possession of a single bottle but rather who had gleaning rights over a specific public space. That is precisely what the BRC and every other state recycling company has been wrestling with rural migrants over ever since Deng's reforms. Who will win in the contest over the spaces where scrap is generated? Over the last four decades this has been a question worth hundreds of billions of dollars.

Rural migrants began coming to Beijing in large numbers in the mid-1980s, selling produce and peddling goods at newly resurgent street markets and jumping at every possible work opportunity: restaurant service, nanny work, garbage collection. Construction work was a huge employer of migrant men; typically working without safety equipment and at best a fig leaf of insurance, rural crews were far cheaper to hire than urban ones. As individuals, migrants had trouble getting permits to reside and work in Beijing, but the authorities facilitated construction contractors' bringing in work crews. Many migrant recyclers first came to Beijing as members of such crews. Boss Lu, a successful recycler from Henan's Gushi county, first arrived in 1987 to work construction. I was introduced to Lu in 2000 by the Chinese Academy of Social Sciences researcher Tang Can, who had spent two years doing fieldwork in Beijing's biggest migrant recycling community at that time, Bajia in Haidian district (aka Henan Village because around 80 percent of the recyclers hailed from Henan).[18] Lu was one of Tang Can's best contacts in the community, and he generously met with me a few times to show me his markets and share his story.

Lu first worked construction, then took a job at a pig farm for 160 yuan a month. One day he struck up a conversation with a man pulling a handcart full of junk who claimed to be making 60 yuan a day collecting scrap. The next day Lu arranged for his family to send him a telegram at his workplace notifying him of the unfortunate death of his grandfather (who had actually died years earlier) and asking Lu to return home immediately. With his two-months' emergency pay, Lu bought a three-wheeled bike-cart and began collecting in Wang Fujing, a touristy commercial area in the heart of Beijing. Every night he pedaled eleven kilometers back to Wohu Bridge, where a community of migrant recyclers was forming centered around a cluster of recycling depots.[19]

As BRC manager Li recalled, it was not long before folks like Lu began making an impression on the BRC's realm:

> From 1988 it was all an uphill battle. From '88 on large amounts of surplus labor from the countryside started entering the city. The cultural level of China's peasants is low, they cannot do anything else. . . . To make money they would steal a couple of bikes, grab a basket and start entering neighborhoods collecting recyclables. SOEs could not compete with independents, because our accounting requirements were strict and we needed three people per collecting group [one on the scales, one on the money, one sorting and packing] to prevent embezzling. It took three SOE employees to do what one self-employed (*getihu*) could do. . . . SOE workers enjoyed

eight hour days, and had to receive overtime pay; independents arrived at 7 am and left at night when no one was selling any more.[20]

Setting aside the spiteful stereotyping, manager Li's explanation is accurate. By the late 1980s BRC employees had long ceased plying the hutongs calling for scrap, and they never developed the habit of servicing new neighborhood businesses. But while the BRC let its bike-carts rust, migrants usurped this symbol of the trade, tirelessly seeking materials and calling on every business and apartment, then schlepping scrap across the city to sell at collection depots. At first such depots were all BRC-licensed collection points because migrants had yet to build ties to industrial buyers, but that changed quickly.

Migrant entrepreneurs quickly created other opportunities in addition to street collection. One of the first sectors the BRC lost to migrants was construction scrap, as manager Li explained: "After reforms every enterprise wanted definite rewards, something to put in petty cash (xiaojinku). The recycling company didn't pay cash to enterprises, but independents did. Especially when it came to construction units selling their scrap . . . this cash payment problem led to our losing that sector."[21] Migrants made similar inroads in other industries, their cash-for-trash networks reaching pretty much everywhere that scrap arose or was in demand by industry. Soon migrant collectors were bypassing the BRC as a buyer and knitting their own networks linking collection, sorting, aggregating, trading, and processing. Moving into these aspects of recycling required knowledge, connections, equipment, and almost always some land, some capital, and a willingness to take financial risks, but by the early 1990s the migrant scrap sector had become an economically stratified and comprehensive supply chain for almost every form of recyclable material. Boss Lu was on the leading edge of these changes, and by the time I met him he had made over a million yuan and become the landlord of an illicit recycling market, renting out stalls to two dozen migrant entrepreneurs, all of whom, like him, came from Henan's Gushi county—the rural county with the largest population in all of China, a low land per capita ratio, and a high rate of poverty. Lu's career can serve as a tour of the sector's economic geography, supply networks, and internal stratification.

Boss Lu started, as most did, at the entry-level job of a collector—the most common, least lucrative, and most strenuous rung in the trade. The poorest collectors could not afford bike-carts and had no money to buy recyclables from residents or businesses, so they scavenged along streets, picking from waste bins and construction sites, lugging sacks on their backs or on bamboo carrying poles. Such scavenging is unhealthful and dirty, but on the positive side, there are no business expenses and everything found can be sold for pure profit. Scavenging on foot was generally a transitional activity for those new to the city and lacking any money or connections; those who did it on a long-term basis were mainly elderly migrants and those unable to handle the physical demands of bike-cart collection.

Bypassing the scavenging stage, Lu jumped directly into work as a roaming bike-cart collector, a "pedaler" (*deng che de*, sometimes translated into English as "recyclist"), cycling through the city looking for scrap to buy. A few pedalers prefer to roam, specializing perhaps in collecting discarded appliances (the highest end kind of residential scrap); but most bike-cart collectors try to establish a collection route and build up a clientele of familiar residents, shops, and businesses until they have customary control over a certain building or turf, at which point they become fixed-point or community collectors. Posted by their office building, shopping area, or apartment complex, community collectors invariably make informal contracts with building managers and, whenever possible, with local police so as to avoid being harassed by them (more on this later). There are no days off; rain or shine, collectors need to maintain a constant presence to secure their turf. Buying scrap from residents at one price (60 cents a kilo for newspaper, 10 cents per PET [polyethylene terephthalate] bottle, etc.), then pedaling it to the edge of town and selling it at the depot for a slightly higher price (70 cents per kilo of newspaper, 11 cents per bottle), collectors' incomes are nothing but the accumulation of those tiny price differences. Some locations are more lucrative than others; in the late 1990s a collector's income could range from 500 to 3,000 yuan monthly, and he or she could save anywhere from 2,000 to 20,000 yuan a year.[22] By the late 1990s every city block, residential compound, and workplace in Beijing was served by a migrant collector, weaving a collection network far denser and more convenient for residents than anything the BRC had ever provided, even in its heyday.

The three-wheel bike-cart (*sanlunche*) was the icon of the recycling trade, defining recycling's public presence and shaping its economic geography and recyclers' daily routines. Each day at dawn collectors pedaled their empty carts (maybe with a spouse or helper on board) from their enclaves at the city's edge to their collection sites in town, commutes that could range from a few kilometers to more than twenty. The entire day would be spent never too far from the cart: weighing and sorting scrap by its side, repeatedly reorganizing and reloading the cart, eating lunch with feet up on the handlebars, stretching out on the cart bed for an afternoon nap, and finally around sunset roping down loads for the ride back out of town. An (over)loaded bike-cart could hold materials piled two meters (six and a half feet) high and weighing more than 200 kilos (441 pounds), and the thousands of recyclers making their return trek during evening rush hour were a public spectacle of endurance (see figure 8). They were the backbone of Beijing's recycling sector, the conduit through which huge tonnages were sorted, packed, and shipped daily. Though recyclers might spend the whole day stationed in a toney neighborhood

FIGURE 8. Informal bike-cart recycler pedaling out to the Beijing suburbs during evening rush hour with a load of mixed recycling. The sign on his handlebars states that he pays high prices for used appliances and provides his cell phone number. Photo by Chen Liwen, 2016. Used with permission.

downtown, their days ended (closer to midnight than dusk) where they began: on the peri-urban outskirts of the city, in the jerrybuilt shacks of migrant enclaves crowded among the grunge of scrap heaps.

After two years as a bike collector, Boss Lu had saved enough cash to open his own wastepaper stall at Wohu Bridge. The economic risks (theft, dislocation, confiscation of goods, fire) were daunting, but the potential returns could be life changing. The seed capital required was substantial: rent for the stall space (10,000–15,000 yuan a year) and a shack to work/live in (1,000–2,000 yuan), a few thousand in ready cash to buy loads from collectors, pay for a few workers (200–500 yuan monthly for each), a business license (a few thousand), and a truck for long-distance hauling (used trucks ran 15,000–20,000 yuan). A stall trader/broker was called a "boss" and was said to have a "sitting" job, but in this case sitting was still far from restful.[23] Stall bosses did not just work in their tiny stall shacks, they lived in them. Work ran 24/7. The busiest time was when the wave of collectors returned from town, from about 6 p.m. to midnight. But recyclers might come by at any time with a big load, and then there were the hours spent processing materials (sort and bale the paper; remove labels and caps from thousands of bottles, etc.), negotiating with buyers, and loading trucks. Moreover, with no protection from the Beijing police, bosses needed to live in their stalls to guard them. With their handful of workers (often just a family member or two), stall bosses spent their days and nights always on duty, catnapping when they could.

Street collectors are relatively immune from price shifts (they buy every form of scrap, and they can adjust the buying and selling price to match the market price), but a stall boss is essentially a small commodities broker heavily invested in one specific material. A big lurch in prices can mean hitting the jackpot or losing one's shirt. Prices climbed rapidly from 1990 to 1994, and Lu did well. In 1992 the city demolished the Henan recyclers' enclave at Wohu Bridge, and the community moved to the Bajia area in Haidian a few kilometers farther from the city center. Lu opened a paper stall in Bajia, but the real money was in metals. The metals trade was still closely guarded by the state in the 1990s, and migrants were banned from getting permits. In order to sell directly to factories, Lu needed an industry insider with Beijing residency, a *tiezhao* in recycler lingo (lit. iron license), to front for him. The license itself cost tens of thousands of yuan, and the sweeteners to the front man cost several thousand per transaction, but Lu made so much money that when he was fined 300,000 yuan for trafficking stolen iron, he was able to pay off the fine just days later in cash.[24]

By the time I met Boss Lu in 2000 he had reached the highest rung in the sector, landlord of his own market, a "big boss": someone with enough economic and social capital to do all the negotiating necessary to open a market and whom other migrant recyclers followed to new turf when the Beijing authorities kicked them down the road. Informal scrap markets never lasted long. Many occupied demolition sites; the same waves of creative destruction tearing down the BRC recycling shops cratered the city with debris fields that made ideal sites for temporary informal recycling markets. Because such spaces were just taken as is, the layouts were often chaotic. Little if any physical infrastructure was installed: paved yards were a rarity; roofing was unheard of; and stalls were separated, if at all, by squat unmortared brick walls. Still, these spaces served their purpose, providing bike collectors with a contained space in which an array of brokers could buy up the various materials they had collected during the day: paper at this stall, ferrous here, copper, plastic bottles, glass, and so forth. Each stall paid a monthly rent to the market boss, anywhere from 1,200 to 7,500 yuan per month, depending mainly on a stall's size and the kind of material it traded.

Lu gave me a tour of his market in Haidian (see figure 9). The twenty-plus "stalls" looked to me more like piles of junk sliding into each other and blocking the market's mud-pitted road. It looked unmanaged, but Lu, having once been in a junkyard fire, was a stickler for fire safety; he strictly forbade smoking and had

FIGURE 9. Boss Lu's scrap market, located in Haidian between the third and fourth ring road, active November 1998–August 2000. Photo by author.

equipped every stall with a fire extinguisher. Indeed, there was a big water tower right in the middle of the market, and during my visit on a stifling summer day, paper piles were being watered down, according to Lu, to prevent spontaneous combustion. Then again, watering down paper was also a common cheat used by paper brokers to make their shipments heavier.

It was July; the market was going to be bulldozed in August. Lu had run it for twenty-one months, longer than any market or stall he had opened since 1990. He said his contract extended for a few more years, but the district was trying to drive him out by endlessly piling on new fees and fines. Real estate prices were soaring, the district clearly had a more attractive and profitable plan for this space, and it was not hard to see why they wanted Lu out.

It was difficult to look at Lu's market and not feel that the government had good reason to view migrant markets as health and safety hazards fostering illicit activity. By 2000 migrant recyclers had decisively taken over Beijing's recycling sector and were providing a valuable free service to the city. They collected and recycled about 20–35 percent of its MSW and thereby saved huge amounts of landfill space; recovered about $1 billion in materials to supply manufacturing; and put money into Beijing residents' pockets by paying them for their wastes. Yet despite these contributions to Beijing's sanitation and wealth, their markets could easily be confused for trash dumps, and the Beijing authorities, as well as most Beijing residents, treated migrant recyclers as an urban nuisance if not as scheming criminals.

That was so because, in many ways, migrant recyclers, by virtue of their very existence in Beijing, were criminals. The household registration (*hukou*) system defined their very presence in Beijing as questionable if not illegal. The specifics of household registration regulations have changed a great deal and a great many times between the mid-1980s and today, and registration status shapes so many aspects of daily life (access to housing, education, health care) and economic activity (licenses for anything—running a business, owning a car, using a bike-cart in the city, contracting land, even [in the early 2000s] registering a cell phone) that it is impossible to list them all here.[25] But it is even less possible to understand how the migrant recycling system evolved and functioned without recognizing that migrants' lives in Beijing have been (and still are) profoundly shaped by second-class citizenship, vulnerable legal status, and social discrimination.

It was technically possible to exist as a legally self-employed migrant in Beijing in the 1990s, but only if one could manage to jump through all the hoops. In 1999, for example, migrants needed four types of identification to work in Beijing legally: a national identity card, a temporary residence permit (about 200 RMB), a work permit (also 200 RMB), and a health card issued by an assigned hospital.[26] Each document was provided by a different bureau, and work permits were particularly tricky to get as recyclers often had no work unit or boss to vouch for them. But these four documents were hardly enough to work as a recycling entrepreneur. Pedalers needed licenses to bring their three-wheeled carts into the city but were frequently denied them; truck and car licenses were available only to Beijing residents. But even if one managed to accomplish all this, registering one's own recycling business was still legally impossible for migrants because recycling was listed by the government as a "special industry" (*teshu hangye*) requiring registration with the public security bureau, for which only permanent residents were eligible. Any market stall or processing business was unregistered or falsely created under a Beijing resident's name. Indeed, finding collaborators among Beijing locals willing to illegally rent spaces, lend their identities, trade materials against work unit rules, and so forth was necessary at almost every step in the migrant recycling trade in the 1980s and 1990s.

All these ways in which *hukou* obstructed the working side of migrant recyclers' lives do not even skim the surface of how it shaped access to things like health care and education. As an example, in theory children living full time in Beijing should have been able to attend Beijing public schools, and a 1998 national law created extra funding for schools that enrolled migrant children. But in fact most Beijing schools concocted "unwritten rules" to exclude migrant children or charged "sponsorship fees" of several thousand to tens of thousands of yuan a year for children lacking Bejiing *hukou* (children with Beijing *hukou* attended school for free). Migrant communities had little choice but to organize their own community-run schools; by 2000 a survey put the number of these schools at around two hundred, serving perhaps forty thousand students. Conditions were generally bare-bones, disorganized, and unstable; these schools had no legal status, were uncertified, and could be summarily closed by the authorities.[27] Rural migrants might well have had their own reasons for preferring to live together in enclaves—shared dialect, cultural habits, kin and work networks—but *hukou* policies made the enclave an imperative of protection and survival.

Discrimination against migrants was not confined to a technocratic maze of red tape; most traumatizing for recycling communities was the custody and repatriation system (*shourong qiansong*). Introduced in 1982, allegedly to help urban authorities shepherd beggars, orphans, and the destitute back to their hometowns, custody and repatriation regulations gave urban authorities the power to detain and deport any migrant lacking a temporary residence permit. In 1991 those powers were expanded to allow police to expel any of the "three noes": no temporary residence permit, no work permit, or no state ID. As the nation's capital, Beijing had a heavy responsibility to serve as China's model of orderliness and culture, and state media praised the city for its generous contribution to custody and repatriation work in 1997:

> Beijing especially has ceaselessly worked to clean up and rectify rental housing, clear out members of the "three noes" and clear out and rectify recycling collectors, junk markets, dance halls, sauna massage parlors and other messy businesses and migrant population enclaves. . . . Through these special clean up and rectification methods, last year 300,000 migrants (*waidi ren*) have been motivated to leave the city, and nearly 100,000 "three noes" have been through Custody and Repatriation leading to over 5000 migrant criminal suspects being detained.[28]

Authorities used custody and repatriation to engage in migrant profiling, performing sweeps of migrant communities to check for papers, then using their mass detention as a pretext to probe for any possible criminality.[29] The "success" of this process in turning up criminal suspects fed the stereotype that migrants were responsible for most of Beijing's criminal activity, thereby justifying more profiling: a self-fulfilling cycle of discrimination. This stereotype prevailed despite the fact that almost every act of supposed illegality by migrant recyclers (renting unpermitted housing and yards, using fake licenses, bribing industrial units to buy and sell scrap to them rather than the BRC) involved Beijing residents and SOE managers as counterparts and accomplices.[30]

Custody and repatriation served as a pretext for terrorizing migrant enclaves. Its enforcement was usually handled not by public security officers, but by joint-defense teams (*lianfang dui*), "grassroots" nonprofessional police assistants who earned less than half a regular police officer's salary and were subject to much lower disciplinary standards. Their night raids on migrant enclaves gave aspiring vigilantes a chance to flex their muscles and extort some cash. During a visit in 2010, my oldest friends in Beijing's migrant recycler community, Mr. X and his wife (Mr. X repeatedly told me not to name him), shared stories with me and some friends about the 1990s:

Mr. X: I don't want to say bad things about my country, but those days, they don't deserve to be called days. After Jiang Zemin rose it got really bad, they didn't see us as people. Before you'd be at home getting a moment rest, eating a little, drinking a little, someone would say they saw the cops coming and no one cared. But then it changed, someone would say "cops" and everyone would immediately start running, like that.

Friend 1: They policed you while you ate?

Mr. X: (a bit bugged at being misunderstood): You wanted to eat [or relax] but you didn't dare, [you were always afraid] they'd arrest you. Back then there was shourong [custody and repatriation], they had the shourong law to deal with migrants (waidi ren). They'd grab a bunch of us, 5, 6, 4 folks, and tie us up together like the Japanese invasion, like in those war movies (laughter).

Me: So in shourong did they send you home, or what did they do?

Mr. X: They . . . ahh, shourong . . . talking about it makes me upset. We had no kind of rights.

Me: Why do you think they did it? What was their reason for arresting you?

Mr. X: They'd say it was their assignment. They were supposed to arrest so many so they got so many. . . .

Mrs. X: At the time we hadn't even finished middle school. . . . We were school sweethearts, we didn't graduate.

Mr X: What graduate? We didn't have food to eat, how could we graduate?

Mrs. X: We couldn't go to school, we had to go work, go work.

Friend 2: When did you come to Beijing?

Mr. X: Before the [1990] Asian Games. When the Asian games were coming they rounded up all the migrants to send them home. Not allowed in Beijing; no good if you don't leave. Then shourong was really intense. . . . [T]hey packed trucks, every day there were several tens of trucks hauling people away.

Mrs. X: Today we're equal, there isn't this "outsider"/"local" differentiation. . . .

Mr. X: [W]e're still not the same. . . .

Mrs. X: I feel like it's a lot better than before.

Mr. X: It's still not good, there's just a lot of foreigners around, they worry foreigners will take pictures (*laughter*).

Me: So with the police so fierce, what did you do to protect yourself?

Mr. X: Simple, we ran! (*laughter*). She (indicating his wife) could really run!

Mrs. X: You mean that time ... when we couldn't get our temporary permit?

Mr. X: We had one, they just ripped it up.

Mrs. X: Sometimes they'd rip it up, sometimes. ... [B]ut that time it was his mother who got me started, she ...

Mr X: My mom was an old woman ...

Mrs. X: I had just had our second child, his mom came up to help us out. I remember one day she thought she saw the cops coming and just took off running. I saw her, I took off too. We both jumped into that big ditch to hide (*laughter*). She was here for a few months. She got a job where she was paid in meals not cash ...

Mr. X: That way they don't let you leave. She was an old lady, working every day for weeks, just crying. She wanted to die. She swore to never come back to Beijing.[31]

In a survey among Beijing recyclers that I conducted in 2010 with the invaluable help of several volunteers from Nature University, fourteen of twenty-nine respondents who had been working as recyclers in the 1990s had been through custody and repatriation at least once. Some were apprehended for not carrying their papers or lacking a bike-cart license, but most said police did not care if they had papers or not, they were still detained. Often it was just a ploy to extort money from them; at other times folks were sent home.[32] Physical abuse was all too common; indeed, the custody and repatriation system finally ended in 2003 after a highly publicized scandal in which a college student named Sun Zhigang was beaten to death while in custody.

It is not surprising that under these conditions migrant gangs emerged, serving both predatory and protective functions. Boss Lu told me he had had a few run-ins with gangs over the years, but that by the late 1990s he was too powerful to mess with. At one market in Haidian in 2000, a stall boss I knew said a gang was extorting 50 yuan on every loaded truck leaving the area; the stall bosses knew that the local police were getting a cut of the money, so they decided not to argue and just paid the fee.[33] But the stall boss also told me that the very same gang was the first to learn of the city's plan to build the fourth ring road right through the middle of the market, and the gang's leaders had hunted down a plot of land for a new market where everyone could relocate—applying strong-arm tactics to prevent splitters.[34] Recyclers rarely discussed gangs with me, but it seemed clear from people's routine behaviors (like sleeping at one's collection turf or stall to guard it) that the threat of theft and physical violence was part of their everyday risk calculations. It is also worth noting that free market entrepreneurialism in the 1980s and 1990s often involved a degree of risk-taking that blurred into a variety of transgressive and even illegal activities; in these years opening restaurants, bars, hair salons, dance clubs, and similar businesses also often involved mixing with what was often called "black society" (*heishehui*).[35]

Wang Weiping, a waste management engineer and a deputy director of the Beijing Commerce Bureau, who produced the only attempted comprehensive study of Beijing's informal recycling sector in these years, enjoyed warning me about the gangs. Wang's 1998 study did not use a survey or statistical models; he mainly relied on interviews with leading members of the informal recycling community, whom he insisted, relishing the mystique, were all gang bosses. Whatever the case, Wang's figures about the sector rang true. He estimated that in 1998 Beijing had eighty-two thousand migrant collectors reclaiming around 800,000 tons of recyclable metals, paper, and plastics and generating over 930 million yuan in profits every year. In addition to bike collectors and scrap markets, his survey described landfill scavenging (fifteen hundred pickers ruled by Boss Du Maozhou of Bazhong, Sichuan) and the gutter oil (*digou you*) trade, in which waste grease from restaurant fryers, grease traps, and sewer drains was collected, processed, and repackaged as cooking oil. (The trade continued into the 2010s and is documented in Wang Jiuliang's film *City Besieged by Waste*).[36]

Wang Weiping's report repeated familiar stereotypes ("we all know, the majority of crimes in Beijing are caused by migrants") but also made the case that migrant recyclers were performing a valuable service for the city.[37] A similar approach became common in other Beijing government documents by the late 1990s:

> [O]n the one hand [they] really did patch up the problem as our recycling network was shriveling. . . . Their cultural quality is low (*suzhi di*), 80% are peasants, they are motivated by personal profit, and their unlawful and undisciplined [behavior] seriously disrupts the safety and economic order of our capital's society. . . . Especially in suburban districts (Chaoyang, Fengtai, Haidian) they gather in "trash heaps," their recycling markets are chaotic, dirty and degraded, bereft of any municipal management. Migrant populations mingle here giving rise to grave and despicable situations. The district authorities ceaselessly chase them away, and they ceaselessly re-emerge. There are none who do not engage in casual theft (*shunshou qianyang*), deal in stolen goods (*shou dao jiehe*). . . . [T]heir criminal activities are endless, public utilities are frequently destroyed, seriously disturbing the capital's economic and social order.[38]

Other documents describe migrant recyclers as "persistently breaking laws and violating regulations. Tax evasion, bribery, theft, and destruction of public property . . . of every kind are plentiful."[39] Like an infestation, migrant recyclers made "even the Public Security and Commerce Departments feel helpless, for although they undertake cleanups three to four times every year, in the end, they do not decrease, but rather increase."[40] Indeed, it became common to refer to migrant recyclers as *huishou youjidui*—recycling guerrilla forces—a pretty ironic metaphor given the CCP's own history. If the story had been told from the migrant perspective it would likely have been one of constantly being uprooted and pushed ever further out from the city center year after year. Our 2010 survey found that stall bosses who had been in Beijing since the 1990s had moved on average six times and often ten times. "Every time you move, that year is just breaking even; you don't make any money until the second or third year at a new place," Mrs. X told me.[41]

THE STATE CHANGES TACTICS: FROM MONOPOLIZING TRADE TO COLLECTING RENTS

By 1998 the municipal-level BRC was mothballed, and the recycling guerrilla forces had won. But as any student of China's modern economy can tell you, SOEs rarely die; they become zombies. The BRC's district-level companies spent the late 1990s reorganizing themselves as smaller shareholder companies and soldiered on under new names: Haidian's company became Kaiyuan, Chongwen's became Tiantianjie, Chaoyang's became Zhongxing and then later Dongdu Zhongxing, and so forth. Each still had some real estate and some equipment as assets; each was still charged with the task of managing recycling in its respective administrative territory; each still advised the district and city governments on how to manage the sector; and each still received assistance in accessing loans and key assets (like land) for its ventures. Many of those ventures were a waste of state funds. The BRC's undead children floated an array of pilot projects aimed at reviving their businesses. The Xicheng district tried providing separate bins for recyclables throughout the district; everything of value was quickly removed by scavengers regardless of which bin it was thrown in. Fengtai tried door-to-door collection, but it proved inordinately expensive.[42] One of the first ideas that turned a profit came out of Chaoyang Zhongxing Recycling.

In 1997 the Chaoyang district government set the goal of demolishing every single migrant recycling market in the district. At the end of the year the district Urban Renewal Office reported on its progress:

> Since 1997 our district . . . has eliminated over 100 recycling stands and rubbish markets, making a great improvement to our district's environment. But [this] did not cause petty recyclers to naturally die off. Instead, in places like Dongfeng village and Mazidian you no longer see a slew of independent recycling traders, but these petty hawkers have adopted the tactic of "retreat from the streets, enter the villages; retreat from the streets, enter the households" and are renting peasant yards to do their trade, creating a new cause of pollution and unsafety. Though these new stalls are smaller in scale, they are more numerous than they were before the clean-up.[43]

The district's frontal assault on the "guerrilla forces" had proved futile.[44] So Chao-yang revised its strategy; if you can't beat 'em, join 'em. Rather than trying to wipe out the informal sector, Chaoyang would become their landlords instead. Chaoyang Zhongxing company would build its own recycling markets and rent stalls to migrants. The authorities would still keep hounding and demolishing migrant markets, but now the goal was to chase migrant recyclers into the arms of the company's safe havens rather than to eliminate them. The Chaoyang company would not do any recycling itself; instead, it would use its status as the state's designated recycler to extract rent from the informal system and present this as a form of urban environmental management. The plan cost 25 million yuan for construction of six market sites and mobilized the concerted efforts of Beijing's public security, commerce, urban planning, and finance bureaus, together with the cooperation of several municipal committees.[45]

In 1999 Chaoyang Zhongxing went into business as the district's exclusively licensed junkyard landlord, its six markets renting out stalls to about 250 migrant scrap dealers. At the largest model market in Yaojiayuan, the grounds were completely paved and walled off from public view; stalls were of uniform size, partitioned by brick walls, and laid out along wide lanes for truck access. There was a separate housing area with single-room quarters and shared bathrooms for migrant workers, as well as offices for market management. According to Ms. Tian, manager of the model market, the company recouped its 25 million yuan investment in less than two years, entirely by collecting stall and housing rents.[46] From the perspective of the recyclers, the company's markets were somewhat less conveniently located than some of the former migrant-run sites (some of which had been located closer to downtown), and the stall rents were slightly higher. But there were perks: the company facilitated stall bosses and their employees' applications for housing, work, and health permits, using its bureaucratic connections to competitive advantage. And the market offered a stable and well-organized site to do business; getting trucks in and out on paved lanes free of debris was a convenience everyone appreciated.

Manager Tian held up the fact that Chaoyang Zhongxing's market was tidier and better managed than those run by migrants as evidence of the superiority of state management. But it was a bogus argument. A week earlier I had visited a market designed along almost identical lines to Chaoyang's model market, built by Boss Lu. After showing me his condemned market in Haidian, Lu had taken me to his new site. Having been forced to move on average about once a year, Lu was all too familiar with the drill of scrambling to find another market space, each time a bit farther from the city center. So this time Lu, always a risk taker, was moving his two dozen loyal stall bosses and their workers more than twenty kilometers west, to the distant suburb of Shijingshan. He had to pay 50,000 yuan a year for the business permit and 200,000 yearly in rent, but he considered it a bargain because the local government gave him a twenty-year contract on the land. The site was still under construction when we visited: systematically laid out and fully paved, with partitioned stalls of uniform size, wide lanes, and a truck scale. Each stall had electricity, running water, and a fire extinguisher. Lu spent about 6 million yuan on construction. Clearly the squalor of Lu's previous markets had had nothing to do with ignorance of how to build and manage a market; the miserable conditions of his early sites were simply a reflection of economic rationality. Facing unrelenting administrative discrimination and the threat that one could be summarily evicted at any time, it would be idiocy to invest any money (let alone millions) in market infrastructure. The chaotic mess of migrant markets was a direct reflection of the fact that their enterprises lacked any security whatsoever—it was, in other words, the result of discriminatory policy, not peasant mentality.

Migrant stall bosses at Chaoyang Zhongxing's market seemed content to work there; the only thing they complained about to me was the training courses they were required to attend in order to rent there. The courses were meant to raise their *suzhi*, or "quality." Several scholars have explored the functioning of "*suzhi* discourse" and its relation to China's postreform neoliberal developmentalism, so I simply assume here that the reader can readily grasp that the term posits the disturbing idea that some groups of people are of objectively higher "quality" than others.[47] As one *Beijing Daily* article published at that time bluntly claimed, "Naturally the *suzhi* of state-owned enterprise employees is much higher than that of small migrant peddlers."[48] To raise their *suzhi*, Zhongxing's tenants were required to take classes including "environmental protection consciousness education; education on the duty of paying commercial fees and taxes; obeying the capital's public security laws; education in how to behave as a qualified citizen of the capital; professional morals; and education in the usefulness of and environmental conservation brought about through recycling resources."[49] Most recyclers I talked to found these classes laughable. As far as they were concerned, Beijing residents produced enormous amounts of trash but were too lazy to do the work to clean it up. Yet according to the authorities, it was migrants who lacked environmental awareness, a claim supposedly proven by the fact that they rummaged through trash bins, congregated in filthy markets, squatted in shanties, obstructed traffic with their carts, and reputedly bilked customers and traded in stolen goods.

In the late 1990s, environmental consciousness was becoming a requisite part of the proper performance of citizenship and possessing high *suzhi*. In part this was a reaction to the growing urgency of China's environmental problems, as runaway industrial expansion was taking an alarming toll on the environment. An added dimension making those alarm bells ring all the louder was that complaints to the

FIGURE 10. Business billboard outside a small scrap market on the north edge of Bajia in Beijing's Haidian district, 2000. Photo by author.

government about pollution issues were rapidly increasing (from 100,000 letters in 1997 to 400,000 in 2002), and such complaints were at times developing into protests.[50] In this context, migrant collectors were said to have taken recycling—that reliable, honest, and patriotic practice of the Mao era—and turned it into a "polluting profession" (*wuran hangye*)."[51] There was very little space in public life or state-run media for migrants to refute this narrative, but while doing fieldwork in 2000 I did stumble upon one effort at a public response to these accusations in the form of a sign that some migrants posted in front of their small scrap market in Bajia (see figure 10). I was unable to get all the words in my shot, but my translation fills in the missing characters (which are easy for any Chinese speaker to guess): "We are not in this for the [money]. We do this to protect our national [environment]" (我们不是为了[赚钱], 我们是保护国家[环境]).

GEARING UP FOR THE OLYMPIC BID

The substitution of state markets for informal ones helped Chaoyang tidy up the problem of renegade waste markets, but it did nothing to solve the unappealing sight of countless unmanaged recyclists roaming Beijing's streets and alleys every day collecting and scavenging scrap. "Our next goal," announced Chaoyang Zhongxing in February 2000, "is to regulate and manage the more than 20,000 roaming collectors [in Chaoyang District], to arrive at having them use uniform vehicles, uniform scales, uniform work clothes, uniform service standards, and uniform collection of item-types, and thereby thoroughly eliminate the traditional 'junk king' phenomenon."[52]

The timing of Chaoyang's proposal was fortuitous. Beijing had just participated in the first round of bidding for the 2008 Olympics. With the International Olympic Committee's vetting process now underway, Beijing officials were eager to create convincing proposals to prove they were committed to combating pollution and providing an environmentally friendly setting for a Green Olympics in 2008.

Based on Chaoyang's initiative, the city convened a group of recycling consultants dubbed the Beijing Materials Recycling Industry Association and tasked them with drafting a blueprint for a comprehensive urban recycling network to be made official policy. Their plan, "the implementation plan for promoting and standardizing the construction of a neighborhood resource recycling system in Beijing," bore the imprimatur of nine city agency and committee seals (commerce, planning, spiritual culture, labor and social insurance, public security, finance, etc.) and was approved to much media fanfare on June 5, 2001, a month before the Olympic Committee's final vote.[53]

I was in Beijing the summer of 2001 as the new network plan was being trumpeted. A *Beijing Youth News* article on the plan ran under the headline: "Banishing the Junk Kings—Their Shouting Will No Longer Be Allowed":

> Those troops of migrant scrap collectors who roam the streets and alleyways will soon fade from Beijing peoples' lives, replaced by a government built, unified, city-wide recycling network. This reporter learned from the Beijing Commerce Committee that the city's eight districts will build 1800 recycling kiosks, about one for every 1000-1500 households. . . . For residents these recycling stalls will be easy to distinguish: all will have the same signage, the same prices, identical scales and measures. Residents will no longer have to worry about the cheating scales so commonly encountered today.[54]

The plan was based on a model being piloted in a comfortable Chaoyang neighborhood by a company called Zhouji Environmental Technology. Zhouji was launched in November 2000; by June 2001 it employed more than ninety migrant collectors and had erected a few fresh-looking blue kiosks in the neighborhood. Zhouji's CEO, Mr. C, welcomed me to his office for an interview. A bronze plaque issued by the city proclaiming Zhouji a "civilizing" and "greening" social influence hung behind his desk. Zhouji's strategy was simple: the company hired the migrant recyclers who were already working in the neighborhood and were familiar figures to residents; issued them a standard set of carts, scales, and uniforms; assigned them regimented work hours and strictly defined turf; and required them to buy recyclables at posted company prices and to sell everything they collected to the company at company-dictated prices.

This model was, of course, preposterous. An informal collector's profit came solely from the differential between the buying and selling price, and Zhouji was taking a cut of that already tiny differential. One employee I interviewed, who had worked in the neighborhood for three years before Zhouji arrived, said he usually brought home to Henan about 5,000 yuan each Spring Festival, but he would be lucky to bring half that now that Zhouji was in charge. I asked him why he joined the company at all: Did it give him greater legitimacy, make his work easier, or pay for his work and housing permits? No, he replied. The only reason he was a Zhouji employee was that he had no choice. The residential compound he worked in contained more than one hundred five-story apartment buildings, but it was completely encircled in walls and fences with only a few well-policed gates, and Zhouji, with the city's support, was keeping the compound closed to noncompany collectors. He either joined Zhouji or lost his turf.[55]

Mr. C showed me the company's list of rules. In its eight months of operation, Zhouji had compiled a six-page list of offenses for which workers could be docked—a list Mr. C told me arose entirely from incidents that transpired with employees: no uniform, 10 yuan; late to work, 50 yuan; sell to other buyers, 200–1,000 yuan first offense, 500–3,000 second offense; hawking (the telltale sign of a "junk king" mentality), 15 yuan; allowing noncompany collectors into company turf, 50 yuan; and colluding with noncompany collectors, 500–3,000 yuan.[56] By August, Zhouji already employed eight roving inspectors, whose job was simply to enforce these rules.[57] Asked if the cost of hiring so many monitors might not make it even harder for Zhouji to turn a profit, Mr. C replied, quite rationally, that the success or failure of his company depended solely on whether it could enforce a leak-proof monopoly on the recyclables in its turf.[58]

Predictably, it could not, and Zhouji fizzled out within another year. The city's fantasy of imposing such a monopoly across all of Beijing met a similar fate, leaving the shells of a few hundred abandoned recycling kiosks scattered about the city. No matter; Beijing, having publicized its commitment to recycling and a green Olympics, won its Olympic bid in July 2001. The policy lessons were fairly clear; staging these green efforts might play well to international committees, but in practical terms the city government's ability to monopolize the use of urban space had its limits. State-affiliated recycling companies could play the role of landlords to migrant recycling brokers and, with significant effort, a coordinated mobilization of urban bureaus and police could squeeze informal recycling markets. But the authorities could not stop migrants from moving through the city and could not stop the goods they carried from moving with them. Plots of land could be owned and rented, and thereby profits could be extracted from the economic activities transpiring on those plots of land, but scrap commodities themselves remained beyond the state and its companies' control, indeed beyond its reach.

CONCLUSION: THE REGIONAL METABOLISM
OF INFORMAL RECYCLING

Seeing the Chaoyang company's scrap market turn a quick and tidy profit, other state-owned district companies quickly followed suit. Haidian opened a fifty-stall market just beyond the third ring road in 1999, quickly filling it with rent-paying migrant brokers. It seemed like a winning formula: spend a few million yuan to pave a yard and divvy it into stalls, and in less than two years you were making pure profit. But by 2004 both the Haidian and Chaoyang companies' markets were bulldozed. The shock waves of land development spreading from the city center had caught up with them. When I visited the Haidian company's markets in 2000, a compound of twenty-story high-end apartments was already going up, with balconies looking right down into the yard. Haidian and Chaoyang had been outer districts in the 1970s; by 2000 they were being enveloped in Beijing's urban core. In a flash, scrap market rents went from looking like fast money to being a waste of prime real estate. It became clear that the city's state-owned recycling companies were not going to dictate the geography of Beijing's recycling system; the real estate market was.

It was fortuitous, then, that at the end of 2002 the State Council canceled a batch of 789 national-level regulations governing an array of businesses, ceding its oversight to lower levels of government, including over recycling. A few months later Beijing removed recycling from its list of "special industries," and the requirement for administrative examination and approval of scrap markets and businesses was canceled.[59] All this is to say, it was suddenly much easier for a peri-urban village to decide to open independent (non-state-owned) recycling markets, and municipal authorities no longer had a mandate to destroy them. This change made it safer for entrepreneurs to invest in building non-state recycling markets and safer for migrants to live and work in them. Of course by 2003 building a scrap market almost anywhere inside the fifth ring road was bound to be a losing investment (land prices and rents were simply too high to sustain one), but for townships and villages out beyond the fifth ring road, in rural districts like Changping, Daxing, and Tongzhou, recycling markets were still tremendously lucrative. A small investment in a scrap yard not only yielded stall rents, it also brought in thousands of pedalers and other recycling workers needing cheap rental housing, stores, and restaurants, all of which would pay rents to local administrative units. The post-2003 recycling enclaves that would emerge beyond the fifth ring were often of such a scale that the scholar Tong Xin has dubbed them "waste cities."[60]

Security for the migrant community improved in another way after 2003 as well. Soon after becoming president of the PRC, Hu Jintao put an end to custody and repatriation. The *lianfang dui* (joint-defense forces) quickly faded from the scene; raids ceased. Of course there were still other urban policing forces to contend with, particularly the *chengguan* (short for Chengshi guanli xingzheng zhifa ju, Urban Administrative and Law Enforcement Bureau), which also had a reputation for harassing migrants, street vendors, and recyclers, but all the recyclers I talked to felt that after 2003 the *chengguan* became less combative as well. Moreover, with the decline in police violence and extortion, the power of gangs within the recycling community all but evaporated because their protection racket was no longer workable or needed. This is not to say that informal recyclers were now granted legitimacy by the municipal government, were supported in their work by the state, or were treated like stakeholders in urban waste management; they were not. But there is no question that life for recyclers in the decade following these reforms (the subject of chapter 7) was far less colored by the constant threat of violence.

Recycling does not stop with collection; it is only a functioning and profitable system when it loops materials into manufacturing. By 2000, Beijing's informal recycling system was making an impressive regional footprint, fueling the growth of processing hubs particularly in the surrounding counties of Hebei. Beijing's wastepaper flowed to the Baoding area, particularly to poorly regulated Mancheng county, which became home to more than one hundred small, often highly polluting paper mills; higher-quality cardboard and newspaper were typically shipped out to bigger plants in Shandong that produced export-quality goods. Beijing's ferrous scrap, the by-product of Beijing's waves of demolition, at first went to feed the enormous Capital Steel complex, but by 2000 it was increasingly shipped out to Hebei's Tangshan, where it supplied scores of small electric-arc furnace enterprises. Waste plastics, growing in quantity at a breakneck pace, gravitated to the rural Hebei county of Wenan, about two hours south of Beijing, where by the early 2000s an estimated ten thousand small plastic processors were sorting, shredding, washing, pelletizing, and remolding what was fast approaching a million tons of scrap resin annually. Some of these processing hubs had historical links to earlier metabolic flows; since at least the early 1920s Baoding region paper mills had survived on Beijing-sourced wastepaper and fiber. And Beijing was not unique; pretty much every city in China went through a process similar to that described in this chapter, so by the early 2000s informal migrant recyclers, despite lacking any large-scale organization to help coordinate their activities, had essentially replaced the state's recycling sector with their own informal network.

By contrast, the SMC's system—which in the Mao era had cast an enormous web of collection networks across the entire nation, reaching into almost every neighborhood in every city in China—had disintegrated. In the terms once used by the state recycling bureaucracy, "society" recycling had been completely usurped by informal migrants. In the industrial sector, once the SMC recycling companies lost their exclusive rights to manage scrap trading between state units, they were quickly cut out of the industrial scrap trade; most factories, foundries, and mines simply started trading with one another rather than through SMC or Materials Bureau channels. But the SMC and Materials Bureau were still the bureaucratic parents of all their state-owned recycling company zombie offspring (Chaoyang Zhongxing, Chongwen Tiantianjie, etc.) throughout the country. In 1993 hundreds of these recycling companies organized into the Chinese Resources Recycling Association (CRRA). In 2001 the CRRA hosted its first international conference for the industry. But as US scrap traders told me, the CRRA conference was not the important scrap trade conference in China; the association that had more clout in the international metals markets was the CMRA, the China Nonferrous Metals Industry Association, Recycling Metal Branch. The old rivalry between commerce and industry continued.

In Beijing, the district-level offspring of the BRC kept experimenting with various strategies to get back into the game. The clever managers at Chaoyang Zhongxing opened a profitable baling station, changed the company's name again, to Beijing Dongdu Zhongxing, and tried their hands at an industrial park in Hebei (see chapter 7). Haidian Kaiyuan spent about a decade and several million yuan trying to create a directory of registered (migrant) collectors whose services could be ordered via a website, but the idea, which in many ways anticipated what the government is trying to do today (see chapter 8), included no mechanism by which it could generate any revenue. In 2007 Chongwen Tiantianjie (TTJ) spent 4 million yuan in city funds on a collection service for high-end apartments and offices, resulting in a staff of forty workers and managers collecting ten tons of recyclables per month—about what four migrant pedalers could collect in the same time with one-tenth the staff and for millions less.[61] Still, TTJ persists today; when I visited Greenpeace's Beijing office in 2018, I was surprised to find that TTJ managed its trash.

7

Top of the Heap

Beijing Welcomes You! (北京欢迎你!; *Beijing huanying ni!*) were words I heard and saw a lot in Beijing in 2008, emblazoned on billboards, broadcast over loudspeakers on busses and subways, and even chirped from taxi meters. I had the good fortune of having an American Council of Learned Societies grant and a visiting scholar position at Beijing University, which allowed me to spend January through July 2008 in Beijing watching the capital gussy itself up for its debut on the global stage hosting the 2008 Summer Olympics. Having family along gave me fresh views into Beijing life. My wife, Cynthia, kept me informed of the city's fairytale overnight transformations: English suddenly appearing on every traffic sign; a scorched stretch of sidewalk magically turning into a tree-lined garden path. She also noticed how construction workers shamelessly ogled her but soon realized they only did so when she had our baby son, Abram, with her; it turned out many migrant workers loved getting the novel chance to coo over a little foreign baby. Abram ate up the superstar attention. He also received lots of Olympic-themed swag from our friends, especially gifts decorated with the Beijing Olympic cartoon mascots the Five Friendlies (see figure 11), one for each ring in the Olympic logo, named Beibei, Jingjing, (Beijing) Huanhuan, Yingying (Welcomes), and Nini (You)!

Of course the "you" in the slogan was not a universal pronoun; some "yous" were not so welcome in Beijing that summer. The city made it clear that access to the Olympic city would be restricted for migrants. Construction companies were to send migrant crews home, beggars would be removed, and "regarding scrap collectors, small beauty salons and other seriously problem-causing low-value trades (低端行业 *diduan hangye*), these migrants population segments will be pushed out (*ji chu*) of Beijing during the Olympic period."[1] For Beijing to rise as

FIGURE 11. Logo for the 2008 Beijing Olympics featuring the Five Friendlies.

a global city meant that certain realities necessary for its functioning, among them its huge informal waste sector (estimated at 150,000–300,000 migrant recyclers and several billion yuan per year in the decade described in this chapter), would need to be temporarily tidied away.

The Beijing Olympics celebrated the PRC's economic rise and ratified the rehabilitation of its international reputation from the last time Beijing had hosted a riveting global media spectacle, the 1989 Tiananmen student movement and massacre. China's economy hit a rough patch after that event, but by 1991 GDP growth was back at an astounding 10 percent, where it stayed, more or less, for the next two decades. Though diplomats occasionally chastened the regime about human rights and Tibet, Western governments and their citizens and corporations were inextricably implicated (as both investors and consumers) in supporting China's rise as an export-oriented manufacturing powerhouse. From 1991 to 2011 China's economy grew eightfold, fueled by low-wage migrant labor and low-cost material inputs and the scrap sector, a quintessential marriage of the two, played an outsized role in that growth. In 2000, the same year that China entered the World Trade Organization, it became the top importer of almost every form of industrial scrap (copper, aluminum, waste paper, plastic) traded on the world market, and it remained at the top of the world's scrap heap as the number one importer of all those materials until, in the summer of 2017, the Chinese government announced a set of strict import bans to take effect New Year's Day, 2018.

This chapter explores the long decade (centered on 2003–13) when recycling in China attained a mind-boggling, fortune-making, and environmentally devastating scale. In Beijing, informal recycling communities operated under a state policy that mixed benign neglect with expedient exploitation. After trying to extirpate informal recyclers in the 1980s and 1990s (see chapter 6), the Beijing municipal government recognized such efforts were doomed to fail. Not only that, having migrants do the city's waste-management work for it was a real bargain. Informal recyclers (1) provided a highly efficient recycling infrastructure at no cost to city governments while diverting 20–35 percent of waste away from disposal, thereby also saving millions in disposal costs (studies confirmed that Beijing's landfills had almost nothing worth recycling in them); (2) were earning and saving enough money to raise the standard of living for hundreds of thousands of poor rural households; (3) on a national scale provided millions of tons of material inputs for Chinese industry; and (4) provided small cash to millions of urban residents (particularly the poor and elderly) in exchange for their scrap.[2] Rather than banish migrant recyclers from the city, authorities adopted a stance of relative accommodation in these years. For many of China's millions of migrant recyclers this meant more business stability and a significant boost in earnings and remittances.

But it is crucial to note that the state never granted migrant recyclers anything like legitimacy. Even as they helped create the biggest recycling sector of any industrial system in the world, China's migrant recyclers were persistently excluded by state policies and denied paths to formal recognition. The informal sector was not informal by default; its informal status and insecurity were repeatedly reproduced by state policies and (in)actions. The premise that informal recyclers were fundamentally incompatible with the state's goals of modernization and environmental protection was so ingrained as a policy platform that it became a meme: "dirty messy deficient" (*zang luan cha*). As an article from the Chinese Resource Recycling Association bluntly declared, "Informal recyclers = dirty messy deficient (收破烂儿=脏乱差; *shou polan'r = zang luan cha*), after so many years nobody doubts this point."[3] In Beijing this equation meant that when the next round of real estate investments was to be made or the next great national event to be held, authorities could unapologetically subject recyclers to rapid and arbitrary dispossession and removal.

While the state's refusal to legitimize migrant recyclers remained a constant, the larger economic context in which Beijing's recycling sector functioned was changing dramatically. What in the 1980s had been a few clusters of intrepid rural migrants picking away at an unraveling state monopoly by the 2000s had become a massive network that veritably monopolized recycling across China (see Map 4), with ranks in the millions (3.3–5.6 million).[4] Informal scrappers had forged supply

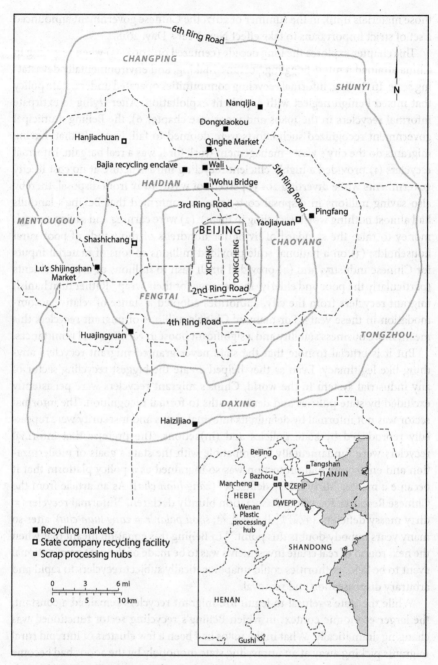

MAP 4. Beijing and Beijing's regional recycling/scrap-processing geography, with key markets and processing hubs, ca. 2010. Map by Bill Nelson.

chains of regional, national, and increasingly international impact, recovering millions of tons of materials and generating the emergence of regional hubs that processed and then fed those materials into countless manufacturing enterprises. Beijing in the 2000s was an "urban mine" at the center of a multi-billion-dollar regional scrap economy: its copper flowed to Tianjin's Jinghai district, stainless and other nonferrous to Bazhou, ferrous to Tangshan, glass to Handan, paper to Baoding, and plastic to one of China's (and the world's) biggest scrap plastic markets, Wenan. Scrap brought these relatively rural hubs a surge of new wealth and often calamitous amounts of unmanaged pollution.

China's climb to the top of the global scrap heap was becoming a race to the bottom where environmental practices were concerned. The government attended to these environmental crises with increasing urgency and in some cases managed to stop or limit some of the most egregious pollution and health hazards. At the same time, the state's knee-jerk scapegoating of informal recyclers resulted in policies of exclusion, crackdown, and discrimination that often had the unintended though predictable effect of driving the worst practices deeper into hiding. Beijing's "Green Olympics" provides both an illustration of and a jumping-off point for exploring how state policies, in the name of exerting control over recycling geographies and economies, reinscribed divisions between informal and formal operators and further tilted already uneven playing fields.

DISTRIBUTIONS OF ACCUMULATION: PROFITS, PROCESSING, AND POLLUTION

One of my first stops after we arrived in January 2008 was to visit Mr. and Mrs. X at their waste Styrofoam stall (a 400-square-meter open-air stall with a 50-square-meter, two-room brick shack with no plumbing that served as home) out beyond the fifth ring road in Dongxiaokou village. I told Mr. X I would take the no. 5 subway line (a new convenience courtesy of Olympic planning) to Lishuiqiao station, then grab the usual ride in a black-market motorbike-taxi to the market, but Mr. X surprised me by showing up in their new black Buick sedan. Our cushioned cruise to the junkyard was a far cry from the first time Mr. X had chauffeured me to Dongxiaokou back in 2004, lurching in his old flatbed truck across debris fields soon to be reborn as Olympic Forest Park. Back then Dongxiaokou market was still being built, and the Xs had only recently moved in after their market near Bajia was bulldozed. It was night when we got to Dongxiaokou, so I did not realize then how huge the market was (160 stalls). Mr. X had taken me to the back of their stall and turned on a bare bulb, revealing a huge pile of Styrofoam crowding a machine the size of an overturned bookcase, a Styrofoam densifier that he had built himself. With a tremendous racket and the heavy sweet perfume of melting plastic, the machine commenced chomping up planks of foam and extruding a small dense blob of warm ooze, which Mr. X turned a few times each minute, slowing building what would eventually become something like a 25-kilogram cinder block of PS (polystyrene) resin. I asked Mr. X how he felt about his new digs. He was confident the market would do good business; it was big and well organized and its owner, Li Bin, was a Beijing businessman who had run markets near Bajia, and he got on well with Gushi folks.

Sitting in their new car in 2008, it seemed the Xs had chosen well. Li Bin's Fuyou Xinyuan Market was one of the biggest and arguably the most successful recycling market in Dongxiaokou village, the largest recycling hub in Beijing, home to five huge scrap markets, with an estimated 20–25 percent of the city's scrap passing through its six hundred to nine hundred stalls (see figure 12). By 2008 about one in three of those stalls' owners had a family car, or rather, a business car, as they were typically used to facilitate meeting with and impressing clients. Regardless, the cars were evidence that a kind of wealth that a few years earlier had only reached a handful of recyclers had percolated to thousands by 2008.

Why were Beijing's recyclers making so much more money in these years? An economist would almost certainly point to the near exponential growth in value of Beijing's recyclable waste output, approximately tripling in both quantity and price between 2000 and 2008, and much of this chapter is caught up in the regional and global economic forces impelling this pole-vault in scale and value. But when I asked Mrs. X about their prosperity since moving to Dongxiaokou in 2004 she had a different answer: stability. Since coming to Beijing from Gushi county in the late 1980s, the couple had always worked hard and made smart business investments, but they were constantly in upheaval. They were evicted every year or two, their markets were torn down, and they were chased to a new spot farther out in the suburbs. Gushi migrant recyclers knew this eviction drill well, but it took its toll on their communities, sending everyone scattering to new locations, upending trading relationships, and putting kids' schooling in limbo. It took a year each time just to recoup losses and rebuild.

Migrant recyclers who lived in Beijing between 1990 and 2003 were forced to relocate every year or two, human mile markers recording the city's ever-widening waves of land speculation and development.[5] It was not that migrant recyclers made no money before 2003, but many spent most of what they made maintaining their businesses and supporting the grandparents and children back home. Being allowed to finally settle down for a few years made investing in one's business and saving up far easier. Stall bosses invested more in hydraulic balers, shears, and forklifts, while market owners increasingly roofed over their markets to help protect materials from weather damage. Of course, district authorities still ran occasional sweeps, inspecting collection sites, checking licenses, chastising and fining violators, and sometimes even confiscating goods or shutting down a collection site. But these sweeps were far less violent and destructive, aimed

FIGURE 12. View down a large stall-style scrap market in Dongxiaokou in Changping district in North Beijing, 2011. Note the wide lanes for truck access, the shacks in each stall where stall owners live, and the range of materials collected. Photo by Kao Shih-yang, ca. 2011, used with permission.

to discipline recyclers not terrorize them and rid the city of them, as in the days of the custody and repatriation raids. Ben Steuer, in a national overview of local regulations on the informal waste sector, corroborates this shift in attitude, finding that prior to 2003, 95 percent of regulations on the sector were strictly prohibitive, whereas after 2003 over one-third of such regulations had provisions aimed at integrating aspects of the informal sector.[6]

The newfound stability of recycling markets was the direct result of the 2003 policy that removed recycling from the list of highly proscribed "special industries" (*teshu hangye*), thereby allowing Beijing's townships and villages to open independent recycling enterprises at their own discretion.[7] By the mid-2000s land prices inside Beijing's fourth ring road were far too high for scrap yards to be an attractive investment, but in peri-urban villages beyond the fifth ring road recycling markets were an attractive low-risk, high-return transitional investment. For recyclers this peri-urban border was also an ideal sweet spot where low land rents and proximity to the scrap-rich urban core met—any closer and rents go up, any farther and transport costs eat into profits. Dozens of peri-urban villages jumped into the sector, but few went all in like Dongxiaokou, flipping from farm country to waste city. The village opened five one hundred-plus-stall markets but chose not to take on the burden and risk of running these businesses directly; instead they leased out acreage to private recycling companies to build and run them. The companies in turn rented market stalls to migrant brokers, each stall an independent business specializing in a specific recyclable commodity (iron and steel, nonferrous metals, paper, PET, other plastic, glass, wood, and [in lower-end markets] used cloth). Recycling companies were junkyard landlords; Dongxiakou villagers were the landlords of junkyard landlords.

Recycling company owners prospered. Beijing native Li Bin, Fuyou Xingyuan's owner, grossed more than 7.5 million yuan a year in rents. Every stall in one of these markets was in reality its own stand-alone business, so every migrant stall owner was legally required to register with the Commerce Bureau. In theory migrants could do so; in reality their applications were almost always rejected.[8] The solution to this problem was that recycling companies like Fuyou Xingyuan were given the authority to register the stall businesses in their markets under their license, an arrangement that was, strictly speaking, not a full licensing— just one of many customary municipal bureau practices that muddied the concept of legality.[9] Essentially, the owners of recycling market companies benefited from the discriminatory practices of the Beijing Commerce Bureau, which prevented migrant brokers from running independent stall businesses and forced them instead to become tenants in licensed markets. So despite the fact that Gushi natives made up around 80 percent of Beijing's stall bosses, almost every market company in the city was owned by a Beijing native.[10]

Scrap markets were the core around which the entire migrant recycling community coalesced. By hosting these markets, the villagers of Dongxiaokou transformed themselves from poor farmers into landlords of a "waste city" that at its peak comprised thirty thousand migrant households employed directly or indirectly by the sector.[11] There were bike-cart collectors, stall brokers and their workers, truckers and truck loaders; then there were all the businesses associated with the sector: hostels, machine tools and hardware, restaurants, truck mechanics, and convenience stores. Dongxiaokou residents were landlords to them all. Some were friendly to the migrants they hosted; others were slumlords. Right across the road from Fuyou Xinyuan market was a shanty complex of 150 one-room brick shacks rented mainly to truck loaders: one water tap per row, pit-style communal bathroom, and nonexistent amenities. The landlord, who had once farmed the spot, told me rent was 200 yuan a month and that his tenants were all criminals.

The majority of the migrants in Dongxiaokou were from Henan's Gushi county; roughly half had been in Beijing for a decade or more. Symbols of Gushi culture were everywhere, from the restaurants advertising Gushi goose, to the dialect used in most transactions, to the little bus station running daily coaches on the 1,000-kilometer (620-mile) trip to Gushi.[12] There were also community-funded schools for migrant children, primarily for elementary years; almost all high-school-aged children went back to Gushi to study because the college entrance exams required students be tested where they held *hukou.* It was almost universally agreed that the schools in Gushi provided a better education than the migrant schools in Beijing, so most parents who could do so left their children back in Gushi with the grandparents.

Recycling was channeling billions of yuan into this migrant community, but living conditions were far from luxurious. Dongxiaokou was a "waste city" that did not sleep; collectors' days began before dawn and often ended after midnight, and trucks ran at all hours. Most recyclers lived in cramped shack housing, two to four persons to a room, without personal bathrooms, running water, or kitchens. Almost all large household items like TVs, refrigerators, and furniture were used discards acquired on the job. In February 2008 I went to Gushi during Spring Festival to get a better sense of how the new accumulation of waste-based wealth was reshaping the county where over half of Beijing's recyclers were from.

During that year's Spring Festival an unusually large winter storm dumped snow as far south as subtropical Guangdong, paralyzing travel in some areas and making it harder for Gushi people to get home. I stayed in the most modern hotel in the county seat, but it had no central heating, so the lobby and halls were below freezing. Local volunteers were in the street shoveling out from the novel two feet of snow. As we headed out to Hongbu township (nineteen villages with the second-lowest average per capita farmland allotment in Gushi; population around seventy thousand, about one-third of whom spent most of the year in Beijing recycling), our driver explained that many of the roads we were taking had only been paved in the last year or two, and the roads between and within villages were all still unpaved. This fact would end up being crucial for understanding how many recyclers, including the Xs, had spent their money over the last decade.

A Hongbu official summarized the township's recent labor history as a kind of snowballing chain migration on steroids. It started in 1983 with 100 workers going to Xinyang; by 1985 there were around 1,000 folks heading to several destinations, and by 1990 nearly 10,000 people were working outside the township, half in Beijing. Hongbu, like Gushi as a whole, was an officially designated "impoverished area" (*pinku diqu*) at the time, and farmers were happy to make any money at all to help meet household needs (*yangjia hukou*). Throughout the 1990s out-migration doubled to 20,000, again with half going to Beijing, largely to recycle. This was the period of building houses back home. "Before 1995, businesses were small; if you came back with 10-20,000 that was good, 50,000 or 80,000 was fucking great (*niubi*)." By the year 2000, someone who came back with 100,000 yuan was a successful boss, and there were one or two millionaires; by 2008, Hongbu had a few dozen millionaires, and total yearly remittances from Beijing approached 200 million yuan.[13]

By 2000 most Hongbu recyclers had stopped building houses in their home villages and instead were buying or building in the Gushi county seat, in Xinyang, or, in exceptional cases, in Beijing. The Xs were typical of this trend; they never built a house in their village, instead buying an apartment in Gushi. Clearly this shift in property investment indicates that migrants were making enough money to move into the cities. But that is not quite the whole story, or even the main one. In the 1990s Gushi's village schools were emptying out, in part due to labor migration; then, beginning in 2001, the national government began consolidating rural schools, closing tens of thousands of primary schools at the village level. By around 2005, parents in Gushi villages who wanted to send their child to a good elementary school, or to middle school at all, had to send them far from the village, possibly even all the way to the county seat. To enroll children in a county seat public school parents often needed to own a residence there, so many migrant recyclers who could afford to bought apartments in town. But even families who sent their children to private schools often bought or rented apartments in town because the quality of county roads meant trips to the county seat could take hours, especially when it rained. Also, by this time educators in Gushi were very aware that kids raised by their grandparents tended to not do well in school, both because they missed their parents and because most grandparents, being barely literate, could not help children with their lessons. Many recyclers, including the Xs, enrolled their children in county seat schools and then paid teachers extra to tutor them, which soon turned into teachers running their own personal boarding after-school programs. The costs of tutors, boarding schools, and apartments in town added up; such expenses absorbed almost all the Xs' earnings into the early 2000s. By 2008, Gushi county's out-migrant laborers and entrepreneurs (about one-fifth of whom, 110,000 or so, were in Beijing) had become the benefactors of several private middle and high schools in the county seat.[14] In short, much of the money Gushi migrants were making handling Beijing's waste was going into trying to better the education of their children.

A map sketching the economic metabolism of Beijing's recycling sector would have to include Gushi as a primary source of labor and a major site of capital accumulation. But why had a group of Henanese won out in Beijing, particularly when all accounts agree that in the early 1990s Hebei migrants predominated in the city's informal recycling? This was the question that animated a fabulous study by Beja and colleagues in 1999 of Beijing's Henan recyclers: "[I]f one seeks to explain why . . . people from Hebei were forced out by those from Henan, one is led to suggest a difference in mentality: Henan people were not afraid to take risks, economic, legal or moral."[15] Personally, I am uncomfortable with the language of mentality, but when I posed this question to Gushi recyclers, many gave this explanation a slight twist: Gushi people took bigger risks because they had no choice but to go all out. Much of this came down to geography. First, Gushi is obviously much farther from Beijing. Hebei migrants could get home relatively easily, which, given the constant displacements and deportations migrant recyclers faced, made lingering at home more tempting. For Gushi migrants a trip home came at a very high cost; those who persisted in Beijing, particularly those who returned even after *shourong* and deportations, were self-selected as highly determined. Second, Hebei villages were close enough to Beijing to become recycling processing hubs. Hebei recyclers had options; they could invest their stakes in collecting in Beijing—a space where they had no rights or leverage—or they could try to shift their engagement with scrap over to their home turf by hauling the scrap back home and opening processing shops or brokering with local factories. Gushi was too far away from Beijing for that, so a Gushi recycler's decision tree was limited to maximizing access to materials and nailing down collection; processing was never an option.

By contrast, in Hebei several processing hubs grew with a ferocious speed matching Beijing's nearly exponential waste generation. My guestimate, based on several related indicators, is that scrap quantities collected in Beijing tripled and total value rose by five to nine times from 2000 to 2008: Beijing's MSW (measured after recyclables had been removed) more than doubled; the size of the migrant recycling workforce was in the ballpark of 150,000 to 300,000, double to quadruple 1990s estimates; the area under urban development in Beijing grew roughly 40 percent; and per unit prices also rose, with the major commodity types (copper, paper, ferrous, plastic) all doubling or tripling in price.[16] Statistical approximations aside, a leap in scale was apparent in the everyday mechanics of the trade. In 2000 recyclers almost universally used bike-carts, but by 2008 about one in three community collectors used a truck. Paper baling operations (average capacity five to ten thousand tons monthly) were unheard of in 2000; the city was ringed by thirty baling stations by 2008, many of them joint ventures or foreign invested.[17] Manufacturing demand for materials pulled scrap prices up, drawing almost every bit of valued material from the city's waste streams, then through regional processing hubs, and from there on to all sorts of manufactures, small and large, local and international.

WENAN: NORTH CHINA'S WASTE PLASTIC RECYCLING CAPITAL

By 2000, Beijing's scrap-processing hubs had developed sufficient economic gravity to pull in scrap not just from nearby Beijing and Tianjin, but from across the region, across China, and even across the globe, transforming these rural counties into sites of both sudden wealth and unconscionable pollution. Figuring out where Beijing's scrap went for processing was easy because most Chinese trucks had the name of the county where they were registered spray-painted on the driver's door. It did not take long to figure out that trucks from Mancheng (in Baoding) hauled paper, Tangshan trucks took ferrous, and Handan trucks took glass. By far the most ubiquitous truck tattoo was for Wenan county; it is not an exaggeration to say that pretty much every load of plastic collected in Beijing (except for PET bottles, which mainly went to Jiangsu) headed two hours south to Wenan for processing.[18]

The roots of plastic processing in Wenan reached back to the early 1980s, when townships were encouraged to shift some of their farm equipment and fertilizer factories into light industry. In Wenan it chanced that a handful of townships experimented with reprocessing industrial plastic scrap (bottle tops, plastic shavings, white goods manufacturing waste, etc.) from Tianjin and Beijing. By the mid-1980s Wenan had three township enterprises that together employed 485 workers and produced 1.9 million yuan of plastic goods. Wenan's Longjie township was being called "plastic town," with four hundred household shops using about thirteen hundred low-tech molding machines to pump out over fifty million plastic doodads like clothes hangers, clothespins, and flower pots.[19] Few could have imagined that this rate of growth would continue unabated for the next twenty-five years. For one thing, where would all the plastic for this dizzying expansion come from? New plastic resins are expensive, so it was really only scrap plastics that could fuel Wenan's workshops. Where would Wenan's farmers find a cornucopia that spewed waste plastic?

The answer was the garbage heaps of Beijing and Tianjin. Wenan was near enough to the large scrap flows in Beijing and Tianjin to access them cheaply, and it was rural and poor enough that environmental enforcement was nearly nonexistent.[20] There were hardly any large-scale enterprises in Wenan. Nearly everyone across thirty villages in the county's southwest part either worked in waste plastics or had a close relative who did, with somewhere between 10,000 and 20,000 household processers and traders employing 100,000 to 200,000 local and migrant employees.[21] Wenan's plastic scrap sector was almost entirely informal: unregistered, unregulated, and tax evading. Plastic shops typically had cheap, ramshackle infrastructure, paid little if any land rents, evaded construction permits, provided minimal protection to their workers, and installed few or no pollution controls.

Wenan's plastic entrepreneurs were local peasants, not *hukou*-lacking migrants, but the industry they built, in its scale and practices, resembled the informal markets of the urban waste trade that supplied it. Some of this was due to the nature of scrap plastics processing. Unlike metals or paper, every step in the plastic recycling process (sorting, shredding, pelletizing, and molding of new products) can be done efficiently on a household scale, often even more efficiently than on a large scale.[22] The machines needed at any step in the process can fit on the back of a pickup truck and are cheap and simple to build; manufacturing them became a vital local industry in Wenan.[23] Other material- and market-related factors helped keep Wenan's plastic businesses small, myriad, and clustered. The postconsumer waste plastic stream is dominated by a half dozen resins (the numbers 1–6 on the bottoms of plastic items), but when industrial, construction, and car scrap are added, there are scores of different resin types. Given the diversity and complexity of scrap flows, it is difficult for waste plastic processors to access a steady supply of high-quality raw materials, and supplies are even more erratic when the main sources are renegade waste pickers. In these conditions, it becomes useful for all parties to have one big market where they can find basically everything and everyone in one place. Were it not for this advantage afforded by a centralized marketplace, plastic shops might (and, when large markets like Wenan were shut down, inevitably did) pop up covertly anywhere, given how small and inexpensive they are to operate and how ubiquitous postconsumer plastics are in urban waste streams.

But none of these factors explains why Wenan's thousands of plastic shops remained informal—unregistered, untaxed, and unregulated—for over two decades, or why local officials countenanced it. One reason was the VAT (see chapter 6). First implemented in 1984, a VAT of 17 percent was collected on a business's revenue, calculated basically as total sales receipts minus total receipts for materials purchased. But Wenan plastic processors had no purchasing receipts because their suppliers were informal recyclers, so they would be forced to pay 17 percent on their total sales, wiping out their profit margins. In 2001 (and lasting until 2008) the state passed a law exempting registered recycling companies from the VAT; but the reform was designed to help SOEs and other large registered companies better compete against informal enterprises that had the unfair advantage of evading taxes, not to help reform informal businesses.[24] To receive VAT exemption, enterprises needed to meet standards regarding their workshops, warehouses, and accounting that Wenan's household shops could not meet, and authorities offered no assistance or amnesty from penalties to help informal shops make a transition. The most viable path for Wenan processors was to bribe local authorities to look the other way. Given that three-quarters of VAT revenues went to the central government anyway, the tax loss to township and county coffers was negligible, so local officials had little reason not to collude with them. One report ventured that of Wenan's estimated four thousand washing/shredding businesses, 95 percent were unlicensed and 98 percent paid no taxes.[25]

Despite the workplace conditions, many of these processors and their workers were highly skilled. Years of experience in the sector meant that most Wenan processors were intimately familiar with markets, supply chains, and the technical intricacies of processing. Many laborers could discern the nearly invisible differences between plastic resins by sight, feel, and smell and could run processing lines without any assistance. Wenan's plastic sector was low wage and labor intensive, had little barrier to entry, and was horribly polluting; it was also peopled by tens of thousands of skilled experts and produced a staggering range of products, from schlocky doodads to high-quality recycled resins.

The regulatory vacuum left plenty of room for despicably unethical practices. In 2003 journalists found that Beijing's medical waste was being sold in Wenan and processed into plastic pellets without sterilization.[26] A 2004 report that found millions of the plastic bags used to hold food were laced with toxic chemicals named Wenan as a supplier.[27] A similar story surfaced about takeout food containers in 2005.[28] Most endangered by the hazardous practices were the local environment and the health of Wenan's residents and shop employees. By the early 2000s it was rumored that none of Wenan's young men were joining the military because they all failed the health screening due to having enlarged livers.[29] Both the pelletizing and molding/blowing stages of plastic processing involve heating plastic to melting temperatures, releasing toxin-laced fumes associated with circulatory ailments, liver disease, and cancers. A clinic doctor who had been serving patients in Wenan since the 1960s described his experience:

> In the sixties, seventies, and early eighties most illnesses around here were stomach problems, diarrhea, things related to diet and water. Since the eighties, high-blood pressure has become extremely common. In the past almost no one had it. In the eighties I started seeing it in people in their forties, and in the nineties I started seeing it in people over thirty. Now I see it in twenty-eight-year-olds. Some people in their thirties have it so bad they get thrombosis and can't move.[30]

Water pollution was also severe. One of the biggest pollution burdens in scrap plastic processing comes at the shredding/washing stage, when waste items (dirty yogurt, detergent or takeout containers; industrial-use PVC (polyvinyl chloride) pipe; wire insulation; agricultural films; etc.) are shredded into small chips and then churned in a bath with detergent and alkaline salts in order to remove contaminating residues and separate plastic types. Wenan's small shops dumped the highly polluted wastewater into nearby ditches and streams (see figure 13). Older residents recalled that up through the 1980s Wenan was known for its many fishing streams, but by the late 1990s the rivers were dead; by the 2000s residents drank only bottled water.[31]

The signs of a mounting health and environmental disaster were undeniable, yet Wenan officials responded slowly. In 2003 they launched the first of several campaigns to clean up the sector, propagandizing and inspecting, fining and warning violators, and shutting down several of the purportedly most aberrant processors. Predictably, the handful of shops forced to close popped back up when the campaigns relaxed.[32] Officials rolled out nine campaigns from 2003 to 2007, fining a total of two hundred shops and summarily shutting down fifty-eight.[33] But these numbers were paltry for a sector ten thousand enterprises strong essentially all of which were violating environmental codes, dumping untreated wastewater into streams, billowing unfiltered plastic fumes in unventilated shops, and dumping tons of unusable waste into ditches and pits.[34]

FIGURE 13. A stream in Wenan's Zhaogezhuang township, the center of Wenan county's plastic processing hub, 2006. Visible in the background are stockpiles of plastic scrap waiting to be processed. Photo by author.

Wenan's irrepressible expansion continued. Fifty-ton-payload trucks arrived regularly from Urumqi and Harbin. By 2006 the flows of domestically generated scrap were matched by loads of imported plastic from the United States, Japan, Korea, and Europe; Tianjin's Tanggu port was a mere ninety-minute drive from Wenan.[35] By the time the Beijing Olympics commenced, Wenan's plastic recycling industry was likely worth between US$2 and 8 billion, handling between one and three million tons of waste plastic annually, about half domestic, half imported. Wenan, an obscure rural backwater had become an integral part of global trade and material flows and one of the most polluted counties in China.

BIGGERING

If, in our post–Cold War globalizing economy, consumption is king, then waste is surely queen. Just as the Walmarting of US consumerism would have been impossible without China's low-wage manufacturing, the same could be said of the single-streaming of US disposal(ism). First introduced in California in the early 1990s, single-stream collection radically simplified residential recycling. Rather than have consumers go through the rigmarole of sorting their recyclables into several separate piles (newspaper, glass, cans, etc.), single-stream let Americans throw all their recyclables into one curbside container, shifting the work of sorting to industrial-scale automated facilities called MRFs (municipal recycling facilities/ materials recovery facilities). Residential recycling was now a cinch; recycling rates doubled from 16 to 34 percent, and by 2010 single-stream had been adopted across over two-thirds of the United States.[36] But large automated MRFs are expensive; with US manufacturing in decline, domestic demand weak, and scrap prices low, how could MRFs ever pay for themselves? Moreover, the materials coming out of MRFs—having been commingled in bags, bins, and trucks before hitting the MRF—are inevitably far more cross-contaminated and of lower quality than separate-stream recycling, forcing more labor costs onto processors and manufacturers. Confined to the context of domestic US markets, single-stream just did not pencil out. Luckily for single-stream, it was just at this moment that Chinese scrap buyers came along who were more than happy to buy what MRFs were selling. Chinese demand made how Americans recycle today possible.

Of course scrap markets have been imbricated in international trade flows for centuries, so it would be absurd to claim the late 1990s marked the first time in history that scrap went global. But the 1990s did mark a milestone when a general principle of the waste trades—that your nearest buyer is your best buyer—seemed to shatter. Scrap is cheap and bulky, so relative shipping costs often determine the bottom line of transactions. But in the late 1990s and early 2000s China seemed to be creating a new normal in which distance no longer mattered.

One of the leading pioneers in grasping the amazing potential of this moment in global shipping was Cheung Yan, aka "The Queen of Trash," the CEO of Nine Dragons paper and China's wealthiest person in 2006. In the 1990s she founded America Chung Nam, a shipping company that specialized in hauling OCC from North America to China. A few years later she started Nine Dragons to turn those old boxes into new ones. By 2001 America Chung Nam had become the single largest exporter by volume of freight from the United States; "[i]n other words, nobody in America was shipping more of anything each year anywhere in the world."[37] In 1995 the United States exported around 400,000 tons of wastepaper to China; by 1999, 1.7 million tons; and in 2007, 9.3 million tons valued at US$1.793 billion.[38]

What explains this explosive growth? From the 1990s to 2010 the US cumulative trade deficit with China topped two trillion US dollars. China became the main factory floor furnishing US consumer goods, but Chinese consumers bought few US-made products. All those goods made in China needed to be shipped in something, hence China's cardboard-box boom, and those boxes were in turn carried on container ships that chugged to US shores, unloaded, and then returned to China virtually empty so they could be filled again with more Chinese products. Shippers call that trip back to China a "backhaul," and an empty backhaul is a big money loser for shipping companies; a load of almost anything at any price is preferable. Why not scrap? Container ships left China heaped with bulging new boxes, then returned stacked with flattened old ones. In the 2000s the economic logic of the backhaul meant it was usually cheaper to ship a ton of scrap across the Pacific than across the Rockies or down the Mississippi. With her two companies, Cheung Yan turned the shipping cycle born of the global trade imbalance into a virtuous circle sweeping prime scrap from the United States to her paper mills in coastal China for next to nothing, and similar logistics applied to other scrap materials. For the first fifteen years of this century, one-half of total US goods shipped to China by weight was some form of scrap, reaching a peak in 2011 at twenty-three million metric tons of secondary materials worth US$11.3 billion, about 11 percent of all US trade to China that year.

Scrap copper, indispensable to China's rise as the world biggest electronics manufacturer, provides another example. From 1992 to 2010, China's scrap copper imports grew over ten times, topping five million tons. The majority of these imports went through ports in south China and Hong Kong to feed Guangdong's huge electronics manufacturing sector, but North China factories also consumed their share, much of which found its way to the obscure rural scrap-processing hub of Ziya, at the Tianjin-Hebei border. Ziya started in the scrap copper trade in the 1980s as a cluster of informal processors sourcing scrap from Tianjin, Beijing, and Hebei. But electronics manufacturing was expanding at a blistering pace, and soon Ziya's recycling entrepreneurs were off to Japan, Korea, and the United States to hunt for more copper. They struck the motherload with industrial waste wire. The labor required in stripping off the wire's plastic insulation to extract the copper made wire processing expensive for countries with high labor costs like Japan and the United States, but Ziya's rural labor made wire stripping a bargain. By 2000, around half a million tons of imported waste wire was making its way to Ziya.[39] Most of that wire was thick enough to strip by hand with the aid of a simple mechanical wire stripper, but superfine wire was too thin to strip, so processors burned off the plastic insulation—laced with polybrominated diphenyl ether (PBDE) flame retardants that release dioxin and other toxins when burned—to get at the copper. Open-air wire burning became rife in Ziya. In the early 2000s the area was shrouded nightly in an acrid fog of plastic smoke (daytime burning was too easily traceable); fruit orchards failed for miles.[40] From the state's perspective the dangers of such pollution disasters were twofold, as they were environmentally damaging public health hazards that could also turn into sources of public complaint and even trenchant protest, undermining political stability.

Ziya was not China's only scrap-processing enclave where a rapid influx of imports brought explosive economic growth while simultaneously turning pollution problems from bad to horrendous. Similar cases came to light in Taizhou, Nanhai, and most infamously in Guiyu, Guangdong province, in 2001, where a hub comprised of thousands of small informal shops dismantling electronics (computers, TVs, etc., aka "e-waste") helped create a toxic nightmare.[41]

Dominant representations, not just in Chinese state media but from foreign non-governmental organizations (NGOs) like Greenpeace, painted a simplified and misleading picture of Guiyu, accusing informal processors of conspiring with foreign traders to illegally smuggle banned forms of "e-waste" into China. But as Yvan Schulz points out in the most comprehensive study on Guiyu to date, such claims were only part of the story and often inaccurate.[42] In fact, the Chinese government explicitly allowed, even promoted, the import of many kinds of electronic scrap (called number 7 Category Scrap [di qi lei feipin] in policy documents) for the purpose of raw material extraction, a practice authorities dubbed "urban mining" (chengshi kuangchan). Waste wire was on the state's list of accepted forms of number 7 scrap, and licensed companies and brokers were issued permits to import it by China's Environmental Protection Agency (EPA).[43] And just as informal recycling in Beijing in the 1990s would have been impossible without a host of willing collaborators (see chapter 6), the same was true for imported number 7 scrap; selling import permits illicitly to informal brokers was just one of many ways licensed companies and SOEs regularly profited by teaming up with informal sector recyclers.

The alarming string of imported-scrap pollution crises in Ziya, Guiyu, Tiazhou, and other places spurred the EPA's Pollution Control Office to action, and in 2001 it mandated a management strategy for these valuable but volatile imports: environmental protection industry parks (EPIPs; huanbao chanye yuan). EPIPs were enclosed industrial parks that exclusively hosted licensed domestic and joint-venture enterprises importing waste commodities for resource extraction. The Ziya EPIP (ZEPIP) was on the list of the first five parks approved.[44] ZEPIP provided infrastructure and administrative assistance to companies leasing yards in the park. In return lessees had to observe a burning ban and demonstrate they had safe methods for handling superfine wire, which meant importing large and expensive (US$500,000) mechanical granulators. The price of a ZEPIP lease and granulator was prohibitive for most local processors, so the vast majority of companies in ZEPIP were joint ventures with no direct local connections; when I asked ZEPIP managers for names of locals with companies in ZEPIP they could not provide any.[45] When I visited ZEPIP in 2006, its seventy-two enterprises imported an astonishing 1.5 million metric tons of scrap annually, mostly waste wire; ZEPIP's profits (from leases and a management fee of 15 yuan per ton) were excellent.[46]

ZEPIP was, by one crucial measure, an environmental success; wire burning was nonexistent in the park, and though the blackened brick pavers of locally owned yards were evidence informal shops were still burning, the practice had steeply declined. But in other ways ZEPIP's insertion into the regional scrap sector could be said to have made regional pollution worse. Most ZEPIP companies were just dismantlers; all they did was strip wire to produce huge piles of plastic and copper, then sell this untreated scrap to unregulated industries nearby.

In 2008, ZEPIP companies sold most of their reported 500,000 tons of copper to thirteen local copper refineries in Jinghai—small, polluting refineries built in the 1990s. ZEPIP's plastic output, 350,000 tons of wire insulation, was almost all headed a short forty kilometers down the road to Wenan.[47]

Moreover, superfines comprised only a tiny percentage of the wire market; the overwhelming majority of ZEPIP wire was hand processed by migrant workers who contracted with ZEPIP companies on a piece-wage basis. ZEPIP companies did not even provide their tools; they brought their simple mechanical strippers with them. In sum, ZEPIP companies were usurping the role of brokers in the sector and turning wire strippers into contract laborers, thereby stripping them of some of their profit margin and all of their entrepreneurial mobility. As ZEPIP managers told me more than once, "We like to say that the most environmentally protective technology is still human labor (*renli*)."[48]

This mechanism, whereby informal entrepreneurs were corralled into becoming a low-cost labor input for formal companies, was not incidental; state policy goals had shifted from attempting to stamp out migrant and informal recyclers to attempting to harness their labor to serve larger formal companies. In his presentation at the International Metal Recycling Forum in 2003, Wang Jiwei, vice-chair of the China Non-Ferrous Metal Recycling Association (CMRA), laid out the reasons behind the government's strong support for the EPIP model:

> The reshuffling of scrap collectors is inevitable. The present scrap collection is quite complete, but the management is very poor and unscientific. . . . The secondary non-ferrous metal recycling and application industry belong to the category of labor-intensive industry, which have been making contribution to the employment issues in our country. . . . [Due to the low cost of China's labor] US$100 per ton cost of production will reduce to US$15 per ton in China, and the dis[as]sembling is even more effective and complete. . . . The centralization of those enterprises in one area [in EPIPs] is for the central treatment of wastes and pollution.[49]

The same people who were automatically branded as "dirty messy deficient" when operating independently, when serving as a piece-work labor force that funneled profits to EPIP companies were the low-pollution solution to China's surplus labor woes, giving China an unbeatable edge on international competitors.

The heads of China's materials and metals ministries-turned-conglomerates took a long view from on high. China was currently in its low-wage manufacturing stage of development, with a labor surplus and materials shortages. Ministry institute experts estimated that China's domestic scrap base—the rate at which end-of-life materials (most importantly metals like copper, aluminum, ferrous, zinc, etc.) were generated—would still be insufficient to meet manufacturing demand for several years; scrap imports would be indispensable and should keep growing until around 2010, at which point China's own scrap generation would be sufficient that imports could slowly level and then taper downward.[50] Until then, China should optimize its competitive advantage in importing scrap, while working hard to limit the attendant pollution. Eventually wages would rise (reducing China's competitive edge) and China's domestic scrap base would grow, and a turning point would be reached (sometime in the 2010s) when scrap imports would fall and domestic collection and processing would scale up, mechanize, automate, and become radically less labor intensive. One cannot help noting that this logical and sensible vision, clearly following trends already laid out by OECD countries, said nothing about the fate of the millions of informal laborers in this process.

WAITING FOR THE POLICY

One morning in early May 2008, about eighty days before the Beijing Olympics were to begin, I saw a recycling couple who doubled as security guards at a nearby parking lot pushing a teetering bike stacked with cardboard between them. When I asked why they didn't just use their bike-cart, they told me that as of May 1 bike-carts were banned inside the fourth ring road. Chatting with other neighborhood collectors, I heard similar reports, though enforcement was inconsistent. One collector recounted how a *chengguan* (urban appearance police) joked with him when he went to buy a pack of cigarettes that he must not want his cart, leaving it alone like that. It was not very funny; Dongcheng district *chengguan* were rumored to be chasing folks out of the district and confiscating carts. Word was that the cart ban would be extended to the fifth ring road starting June 1.

The cart prohibitions seemed a bit illogical to me, not just because in my opinion the government was mistaken about how foreigners would react to Beijing's "recyclists," who provided environmental services while emitting less pollution than even the cleanest of the city's Green Olympic fleet of natural-gas vehicles. I also wondered how the city would manage if recyclists were truly banned. Truck collectors might fill the gap, but as of July 1 all motor vehicles would be restricted to either odd or even dates based on their license plates, and trucks were barred from many activities unless they had a coveted green certificate confirming they were emission compliant and approved as necessary for urban management. Approval for informal recyclers typically would be denied, though bribes and connections could make many things possible. Rules about street collection sites remained vague: Can recyclers be on the sidewalk? Are certain neighborhoods off limits? Will they need a uniform or badge? It all seemed to me to bode ill for recyclers, and a few did tell me they were going home for the summer. But most said they would wait and see. When I asked how they would manage with all the restrictions, many told me I was overreacting. The regulations would overreach. The authorities would come down hard at first, then soften. The city's neighborhoods would need recycling, loopholes would be made. Come July, depending on the specific situation—Will the neighborhood committee controlling my turf demand a higher fee? Will the markets I frequent stay open?—they would decide whether to stay or go home. Over the following months I realized they had been giving me a basic lesson in Chinese political science.

Shooing recyclists from roads was only a minor detail in Beijing's comprehensive pre-Olympic spring cleaning. The city was humming with environmental awareness activities. There was the daily news countdown to the June 1 ban on free plastic bags, with debates over how much stores should charge for the new compostable substitutes, essays advocating for shoppers to return to using reed baskets, and reports of grocery stores raided by hoarders as the end of the free bag era drew nigh (many people reused them as garbage bags).[51] In schools, the Olympic curriculum had students conserving water, planting trees, and holding essay competitions on preserving the environment.[52] A hotline was created to report instances of pollution to the city's scenic lakes and canals, and weekends were full with volunteer community greening activities.

For its 2001 Olympic bid, Beijing had pledged to deliver a Green Olympics to the world, committing to a full-body environmental makeover that would be seven years and US$17 billion in the making. The bid included seven environmental promises benchmarked and monitored by the United Nations Environment Programme (UNEP):

1. Greening: planting thirty million trees and adding ten thousand hectares of green space;
2. Water: improving drinking water quality and achieving 90 percent sewage treatment;
3. Air: relocating two hundred factories and shutting down the flagship Capital Steel complex, responsible for producing one-tenth of Beijing's particulate matter;
4. Transport: reformulating fuel standards, removing forty thousand old taxis from the roads, converting 90 percent of city busses to natural gas, and opening new subway lines;
5. Energy: replacing and renovating thousands of coal-burning boilers and furnaces and expanding natural gas supply;
6. Venues: designing Olympic facilities to achieve LEED standards; and
7. Solid waste: "The Beijing bid committed to the establishment of a safe urban domestic waste disposal system capable firstly of sorting, or classifying, 50 per cent of all domestic solid waste in the city, and secondly, able to recycle 30 per cent of all domestic solid waste produced within the city by 2008."[53]

This was a bold commitment considering that the city for all intents and purposes did not have a municipally managed recycling system any more.

Beijing's Olympian waste-sorting goal was mandated at the national level through a Construction Bureau policy designating Beijing one of the country's Eight Trash Sorting Pilot Cities in 2000. Over US$1 billion went toward Beijing's Olympic waste programs, which included expanding landfill, incinerator, composting, and hazardous waste facilities, but the heart of the effort was mobilizing half the city's seventeen million residents to sort their garbage into three streams: recyclable, kitchen waste, and other (garbage). Some 300,000 trash sorting charts were printed for hotels and restaurants; Dongcheng district gave away 40,000 trash-sorting-themed calendars; communities gave awards to their star sorters; volunteers rallied and coached their neighbors; district officials conferred, evaluating participation surveys; and hundreds of thousands of color-coded bins were distributed to 2,255 residential communities and 2,600 work units (schools, hotels, restaurants, offices).[54] Over the intervening years occasional reports noted that some communities were falling short, making it all the more vital that each individual citizen realize that his or her own personal commitment counted: "Garbage classification embodies civilization, but to achieve this kind of improvement, it must be integrated into our living habits. It is only when people come to the self-realization that they are 'sorter #1' of their garbage that the subsequent steps of properly sorted collection, properly sorted treatment and properly sorted reuse can achieve seamless integration."[55] But apparently the city met this challenge of educating and motivating nine million individual residents to change their habits; according to the UNEP's 2009 assessment, despite some imperfections, the city achieved 52 percent sorting in 2008.

But that was hogwash, as was all the handwringing about public consciousness. None of it mattered because it was all a show. I visited several model communities throughout 2008, peeking into bins, and saw no evidence of sorting. But that was not the point; in reality, even had every Beijing citizen sorted the trash perfectly, there was no collection, transport, or treatment infrastructure behind the façade of colored bins. Neighborhood trash collectors regularly put all the wastes together into one truck, and the city's garbage transfer stations had no means of keeping wastes separate. Whatever residents did at the community level, the final product was mixed garbage. It took years before journalists had either the information or the guts to reveal that "from 2002 when trash sorting was publicly promoted, the problem of sorted trash being mixed back together was severe."[56] And the charade did not end with the Olympics in 2008; Beijing launched a sequel in 2009. By 2011 the city had spent another 400 million yuan equipping twenty-four-hundred residential communities with color-coded bins (enough to cover about 50% of the city).[57] As if the mere existence of those bins made self-sorting a reality, authorities (again) proclaimed that 50 percent of the city was now sorting their trash. Soon afterward a Qinghua University study found that only 4.4 percent of residents were using the cans properly.[58] But yet again, participation rates were a distraction. When the Beijing NGO Friends of Nature surveyed residents, they found a major reason residents gave for noncompliance was seeing trash collectors toss their carefully separated "organic," "recyclable," and "nonrecyclable" waste into the same truck. Subsequently confirmed in countless news reports across all eight pilot cities, this quandary has been dubbed "first separate, then mix" (*xian fen, hou hun*).[59] "As CPPCC (Chinese People's Political Consultative Conference) National Committee representative Liu Xiaozhuang explained in 2017, 'Many cities' so-called "trash sorting" has just been putting out a bunch of recycling cans.' In Beijing, Hangzhou, and the other model trash sorting cities this has been common practice."[60]

For Beijing's migrant recyclers, the Olympian waste-sorting pantomime was inconsequential, as it hardly interfered with their work. Nor did informal recyclers harbor any illusions that they would be involved in the other major component of the Green Olympic waste management plan, providing Olympic venues and accommodations with recycling services. The city handed those valuable contracts to its SOEs. Locking informal collectors out of Olympic spaces was easy; access to them was already highly restricted. Three SOEs (Chaoyang's Dongdu Zhongxing Recycling, Haidian Recycling, and Incom Recycling, based in Shunyi district) were awarded the Olympic venue contracts (much to the chagrin of at least one independent Fengtai recycling company manager who was not cut in on the deal).[61] The chosen SOEs expanded their truck fleets, festooned their baling stations with Olympic banners, and staffed up temporarily to enjoy their monopoly on a brief paper and plastic waste bonanza.[62] As summer approached, the newspapers touted how the Olympic spirit was raising Beijing's recycling game to a higher level. Coca Cola and Incom jointly pledged to recycle every PET bottle disposed of at Olympic venues—this in a city where people joked how a PET bottle tossed anywhere would disappear into a picker's bag in under ten minutes.[63] The Haidian company "raised" (*chouji*) 3 million yuan to purchase forty vehicles to ensure that residential recyclables in the district would be removed the same day they were collected—as if informal collectors had not done exactly that every day of the year.[64] In July, with many informal collectors having been chased out of town, the Commerce Bureau used the *Beijing Evening News* to inform the public that the Haidian and Chongwen Tiantianjie companies were providing same-day single-call (or web-order), at-your-door recycling collection by "uniformed workers, bearing logos and accurate scales"; a few days later a follow-up article asked residents to please be understanding if the service was actually taking multiple days and repeated calls—the companies' were short on capacity.[65] In some cases, real estate companies blocked SOE collectors from entering their compounds, demanding they first pay a fee to access the communities' recycling, apparently not realizing that the customs they used with informal collectors were inappropriate to use with SOEs.[66]

The reader might wonder if perhaps these efforts to displace informal recyclers were based, if even slightly, on environmental considerations. After all, informal collectors sold their scrap into networks that included highly polluting processors, and perhaps SOEs were more responsible. They were not. From 2004 to 2008 I repeatedly visited SOE facilities, interviewing their managers in Daxing, Haidian, Chaoyang, and Chongwen, each of which still ran recycling operations. Daxing opened a seventy-stall market in 2004; Haidian maintained a fifty-stall market in Shashichang and a baling operation in Hanjiachuan; Chaoyang Dongdu Zhong-xing closed all its stall-style markets in 2004 (see later in the chapter) but managed to flip its Yaojiayuan site into a baling station; and Chongwen Tiantianjie was still bleeding red ink marketing customized recycling collection services to high-end clients. Company managers all seemed to me sincerely distressed by the pollution problems in processing hubs, and with few exceptions, they claimed that this made it imperative that the state wrest back control over the sector. I would invariably ask in response whether their companies made special efforts to sell to cleaner processors, and the answer was always "No," they needed to make money like any other business and sold to whoever offered the going price. This was not just true for the stall-style markets, where these SOEs could be said to have no control over migrant stall owners' business choices; it was true for the baling stations and collection services the SOEs owned outright. These managers claimed that until the government introduced policies that enabled them to verti-cally integrate with specially designated processors, they had no alternative. Only government policies could alter the playing field, weaken the informal sector's market advantages (tax evading, no pollution controls, etc.), and stop scrap from leaking into it; until these policies were issued, all they could do was wait.

Vice Director Wei of China's CRRA also seemed a bit jaded about the potential for China's formal recycling companies to change the status quo, even though in theory creating that change was why the CRRA existed. We met in mid-May 2008, a week before CRRA's annual international conference, and Wei walked me through the association's history. Founded in 1993, the CRRA emerged out the Materials Bureau (which had overseen recycling companies, particularly in rela-tion to allocating industrial materials during the Mao era; see chapters 4 and 5) and was created to help the bureau's recycling companies navigate the uncharted waters of market trade. As of the 2000s, the CRRA's main purposes were to facili-tate information flows and networking among domestic recycling companies and to represent the collective interests of its members to the state—essentially to lobby the government on recycling policies. Unfortunately, Mr. Wei explained, the CRRA was not nearly as powerful as analogous associations like the Institute of Scrap and Recycling Industries (ISRI) in the United States or the Bureau of International Recycling (BIR) in Europe. In practice power flowed in the other direction; the government treated the CRRA as a means to disseminate and help enforce regulations, while CRRA member companies generally saw little value in using the association as a collective voice to push for self-governance. Instead, most members found it more expedient to pursue their interests through their own individual connections with state authorities. This struck me as odd. The domestic recycling sector was, by 2008, dominated by thousands of independent enterprises with limited access to the government, and these independent recyclers surely might benefit by having a collective voice. Was the CRRA open to non-SOEs? I asked. Mr. Wei said it was. How many members were non-SOEs? He replied, basically, none—the association had only been admitting them for a year or two. In fact, of the CRRA's seven hundred-plus members, more than 90 percent were still direct descendants of the Materials Bureau. Three decades of reforms had hardly eroded the fossilized, bureaucratic identities of state scrap sector companies. In fact, a separate association of recycling companies, the China Nonferrous Metals Industry Association, Recycling Metal Branch (CRMA), represented companies from the old Industrial Bureau. The CRMA held an annual shindig as well, a more influential affair than the CRRA's according to all the international scrap traders I spoke with, as the CRMA's members were titans of the highly lucrative nonferrous metals world. The era of the command economy was long over, yet the rivalry between commercial and industrial bureaus lived on—with, sadly for the CRRA, the industrial side coming out on top.

A week later I got a fuller look into the CRRA's world at its international conference in Dongguan, a manufacturing center in South China. The hotel lobby, with its van-sized tropical fish tanks and free spreads of sushi and piped whipped-cream dessert bites for badged conference attendees, was an interesting setting to talk about waste. Conference sessions featured Chinese and foreign analysts forecasting commodity price trends (their bullish predictions were dashed months later by the global financial crisis) and Chinese government experts sharing data on China's scrap generation and explaining import policies. The real action was not in these PowerPoint sessions but down in the lobby, where deals were being cut. A nonferrous metals broker from California broke it down for me, explaining that, at the volume at which the scrap import/export trade operated, it was less like a junkyard cash trade and more like a commodities market. Companies sat on materials waiting for price shifts and used hedges to protect against price fluctuations over the month that passed between purchase and delivery. Gaming customs inspection was also crucial. Everyone in a trade profited if they could lowball the customs tax by passing off a shipment as lower value than it actually was, so dealers typically threw a lot of poor-quality scrap on top of a high-quality shipment to fool inspectors. And those who really wanted to avoid the customs hassle shipped through Hong Kong, where inspectors were notoriously corrupt and did not even bother to look. Even North China companies sometimes shipped through Hong Kong; the money saved on customs duties made up for the extra thousand miles of shipping costs. None of this was news to anyone in the lobby but me. These were open secrets, the international trading equivalent of how informal sector collectors used tampered scales or waterlogged their cardboard; it was just how things worked.

CRACKDOWNS

They can't control the government connected enterprises, so they control the small common peoples' enterprises.
—MR. X

Back in Beijing, as June wore on, migrant recyclers waited for the next policy shoe to drop: the recycling market crackdown. That the authorities would start closing and bulldozing markets was certain; they had made their intentions clear in the 2007 "Beijing Commerce Bureau Notice to Further Increase Efforts to Eliminate Illegal Recycling Stands and Markets," which explicitly set the Olympics as the cleanup deadline.[67] But aside from conveying the city's hard-nosed resolve to banish illegal markets, the notice left recyclers, and me, wondering what exactly made a market "illegal" . . . or legal, for that matter?

The deregulation of 2003 had given the greenlight to open independent markets as long as they had land contracts and Commerce Bureau licenses, but it had left the city in a planning mess. City authorities had abandoned the failed policy of stomping out all non-SOE markets (see chapter 6) but had no new policy to fill its place. There were still scores of unpermitted recycling stalls and small markets that predated 2003, many of which looked like waste dumps; then there were post-2003 independent markets, ranging from the large, well-planned and licensed facilities in Dongxiaokou to gray markets with little infrastructure that were clearly taking advantage of the relaxation on enforcement. This junkyard hodgepodge was a far cry from the city's vision of a network of large, efficiently designed, scientifically managed markets located in proper land-use zones, equally distributed in a ring just beyond the fifth ring road.

The lack of policy coherence soon turned acrimonious in 2004 when a District Planning Commission, charged with pre-Olympic urban improvements, ordered the posthaste demolition of thirty-eight recycling sites in the area outside the fourth ring road.[68] The list included all of Chaoyang Dongdu Zhongxing's markets, leaving the SOE no lead time and providing no funds or land for new markets. Dongdu Zhongxing lobbied Vice-Mayor Zhang Mao, who pressed for an investigation, resulting in the Municipal Planning Commission publicly faulting the District Planning Commission for inappropriately applying the demolition order, not just to markets without licenses and those (allegedly) in violation of their licenses, but even to Dongdu's sites that were (allegedly) fully legally compliant. But the admonition did not save Dongdu's markets, which were bulldozed, and no relocation sites were provided; only one corner of the company's Yaojiayuan site was saved, upgraded to a baling station.

The upshot was that the Municipal Planning Commission got cracking on a master plan for the sector. In spring 2006 it announced it was "hastening to complete the 'Beijing city plan for the layout of recycling facilities'. . . . To be completed before year end. . . . [It] will determine the specific siting for stall-style markets (集散地 *jisandi*) (processing centers [综合处理中心 *zonghe chuli zhongxin*]) at the center of the recycling system's construction."[69] As the reader can see, there was some muddling of terminology regarding the facilities around which this plan revolved, but be that as it may, a list was supposedly in the offing. And indeed, in late 2006 the commission shared its bold vision, charting the future of Beijing's recycling into 2020. The commission proposed a comprehensive closed system eliminating all the "dirt mess and disturbances" of the present system: two thousand collection sites across eight districts, each serving one thousand to fifteen hundred households, would send materials to a network of large sorting centers (the promised permanent market sites), which would then directly hook up (*zhi gua*) with processing factories in Hebei through municipally supervised "direct distribution" (*zhijie peisong*). This last bit was the policy piece all the district SOE managers kept saying they were waiting for: state-managed vertical integration. The proposal also clarified the earlier terminological muddle somewhat; stall-style markets were to be phased out. "Specialized sorting centers will gradually replace stall-style markets . . . the city developing about 10 such centers." The terminology was clearer, but the promised list of sites was not provided.[70] Another year passed. When the 2007 notice demanding the elimination of illegal markets before the Olympics came out, there was still no finalized list of sites, yet it defined as illegal "markets not in the plan and lacking licenses." Plenty of markets had licenses, but no market was in the plan, so by the 2007 notice's definition, no market in Beijing was legal.

The Olympics would come and go before a finalized list ever materialized. In fact, it never really did; over the coming decade some draft lists were circulated but never finalized. The problem was simple. No village, township, or district government wanted to be on the hook for assigning a massive piece of land to be permanently consigned as a recycling center; it was a huge money looser. Beijing's ever-widening ripples of rising land rents were already engulfing the fifth ring road and would soon reach the sixth and beyond; nobody wanted to be stuck with a huge, permanent low-rent site obligated to service the city.

On the other hand, the city's recycling companies could dream of nothing better than getting on that list. With the Olympics fast approaching, recycling companies were still furiously jockeying for position. District SOEs had the inside track with the government, but the land price problem put districts inside the fifth ring road largely out of the running. Li Bin was determined to keep his markets in Dongxiaokou intact through the Olympics and get at least one of his sites, a massive plot of land in Nanqijia, way out near the sixth ring road, on the final list. Two Beijing University professors and I visited Li Bin at his Fuyou Xingyuan market to talk about his plans. His unpretentious office was right in the middle of the market, where he could keep his eye on the truck-weighing station. Over the clamor of the lurching scales, he laid out a savvy take on the sector and his ambitions. Li Bin's favorite adjective was "pathetic" (*beiai*); SOE recycling companies' understanding of the business was pathetic, the average Beijing person's laziness was pathetic, his own position of supplication to the authorities was pathetic. But his businesses were not pathetic. Li Bin was proud of his markets and frustrated that he could not get any access to officials higher than the township level; district and city officials brushed him off. Still, he had his ear to the ground. He knew the city wanted stall-style markets to transition to "sorting centers" and knew better than I did what that meant: bringing in large equipment like balers and grappling cranes to at least provide the impression of industrial scale and reduced labor. He had already consolidated eight stalls in Fuyou Xingyuan into a paper-baling operation under his ownership and was planning a huge steel yard and paper operation for Nanqijia. But he was under no illusions about the future of the Fuyou Xingyuan market; despite its being reputed to be Beijing's highest volume recycling market, the village was planning to demolish it in three years to build high-rise apartments. Li Bin's scaled-up paper operation was not going to save the market, but it showed he knew which way the wind was blowing. And Li Bin agreed with the policy direction and its scaling-up vision. He too imagined a near future when his company would reach directly into communities to collect their recycling, limiting the number of migrant intermediary collectors and brokers who ate into profits. The future demanded a bigger, more industrial scale. In the future Li Bin imagined, the loyal Gushi stall bosses who had followed him to Dongxiaokou would swap their independent businesses to become managers or small shareholders of Li Bin's company.

Li Bin had no doubt his markets would survive the Olympics, and they did. The government policies and bans promised more than they could deliver; the recycling sector remained a messy, negotiated space of informal rules and connections. When the crackdown came in late June, it generally conformed to predictions, with many ramshackle markets summarily flattened, while those with better facilities (revealing their better connections and larger investments) were spared and temporarily shuttered. On June 25 I went out to Pingfang to meet a manager of two large independent markets there. The markets had been ordered to hang huge, plastic-canvas Olympic posters over their market gates, making them impassible. Dozens of collectors on loaded bike-carts clogged the road, debating what to do with their hauls: bike another five miles out to Tongzhou and hope to find an open site there, or try to cajole their way in here.[71] The bigger of the two markets, about eighty stalls in an unreconstructed, half-demolished factory site, had already been flattened; the manager told me he and the market's owners had been held by the police for two days until they agreed to sign off on the demolition. Their smaller, better-tended site was still running a few trucks at night.

By the time we left Beijing in late July, about a week before the breathtaking Olympic opening ceremony, around half our neighborhood's recyclers had folded up shop. One had decided to pay an extra few hundred yuan to the real estate company for an official price list and a uniform so he could masquerade as a city-registered collector. The day before we left for home I heard that the couple with the parking lot security gig had gotten into a scuffle with the *chengguan*; they had been using the lot to bring in unpermitted trucks, loading them up in the wee hours and smuggling recyclables out to Tongzhou.

HARD FALLS

I did not get back to Dongxiaokou to see the Xs again until Christmas Eve, 2010. It would be the last time I would see them in a market stall. Just as Li Bin had said, the village was getting ready to kick out the stall owners and demolish the market within the coming year, and rumors about the removal negotiations were rampant. It did not simplify things that a key player in those negotiations, Li Bin, was now in prison, convicted of plotting the murder of a villager who had refused to forfeit control over some land Li Bin wanted for his market out in Nanqijia.[72]

That was not the only change at the Xs' market stall; their tiny, two-room shack was different too. A corner had been turned into a shrine. I had never known the Xs to be religious, so I asked why it was there. Mrs. X told me it was for her; Mr. X had suffered a bout of thrombosis-caused paralysis—the plague of so many plastic processors—and she had taken to praying for his health. While Hebei's scrap-processing hubs were all profoundly and hazardously polluted, this was not a major characteristic of most recycling markets in Beijing, where minimal processing occurred. Certainly there were dangers in collecting and dealing scrap, including cuts and punctures from glass shards and metal splinters, accidents with equipment and trucks, and skin ailments among cloth collectors, and some PET stalls shredded their stock before shipment, then piped the dirty water into the sewer. But generally the recycling collectors and stall bosses in Beijing I questioned—and I asked almost anyone I talked to for more than ten minutes—felt they had no health problems from their work. However, Mr. X's blood pressure and thrombosis symptoms were rampant in Wenan workplaces that melted plastic, and that, of course, is what Mr. X's polystyrene condenser did. Happily, Mr. X seemed perfectly well and in good spirits, maybe even a bit healthier than usual now that he was on medication and watching his diet.

We spent the night catching up. The Olympics had been bad for business, but the Xs took that as a given. Unfortunately, several weeks later the global financial crisis struck, throwing the brakes on global trade flows and sending scrap commodity prices into a tailspin. The effects were felt at all levels of the sector. The virtuous cycle of trans-Pacific scrap shipping turned into a vicious circle: US consumers stopped buying Chinese goods, shipping containers stopped coming to the United States, and the cheap backhaul suddenly disappeared. Getting scrap to China was no longer a bargain. By December 2008, Nine Dragon's share price had plummeted from HK$26 to 81cents a share, and its credit rating was downgraded to junk bond status.[73] On the streets of Beijing, recycling prices tumbled and stall owners were stuck selling materials at a loss.

By 2011 most of Beijing's recycling prices had recovered, but it seemed that Beijing's plastics recyclers could not catch a break; in the summer of 2011 an unprecedented crackdown in Wenan sent the entire North China waste plastic sector for another tumble. That spring, the irrigation water from Wenan county's Xiaobai River was so toxic it wiped out thousands of acres of crops.[74] Wenan's approximately two to three thousand shredding/washing shops were named as the culprit.[75] There was no easy fix to the sector's water pollution dilemma. No single Wenan shop was nearly big enough to merit, let alone profitable enough to build, its own water treatment facility. The piecemeal crackdowns Wenan authorities had engaged in for a decade were pointless in regard to this environmental matter. Wenan had thousands of shredding shops; punishing a handful of them each year had no meaningful environmental impact and offered no solution to the underlying problem.

But the county government's response to the 2011 incident was different. On June 28 the County Party Committee released a document emblazoned in red characters announcing a "special action plan launching countywide normalization of waste plastic cleaning enterprises."[76] Under the newly arrived county party secretary, Li Keliang, Wenan launched a massive crackdown bent on eliminating every shredding and washing enterprise in the county. Secretary Li, having served his entire career in Langfang prefecture, of which Wenan was part, was no doubt familiar with the sector and understood that these shredding shops were an indispensable link in the sector's supply chain; their elimination would cripple the area's ten to twenty thousand recycling businesses. In taking this dramatic step, Secretary Li was clearly prioritizing environmental protection over GDP in a manner that Wenan's previous secretary had not, and while it is impossible to say what Li's motivations were, one can certainly speculate that changes in cadre evaluation criteria after 2006 that elevated the importance of environmental protection likely played a part in this shift in priorities; there is no question the government was increasingly concerned about pollution and was trying to get local officials to feel that urgency personally.[77]

The countywide shutdown required mustering the dedicated efforts of nearly every Wenan government bureau and employee for months. A wave of daily news conferences and propaganda activities began on June 29 and did not let up until September. Throughout July, through an unrelenting series of meetings highlighted daily on the county TV news, officials laid out the crackdown's scope. All roads in and out of the county would be policed, and trucks carrying plastic scrap bound for Wenan would be turned away; any trucks bearing plastic loads found within the county borders would be severely fined; and all shredding shops in Wenan were to be permanently closed. Notices were issued to each household in the area, and on a staggered schedule every township and village was told the date by which every plastic shredding shop was to be closed and fully dismantled. All unpermitted buildings were to be torn down; all unpermitted water outlets were to be plugged; all unpermitted access to the electric grid was to be cut; and all shredding, washing, and drying machinery was to be removed or physically destroyed and disposed of by the owners themselves. The two-page notice continued:

> [Residents] who after this date continue engaging in production and polluting the water and soil environment will be fined between 20,000 and 200,000 yuan as set in the PRC Water Pollution Prevention Law. . . . Concurrently, several county party and county government formulated policies providing special benefits will be implemented to attract enterprises and production and processing households to develop Dongdu Environmental Protection Industrial Park.[78]

According to the notices, Wenan's shredding shops had an alternative; they could move into Wenan's own local EPIP, Wenan Dongdu Environmental Protection Industrial Park (WDEPIP; the Dongdu stands for Chaoyang Dongdu Zhongxing company, a co-investor in the park). The 3,700 mu (2.5 square kilometer) park was not new. It had been built in 2006, just a couple of years after the banner success of ZEPIP in neighboring Jinghai. But unlike its successful neighbor, WDEPIP stood empty for five years. WDEPIP was built, not in the plastic processing hub on the county's west side, but rather twenty kilometers away from there, on the relatively sleepy east side.[79] When it opened in 2006, WDEPIP's promoters forecast it would draw in 1.4 billion yuan of investment in the first three years, but even the vice-chairman of the CRRA was dubious: "What is this 3,700 mu idea? That's approaching the size of a small township. . . . [What are] regular real estate companies doing designing this highly specialized project? Its future looks very murky."[80] That skepticism proved warranted; WDEPIP was a flop. Site visits between 2007 and 2009 found it remained little more than a grid of empty paved streets cutting between equally empty lots. The park was ill-conceived. Why would thousands of household plastic processors in west Wenan, twenty kilometers away from WDEPIP, whose workshops were either jerrybuilt add-ons to their own homes or built in their own villages (meaning they paid next to nothing for land use), spend hundreds of thousands of yuan (the minimum lease at WDEPIP was 300,000) to lease land on the other side of the county for the main privilege of having to register and pay taxes and fees on their businesses? And why would any outside investor ever start a plastic-processing business in WDEPIP knowing that twenty kilometers down the road were more than ten thousand tax-dodging competitors with almost no overhead vying for the same materials?

That flawed economic logic had not changed with the crackdown; for Wenan processors, uncompensated demolition still made more sense than moving into WDEPIP. From July 20 through early August 2011, the Wenan news replaced its coverage of propaganda meetings with footage of residents sledge-hammering concrete washing tubs, slicing through shredder rotary belts, smashing feeder boxes, and loading machine carcasses onto trucks for disposal. The park remained empty. Internet chat forums quickly became a semi-anonymous sphere for residents to debate the crackdown:

> Liu Hong the Crazy (刘洪也疯狂) [posted July 13, 2011]: Has the leadership group of Wenan county's government been kicked in the head? Have you thought to put yourselves in the shoes of the common people? . . . When you stop the plastic, what are we going to eat? Have you prepared the bowls and chopsticks for several tens of thousands of people? I hear you want all the shredding factories to move to Dongdu. This is where my buddies most admire you. . . . Let's say every shredder comes. Have you calculated their costs? Can you accommodate all of them? . . . If the processors follow them to Dongdu, you are implying that the entire west of Wenan should move into east Wenan? . . . Plastic's pollution we all can see, and we know how serious it is. We also want to rectify this, but please give us a solution plan, seek out some suggestions from the common people. We support your rectification, but please take a moment to think about it from our perspective.

> 鬼见愁 hjh [posted August 1]: Stop saying you're so pathetic. You all have made a lot of money. . . . County Secretary, I support you.

> LDPE pellet (低压瓶盖颗粒) [posted September 18]: Your Wenan has moved to our Baoding! Each day come several trucks, big loads, who knew? I can help you find a processor. Call . . . [81]

In the short term the ripple effects of Wenan's shut down were felt across North China. In August 2011 prices for scrap plastics in Beijing fell 50 to 90 percent, and many Beijing recyclers stopped collecting plastic from city residents.[82] For several months the bulk of Beijing's plastics went to the landfill, until processors relocated and the sector revived.[83] Wenan had been successfully closed down, but from the regional perspective the shutdown's main effect was to compel waste plastic processors to seek cover in less tightly guarded corners of the province. Covert clusters of plastic shops soon sprang up around Beijing's sixth ring road, and Baoding experienced a scrap plastic boom.[84] Though Baoding never approached the scale of Wenan as a processing hub, the practices there were at times just as appalling as anything found in Wenan; open burning of plastic wastes soon became a common problem in Baoding, leading to repeated uncontrolled fires that endangered residents and their property, and in one case asphyxiated more than five hundred chickens on a nearby farm.[85]

As the secretary of the Chinese Plastics Processing Industry Association, Ma Zhanfeng, had explained in a 2009 interview, two years before the Wenan crackdown, shutting down Wenan would not solve the problem: "Scrap plastic, like other waste materials, is by nature dirty. . . . If you talk simply of eliminating it, the waste plastic will just flow from Wenan to someplace else; it can't just disappear. For scrap industries that have great market demand, banning them is not as effective as improving their technology and strengthening their management."[86] Being a spokesperson for plastic processors, Ma would not be one to recommend the sensible solution for reducing plastic waste generation, manufacturing less plastic to begin with, but he was at least correct that banning plastic recycling does not make the sources of plastic waste disappear.

The Wenan case, as well as many of the policy processes described in this and the previous chapter, could be summarized as the state's exacerbation of an environmental race to the bottom by its persistent (re)production of the informal as illegal. The state's production of the informal as illegal was (and is) not merely a discursive act, because when the Chinese government treats informal sectors as illegal, it profoundly shapes conditions and behaviors in those sectors. The informal/formal division is neither a natural outcome of market forces nor a foreordained by-product of a transitional economy. Even less so is it an accurate representation dividing law-abiding actors from law-breaking ones. Rather, the formal/informal division is a persistently reinforced and malleable policy tool, regularly reinvented and renewed to shore up privileged political, administrative, and business networks against a wide range of outsiders (who are often, not coincidentally, business competitors) by labeling them not just as vaguely inferior (uncivilized, unmodern, "dirty messy deficient") but as polluting criminals. So branded, informal enterprises can be shut down at any moment, their assets confiscated and destroyed without compensation, conditions that predictably result in informal shops cutting costs in ways that negatively impact the environment and health. Perhaps most important of all, informal entrepreneurs are not only barred from government-run professional associations but are banned from creating such associations themselves; they are deprived of any role as stakeholders in shaping the policies that affect their sector. We find this dynamic throughout China's informal waste and recycling sectors. As Yvan Schulz concluded in his study of informal "e-waste" recyclers, "the discourse of environmental protection, which serves to justify restructuring the 'e-waste' recycling sector, should not be taken at face value. Above all, it is an asset that certain actors mobilize—alongside scientific and media authority, state power, corporate funding, etc.—to advance their own interests."[87] The EPIP model fits this description well. On the one hand it offered a potential step toward better environmental protection: gathering processors into one place for closer oversight, enabling the concentrated use of pollution remediation facilities like water treatment plants, and ensuring that shipments passing through customs go directly to licensed facilities rather than quickly dispersing into the informal sector. But the model was based on a kind of magical thinking that the park's walls miraculously separated companies inside from the informal sector outside. ZEPIP companies declared themselves "green" because they produced little pollution inside their yards, but their profits were derived from selling the materials they produced to polluting copper refineries and informal shops outside the park. The quarantining of the "good" parts of recycling from the "bad" parts was never plausible, and as we have seen, the state-managed portions of the supply chain were just as vulnerable to corruption as the rest of the sector. Moreover, the recycling sector was dependent on the informal sector to provide not just cheap labor, but also expertise in materials sorting, processing, and marketing. The informal sector was the goose that turned scrap into golden eggs, and the EPIP model mainly served to hide the goose on the other side of conceptual or physical walls. The EPIP model could not change or disguise the fact that by promoting massive scrap importation and "urban mining" the state was choosing rapid GPD growth over environmental protection.

The 2000s saw the Beijing municipal government repeatedly getting out ahead of itself about recycling, making policy pronouncements that it proved unable to deliver. Hundreds of millions of dollars and twelve years of effort were expended on residential trash-sorting campaigns that resulted in no waste diversion, instead undermining public confidence as the "first sort, then mix" phenomenon went unaddressed. Of much greater consequence to the lives and work of hundreds of thousands of migrant recyclers, city authorities incessantly revisited grandiose plans for building a rationalized modern recycling network, using their vision as an excuse to repress migrant collectors and brokers when their removal was convenient, all the while channeling hundreds of millions of yuan in funding, contracts, and land deals to poorly performing SOEs.

Recycling is far from the only sphere in which China's local administrations have faced challenges enacting policies that, were they fully implemented and enforced, might have been salutary to environmental and social well-being. Indeed, there is a large scholarly literature analyzing the problem of implementing the government's often idealistic environmental policies on the ground. This literature explores how local officials are often inadvertently incentivized to choose profit over environment, or how China's overlapping and fragmented vertical and horizontal administrative structures (tiaokuai) conspire to defeat policy effectiveness.[88] We have seen plenty of evidence substantiating both arguments, and the *tiaokuai* problem in particular seems an apt description of recycling in Beijing, where the concrete manifestations of everyday recycling involve so many different governing offices: commerce, sanitation, urban planning, environmental protection, and transport. But as important as these internal governance mechanisms surely were (and continue to be), when we look at the recycling sector altogether over this period, it becomes clear that analyzing the details of each specific bureaucratic snafu, while surely enlightening, misses the forest for the trees in the governance of this sector.

Instead, I argue that there are three more sweeping assumptions or orientations that combine to produce these consistently ineffective and often unjust policy outcomes in the recycling sector: a dismissive and discriminatory devaluation of rural migrants, a favoring of state system insiders over outsiders (*tizhi nei* vs. *tizhi wai*), and a teleological view of modern development. The reader by now needs no more data on the pervasive bias projected in word and deed regarding the "dirty messy deficient" and "low *suzhi*" nature of migrant recyclers; we have also seen throughout the last two chapters how, despite years of economic reforms, officials consistently excluded nonstate (*tizhi wai*) players and even clung to old ministry identities. It is also almost too easy to see what motivates the consistent reinscription of these orientations—just follow the money.

Still, the third orientation, a seemingly unquestioned teleology of what constitutes modern development, plays a crucial role in justifying the other two orientations as rational, inevitable, and socially and environmentally beneficial. From the lofty heights of macroeconomic forecasting and planning, China's hugely successful stint as the world's factory in the 1990s and 2000s was never the final destination; China was not supposed to remain a low-wage, low-value-added manufacturing center forever. This was merely a crucial step to move China toward future prosperity. With such rapidly and consistently rising GDP, it was inevitable that China would see rising wages, greater urbanization, and the accumulation of a resource base, all enabling a transition to higher-wage, higher value-added, scaled-up, less labor-intensive, and hopefully less environmentally damaging, production. As this teleology manifests in the waste management and recycling world, waste pickers, hand processors, community bike-cart collectors, and stall brokers with small-scale equipment are all viewed necessarily as transitional; they are not worth investing in because they are destined to be supplanted. Beijing's informal recyclers often mocked the incompetence of the city's recycling companies and officials, for their obvious lack of knowledge about materials, processing, and markets. But from most officials' perspectives the skills and expertise of informal agents were of little consequence; indeed, many officials did not even seem to recognize that these skills and expertise existed and just treated informal recyclers as unskilled "human labor" (*renli*) soon to be replaced by scaled-up technologies and automation. From this perspective, to treat informal recyclers as expendable and unworthy of support or investment is not an expression of bias; it is simply to understand the imperatives of economic development.

I argue that these orientations conspire to foreclose as unthinkable the possibility of recognizing informal sector actors as stakeholders and bringing them to the table. I am not arguing that doing so would have resulted in easy solutions to the corruption and pollution in the sector. But given the large amounts of money and effort the Chinese state has thrown into ineffective schemes, backfiring crackdowns, and propping up SOEs while environmental degradation raged in marginalized and poor communities, it seems unfortunate that the possibility of cooperation was never even broached. Moreover, it is important to point out that the idea of reaching out to and cooperating with the informal waste sector in so-called developing countries is far from novel; a landmark 2007 report bringing together research from six countries (Peru, India, Romania, Zambia, Philippines, and Egypt) argued that in every case a policy approach based on respecting informal waste workers as stakeholders and seeking cooperative solutions with them was not just more ethical and environmentally beneficial but more cost effective than policies based on criminalizing and eliminating them.[89] That such well-researched approaches have been absent in Chinese policy and academic circles seems indicative of either a refusal to see these developing countries as potential peers or a rejection of the very notion of legitimizing informal waste workers as politically unthinkable.

Be that as it may, if China's recycling SOEs and local authorities were all waiting in the 2000s for state policies to direct them toward a modernized, scaled-up, less labor-intensive plan for the recycling sector, then those state policy makers were themselves waiting for the economic indicators (urban land prices, wage levels, resource bases) to show that China had reached the point where the domestic economy was ready to make that shift. As shown in chapter 8, that time, apparently, is now, and the policies are here.

8

No Longer the World's Garbage Dump!

Most of us hardly give a thought to what happens to our trash after we throw it out, until something throws it back at us. Usually the boomerang effect is local: a racoon knocking over the bins or a municipal strike that stops garbage pickup long enough to remind everyone what rotting trash smells like. But recently the boomerang has been global. "Your Recycling Gets Recycled, Right? Maybe, or Maybe Not," ran a *New York Times* headline in spring 2018.[1] By then the upheaval in global recycling markets was forcing people across the planet, from New York City to Thailand, from London to Vietnam, to wake up and smell the garbage. The trigger for the global recycling crisis was China's ban, issued in January 2018, on importing "foreign garbage" (*yang laji*), aka scrap. While few outside the recycling industry had paid much attention as China amassed a waste empire early in this millennium, China's shutting its ports to imported scrap has been a rude awakening for US, European Union (EU), and other OECD nation consumers, who are now realizing that they have been making a lot of trash and have no clue where it has been put. The ban has washed the wastes from these rich countries to the shores of developing nations throughout Southeast Asia, inundating them with more scrap than they have capacity to manage, and recently several of these countries have been following China's lead, closing their ports to waste materials and even sending loads of contamination-laden materials back to the wealthier lands from whence they came.[2]

China's initial "foreign garbage" ban listed twenty-four categories of waste, most significantly many kinds of recovered plastic and "mixed paper," the main outputs of OECD countries' residential recycling systems. In 2019 the list expanded to thirty-two categories, and China's Ministry of Ecology and Environment (MEE) insists that its goal is to reach zero waste imports by the end of 2020. All told, that dramatic claim might be somewhat mushier than it sounds; the term *waste*, as the reader by now is all too aware, can be quite flexible.[3] The MEE's Qiu Qiwen recently explained, "If solid waste . . . meets the requirements of China's import standards and doesn't contain any hazards, then it can be treated as common commodities, not waste."[4] Still, call them *wastes* or *commodities*, imports of scrap materials plummeted by 47 percent in 2018; as of January 2020 scrap plastic imports were down 99 percent from their 2017 levels, while imports of recovered fiber (scrap paper) in 2019 were 39 percent of 2017's figures, and brokers generally view as credible China's claim that paper imports could fall to essentially zero by 2021.[5]

While the "foreign garbage" ban has upended the global recycling sector, it coincides with another policy shift that, though receiving far less attention in Western media, is arguably just as significant: the thorough restructuring of China's domestic solid waste management system. At the heart of China's monumental domestic waste management rebuild is what I will call "the merge," short for the phrase "merging of two networks" (*liang wang ronghe*)—a policy aimed at merging the two long-separate bureaucracies that have been at the core of this study: MSW, managed by the sanitation bureaucracy, and recycling, which since 1949 has been overseen by the Commerce Ministry. Unlike the patchy array of waste reforms and crackdowns of the 1990s and 2000s, this coordinated policy emanates from the highest levels of government. National garbage sorting is one of Xi Jinping's signature campaigns, attested to by a barrage of policy documents, speeches, media campaigns, and even animated rap videos like *Six Things Xi Jinping Cares About*.[6] Central state funding for "the merge" over the current five-year plan approaches 300 billion yuan, and that is without local government and corporate investment added in. This massive infrastructure reform aims to permanently replace the informal recycling system with municipally planned source separation, beginning at the level of household trash fees and sorting bins and stretching all the way to waste-to-energy (WtE) incineration and circular economy industry parks (CEIPs; *xunhuan jingji chanye yuan*—something like a domestically focused version of the EPIP model described in chapter 7). As this chapter explains, the import ban and the network merge are fundamentally linked policies, and neither can be fully understood without the other; hence, below I refer to these linked policies as "the Ban + Merge."

The Ban + Merge are being undertaken at tremendous cost. The purported aims are minimizing waste generation, eliminating polluting practices, and maximizing resource recycling in the name of developing China's "ecological civilization" (*shengtai wenming*). The state wishes to root out polluting forms of scrap processing—particularly unlicensed processors that operate with little or no pollution remediation—while installing a comprehensive infrastructure in which state-owned or -affiliated companies gain monopoly rights over wastes, in return for which they are ostensibly obligated to process them in accord with MEE standards. As of summer 2020, the ban has settled in as the new normal for global scrap markets, while the merge remains a work in progress.

This chapter begins with a discussion of the buzzword *ecological civilization*, the guiding vision that all these waste-related reforms are said to advance. It then sketches the ban and its effects on global and Chinese recycling markets, then moves on to outline the merge and explain how the Ban + Merge, described by one expert as a "one-two punch" to the informal recycling sector, are meant to reinforce one another.[7] Finally, the chapter surveys several aspects of the merge, exploring how the massive wave of state investment is reshaping China's domestic waste sector, transforming the disposal habits of urban residents, and perhaps dealing a disabling blow to Beijing's migrant recycler communities.

Since around 2012, Beijing's informal recycling sector has faced increasing headwinds. No reliable numbers exist, but many old-hand recyclers in Beijing estimate the city's migrant recycling community has shrunk by as much as 70–90 percent over the last decade. Attrition in Beijing began with a round of scrap market demolitions in 2012–13 paired with a return to the 1990s-style policies of prohibiting the building of any new scrap markets—a policy that in its current iteration has been easier to effectively enforce, as land rents inside the sixth ring road are now generally too high to make scrap markets an attractive investment.[8] Added to the fact that markets were getting fewer and farther between, scrap commodity prices slumped from 2013 to 2017, in part due to China's slowing GDP growth. Then, in December 2017, Beijing was shaken as the city government unleashed an unprecedented wave of mass evictions targeted at migrant communities. The evictions were supposedly undertaken for public safety. On November 18, 2017, a fire broke out in an unpermitted apartment building in a migrant enclave in Beijing's Daxing district, claiming nineteen lives. Authorities used the tragedy as justification to launch a blitzkrieg on unpermitted construction, summarily evicting an estimated one million migrants from their homes, throwing many into the street in the middle of winter. Many Chinese and international onlookers were appalled and seized upon a phrase the government repeatedly used to characterize the evicted communities—low-value population (低端人口, *diduan renkou*)—turning it into a human rights meme. It is an interesting term. The adjective low-value, *diduan*, is most commonly paired with economic terms like brand (*pinpai*) or sector (*chanye*). Informal recycling is, of course, a paradigmatic "low-value" sector, and the phrase "low-value population" was being bandied about in describing migrant recyclers for decades before it suddenly became politically taboo in late 2017. But even if officials now avoid uttering that exact phrase, it is no secret China's leadership remains deeply anxious about low-wage and informal workers, for they are precisely the sectors that government economists insist must wither and be replaced by higher-wage and higher-value-added jobs if China is going to move from being a low-wage manufacturer to a middle-class society.

For Beijing's recyclers, the dehumanizing rhetoric and bullying meted out during the 2017 evictions was extraordinary for its scale but not for its methods or message. Recyclers today continue to be caught in the tumult of creative destruction that is the material manifestation of China's economic rise. The question for migrant recyclers in many respects remains the same today as it was in the 1990s: Will the opportunities and wealth these paroxysms of creative destruction are supposed to unleash be sufficient to make the violence of these processes worth weathering? More generally, in what follows I attempt to provide an overview of where these policies might be leading China's waste sector, where environmental and social concerns might indeed be gaining important ground, and where policies seem more geared to benefiting investors than the public or environment.

ECOLOGICAL CIVILIZATION AND SIMULATION OF PUBLIC OPINION

To many US environmentalists, the Chinese state's embrace of the rhetoric of sustainability, when compared to their own government's promotion of environmental deregulation and climate change denial (particularly under Republican administrations), sounds innovative and even inspiring.[9] In 2007, at the CCP's 17th Party Congress, President Hu Jintao brought the phrase "ecological civilization" into the national limelight. A decade later, at the 19th Party Congress, Xi Jinping—wielding greater lung capacity and political power than Hu ever showed—spent much of his three and one-half hour oration preaching ecological civilization's preeminence and, a few months later (at the same meeting at which Xi was anointed president for life) "ecological civilization" (along with "Xi Jinping thought") was formally written into the Chinese constitution. Since then the phrase has echoed across state media. Riding the rhetorical froth has been a raft of tangible reforms: the consolidation of environmental governance under a new mammoth MEE; the replacement of pollution fees with a more robust environmental protection tax; tighter air pollution monitoring that has given Beijing more blue sky days than it had seen in decades; and in the solid waste world, the Ban + Merge and "mandatory trash sorting" (qiangzhi fenlei) campaigns.

While debate swirls around whether the government is truly committed to "ecological" values, the word civilization also deserves scrutiny. In China today, the word regularly serves as a dainty justification for extrajudicial state violence, from the detentions and forced reeducation of one million Uyghurs in Xinjiang (in the name of socialist and modern civilization) to the violent eviction of migrants in Beijing in December 2017 (to build a "civilized city"). Xi Jinping did not invent the use of *civilization* as a rationale for oppressive assimilationism and sweeping acts of extrajudicial repression and confiscation—indeed, such uses of *civilization* are not unique to the modern Chinese state; the long and violent histories of European and US colonialism could easily be cited as exemplary in this regard—but Xi has weaponized the application of *civilization* against extraordinarily large portions of China's citizenry.

Of course, the preferred mechanisms by which ecological civilization is deployed are not militarized brutality but economic policies. According to Xi Jinping, the meaning of ecological civilization can be distilled as "green waters and green mountains are golden and silver mountains" (*lü shui qingshan jiushi jinshan yin shan*), equating sustainable development with economic prosperity. As Heidi Wang-Kaeding astutely puts it: "Ecological Civilization reinforces the symbiosis between economic development and environmental protection. It highlights the functional logic that commodifies environmentally friendly projects."[10] She further notes that this "harmonization between environmental and commercial interests has induced domestic players to jump on the bandwagon of Ecological Civilization"; as we will see, the corporate waste sector is fully on board.

There is no question that in concentrating its attention on the environment, China's leadership is responding to a major concern of Chinese citizens, both rural and urban. Exposure to health-damaging pollution, or the risk of such exposure, spurs hundreds of protests throughout the country every year. These problems arise, it is argued, because for the last few decades GDP has been valued over environment and health. In building an ecological civilization it is claimed such trade-offs will no longer be countenanced; only win-win projects that nurture the environment will be fostered. I am not alone in approaching these claims with some skepticism, but before looking into the specifics of these projects in the waste-space, I look briefly at the state's curation of public opinion in the environmental realm.

The policy discourse decrying "foreign garbage" reveals a state deft at claiming responsiveness to public opinion. I argue instead that the state produces a simulacrum of public opinion, acknowledging that environmental problems exist while simultaneously using threats and censorship to pare down the rough multiplicity of anxieties and debates regarding pollution problems, shaping them into a self-justifying call for nationalistic, state-guided solutions. The state's use of Wang Jiuliang's film *Plastic China* (塑料王国 *Suliao Wangguo*) is a case in point. While the *New York Times* article "China's Environmental Woes, in Films That Go Viral, Then Vanish" painted a picture in 2017 of Wang's film becoming a spontaneous public sensation only to be banned by state censors, in fact, state media helped set the stage for *Plastic China* to go viral in the first place.[11] For two years before *Plastic China* was released, Wang Jiuliang repeatedly appeared in state media showing clips from his documentary, raising public awareness of both plastic pollution and his coming film.[12] This dynamic—the state publicizing a film on a sensitive environmental issue and then banning it only days after its "viral" release—is not unique to Wang Jiuliang's work; Chai Jing's documentary on air pollution, *Under the Dome* (*Qiongding zhi xia*), had a similar trajectory. There is plenty of evidence indicating that in both cases this pattern of state promotion followed by censorship was unintentional, that in both cases it was the result of disagreements/ miscommunications between different propaganda offices, but the fact is that this cycle (first publicity, then censorship) still creates the simulacrum of public opinion the government desires. The state allows members of the public to raise a sensitive matter only to foreclose the terrain of analysis as soon as the discussion risks raising any complex and potentially trenchant political critiques. This is not to say that Wang Jiuliang is in any way responsible for the co-optation of his work. *Plastic China* is, in my opinion, beautiful, persistent, deeply ethical art with layered meanings far beyond any simple nationalism. But it is precisely those layers of meaning the government finds threatening. This does not mean China's state policies are incapable of achieving salutary effects that benefit the public—as we will see, the scrap import ban, while a mixed bag, is helping transform the global policy discussion on plastic use—but China's publics are never allowed to delve where problems lie, explore their complexities, or debate what actions should be taken. Rather, the government uses a curated simulation of public expression so it can present its policies, not as the unilateral decisions they actually are but as sensitive and technically expert responses to the public's supposed plea for the government to protect their well-being.

THE BAN
Getting Finicky

Though the war against the "trashing" of China has two fronts, domestic and international, it is the international one that has grabbed global headlines. The severity of the ban took many in the sector by surprise, but it was far from a sneak attack; there were signs over the years that a war on "foreign trash" was coming. In late 2012, foreign scrap brokers began to notice that customs officials at the Guangdong and Shenzhen ports were scrutinizing waste loads with a new perspicacity, leading to a sharp slowdown in scrap imports into those two ports.[13] It turned out this was a preview of a national-level tightening of enforcement, dubbed Operation Green Fence (绿篱行动 *lü li xingdong*), launched in February 2013. No new regulations were drafted; the operation simply stepped up customs inspection and enforcement of regulations already on the books—checking to make sure manifests were properly filled and that materials met contamination limits. All kinds of wastes were inspected, but the focus was plastics. Inspectors began enforcing a 1.5 percent contamination limit, a very high standard, especially for mixed plastic loads originating from US single-stream collection, which typically are heavily laced with food residue, oil, and unwanted rubbish. In the first four months of Green Fence, fifty-five scrap transactions totaling seventy-six hundred tons of material, largely mixed plastics, were rejected at port and "returned to sender" at great expense to said sender. With the United States shipping twenty million tons of scrap to China per year at that time, the rejection rate was tiny, but for export-ers who had grown complacent after years of sending substandard loads with no repercussions, it was a shot across the bow. The sector was shaken; after a decade of uninterrupted double-digit growth, China's plastic scrap imports in May 2013 dropped 5.5 percent, while the price of mixed plastic fell from $140 to $20 a bale.[14] In response, many US recyclers started putting in the extra effort to sort and clean their materials better. Demand and prices on well-sorted and cleaned bales stayed steady. In sum, Green Fence succeeded somewhat in getting foreign dealers to stop sending so much low-quality, pollution-loaded scrap to China.

But the effect of Green Fence on reducing pollution in China's scrap process-ing was limited. At first both Chinese and foreign reports found that Green Fence had "driven out of business many small operations and many facilities in south-ern China."[15] But the effects in reducing pollution were at best partial and short lived. Wang Jiuliang shot his film *Plastic China* during the years of Green Fence enforcement, documenting hellishly polluting plastic shops that still sourced exclusively from imports and seemed to have no run-ins with the law; as discussed in chapter 7, even the 2011 shutdown of the huge processing hub of Wenan only caused a short-term decline in the sector, as informal shops quickly popped back up in other poorly regulated areas.

Imports had fully recovered by the time the state announced a reprise of Green Fence in late 2015. This time enforcement focused less on the ports and more on domestic plastic processors: "All provincial offices of China's Environmental Protection Bureau have been charged with the responsibility of undertaking spot inspections of scrap plastic users . . . to assess for any illegal behavior."[16] Scores of plants were shut down, only to have others spring up in their place; something bigger was needed.

Slamming the Door

Four years after Green Fence, the new normal of China's scrap trade was not terribly different from the old one. Overall, imported scrap was of somewhat improved quality, and port inspections and crackdowns on informal processors were more frequent, but domestic processing, particularly in plastics, remained largely informal and import volumes huge. When the next round of crackdowns, dubbed National Sword (国门利检 *Guomen li jian*), was announced in February 2017, it was expected to be Green Fence redux. But the drumbeat soon quick-ened; in early April several Chinese ports were said to be opening and inspecting every incoming container of scrap, and on April 18, state media reported that the Central Leading Group for Comprehensively Deepening Reforms (chaired by President Xi) recommended that "regulations should be enhanced to significantly reduce the *categories* and volume of waste imports."[17] This was a big deal, signaling that customs would move from controlling scrap on a shipment-by-shipment basis to banning entire categories of scrap outright. The US trade publication *Resource Recycling* looked to recycling brokers for their reaction: "Some observers are not convinced China will take the dramatic measure of effectively blocking such a massive import market. 'I don't think such a ban will happen as it would be chaotic to the global recovered paper industry, including the Chinese mills,' said Bill Moore of Moore & Associates."[18] But bring on the chaos they did. On July 18, 2017, China notified the WTO of its intention to ban twenty-four types of waste by the end of the year, including several kinds of plastics (mixed plastic, PE [polyethylene], PS, PVC), mixed paper, and textiles.

The math of the ban was jaw dropping. In 2017, before the ban, in just its first round of issuing import permits, China's Ministry of Environmental Protection approved the import of 3.5 million tons of scrap; in 2018, after five such rounds the total was only 21,300 tons.[19] In the first half of 2018 the United States sent 3 million fewer tons of scrap (all kinds) to China than in 2017, and plastic scrap exports out of the port of Los Angeles to China and Hong Kong for January 2018 fell 96 percent on the year.[20]

Cities across the United States, the EU, and Australia had nowhere to send the recycling they collected. Ziggurats of scrap bales piled up in ports up and down the US West coast. Hundreds of cities and counties reeled from the punch, some bleeding cash (Fort Worth saw a $1.4 million turnaround in its recycling budget), some slashing their recycling programs (Sacramento, CA; Twin Falls, ID; Lincoln County, Maine; etc.), others sending loads of scrap to landfills and incinerators (Ketchican, AK; Phoenix, AZ; Honolulu, HI; etc.), and some hiking fees to cover their losses (in MA, NY, CA).[21] Plastics were not the only sector to take a hit; many recyclers were paying $30 a ton to have mixed paper taken off their hands, and OCC fell from $150 a ton in 2017 to $70 in 2018 and $28 in 2019. Many US consumers saw their trash/recycling fees bolt upward; others saw the plastic and paper they had diligently sorted to recycle sent to the landfill instead, turning what they imagined had been deeds of environmental conservation into acts of wasting and polluting.[22] There have been some indications that these rock-bottom prices might spark a small resurgence in recycling processing in the United States, with both domestic and foreign companies exploring investing in US operations. For instance, at the very same time in spring 2018 that China's cardboard and paper giant, Nine Dragons, was forced to idle paper recycling lines at home due to supply shortfalls caused by the ban, the company purchased a paper mill in West Virginia. Five other large US recycling plants were contracted by Chinese investors in August and September

2018, including a $150 million investment in a Kentucky paper mill and $75 million in a North Carolina plastics plant, and a few US companies have expanded capacity as well.[23] While these glimmers of investment are signs that perhaps in several years US scrap processing might experience a small revival, thus far they have provided little help with the glut of scrap confronting US recycling since the ban.

As soon as it became clear the ban was coming, US and EU scrap brokers started scrambling to find alternative markets. From the perspective of the supply chain, China's import ban merely forced one link—material cleaning and preprocessing—to relocate abroad; once the tons of dirty discarded plastic tubs, packaging, and other items had been processed into clean flake or pellet, they could be reexported to China as production materials.[24] The obvious first place to look for alternative processors was Southeast Asian countries. Close to China, with plenty of cheap labor, Association of Southeast Asian Nations (ASEAN) members also had the advantage of being exempt from many Chinese import tariffs, so they could reexport processed materials to Chinese manufacturers at a competitive price.

It was not just OECD brokers selling scrap who did the math and came up with Southeast Asia as the solution; Chinese scrap plastic processors had read the writing on the wall and were already jetting to Southeast Asia to set up shop. The shift was underway within months of the government announcement, even before the ban was fully in place. Comparing 2017 to 2016, Thailand saw PE scrap imports jump 876 percent, PVC 128 percent, and mixed plastic 150 percent; for Malaysia PVC rose 407 percent, mixed plastics 292 percent, and PE 132 percent; and Vietnam's PET imports increased 137 percent and its PE 166 percent.[25] Shipments from the United Kingdom to Malaysia tripled.

But the outlook for relocating to ASEAN countries quickly soured. Vietnamese ports were soon inundated, and customs violations were rampant. As violators had their permits to import revoked, thousands of unclaimed containers accumulated, jamming ports. By June 2018, Vietnamese authorities announced their own temporary plastic scrap ban and floated plans to make it permanent by 2020.[26] In Thailand, after a wave of permit abuses and a high-profile bust of e-waste scrap processors, the government banned all plastic and e-waste imports; US exporters sent only 1.5 million pounds of recovered plastic to Thailand in July 2018, compared with 27.1 million pounds in June and 41.6 million in May. China's neighbors are also refusing to be trashed. The crescendo of international voices for a scrap plastic ban culminated in May 2019 with plastic being added to the list of substances controlled under the Basel Convention on the Control of Transboundary Movements of Hazardous Wastes and Their Disposal.[27]

Processors React

Turning to China, is the ban having the desired effect of strangling the supply flows headed to polluting processors and helping root them out? On January 22

允许进口？没有许可证管制？这些字眼是不是让您觉得特别辣眼睛？是的，菲律宾就是这么任性！

更劲爆的是：菲律宾当地进口塑料加工企业比较少，待开发的市场潜力巨大。

What? 连小编都有点心动了，您不信？不信来跟我们走一趟！

杜特尔特总统邀请您去菲律宾投资！

FIGURE 14. Portion of an internet advertisement posted by the official WeChat account of China's Scrap Plastic Association in November 2017 for a December tour of the Philippines to scout out opportunities for plastic processing. From https://mp.weixin.qq.com /s?__biz=MjM5MTM5NjM4NA==&mid=2662314791&idx=1&sn=f3d56d96628b27 ff29ceefb17d43c1bb&chksm=bded34688a9abd7e98ae27d3966910a8ecc3b6932f1d77feeb 31def349c63e23f8f44edbaa9f&scene=21#wechat_redirect.

and 23, 2018, China Central Television (CCTV) aired a pair of undercover reports on the waste ban, orchestrated reconnaissance missions complete with night-flying drones, clandestine filming, and journalists impersonating buyers. The first report focused on Ziya Environmental Protection Industry Park in Tianjin (ZEPIP; see chapter 7), a state-managed industrial park that for a decade had been dedicated exclusively to processing imported scrap, much of which was now cut off. Reporters saw no signs that ZEPIP companies were violating the ban but did find many companies were in dire straits trying to transition from foreign to domestic supply chains; managers complained that China's domestic scrap was of insufficient quality to replace the imported materials on which they had depended.[28] The second report investigated the notoriously polluting county of Wenan and ferreted out a cluster of informal plastic shops from which noxious fumes billowed into the night air. This was happening despite the fact that Hebei was under the tightest ever "blue sky" restrictions on air pollution; the rogue processors had informants inside the local government warning them about inspectors before they arrived.[29] The higher-ups take measures, those below have countermeasures (*shang you zhengce, xia you duice*), as the saying goes. Still, there was no sign any of this scrap was imported; it was all clearly domestically sourced, so at the very least the ban almost immediately narrowed the options available to rogue processors.[30]

For those informal processors with more capital and better foreign connections, opening processing shops in Southeast Asia looked more promising than playing dangerous games of cat and mouse with the government. It was entirely predictable that China's informal processors, with their inexpensive equipment, their long history of dodging state authorities, and their familiarity with foreign supply chains, would be quick to search out overseas locations where they could continue processing, profiting, and polluting. Within weeks of the ban's announcement in July 2017, online advertisements appeared hawking group tours for Chinese plastic processors interested in scouting for factory locations in the Philippines, Malaysia, Vietnam, and Thailand (see figure 14). But these tours were not organized by shady informal scofflaws; they were being planned and led by the state-affiliated China Scrap Plastic Association (CSPA). It was not criminal polluters from Wenan and Guiyu but the CSPA that was selling weeklong "inspection tours" complete with meetings with foreign officials to discuss import regulations and other matters. Here is some of the catnip the CSPA dangled for its package tour of the Philippines:

[Webpage title] President Duterte says, "Come to the Philippines to process your plastic scrap, a huge quantity of materials awaits Chinese entrepreneurs!"

Though a signatory of the Basel accords, *the Philippines allows the importation of plastic wastes. In fact, it is the only South East Asian country that imposes no licensing controls. They allow imports? Without any permit control?* Don't those words give you especially "spicy eyes" (辣眼睛 *la yanjing*)? It's true. The Philippines is just that headstrong![31]

Not every ASEAN country was touted as an unregulated paradise. Tour materials for Thailand emphasized its advantage of having strong Chinese business networks already in place, but cautioned that Thailand's port and environmental authorities needed to be taken seriously. In its dozens of tour reports and advertisements, the CSPA framed the shift of processing overseas as part of "One Belt, One Road" ecological developmentalism.[32] Thai, Malaysian, and Vietnamese authorities begged to disagree. A raid in October 2018 outside Kuala Lumpur shut down three illegal plants, two of which were owned by Chinese nationals.[33] A spring 2019 report from the environmental NGO Global Alliance for Incinerator Alternatives documents the devastation caused by the tsunami of plastic processing and waste burning that inundated port-adjacent villages in Malaysia, Thailand, Vietnam, and Indonesia; Chinese partners were active in almost every case.[34]

Ripple Effects

Seeing that a blanket ban is inflicting damage across the Chinese economy, crippling not just small, shifty polluters but also registered companies in state industrial parks like ZEPIP, the question arises: Why would the state choose such a strategy? As Adam Minter has argued, if the goal is pollution prevention. then banning scrap imports seems misguided; it either forces companies to substitute lower-quality and more polluting domestic scrap or shift to virgin materials, which are more polluting and energy intensive to produce than using recycled materials. Both alternatives entail higher overall environmental costs than using imported scrap.[35]

But Minter's calculation, though accurate, is not the one China's planners are making. The state is not comparing domestic to imported scrap but looking at the country's overall materials markets and resources. Compared to twenty years ago, China has more than quadrupled its available domestic scrap arisings—from huge new flows of postconsumer plastics and paper to a massive expansion of metals from end-of-life durable goods and building demolition. Hence, in theory China is much closer to being able to supply all its own scrap demand. So state planners ask: "With today's massive domestic scrap material base, why import scrap at all? Scrap requires processing which always has local pollution costs; shouldn't we only import clean virgin materials instead? OECD countries hardly import any scrap; why should we?" This logic is certainly not environmentally beneficial from a global perspective (increasing the use of virgin materials increases environmental costs from mining, deforestation, etc.), but it makes more sense from a national one. Banning scrap means that imported materials will only raise the overall quality of materials used in China's manufacturing rather than add to the country's pollution load. Ecologically, the ban quickly increased demand for more costly (both economically and environmentally) virgin materials; the third quarter of 2018 saw the biggest exports of virgin PE plastic resin to China in history.[36] Though the environmental costs of producing virgin PE are higher than for recycling it, those costs have been shifted outside China's borders.

But the environmental calculus is not the whole story, nor the most important one, from the global environmental perspective. Two years on, it has become clear that China's ban has helped catalyze an impassioned global debate on plastic pollution. Environmental scientists, biologists, and activists have been documenting the myriad hazards of plastics to the environment and human health for decades, but China's ban has helped raise these concerns to new levels of attention, outrage, and political action. When Southeast Asian nations followed China's lead with their own import bans—returning hundreds of containers of waste plastics back to the OECD nations whence they came and sharing images of villages buried under piles of imported trash—the scales of public opinion in OECD nations began to tip. In May 2019 the Basel Convention on the transboundary movement of hazardous wastes was amended to include plastic waste under its processes of monitoring and regulation.

But arguably most important is that the ban has helped push the international conversation on plastic pollution up the supply chain, beyond the questions of disposal and recycling and on to questions of how best to reduce or even eliminate the manufacturing and use of disposable plastic products and packaging. In the wake of China's ban, the EU endorsed the Strategy for Plastic in the Circular Economy, which included eliminating single-use food utensils, reductions in food containers and packaging, and mandates for recycled content in plastic products, and California has drafted similar legislation.[37] And China's National Development and Reform Commission (NDRC) is drafting similar policies as well, with goals like banning plastic foam takeout containers, plastic utensils, ultra-thin plastic bags, and all products containing plastic micro beads by 2022.[38]

There is no denying that within China, the ban comes with economic costs. Countless Chinese manufacturers have built supply chains around plastic, paper, and metal scrap for decades, and suddenly cauterizing the inflow of tens of millions of tons of materials has inflicted collateral damage across a broad swath of the economic landscape. Why would China's government choose to impose this kind of self-inflicted wound on its economy? This is where escaping the "middle-income trap" comes in. China's "development miracle" since the 1980s was built on the backs and sweat of China's huge pool of inexpensive labor. But after decades of successful growth, that economic model's potential is tapped out. To continue raising GDP per capita, China must advance into higher-profit, higher-wage sectors. Recycling, especially informal recycling, is a textbook labor-intensive, low-wage, low-profit sector, and the state hopes to hasten its atrophy with the ban. As a leading government policy expert explains it:

> In the short-term, the renewable resources processing and utilization sector will sustain a definite shock. After a period of pain, a large number of low-end (diduan) enterprises must face their fate and shut down. But in the long run it is a major opportunity to contribute to industrial agglomeration, improving the level of our technology, management, environmental standards and product quality.[39]

Markets will collapse, and costs will rise, but large companies favored with government loans and soft budget constraints can weather the storm; small, private entrepreneurs with thin profit margins will struggle mightily and mostly fail. And that is the whole point. From the state's perspective, those small, diduan companies need to be weeded out. At the same time, if all works out properly, it is hoped that domestic waste management policies will foster market spaces enabling high-tech and state-owned companies to wrest back control over China's own huge domestic waste streams and put them to profitable and environmentally responsible use; that is the goal of "the merge."

THE MERGE
A New Waste Regime

From the vantage of overall material flows, "the merge" is intended to fill the vacuum caused by banning "foreign trash" with China's own domestic scrap. Such a macro view on overall commodity flows is not new for the Chinese state; the intense concern over recycling in the Mao era was closely linked to China's inability to access resources in international trade. And as discussed in chapter 7, scrap import policies in the 2000s were based on long-term forecasts that after a few decades of importing scrap, China could shift to relying on its own domestic scrap base. That time has apparently arrived. The ban therefore goes hand in hand with the comprehensive restructuring of China's domestic waste management system: "the merge" bookends "the ban." The ban is intended to "provide market space and a channel for recyclable materials extracted from the domestic waste stream, serving as a market traction mechanism."[40] Indeed, such effects began immediately as the ban settled into place, with Beijing's street prices for recyclables like cardboard and plastics rebounding for the first time in years soon after the ban was implemented.[41] The rise in domestic scrap prices is meant to incentivize companies to invest in the sector, promote innovative technologies, and tender bids for urban waste management contracts. The hope is that if domestic waste sector reforms are properly managed, domestic scrap will replace imports, and the entire sector will leave low-value materials and processing behind and concentrate on extracting high-value materials for environmentally responsible processing. These hopes ride on how well the domestic half of the waste management reforms proceeds.

What distinguishes "the merge" from decades of earlier waste policy reforms is the colossal size of government investment and the steadfast effort, originating from the very highest reaches of state, to assert unified control over all forms of waste. The current thirteenth five-year plan (2016–2020) put 252 billion yuan into solid waste infrastructures, 20 billion of which goes to Beijing.[42] The nation's incineration industry, dubbed a "pillar industry" of the plan, has received 340 billion yuan in central government investment in the last decade alone.[43] And over 70 billion yuan from the current five-year plan is being spent on public-private partnerships (PPPs) with corporate investors to provide residential and commercial garbage sorting and collection, "smart" bins and data systems, and waste treatment and processing facilities.

These reforms are referred to as "merging two networks" because the PRC state is attempting to merge recycling and trash management into a single comprehensive system for the first time since its founding. Beginning in 1949, recycling was administered through a network of units governed and licensed through commerce and industry bureaus, while garbage was handled by a separate network of offices covering environmental sanitation and urban management. Despite much bureaucratic reshuffling, this fundamental split between managing "trash" and managing "recycling" persisted for nearly seven decades. Even though the composition of urban MSW changed radically over those years—from mostly coal residues with only a small fraction of salvageable scrap in the Mao era, to an increasingly massive and incredibly diverse flow of materials, about 50 percent of which today are postconsumer goods and packaging (paper, plastics, bottles, aluminum cans, discarded electronics, etc.) potentially worth tens of billions if salvaged for recycling—the administrative division of garbage and recycling held firm. As a result, extracting recyclable resources from MSW was administratively outside the mandate of the sanitation bureaucracy, while at the same time government recycling companies had no authority to collect or dispose of MSW. Rushing in to fill the gap, millions of migrant laborers and entrepreneurs gained access to and eventually monopolized the postreform flood of recyclables that fell outside the mandates and street-level infrastructures of either the commerce or sanitation bureaucracies. Now, after seventy years, the state is attempting to merge these two systems, hoping that it can regain control over the nation's fragmented, problematic, and lucrative waste-scape.

Just as Zsuzsa Gille's theory of waste regimes would predict, such a fundamental restructuring of the waste management apparatus necessitates a redefining of waste itself, and the state's leading policy consultants are doing precisely that. Liu Jianguo, professor at Qinghua University's School of Environment, is among the most prominent experts shaping the state's waste policies. At a forum organized in interview format, he immediately begins by redefining waste:

Questioner: Many people say garbage is "misplaced resources" and sorting garbage is simply doing a good deed, so we should use incentives like point reward systems to encourage people to do more of it. What do you think?

Liu Jianguo: Garbage is an entirely material thing; to speak abstractly about garbage as a resource is meaningless. I won't deny that garbage actually includes some resources in it, but these are strictly limited by spatial and temporal conditions. You can resourcify (*ziyuanhua*) garbage, but only by paying the corresponding economic and environmental costs. Products must have a market space, but if the capital investment needed is too high, the environmental costs too great, or the product has no market, this kind of resourcification is self-deceit. If we over-emphasize that garbage is misplaced resources, it will actually not benefit our promotion of [garbage] sorting. If garbage is a resource, then it would only be right to encourage me to produce more garbage, why would you want me to reduce it? If garbage is a resource, and then you also want me to sort it, aren't you just giving me more trouble? If garbage is a resource, shouldn't you pay me for it rather than charge me a fee? It makes no logical sense. Let's rethink this from the oppo- site [angle]: If we say garbage is a source of pollution, we are all each garbage producers. This means we are pollution makers, and producers have responsibility, polluters must pay the costs. Then it quite naturally comes from this that we each should join in reduc- ing our garbage, sorting it, and paying for it. So, I always take the position that *garbage's core attribute is a source of pollution.*[44]

Liu's point is that if our goal is to reduce the ever-rising volume of waste flows, then we need to redefine waste as a cost, not an asset. In the past, China's trash fees had been flat rates that did not differentiate between profligate and low-waste behavior. Under the new fee structure, garbage is a liability, and the more you make, the more you pay. In the Mao era, under the socialist "cult of waste," it was said that there was no such thing as true trash; waste was said to be a "misplaced resource." In other words, trash was defined as unsorted recycling, an untapped asset that had yet to be raised to its full potential value. The new definition now being promoted by the state reverses this definition: recycling becomes, in essence, pollution-remediated garbage; recycling is form of waste, a liability that has had its environmental cost momentarily nullified.

But there is something more at work here than merely converting trash from an asset to a cost. Household trash and the recycling that might be culled from it are being redefined not merely as costs, but specifically as *pollution.* Pollution is a hazard to public health and the environment that must be properly handled and regulated. This radically redefines not just the nature of recyclables as objects, but also the act of engaging in recycling outside of government-imposed bylaws. By defining recyclables as prima facie pollutants, the state turns informal recyclers from petty traders evading commercial taxes (which is how they were framed under the waste regime of the Mao era) into prima facie pollution dumpers, thereby justifying the extirpation of all aspects of informal recycling in the name of environmental protection. To engage in recycling without proper government approval is now (again) illegal.

This casting of informal recycling as the enemy of ecological civilization is, I argue, the "core attribute" of the new definition of waste as pollution. As we will see, though some merge reforms certainly have potential environmental benefits, some are rather obvious boondoggles, and many are riven with internal contradictions and may prove less "sustainable" and more polluting than the informal systems they purport to improve. I assert that this is because the merge is as much about eliminating informal laborers and businesses in order to take control of a sector that promises exorbitant and guaranteed profits—large loans and financing for infrastructure builds and start-up funding on the front end and decades of mandated fee obligations and subsidies for waste treatment and waste management services on the back end—as it is about gaining oversight over pollution control. Or, to put it slightly differently, when pollution and the informal sector are seen as synonymous, the differentiation between eliminating informal actors and reducing pollution is essentially nonexistent.

In one respect the merge has already been accomplished in Beijing. Beginning in July 2016 the Municipal Commission of Urban Management (Beijing shi chengshi guanli weiyuanhui) took on the role of planning, overseeing, and coordinating both the city's MSW and its recycling. But in practical terms the merge has hardly begun. Merely placing recycling and MSW under the umbrella of the commission's purview did not alter the reality that as of 2016 the recycling sector was still almost entirely informal and beyond any actual state oversight, nor did it simplify the bureaucratic labyrinth of offices (environmental protection, commerce, transport, construction, land use, and so forth) that still have key roles in overseeing MSW and recycling enterprises and their activities.

The objective of the merge is to place all aspects of urban solid waste collection, disposal, and processing under formal state management. The State Council's Domestic Waste Classification Implementation Plan laid out this objective, assigning forty-six cities responsibility to pilot comprehensive and replicable models of waste separation covering all residential, government, and commercial units by 2020. The models must cover all stages of waste management, including WtE incineration, kitchen waste utilization, and scrap recycling industrial parks. City governments must promote and manage financing for these infrastructures, design and implement quantity-based fee structures, and facilitate the use of online-to-offline (O2O) systems such as apps to request recycling and e-waste pickup and to track data on household waste generation.[45] Investment in, construction of, and operation of these infrastructures will largely be contracted through PPPs—so the billions of yuan in government money will be used to attract billions more from local governments and investors. The state will set the policies, plan the overall system, and perform regulatory oversight; companies will compete for contracts to deliver the actual services, thereby promoting competitive efficiency and creative solutions.

What follows are sketches of several components of the merge: "e-waste" disposal, O2O collection, residential garbage sorting, incineration, and recycling. All five areas have seen a modicum of state-guided investment over the past decades, but nothing compared to the current bonanza. The link between the new policies and profits is hardly a secret. Within two weeks of the State Council's March 2017 announcement of the forty-six cities waste plan, stock prices for several publicly traded waste management companies bounced upward, including Beijing Capital Co., which doubled (4.31 to 8.33 yuan per share) and Tianjin Capital Environmental Protection Group Co. Ltd., which nearly tripled (8.16 to 22.66 yuan per share). Summer 2018's biggest winner on the Shanghai exchange was the waste management company Dynagreen, which surged 500 percent. In the first week of September 2018 alone, sixty-two waste-sorting service procurement announcements were issued by cities across the country.[46] In 2019 more than eighty-three hundred new waste-related enterprises were created, an average of twenty-three new companies daily.[47] Amid this flood of investment and policy development, the merge is still very much a work in progress, hence the somewhat fragmented nature of the sketches that follow.

E-Waste, by Any Other Name

I start with e-waste, a uniquely high-value segment of the postconsumer discard stream and a striking example of how China's state policies articulate with international trends. This sketch, far too short to delve into the complexity of this sector, is indebted to the work of a handful of scholars, journalists, and activists— Adam Minter, Yvan Schulz, Josh Lepawsky, Anna Lora-Wainwright, Chi Xinwen, Robin Ingenthron, Chen Liwen—who have been fighting an uphill battle trying to dislodge the received wisdom dominating media and policy discussion of the "e-waste" problem both in China and globally.[48]

The average Chinese consumer generates about one-fourth the e-waste (discarded air conditioners, refrigerators, washers, televisions, computers, cell phones, etc.) of the average American, but with four times the US population, China more or less ties the United States as the world's largest aggregate e-waste generator, at more than seven million tons annually and growing. But looking at Chinese media, one might imagine that China's domestic e-waste was not problematic, that the only e-waste in China that created pollution was e-waste that originated from rich countries and was smuggled across the borders by foreign Mafiosi in cahoots with rogue Chinese processors. China's state media blame e-waste pollution almost invariably on foreign countries "dumping" their e-waste in China illegally. The reason for this bias is fairly obvious: China's domestic e-waste glut is the inevitable by-product of the county's booming appliance consumption, which is highly valued both because electronics manufacturing is a vital motor of China's modernization and because citizen consumption of these items is symbolic of China's growing prosperity. For state media to decry the mismanagement of China's own e-waste arisings would come uncomfortably close to throwing shade on the state's greatest claim to legitimacy: economic growth. Far more surprising is that international scholarship and policy representations of

China's e-waste problems are similarly myopically fixated on an alleged plague of OECD "dumping," while hardly any attention has been given to China's domestically generated e-waste.

This representational imbalance dates back to how China's e-waste woes first burst into the international spotlight, through a 2002 report titled *Exporting Harm* from the US-based NGO the Basel Action Network (BAN). The report documented the horrific pollution unfolding in a cluster of villages in Guiyu, Guangdong province, which had grown into a massive hub for the informal processing of e-waste, much of which was (at that specific time and place) imported. In the wake of this nightmarish revelation, the Chinese government immediately explored solutions to avert such disasters and quickly started building a state-subsidized and regulated e-waste dismantling system based on OECD models. In the first wave of this effort, $51 million was invested in four state-of-the-art factories that mechanically shredded electronics and sorted that shred into commodity fractions (copper, ferrous, plastics, etc.) for recycling—precisely the kind of processing done by the leading e-waste disposal companies in the United States and EU. By 2006 these factories were up and running, but there was a problem: they could not get their hands on any e-waste to process.[49] Informal migrant recyclers dominated urban e-waste collection, buying old appliances and electronics the same way they bought other recyclable scrap, through community and roaming bike recyclers; the state's model factories could not offer high enough prices to access the supply chain.

How did China's informal sector processors manage to pay so much more for e-waste? The explanation that Chinese government analysts arrived at was essentially identical to that provided by environmentalists in the United States and Europe who, horrified at the sight of the e-waste from their own countries decimating places like Guiyu, had asked basically the same question: Why are informal processors in places like Guiyu and Ghana ending up with our e-waste? Their explanation, epitomized in BAN's *Exporting Harm* report, went like this:

> After possibilities for re-use have been exhausted and a computer is slated for disposal, its worth in the marketplace will likely have been reduced from over 1,000 dollars to very likely a negative value. Indeed most recyclers, due to the costs of dealing with the disposal of non-recyclable parts and the expense of dealing carefully with the toxic waste components of old computers, will not take your computer unless you are willing to pay them to take it.[50]

In other words, in relatively rich OECD countries the ecologically *responsible* processing of e-waste generates no profit because environmental protection costs are higher than any profit to be made from selling the scrap. By contrast, *irresponsibly* processing e-waste through cheap, highly polluting methods like acid baths, wire burning, and toxic waste dumping can be quite profitable. Hence, *Exporting*

Harm claimed, 50–80 percent of OECD e-waste (a figure that would echo in policy reports and debates for over a decade despite the lack of any empirical evidence supporting it) flowed from places like the United States and the EU to backwaters in the Global South, where environmental enforcement was weak to nonexistent.[51] This was the pollution haven hypothesis, and Guiyu was its international poster child; in fact the cover of *Exporting Harm* is a photo of a child sitting on a pile of Guiyu's e-waste. BAN's solution to this problem, which also was the solution codified in the Basel Convention, was an international ban on the movement of e-waste from OECD to non-OECD countries. Chinese analysts came to a similar conclusion: the reason their new state-of-the-art e-waste shredding factories could not get their hands on any e-waste was that they paid for pollution remediation while dirty informal processors just dumped their pollution and thereby could pay more for e-waste and still turn a profit. Unfortunately, BAN's explanation of what caused OECD e-waste to flow into non-OECD informal sectors was wrong, and so too was the application of this logic to China's domestic e-waste markets.

Much of the problem lies with the term *e-waste* itself, or in policy-speak, waste electrical and electronic equipment (WEEE). Both these terms dub the items in question "waste," implying they are beyond reuse or repair. A far more apt term for WEEE/e-waste would be DEEE, where D stands for "discarded." This is because a large portion of discarded electronics are not "waste" at all, but in fact are quite repairable. The questions at issue are repair, reuse, and resale by whom, at what price, and for what markets. I ask the reader to simply judge from your own experience with appliances, cell phones, and computers: Do you discard these items because they become utterly useless or because they become outmoded or too expensive to diagnose and repair? But in many marketplaces throughout the world, including China, there are skilled technicians who know how to repair and refurbish used equipment, are doing so for much lower wages than technicians in OECD countries, and have ready access to consumers happy to purchase used electronics. To grossly simplify across product types and brands: in urban China today about 50 percent of the electronics and appliances collected by informal recyclers are channeled for repair, refurbishing, and resale to millions of customers (mainly migrant workers and residents in third- and fourth-tier cities) who cannot afford new models. That figure was closer to 90 percent in the 1990s and around 70 percent in the 2000s.[52] These used devices are much cheaper than new ones, but they sell at prices far higher than could be fetched were they simply thrown into industrial shredders and reduced into commodity fractions of scrap metal and plastic. And this is why China's informal migrant junk collectors have been able to pay much more for DEEE than their formal competitors, who treat all DEEE as if it were WEEE and shred it. Note also that this explanation applies globally as well. When UNEP analysts finally produced a comprehensive piece of field research in 2015 aimed at documenting the EU's WEEE flows, they discovered that more than 73 percent of the presumed WEEE heading from the EU to African and other developing countries for alleged toxic dumping was actually fully working DEEE heading abroad for reuse.[53] Whether in Europe or China, the main economic driver that keeps most DEEE circulating in the informal sector is not the savings on pollution control costs, it is the profit made on repair, reuse, resale, and component harvesting.[54] In Beijing's informal DEEE sector there is a complex harmonizing of thousands of entrepreneurs whose combined marketing and technical skill sets enable the efficient differentiation of which units can be repaired and resold profitably and which cannot.[55] China's state-subsidized e-waste processors lack these capabilities; their factories—modeled on e-waste processing factories in the United States and Europe—are designed only to dismantle and mechanically shred what they receive: DEEE comes in; piles of commodity-grade plastic, copper, aluminum, and so forth go out.

This model of processing is not unique to China; it is the hegemonic model in OECD countries. Justifications for this approach include that it protects intellectual property rights and prevents components from being harvested and resold as counterfeits, it prevents private data theft, and it conforms to environmental protection standards. On the other hand, this model insists on the destruction of units and components that could readily be repaired and reused, foreshortening the lifespan of goods. Destroying perfectly usable goods hastens product turnover and speeds up consumption. From a product life-cycle perspective, this model promotes increased resource extraction and planned obsolescence, all under the banners of environmental stewardship and social justice. OECD nations can boast that they do not send their e-waste out to pollute poorer countries, that they take care of it at home through ethical recycling.

Yvan Schulz has dubbed this model "shredder ideology," and it fits just as nicely into Chinese state visions of ecological civilization and its goals of resource recovery (*zaisheng ziyuan*) and urban mining (*chengshi kuangchan*) as it does with OECD models of corporate environmentalism.[56] Previous chapters have shown how the domestic context in China has resulted in the criminalization of the informal recycling sector; what the case of DEEE shows is how China's domestic politics of scapegoating informality can also fit snugly with OECD interests, policies, and discourses, each reaffirming the other. It is not only the Chinese state that for reasons of political power, economic advantage, and cultural bias excludes informal stakeholder experts from their deliberations and criminalizes them with its policies.

Returning to the sketch of China's e-waste management policies, having adopted the shredder ideology and technologies in the early 2000s, the Chinese state still lacked a mechanism to channel sufficient flows of e-waste to its facilities. In 2009, again looking to OECD solutions, the government announced it was designing an extended producer responsibility (EPR) system. Under EPR, original equipment manufacturers (OEMs), both domestic and foreign companies selling new units on the Chinese market, have to pay fees into a fund that is used to subsidize the "take back" of e-waste by state-approved WEEE disposal companies. After a few years of negotiations with OEMs, in 2013 state-approved WEEE disposal companies began being paid on a per unit basis (85 yuan for a TV, 80 for a fridge, etc.) for each item they documented shredding. The subsidy essentially amounted to the state purchasing the supply chains for these companies. In 2013 the government oversaw the dispersal of 629 million yuan to WEEE disposal companies. Immediately, investors stampeded into WEEE processing; the number of state-subsidized WEEE dismantling plants leapt from 43 in 2012 to 109 by 2016.

The subsidy was intended to help formal companies compete against informal collectors and wrest access to the DEEE supply chain from them, but ironically the subsidy has actually led to cooperation between the formal and informal sectors. Indeed, the subsidy has played out in such a way that it has made the formal companies dependent on the informal sector to do their collecting for them. Informal collectors offer extremely convenient service, coming to residents' homes, picking up their DEEE, and paying for it immediately in cash. They then sort out what can be profitably repaired and resold and consolidate what is left to sell to the formal WEEE dismantling companies. In 2016 the state forked out 4.7 billion yuan in subsidies to formal WEEE disposal companies, much of which flowed through them into the pockets of informal collectors.[57]

This situation, a fortuitous policy accident in which informal and formal sectors coexist, I argue has resulted in a better system environmentally than would have been the case had the subsidy policy actually succeeded in its goal of eliminating informal DEEE collectors and putting the entire DEEE stream into the hands of formal companies so they could shred it all. In that scenario, the 50 percent of units currently going to reuse and resale would have vanished into the shredders. It is precisely these kinds of better solutions that, I argue, could exist in many parts of the recycling sector if policy makers would bring informal stakeholders to the table. The irony is that even when this kind of happy accident occurs, government policy experts seem unable to recognize it; as illustrated in the next section through the story of a company called Banana Peel, the state is still spending millions on ill-conceived attempts to root out informal DEEE collectors.

Online-to-Offline Recycling

Collection is almost always the highest cost of residential recycling systems, accounting for 55–80 percent of operating costs due to the high cost of infrastructure (receptacles, etc.), transport, and labor. Collection seems simple, but it is pivotal because whoever controls it controls the materials themselves and therefore has leverage over everything that follows. Back in the 1990s the BRC had tried desperately to intercept residential recyclables before they entered the hands of migrants, to no avail; the state companies simply could not compete with informal collectors' rock bottom labor costs and tireless work. But with the rise of internet apps and smartphones, the dream of intercepting scrap before informal migrants can get it has revived, with a techno-twist of reducing or even eliminating human labor (costs) through automation.

Almost immediately upon the release in May 2016 of the central government's circular "Suggestions for Transforming the Resource Recycling Industry," with its ballyhoo for "Internet + Recycling" solutions, droves of "smart recycling" start-up companies sprang forth "like mushrooms after the rain."[58] Recycling robots parachute into urban communities accompanied by heroic news coverage and child-filled photo ops. Within months they usually fade silently from public view, unused. O2O "smart" recycling concepts fall into two main approaches: (1) automated installations, in the form of machines, varying in size from vending machines to wall-length stations, that automatically collect recyclables, record transactions, and reimburse users with scrip or money, or (2) apps that connect residents to recyclers to coordinate convenient home pickups.[59] Both systems are advertised to consumers as making recycling more efficient and reliably "green," meaning purportedly all DEEE and recyclables collected will be processed in environmentally safe contexts. The pitch to investors is that these O2O schemes will solve the riddle of recycling's "last mile" and find that miraculous vacuum-tube passageway where recyclables whisk directly from residents' hands to be plunked into the hoppers of corporate aggregators/processors, eliminating all those pesky labor costs that interfere with profitability. But the magic has proven elusive; "Zaishenghuo, Xiandou, 9 Beike, etc., enterprises have all tried or are trying this kind of trash sorting and recycling project, but from beginning to end none have found a profitable model."[60] Beijing's most touted O2O duds include Zaishenghuo (released its app in 2015, vanished by 2017) and Taoqibao (similarly missing as of 2017). The most venerable O2O company in Beijing is Incom (Yingchuan), whose vending machines collecting empty PET bottles have gathered dust in Beijing subway stops and gated communities since as far back as 2003. A 2018 *China Daily* piece on Incom unwittingly betrayed the company's failed business model by boasting that in fifteen years of operation they had recycled an astonishing total of fifty-four million plastic bottles—about as many PET bottles as Beijing residents discard in three weeks.[61]

DEEE, being far and away the highest-value segment of the residential discard stream, is the darling of these O2O start-ups' efforts. In the summer of 2016 the scholar-activist Chen Liwen spent several weeks following a pilot start-up geared toward DEEE called Banana Peel, a child company of Beijing's biggest formal e-waste disposal company, Huaxin. With support from Beijing's Development and Reform Committee, Banana Peel received 2 million yuan to provide recycling services for thirty-four residential communities in the city's Yizhuang Development Zone.[62] Banana Peel focused on DEEE collection, but its app included the whole panoply of residential recyclables (paper, plastic, glass, used clothes, furniture, etc.), hoping in this way to expand its revenue stream. Banana Peel hired twenty-two employees (eight managers and phone/computer operators, fourteen collectors); customized fourteen collection carts, two vans, and a truck; and provided free recycling bins to residents who downloaded the app, about eighty thousand people. To ensure employees did not cheat the company, collectors had to itemize and weigh all items collected and photograph all DEEE, then send the pictures to management, making pickups excessively time-consuming. On average the company collected fewer than a dozen DEEE items and about 2,000–3,000 yuan worth of mixed recyclables per day; at that rate it was losing 30,000–60,000 yuan monthly just based on wage costs alone. Perhaps most comically, the company had no idea how to sell the non-DEEE recyclables it collected and was forced to rent a warehouse and find experienced migrant recyclers to manage the recyclables.[63]

Yet O2O continues to enchant China's financial sector. Recently making headlines is Little Yellow Dog, which raised over 1 billion yuan in its A-round of financing in June 2018. The company aims to fully automate recycling collection by installing walls of five "smart" sorting bins (paper, plastic, glass, hazardous waste, metals) in residential communities. The phalanx of tamper-proof smart bins costs 250,000 yuan for a full set, but the company calculated that it could recover this investment in hardware in under a year.[64] Bins would supposedly reject bottles with liquids in them, refuse to pay out for poorly sorted materials, automatically spray deodorizing scents in summer, and when 80 percent full, automatically signal headquarters for a pickup.[65] By January 2019 thousands of machines had landed in communities throughout major cities including Beijing; by April they had all stopped working. After three months of not paying its employees and still failing to make its bank payments, Little Yellow Dog's accounts were frozen and its machines shut off.[66]

Trash Sorting, with Teeth

The merge is intended to thoroughly restructure China's networks of urban garbage disposal and recycling into a unified, comprehensive system. The efficacy of this integration of two separate bureaucratic/material networks rests on transforming one simple behavior: the everyday waste disposal of every urban resident in China. At present, this human cornucopia pours forth a tremendously complex commingled stream of solid wastes. To merge recycling and trash disposal into a unified system, China's urban populations will need to be trained to self-sort all the wastes they generate into the state's designated four separate streams: wet (kitchen) waste, dry waste, recyclables, and hazardous wastes.[67] Without high levels of reliable public participation, these streams will be cross-contaminated, so mechanisms for instilling, monitoring, and enforcing proper community sorting are imperative. Data management systems to track and tabulate every household's waste disposal fees, penalize shirkers, and award recycling credits will also be needed. Each material stream will require dedicated containers, hauling and processing infrastructures, monitoring, and last but certainly not least, financing mechanisms. There is a lot of money to be made providing all that; analysts estimate 2020 spending on containers and hauling alone to tic up 8.4 billion yuan over 2019 totals.[68] Forty-six cities, including Beijing, Tianjin, Chongqing, Shanghai, and every provincial capital, were tasked to achieve this unified and functioning system by the end of 2020; cutting to the chase, with the notable exception of Shanghai, as of January 2020 none appeared close to reaching that goal.

By fall 2018, Beijing had eighty-four model neighborhoods employing a total of 27,800 trash-sorting coaches, a mix of retirees, community sanitation workers, and informal recyclers working as educators, sorting assistants, monitors, and laborers performing a "second sort": going through bins to catch misplaced items.[69] With so many thousands of assistants poring over the trash, sortation improved, but left to their own devices, average Beijing residents were still confused about how to sort their garbage. A report on a model Chaoyang neighborhood that had been sorting for over eighteen months found residents were still just "pretending to sort."[70] Beijing was not unique; every pilot city was having trouble inculcating trash-sorting habits into their millions of residents—every city except Shanghai.

Exit the trash coaches, enter the trash cops. Beijing's MSW regulations dated back to a 2011 ordinance, and there was no provision in them enabling the city to fine residents who failed to properly sort their garbage. Shanghai, in contrast, realized the merge demanded tougher measures and revised its MSW regulations to make punitive fines the centerpiece. That quickly caught everyone's attention. The day of reckoning arrived in Shanghai on July 1, 2019, with state media declaring China had now entered the "era of forced trash sorting" (*laji fenlei qiangzhi shidai*): "Today, what is being called 'history's strictest' trash separation measure, 'Shanghai garbage separation management regulations' will be enforced, according to which individuals and work units must sort according to regulation or face punishment."[71]

It is not an exaggeration to say that garbage sorting was the single biggest event in Shanghai in 2019, involving a state campaign blitz the likes of which had not been experienced since the Mao era. There were months of news coverage in preparation for the change, explaining the sorting categories; celebrating the arrival of new bin ensembles here and automated trash-eating machines there; interviewing volunteer squads and anxious tenants; and following the trash police on their daily rounds inspecting bins, issuing warnings, and praising a sort well done. There was also an explosion of videos, blogs, and commentaries on social

猪可以吃的　　猪都不吃的　　猪吃了会死的　　卖了可以买猪的

厨余垃圾　　其他垃圾　　有害垃圾　　可回收物
Kitchen Waste　　Other Waste　　Harmful Waste　　Recyclable

FIGURE 15. One version of the Piggy meme on how to sort garbage in Shanghai, circulating on social media summer 2019.

media from Shanghai residents bracing themselves for the new regimen, including ingenious and humorous memes and songs about garbage sorting. In part this was because the new system could be pretty complicated (sunflower seed shells, being organic, are "wet waste" and crab shells are too, but oysters shells are "dry waste," etc.). One meme that went viral was a method for figuring out what to throw into what category bin: wet waste, a pig can eat it; dry waste, a pig cannot eat it; hazardous waste, a pig will die from eating it; recyclable waste, sell it and you can buy a pig! (See figure 15.)

Only days after Shanghai made garbage-sorting history, the head of Beijing's Commission of Urban Management, Sun Xinjun, announced that Beijing would be reviewing its old MSW regulations and revising them; now that Shanghai had pulled off its punitive law without chaos or protest, Beijing would follow suit. A few weeks later the *Beijing Evening News* compared the extent to which trash sorting permeated the lives of Beijingers versus Shanghailanders. The writer notes that in Beijing the installations of automated bins were attracting public attention and that some people had begun carefully sorting their garbage; by contrast in Shanghai,

> whether in People's Square or strolling on Nanjing Avenue, in big boulevards or narrow alleys, every waste bin has a sorting diagram; every subway train trash can has been replaced by waste sorting bins; turn on the TV and every day there is a program on trash sorting; every evening at 6 pm every apartment building has a resident aunty with a bullhorn playing a continuous loop about paying attention to trash sorting. . . . When people meet up and start chatting, everyone, without even thinking, ends up talking about trash sorting. . . . Since trash sorting started Jiang Jiayi has

stopped drinking boba milk tea. "It's just too much trouble," she sighs; the tea you haven't finished has to be poured down the drain, boba pearls go in the wet waste, the cup lid in the recycling, the cup itself tossed in the dry waste.[72]

As of May 1, 2020 Beijing residents also began asking themselves if they really want that cup of milk-tea; Beijing's revised MSW ordinance, which began on that date, includes nearly identical procedures and penalties as Shanghai: fines of 50–200 yuan for individual residents and 1,000–5,000 for businesses.

Given that Shanghai is recognized as the model to emulate and is about a year ahead of every other Chinese city, it is a good place to begin trying to understand where the merge might be heading. After six months of garbage sorting, 90 percent of Shanghai's residential communities were reported to have achieved the city's standard for sorting.[73] That is no small feat. Enforcing effective sorting is all the more difficult because most of China's urban residents live in apartment complexes with communal trash collection, meaning that one refractory trash-tosser can ruin everyone's hard work. Monitoring is therefore crucial. On the tech side, many bins now require quick response (QR) code swipes to open; this helps track fees for trash and rewards for recycling and might help assign blame for con-tamination. Many companies are also experimenting with putting personalized QR codes on the trash bags themselves to track each household's behavior. But there is also a human, labor-intensive side to disposal training and surveillance. Residents can no longer just take out the trash whenever they like; they can only do so at scheduled morning and evening disposal hours (around 6:00–8:00 a.m. and p.m.), during which community coaches supervise the activity. Were such labor fully paid or made the responsibility of waste management companies, the cost would be quite high. Real estate companies can, if they choose, pay workers to help manage these services, but the ground troops in most communities will be volunteers, often mobilized by grassroots Party activists. The proposed goal is that Shanghai will reach one million garbage-sorting volunteers by 2021.[74] Looked at with regard to labor, the garbage-sorting campaign aims to shift the labor involved in the sorting of wastes/recycling from workers and informal recyclers to a public who will do it for free. A sociologist colleague put it differently; she views garbage sorting as Xi Jinping's version of the "loyalty dance" honoring Chairman Mao that was promoted during the height of Cultural Revolution zealotry—a daily ritualized performance of ideological legitimation.

Assuming that these new habits of disposal take hold permanently, what is the point? How is the segregation of urban wastes going to help achieve the goals of waste reduction and "resourcification"? The answers are multiple and also, in many ways, not yet settled, and that is in part because the government realizes, quite rightly, that this is a huge experiment and best practices cannot be predeter-mined. A brief exploration of the question of what to do with wet wastes provides a glimpse of the wide range of possibilities, from environmentally utopian to rather dismal.

Of the merge's four waste streams, wet waste (*shi laji* aka "kitchen waste," *canchu laji*) is the new kid on the block. Chinese cities have had decades of experience landfilling and incinerating "trash," collecting and reprocessing "recyclables," and collecting household "hazardous wastes" such as batteries and florescent bulbs through niche infrastructures, but no Chinese city has ever confronted a daily flood of segregated, soggy organic wet waste refuse on the scale the merge is creating. From the business side, this is a huge opportunity; it is predicted that the year 2020 could see over 22 billion yuan invested in kitchen waste treatment.[75] What will these treatment facilities entail? One possibility is biogas plants that will feed into local energy grids and receive, like WtE incinerators, renewable energy subsidies. Another is composting facilities to create fertilizers and soil applications for farming, forestry, and landscaping. At present the composition of the wet waste stream is still too contaminated and underresearched to permit using its products for agriculture, but if effective composting can be achieved at urban scale, it could mark a dramatic resurgence of circularity in China's rural-urban metabolic cycle. On the other hand, it is also possible that composting will prove impossible at scale, saddling cities with an expensive public nuisance. Kitchen waste is heavy and expensive to transport; within an hour or two of hitting outdoor bins, particularly in the summer, it turns into a stinky, corrosive stew. Shanghai officials have already received complaints and are contemplating issuing special trash bags that can be cinched closed. Of course those will eventually need to be designed to be compatible/compostable with any future treatment processes; meanwhile such bags can easily disguise poorly sorted waste. A recent article describing work on a waste sorting line at the Shanghai train station tries to convey to readers what handling bags of poorly sorted waste can be like: "I felt terrible about myself when I started working here. It wasn't just the unbearable smell of the garbage. One slip and you can get cut by some piece of broken glass in the trash bag, or sometimes you have to pick out a plastic bag filled with some kid's poop."[76]

In sum, the future of wet waste management is an open question. But it is worth noting that even should biogas and composting fail to prove cost effective, the simple fact that wet wastes will be separated from dry should deliver one significant benefit: hopefully it will help make China's incineration sector less polluting than it has been up to now.

Incineration

In its ever-growing list of waste superlatives, China has the largest and fastest growing incinerator sector of any country in the world, accounting for more than half of all incinerator construction on the planet since 2009, with a capacity today of over 440,000 tons daily.[77] Beijing alone has built three new incinerators in the last several years, with the largest, Lujiashan, costing 2.1 billion yuan. The state treats WtE as a sustainable technology, and in addition to financing PPPs for incineration construction provides sustainable energy credits to incentivize investment. But incinerator infrastructure is expensive, and once built a WtE plant typically has to operate for a minimum of twenty to thirty years to realize return on investment. In other words, incinerators demand to be fed garbage for decades. On the basis of this fact alone it seems rather paradoxical that incineration would be central to a waste management plan the primary goal of which is purported to be waste reduction. But according to the state's version of environmental accounting, by burning garbage to produce energy, WtEs can be considered both a form of waste diversion (away from landfilling) as well as a source of green "renewable" energy (*kezaisheng nengyuan*). Indeed, many of Beijing's largest incinerators—Lujiashan, Asuwei, Gao'antun—have been redubbed CEIPs. Many critics have pointed out how problematic it is to claim that WtEs create renewable energy because (1) the burning process emits CO_2; (2) the waste being burned includes substantial amounts of plastic (10–15% of the typical urban waste profile), which is made from fossil fuels; and (3) many of China's incinerators shovel in large amounts of coal with their trash to get them up to burning temperatures.[78]

Several anti-incinerator protests in China's cities have made international news over the years, most recently one in Wuhan in July 2019. But protests in more rural areas typically get little attention. In April 2018 in Jiujiang, Jiangxi province, villagers started a vigil, camping in their fields for months trying to stop the building of a WtE plant on their land—paddy fields next to a wildlife refuge. The project was contracted to China Everbright International, a state-owned conglomerate, Asia's largest investor in WtE projects, and a member of international ethical investment groups including the Dow Jones Sustainability Index. In early November police stormed the protestors, beating some farmers bloody in the streets and arresting several. The Jiujiang protests were not covered in the Chinese media and were hardly mentioned in the foreign press. The protestors have worked meticulously with the assistance of volunteer lawyers to stay within the lines of national law; they have simply been insisting the state follow its own regulations regarding environmental protection and information transparency.[79]

Urban protests are harder to expunge from the media sphere. The opposition movements in Beijing against the Liulitun incinerator in 2006 and the Asuwei complex in 2012 were often characterized, particularly within the Chinese media, as middle-class NIMBY protests motivated by local residents concerned that poor neighborhood air quality and icky odors would negatively impact their real estate values. But, as Amy Zhang argues, this framing misses the point; these protests are first and foremost expressions of a "social critique of the politics of urban infrastructure."[80] The crux of the protests is a distrust regarding who profits and whose well-being and prosperity are damaged by these projects, a distrust grounded in a pattern of government dishonesty and failure to meet legal requirements. The Everbright company, for instance, operates twelve WtE plants across China and is building half a dozen more. A survey of ten of its plants by Chinese NGOs in 2015 found that none properly stabilized or safely disposed of its fly ash; eight had large amounts of unburned trash in their slag (plastics, whole shoes, etc.), evidence that they failed to reach proper temperatures. In several instances, villages located less than a kilometer from one of Everbright's WtEs reported an increase in child respiratory ailments, decreased harvests, and in two cases, spiking cancer rates confirmed by local doctors.[81] But there is no reason to pick on Everbright; failure to meet standards has been veritably universal in the sector. A 2017 survey that obtained data on twenty-seven incinerators found that over a twenty-five-day period regulatory emissions limits were exceeded 2,533 times.[82]

The failure to operate WtEs according to proper standards is directly related to the fuel they burn. Up until very recently, China's incinerators have been fed untreated mixed MSW, which is typically over 50 percent kitchen waste. Food waste has a high water content and therefore a low calorific value—try setting a watermelon rind on fire. If incinerators do not reach a high enough temperature, they emit much larger amounts of toxic chemicals, including dioxins. This is why finding identifiable objects in incinerator slag is so disturbing, as it clearly indicates failure to reach a safe burning temperature. One would have hoped that the state would structure incinerator fees to incentivize reaching safe burn temperatures, but for most of the last decade it did not. WtEs have two major revenue streams: a fee for every ton of waste they dispose of (the tipping or gate fee) and a fee for every unit of electricity they produce. Both fees have been problematic. Tipping fees have been based purely on the weight of trash delivered to the WtE's gates, with no restrictions on the waste's content, so maximizing tonnage by accepting water-heavy wastes has translated directly into more revenue. And renewable energy fees were available to WtE plants even when they added large amounts of coal to the trash to make it actually burnable. On top of all this, state oversight of the bidding process in the sector has been notoriously lax, with competing companies lowballing one another on tipping fees in order to win contracts, charging as little as 20–70 yuan (US$3–10) per ton (similar fees in Europe and Japan run around US$100).[83] As one industry expert admitted, "When it's that cheap, you definitely are not burning it in a clean way."[84]

Troubling as this all is, there have been signs recently that the government is taking problems in the sector more seriously. In 2019 the Ministry of Finance requested that inefficient and highly polluting WtEs have their renewable energy subsidies reduced or even terminated (WtEs that meet state standards will continue to be subsidized).[85] And in early 2020 MEE officials announced that evidence of breaches of emissions standards collected by automatic monitoring equipment is now sufficient to charge WtEs with polluting and impose penalties (WtEs have automatically monitored their emissions for years and even posted the data in real time on electronic billboards, but those data could not be used to punish operators).[86] But it is arguably the merge's garbage-sorting campaign that has the greatest potential for cleaning up the incinerator sector; by drastically reducing the water content in WtE feedstocks, garbage sorting will hopefully help WtEs burn at higher and safer temperatures. For better and for worse, the state has embraced incineration as its main urban waste solution, given which one can only hope that the trash-sorting campaign will be successful enough to at least get burn temperatures higher and thereby reduce the risk WtEs pose to the many millions living within breathing range of their chimneys.

Recycling Recriminalized

Given that the most publicized rationales for implementing the Ban + Merge are to put an end to the polluting of informal processors and improve China's domestic resource recovery, it is notable that compared to the merge's other project areas (community sorting, incinerators, O2O), the state-licensed recycling infrastructure has been rather slow to take shape. Actually, the decision to put off developing the recycling piece of the merge until after the other pieces are in place is probably wise; city planners are waiting to see which PPPs prove successful at managing the complexities of handling waste sorting before committing to long-term contracts and land leases for recycling facilities. It would be foolish, for instance, to contract an O2O company to build a sorting center to manage all the recycling it collects only to have its machines turn out to be a flop. In fact, when Little Yellow Dog when bankrupt last year and its machines suddenly froze in communities across Shanghai, it was informal recyclers who came to the rescue, paying residents for their recyclables and carting them off.[87]

As of summer 2020, Beijing still seems far from having a comprehensive formalized recycling network, and even Shanghai is still in the early stage; but what can be gleaned from developments thus far? At the level of collection, recycling is still in limbo. Companies contracted to handle sorted residential wastes have begun accessing some recyclables, but there are plenty of informal collectors still at work. Indeed, many of the companies implementing the merge are hiring informal recyclers and community trash collectors as the basis of their workforce:

> Mei Tao, responsible for "merge" projects in [Shanghai's] Hongqiao district, says in the future they will absorb a portion of roving recyclers: "The transformation from 'Junk Kings' to 'Regular Army' [*zhenggui jun* literally "formal (as opposed to "informal") military"] is a step forward in the recycling of renewable resources. Those we absorb will be equipped with electric tricycle carts, they will have formal logos and if some residents call them they will go directly to their communities; everything will be according to formal standards."[88]

In reality, however, it is unclear if collectors working in merge projects are always passing the recyclables they help sort on to the contracted companies that employ them; some seem to be skimming off the highest value materials to sell in informal networks.[89] Informal collectors still station trucks in alleys and side streets, buying bottles, carboard, DEEE, and other materials from residents. The number of collectors has fallen drastically, possibly by as much as 80 percent, but for those that remain, business is robust.

Moving up the supply chain to the aggregation/baling/trading stage, though policy documents claim that every city is supposed to have a comprehensive network of district sorting centers (*qu fenjian zhongxin*) for recyclables by the end of 2020, only a few such centers have opened in Beijing to date. I only know of two facilities that have the stamp of municipal approval to manage recycling in the new system, both with footprints dating back over a decade. One is a Huanjingyuan recycling market. Located between the fourth and fifth ring roads near rail lines that make the site unfavorable for commercial or residential use, the facility, opened in 2003, is the longest continuously running, large-scale recycling market in Beijing. Huanjingyuan is contracted to provide waste-sorting services for a large part of Fengtai district and has recently installed an automated waste-sorting system—the kind of labor-assisted system of conveyor belts, shaking screens, magnets, and balers found at MRFs in the United States, EU, and other places. The second facility is the Haidian district SOE's Hanjiachuan facility, which first opened in 2008 as a baling yard to handle recyclables during the Olympics and is now a designated center for low-value and "bulky item" recycling. There is also a handful of approved small pilot facilities, mostly between the fifth and sixth ring roads, run by new recycling start-ups. One that has gotten a good deal of attention is Love to Sort (Ai Fenlei), which was founded by Xu Yuanhong, the son of Gushi migrant recyclers who grew up recycling with his parents in Dongxiaokou, then went off to college, but decided to return to the scrap yard.[90] While informal migrants face more obstacles than others in getting local approval to form merge program PPPs, Xu Yuanhong's example demonstrates that transitioning from informal to formal is possible; should Love to Sort and similar companies in other cities emerge and be successful, one might imagine that such companies could offer relatively welcoming spaces in which informal migrant recyclers might continue to operate.

On the other hand, informal recyclers who do not have the financing and social capital to make the transition to formal companies are facing increasing pressure in Beijing. The city's informal market network has been largely bulldozed out of existence. After a decade of tolerating the construction of stall-style markets and sorting centers, in 2013 the city included recycling facilities in its list of enterprises barred from any new construction.[91] From 2013 on, as scrap markets were demolished and converted to higher rent investments, no new ones were built to replace them—at least not new ones with permits. In 2016 the city undertook a thorough sweep of the sector, identifying and demolishing eighty-one recycling facilities, leaving Huanjingyuan the sole recycling market/sorting center still standing inside Beijing's fifth ring road.[92] With the evictions of 2017–18, the demolition sweep was redoubled and reached to the sixth ring road. Every month or so, one or another small "criminal gang" is caught running a baling station in an abandoned building or stashing piles of rebar and cardboard under a freeway overpass; their equipment and materials are confiscated, and in some cases those involved are arrested.[93]

Of course, in terms of environmental damage it is not scrap collection or sorting but scrap processing that is the most pressing concern, as that is the stage at which truly egregious polluting often occurs. The government often states that the chief goal of the Ban + Merge is to deprive small, informal, polluting processors of market space and create a formal corporate processing sector in their stead. As a basis for this new processing sector, the NDRC has designated fifty industrial parks as resource circular use bases (RCUB; *ziyuan xunhuan liyong jidi*), two of which—an "urban mining" industrial park in Tangshan and an SMC-managed park in Hebei's Dingxian county—lie within easy reach of Beijing. I have not been back to the Bejing area since 2018, so I cannot say with any certainty how these parks are performing economically or environmentally. Nor can I say with any confidence how the informal processing sector is fairing; my guess is not very well, though it is also certainly far from dead. The plastic processing sector in the Beijing area when I visited in 2018 was in straitened circumstances. Processors who used to manage shops with machines running 24/7 were now cautiously and rather secretively contracting one job at a time, but business continued.

The last time I saw Mr. and Mrs. X was in their small Beijing apartment out near the sixth ring road in February 2018, a few months after the demolitions and forced evictions following the Daxing fire. They told stories of friends losing their homes and recycling yards, but the conversation turned, as it so often does, from bitter to humorous as they began teasing one another in an ongoing debate. Mrs. X was trying to convince her husband to open another scrap polystyrene stall, but Mr. X refused. Mrs. X's family, including her two brothers, are all in the recycling business, but for years Mr. X has been the family CEO, securing jobs for siblings and in-laws and making the main business decisions. With the sector in turmoil, no one in the family was working, but Mr. X was not up for coming to the rescue by jump-starting his PS processing business. It was not because of the economics; they would make a killing. Demand for PS resin was strong and prices high because of the import ban. The boom in online shopping and deliveries made for ample supply and strong demand. But informal recycling was being treated as a virtual crime in Beijing. Scrap markets of any kind within the sixth ring road had nearly vanished, collectors were being harassed by *chengguan* (urban management police), and trucks hauling recycling were having their loads confiscated on the thinnest of pretexts. This meant there was virtually no competition and that PS on the street was practically free. Mr. X guessed they could easily turn over materials at 100 percent profit per kilo. But it was too risky; he did not want to worry about dodging cops or getting ratted out by someone and having his compressors confiscated. Many recyclers were taking the risks. They had changed things up, switching from open-bed trucks to fully closed ones (less hauling capacity, but no one knows what you are carrying) and traveling on highways (blending into other traffic instead of sneaking on back roads). Businesses were not clustering in markets very often—those were too visible and immediately got shut down. Instead, folks were finding their own hidden corners—occasionally right in the heart of the city, but more often out beyond the sixth ring road and as far out as Miyun. Deliveries were coordinated through phone calls and text messages, and turnover happened in under twenty-four hours. Scrap was collected during the day, shipped out to the baling/processing point at night, and packed out by dawn; this way no big scrap yard was needed, and materials were not stockpiled. Truckers and stall bosses formed text-messaging chat groups to keep track of which new depots were opening and which ones were being shut down. They also shared nightly intel on where traffic cops were inspecting trucks and the best alternate routes.[94] The money was good, but operations were expensive; equipment like balers and forklifts had become the norm, and one could lose all that expensive equipment if caught. When I asked Mr. X how others were handling the situation, he gave me a tour out his apartment windows of a few sites where recyclers had recently folded up shop, then showed me pictures of a baling station someone he knew was running out in the hills of Miyun. But he said most folks were like him, biding their time to see where things were going.

CONCLUSION

Regarding informal waste workers, the Ban + Merge have largely involved applying steroids to the familiar toolkit of bans, criminalization, discrimination, and proletarianization (turning the "guerrilla force of junk kings" into "regular armies" of waste company employees) that have generally failed to eliminate the sector in the past. But things already look quite different this time around. Perhaps in part this is because during the first long decade of the twenty-first century (see chapter 7), the state was less interested in eliminating the sector than in containing it, only occasionally orchestrating its temporary disappearance for spectacles like the Olympics. The enormity of the Ban + Merge as a platform for investments, mass campaigns, and stiffly prohibitive policies seems to signal a shift in goals, from containing the informal sector and managing its worst crises to fully rooting it out. Then again, as often as the state has insistently drawn and redrawn lines meant to divide the formal and informal over the last three decades, in practice such distinctions have proven impossible to rigorously enforce. Indeed, as we have seen, since the 1990s formal sector recycling companies have never shown themselves to be up to the task of successfully managing recycling without depending upon the very informal sector collectors, brokers, suppliers, and processors they so adamantly disavow.

I have argued throughout that informal urban collectors, scrap brokers, DEEE repair workers, and so forth are hardly the uncitizenly mass of polluting gangsters they have been portrayed as (though certainly some are involved in polluting, and some have been gangsters), and that policies could have been (and still could be) more successful, environmentally sound, and socially just by cooperating with informal stakeholders. But one has to acknowledge that in one crucial way the Ban + Merge is almost certainly working where previous efforts failed. It seems indisputable that the Ban + Merge is resulting in a steep decline in informal scrap processing—surely in the Beijing region—and this also means a decline in the polluting and health-damaging consequences produced by that sector. But this is not to say that overall the pollution related to waste management and recycling will necessarily decline, for there is no evidence that registered corporations and SOEs will be accountable environmental stewards. China's large-scale, tax-paying, registered, and state-subsidized incineration industry will probably never be investigated sufficiently to get an accurate understanding of its health and environmental destructiveness over the last decade. An environmental accounting of the current profusion of giant O2O garbage robots would almost surely show them to be a colossal waste of resources, and it would be foolish to assume that the new RCUBs and CEIPs will process scrap more responsibly than did the EPIPs that preceded them. On a very brief visit I made to Guiyu in 2018, it was clear that the companies dismantling DEEE inside Guiyu's supposedly closed CEIP were selling enormous amounts of scrap plastic to unregulated shops throughout the surrounding townships (much like ZEPIP in chapter 7). And when Yvan Schulz and Anna Lora-Wainwright tried to assess conditions at the Guiyu CEIP, they were barred from visiting.[95] In other words, it would be foolish to assume that, even if the Ban + Merge succeed in eliminating large swaths of the informal sector, the polluting practices that have been stereotypically attributed to them will be eliminated as well. Informal recyclers may have held a veritable monopoly over China's recycling sector for the last few decades, but they hold no monopoly over waste pollution.

Whither Beijing's Recyclers?

In early 2018 I went with scholar and activist Chen Liwen to visit Gushi to check in on the families of old friends we had made over the years and to try to get a sense of how the pressures from Beijing's mass evictions and waste sector reforms were affecting people back home. Were recyclers giving up on Beijing, heading home to do business in Gushi, or seeking work in other cities? We only had two days, enough time to talk to about twenty-five people who had links to Beijing. They were easy to find: high school kids who spent summers in Beijing living near the scrap markets with their parents; drivers working for Didi, China's Uber; middle-aged men and women who were spending a spell back home looking after aging parents. We visited a grandpa we knew who had worked in Beijing collecting used appliances and was now back in Gushi watching his grandchildren and running a small washing machine repair shop on the side. Most folks were in a holding pattern. Almost everyone agreed that Gushi was a decent place to retire but offered few business opportunities. Though Gushi county seat has become quite prosperous—in part due to the remittances of Beijing recyclers—the area has little industry, and retail is getting squeezed out by Alibaba and online platforms.

In many ways I feel that I learned even more about Gushi after we left. Chen Liwen published a blog, and she was posting every few days about our trip. She wrote a lovely post about what she found in Gushi, about the thousands who had worked for decades to contribute to keeping Beijing clean and trash free but who were now out of work and unsure where they would land. She was surprised by the response. Usually she got from two hundred to two thousand readers for a blog post and never more than three thousand, but for her Gushi post the number reached six thousand after a few days. It eventually topped twenty thousand views, making her fairly certain that Gushi folks were reposting it to share with their friends. The personal responses confirmed her hypothesis:

> "Reading this letter my tears started to flow. I sacrificed my youth (*qingchun*) to help Beijing clean up its waste."
>
> "Even though this work is dirty and exhausting, to make a living we have to persevere through it. It's easy to say 'change your profession' but hard to do, with 20–30 years of doing this it is hard to understand how to do anything else. We have no choice but to hope the government bureaus give recyclers a little space, stop the squeezing, the suppression, give the common folks who do this some space to exist."

It was moving to see how touched these readers were by a short blog appreciating their work and reflecting their stories. It brought home to me how rare it is for migrant recyclers to receive any public affirmation outside their own communities.

Like Chen Liwen, photo journalist Wang Jing has spent a lot of time over the last decade getting to know Beijing's recyclers, visiting their markets, talking to them, and photographing their daily lives. In August 2017, Wang Jing shot a series of photographs in which he returned to about twenty recycling markets that he had previously photographed, all of which had since been demolished. He brought with him large framed prints of photos he had taken at those same sites when they had been bustling with activity, and in many cases he also brought along the recyclers he had captured in those photos and had them hold the old image while standing in the now abandoned, sometimes beautifully overgrown spaces, where the markets had been. That series of photos, of which figure 16 is one, conveys layers of melancholy, pride, and accumulated everyday labor. One is startled by the jarring transience of Beijing's landscapes; reminded of the recurring willful erasure of migrant recyclers from the city's history; and also inspired by the persistent, vibrant, and often joyful flash of memory. Wang Jing's series speaks to how migrant recyclers made inhospitable spaces into homes, only to lose them again and again. It also made me realize how the erasure of history contributes to the incessant reproduction of informality and marginalization that migrant recyclers have experienced throughout the last forty years of reforms. The government has changed its policies toward migrants over these decades, generally for the better. *Hukou* restrictions have become much less punitive, the custody and repatriation system was dismantled, discrimination against migrants is far less common in the media, and its articulations are less outrageously degrading. But such improvements in no way address the damage these policies did. There is no compensation ever given for all the lost homes and businesses. These past losses and abuses are not included in the official record; they are forgotten, erased from public memory. Decades of confiscations, eviction, and abuse leave layer upon layer of scars, and the current socioeconomic playing field inherited from these erased pasts is profoundly tilted and unequal. Migrant communities

FIGURE 16. Demolished scrap market in suburbs of Beijing, from a series of more than 20 photographs taken by Wang Jing in 2017. Each photograph in the series contains within it a photograph of the same place taken in 2012, when that location was the site of a thriving recycling market. Used with artist's permission.

remember these experiences and know their lives have been shaped by them and that they have arrived at their current places in society by passing through them. But the greater public cannot even see the history that is right in front of them. Like the enclaves in which migrants worked and lived, that history is not just erased/demolished; it is soon built or grown over with something else.

I cannot say with any certainty what the state of recycling in Beijing will be by the time this book actually comes out in print. As I write this in spring 2020 under the shadow of a pandemic, attrition in the informal sector has been severe, but thousands of recyclers are still at it in Beijing, and thousands more are waiting to see what the future brings. The "waste cities" of the early 2000s are likely never to return. The question is whether the informal sector's new configuration—small yards located at tremendous distances from the city (out of reach even for an Olympic cyclist); same-day collection, baling and shipping coordinated by phone calls and text messages—will weather the merge reforms or be weeded out. Rather than predict the outcome (which I would doubtless get wrong), I think the question itself—"Given a snapshot of the sector, can we tell which way will it go?"—might return us to some of the themes of this history.

This history can be seen as sketching two somewhat contradictory premises about the recycling/reuse/waste "sector" of urban-centric economies. On the one hand, the practices and economics of the waste sector cannot be understood without also understanding the economy as a whole, the entire cycle of material-metabolizing processes from production (both agricultural and industrial) through trade and consumption to disposal, recycling, and reuse. To use the Marxist term, recycling and waste must be understood in the context of the mode of production. This study has used reuse/recycling/waste economies as a lens through which to better understand the larger mode of production. Hence in the Republican era the materials and processes of reuse/repair/recycling were entangled mainly with agricultural and handicraft modes of production. Socialist industrialization saw the cycle of food wastes (including digested food) damaged and eventually broken, while other material cycles shifted away from handicraft reuse and decisively in the direction of recycling to make material inputs available for industrial processes or mass recirculation (as in cases like the mass reuse of bottles and cardboard boxes). Regarding the reform era, it is somewhat ironic to see the Chinese state issuing the battle cry "China will no longer be the world's trash can!" because, of course, the Chinese state was explicit that its aim in the late 1990s and 2000s was to make China the world's factory—and being the world's factory and its trash can were in fact two sides of the same mode-of-production coin.

On the other hand, as we have also seen, reuse/recycling/waste sector practices rarely fit seamlessly into the dominant mode of production. The sector is very often a space wherein a mode of production's acute contradictions and mismatches emerge in bold relief and marginalized groups engage in material and economic practices incongruous with the dominant political economy. Examples are the uneducated shit hegemon who becomes wealthy on human wastes and parades around town in a scholar's robes; the model BRC worker who is praised for doing a great service for Socialist industry but whom no one is willing to marry; and the recycling collector pedaling a three-wheeled bike-cart through the automobile traffic jams in the 2000s, whose legs and hands help produce a material stream upon which China's propulsive industrialization depends. Recycling/reuse/waste practices cannot be divorced from the larger economic context, yet they also often fail to conform to the dominant modes in which they are embedded.

Beijing's recycling sector at this historical moment is no different, both reflecting the dominant modes of capitalist manufacturing and consumer practices in China today and also upsetting them. In asking what will determine the fate of informal recycling in China today, we are in essence asking which forces in the current political economy—the dominant modes of production, or other internally contradictory vectors—will be of greatest importance in shaping the sector. There are many elements that could play decisive roles. Market demand for materials is a powerful force; as long as manufacturers are buying, recyclers will be collecting. What specific materials will be in circulation, however, is more time/place specific. Now that China's biggest cities are no longer convulsed by waves of demolition and construction, iron, steel, and other scrap metal arisings are shrinking, while online shopping has caused circulation of paper, cardboard, and plastics to surge, becoming the staples of the recycler's diet. The Chinese government would like to coax (or shove) the recycling sector to move in lockstep with its vision of a restructured, higher-profit, higher-wage, and higher-tech mode of production. But that remains an uphill battle, because in the context of China's gaping economic disparities, the liminality of recycling presents an economic opportunity to the hundreds of millions lagging behind in China's economic rise.

If the previously described economic forces (large supplies of waste materials, high demand for them, and a relatively poor population willing to do the work) played out in empty space, informal recycling would continue to thrive. But recycling does not occur in empty space. It is, as we have seen, always inextricable from specific geographies, from capillaries of collection that reach to the urban cellular level (households, alleys) through nodes of exchange (markets planned and unsanctioned) to organs of processing. Over the last four decades the Chinese state has expended much effort to regulate and take control of scrap geographies—restricting collection, uprooting markets, forbidding shipments, demolishing shops, and confiscating materials and equipment. Yet state control, even after decimating crackdowns such as that in Wenan in 2011, has usually been temporary; new wastes unavoidably and continually emerge, and informal recyclers develop new techniques to access, trade, and move them. The Ban + Merge are attempts to assert control over scrap flows and geographies on an unprecedented scale but are largely cut from the same cloth as earlier policies. Perhaps today we are witnessing the battle in which the state finally wins its war with the informal "guerrilla army," but the strategies we are seeing have never yielded a decisive victory before.

But there is another factor, a wave of state policies not directly related to waste processing and scrap geographies that might play that decisive role: the state's coordinated efforts to harden cities, restrict their population size, and make them inhospitable for low-income migrants of any stripe. The Ban + Merge policies have clearly made working in the recycling business much more difficult for migrants, but the biggest difficulty many migrants in Beijing face these days is not making a living but being able to live. China's urban real estate prices have risen beyond affordability for the vast majority of the populace. For poor migrants, housing in China's major cities is unaffordable, and crackdowns on unlicensed rental arrangements and unpermitted construction have made finding a place to live extremely difficult. That, along with the sprawling geography of urban recycling circuits—the distances one needs to be able to traverse every day and still manage to get back to some form of housing—is making living in the city all but impossible for migrant recyclers. They have never been demanding about where they live; single-room shacks next to garbage markets have been fine, but even that spatial arrangement is becoming increasingly rare.

In sum, if the informal urban recycling sector is eliminated, it will probably be as much due to the state getting control over recyclables or the geography of recycling as to the state eliminating the recyclers themselves. And if this proves to be true, it would make some historical sense. Both in the Republican era and in the post-Mao reform decades, Beijing's recycling/reuse sector was largely informal, comprised of impoverished migrants hoping to eke out a living by applying labor to the city's material surplus. Their being able to make that living was premised on their ability to actually find places to physically abide in the city, whether that meant sleeping on the floor of a neighborhood temple or in a shack in a peri-urban village. The only time the Chinese state ever managed to actually claim monopoly control of the scrap sector was in the Mao era, when the systems of household registration and rationing tickets made it nearly impossible for rural migrants to settle for any prolonged period in urban areas. Even then, the main informal actors when it came to night soil management were peasants who avoided government attention by staying with their relatives and not registering. So perhaps this is what we will learn in the coming years: that sustained state-managed control of China's urban scrap sector is only achievable once it becomes all but impossible for poor migrants to live in the city. There is no question that government policies—*hukou* regulations, restrictions on kinds of construction, and so forth—play a part in expelling rural migrants from urban spaces, but by far the most powerful mechanism of exclusion today is not any set of government policies, but simply the real estate and rental markets that make urban housing available only to the rich. If the Chinese government does in fact succeed in making its leading cities unlivable for the poor, the government can indeed be proud that not only has it joined the wealthy and developed OECD nations in asserting nearly monopolistic control over its urban waste management, but it has joined those nations also in their great achievement of creating top-tier global cities in which only the rich can afford to live.

Timelines of Selected Events in the Recycling and Sanitation Bureaucracies, 1949–2000

RECYCLING

1951   Copper becomes the first state-managed scrap material, by China Native Goods Company.

1952   Copper management is moved to the All-China Federation of Supply and Marketing Cooperatives (SMC).

1952–55   Rubber, paper, and cloth scrap are placed under SMC management.

1955   Under the SMC the Beijing Scrap Management Office is established. Also, the Beijing Handicraft Cooperative creates a Used Goods Management Office. Most recycling businesses are still private. Recycling is designated a "special industry" (特殊行业).

1957   The Beijing Scrap Company (BSC 北京市废品公司) is established, jointly managed by the SMC and the Materials Bureau (物资局), with exclusive rights over commerce in scrap.

1958   Nine district-level BSC companies are established, and all employees are made state employees.

1958–59   The BSC municipal-level office is disbanded for one year; the SMC is merged with the Commerce Bureau.

1962   The SMC and Commerce split, and the BSC is placed back under the SMC.

1963   The BSC is returned to joint SMC and Materials Bureau management. Beijing scrap metals collection and allocation are placed exclusively under BSC and Materials Bureau control.

1965   The BSC changes its name to Beijing Recycling Company (BRC 北京市物资回收公司).

1968   The Beijing SMC is merged into the Second Commerce Bureau (二商局).

1971   The BRC is placed under the Second Commerce Bureau.

1979   The SMC is split out from Second Commerce Bureau, and the BRC is placed under the SMC.

1982   A reiteration is issued that all Beijing scrap metal commerce is still under BRC management only.

1986   District BRC companies are decoupled from the municipal BRC.

1987   There is a shift from prescriptive allocation of scrap ferrous to looser guided planning.

1989   Beijing ends nonferrous planning.

1992   Beijing ends ferrous planning. Price controls for both ferrous and nonferrous are ended.

1992–94   The BRC stops collecting and processing glass, bottles, bones, human hair, and rubber.

1994   The city enforces the "three license" (三证) policy in an attempt to stop informal scrap trading.

1999   The municipal-level BRC is mothballed. District-level companies continue to function under various shareholding arrangements, adopting new names and business strategies.

SANITATION: GARBAGE AND NIGHT SOIL MANAGEMENT

1949   Cleaning teams and the Number One Sanitation Truck Depot are established under the Beijing police.

1950   Urban Environmental Sanitation is placed under the Beijing Engineering Sanitation Bureau.

1953   Beijing's last privately owned night soil yards are closed; night soil is fully under state management.

1954   Environmental Sanitation is placed under the Above/Below Watercourse Engineering Bureau.

1959   Environmental Sanitation is placed under the Beijing Public Sanitation Bureau.

1964   Environmental Sanitation is raised to bureau level (ESB). The city begins eliminating household privies.

1967–78   The ESB is eliminated. Waste management is placed under the Beijing Utilities Bureau.

1974   Eighty-five thousand household privies in urban districts are replaced with truck-accessible public toilets and the need for laborers carrying night soil buckets and scoops in Beijing ends.

1978	The Environmental Sanitation Bureau is reconstituted.
1985	Districts are made responsible for disposal of their own garbage. ·
1994	Beijing opens Asuwei, the city's first sanitary landfill; others quickly follow.
2000	The Beijing ESB is dissolved; entities under it (sanitation truck fleets, etc.) become SOEs. Waste management is placed under the Municipal Administration Commission.

NOTES

ABBREVIATIONS FOR SOURCES USED IN NOTES

#1QJCZ   北京市第一清洁车辆场环境卫生志, 1949–90 [*Beijing shi di yi qingjie che liangchang huanjing weisheng zhi, 1949–90*; Beijing municipal Number One Sanitation Truck Depot environmental sanitation gazetteer, 1949–90]. Edited by Ji Hong. Beijing: n.p., 1994.

BJGXSZ   北京市　商业卷　供销合作社商业志 [*Beijing zhi Shangye juan Gongxiao hezuoshe shangye zhi*; Beijing gazetteer, business collection, Supply and Marketing Cooperative business gazetteer]. Edited by Beijing Local Records Compilation Committee. Beijing: Beijing chubanshe, 2003.

BJHWZ   北京志　市政卷　环境卫生志 [*Beijing zhi Shizheng juan Huanjing weisheng zhi*; Beijing gazetteer, urban administration collection, Environmental Sanitation gazetteer]. Edited by Beijing Local Records Compilation Committee. Beijing: Beijing chubanshe, 2002.

BJMA   北京市档案馆 Beijing Municipal Archives

CCTV   China Central Television

RMRB   人民日报 [Renmin Ribao people's daily]

RR   *Resource Recycling* at https://resource-recycling.com/recycling

XCHWZ   北京市西城环卫史志 [*Beijingshi Xicheng Huanwei shi zhi*; Beijing Xicheng District Environmental Sanitation history gazetteer]. Edited by Beijing Xicheng District Environmental Sanitation Management Bureau. Beijing: Beijing shi Xicheng qu huanjing weisheng guanli ju, 1987.

ZGGXSXB   中国供销合作社史料选编 [*Zhongguo gongxiao hezuo zongshe shiliao xuanbian*; China Supply and Marketing Cooperative selected historical materials]. Edited by Quanguo gongxiao hezuo zongshe. Beijing: Zhongguo caizheng jingji chubanshe, 1986.

INTRODUCTION

1. Ralph Linzner and Stefan Salhofer, "Municipal Solid Waste Recycling and the Significance of [the] Informal Sector in Urban China," *Waste Management & Research* 32, no. 9 (2014): 896–907.

2. Zsuzsa Gille, *From the Cult of Waste to the Trash Heap of History* (Bloomington: Indiana University Press, 2007).

3. Josh Lepawsky, *Reassembling Rubbish: Worlding Electronic Waste* (Cambridge, MA: MIT Press, 2018).

4. Adam Minter, *Secondhand: Travels in the New Global Garage Sale* (New York: Bloomsbury Publishing, 2019).

5. Brian Wynne, *Risk Management and Hazardous Waste: Implementation and the Dialectics of Credibility* (Berlin: Springer-Verlag, 1987).

6. Mary Douglas, *Purity and Danger: An Analysis of Concepts of Pollution and Taboo* (New York: Praeger, 1966), 36.

7. Zsuzsa Gille, "Of Fish Feces, Shamanic Bowls and Chimpanzee Scraps: Extension vs Precision in the Concept of Waste," *Worldwide Waste: Journal of Interdisciplinary Studies* 1, no. 1 (2018): 1–2, https://doi.org/10.5334/wwwj.22.

8. Risa Whitson, "Negotiating Place and Value: Geographies of Waste and Scavenging in Buenos Aires," *Antipode* 43, no. 4 (2011): 1414–15.

9. Kate Parizeau and Josh Lepawsky, "Legal Orderings of Waste in Built Spaces," *International Journal of Law in the Built Environment* 7, no. 1 (2015): 21–38.

10. Gille, *From the Cult of Waste*, 11–37.

11. Susan Strasser, *Waste and Want: A Social History of Trash* (New York: Henry Holt, 1999).

12. Vance Packard, *The Waste Makers* (Brooklyn, NY: Ig Publishing, 2011).

13. Joshua O. Reno, *Waste Away: Working and Living with a North American Landfill* (Oakland: University of California Press, 2016).

14. J. B. R. Whitney, "The Waste Economy and the Dispersed Metropolis in China," in *The Extended Metropolis, Settlement Transition in Asia*, ed. N. Ginsberg, B. Kopple and TG McGee (Honolulu: University of Hawaii Press, 1991), 177–91.

15. Note that the Chinese term 废旧物资 (*feijiu wuzi*) does not directly correlate to the English word *recycle*, and 回收 (*huishou*), another word that I often translate as *recycle*, would more literally translate as "take back." There are many interesting and significant differences in what these terms denote and connote that are often lost in translation; throughout this book I only point to a few examples when they are crucial to the argument, but far more could be said. See especially Adam Liebman, "Reconfiguring Chinese Natures: Frugality and Waste Reutilization in Mao Era Urban China," *Critical Asian Studies* 51, no. 4 (2019): 537–57.

16. Minh T. N. Nguyen, "Trading in Broken Things: Gendered Performances and Spatial Practices in Vietnamese Rural-Urban Waste Economy," *American Ethnologist* 43, no. 1 (2016): 116–29.

17. Dorothy J. Solinger, *Chinese Business under Socialism: The Politics of Domestic Commerce, 1949–1980* (Berkeley: University of California Press, 1984).

18. Elizabeth Economy, *The River Runs Black: The Environmental Challenge to China's Future* (Ithica, NY: Cornell University Press, 2004), 49. For other examples of this starkly condemning narrative, see Vaclav Smil, *The Bad Earth* (Armonk, NY: M. E. Sharp, 1984); and Judith Shapiro, *Mao's War Against Nature: Politics and the Environment in Revolutionary China* (Cambridge, UK: Cambridge University Press, 2001).

19. Sigrid Schmalzer, *Red Revolution, Green Revolution: Scientific Farming in Socialist China* (Chicago: University of Chicago Press, 2016); and Sigrid Schmalzer, "Layer upon Layer: Mao-Era History and the Construction of China's Agricultural Heritage," *East Asian Science, Technology and Society: An International Journal* 13 (2019): 413–41.

20. In addition to scholars already cited in this introduction—Gille, Lepawsky, Reno, MacBride—who all make this point, Max Liboiron has made it fundamental to her scholarly interventions, many of which can be found at the *Discard Studies* blog she curates.

21. Samantha MacBride, *Recycling Reconsidered: The Present Failure and Future Promise of Environmental Action in the United States* (Cambridge, MA: MIT Press, 2011).

22. Some of these topics have recently been pursued by some wonderful scholars. Kao Shih-yang conducted groundbreaking (in both senses of the word) research into Beijing's construction waste: "The City Recycled: The Afterlives of Demolished Buildings in Post-War Beijing" (PhD diss., University of California, Berkeley, 2013). Chen Liwen provided the first overview of Beijing's discarded appliance network in "E-Waste Recycling in Beijing and the Impact of China's WEEE Directive: Competition or Collaboration Between Informal Recyclers and Authorized Recycling Enterprises" (master's thesis, Memorial University of Newfoundland, 2019). Tong Xin at Peking University continues to produce excellent research on e-waste and recycling in China and Beijing. Jennifer Altehenger, in *Fibre Fever: Raw Materials, Waste, and the Dilemma of Economization in China's Great Leap Forward* (Washington, DC: Association of Asian Studies, 2018) delves into comprehensive resource use in the furniture industry. Dozens of studies on China's waste issues and recyclers that I have not directly cited here would reward exploration; one that should not be missed is Hu Jiaming and Zhang Yiying, *Feipin shenghuo* [Scrap life] (Hong Kong: Chinese University of HK Press, 2016).

RECYCLING OF A DIFFERENT SORT

1. Pan Gong, "Da gu er de shenghuo zhihui" [A drum beater's life wisdom], *Beijing Jishi* [Beijing document], no. 7 (2009): 80–82.

1. DREAMS OF A HYGIENIC INFRASTRUCTURE DEFERRED

1. Quantities are based on best guesses from profiles of municipal solid waste (MSW), night soil, scrap, and used goods, mainly from the *BJHWZ* and an unpublished memoir of a Beijing Recycling Company (BRC) manager. *BJHWZ* estimates garbage at one thousand tons daily for the Republican era (p. 50), with around 80 percent coal ash and dirt, though with much more fruit and vegetable waste in summer, while night soil likely averaged over seven hundred tons daily (p. 63). According to all accounts, many more scavengers collected scrap than used goods, though used clothing and cloth scraps, if counted as a single category, perhaps outweighed any other scrap.

2. Shi Mingzheng, "Beijing Transforms: Urban Infrastructure, Public Works, and Social Change in the Chinese Capital, 1900–1928" (PhD diss., Columbia University, 1993), 134–40.

3. This was common in Paris, for example. When the Parlement in 1721 began assessing property owners for the costs of sewer cleaning, the levy only spurred residents to dump more waste, eventually prompting the imposition of fines for dumping in 1736. Donald Reid, *Paris Sewers and Sewermen: Realities and Representations* (Cambridge, MA: Harvard University Press, 1991), 13.

4. Shi, "Beijing Transforms," 152.

5. Wang Weijie, "Jiu shi Beijing cheng wushui dui huanjing de wuran" [Old Beijing's sewer water's pollution of the environment], *Huanjing Kexue* [Environmental science] 7, no.6 (1986): 90–91.

6. Wang, "Jiu shi Beijing cheng wushui dui huanjing de wuran," 90. The Chinese of the verse reads: 街衢下列行水沟, 道旁错落露沟头. 积秽所入淤不流, 一岁一开夏整修.... 窈然深黑恶气腾, 往往沟夫死络绎. 疫气流行借沟气, 月令触犯人身灾.

7. Shi, "Beijing Transforms," 144.

8. Shi, "Beijing Transforms," 292.

9. Ruth Rogaski, *Hygienic Modernity: Meanings of Health and Disease in Treaty Port China* (Berkeley: University of California Press, 2004), 187.

10. Ruth Rogaski, "Hygienic Modernity in Tianjin," in *Remaking the Chinese City: Modernity and National Identity, 1900–1950*, ed. Joseph Esherick (Honolulu: University of Hawaii, 2001), 30.

11. Sidney Gamble, *Peking, a Social Survey* (New York: George H. Doran, 1921), 122.

12. Janet Y. Chen, *Guilty of Indigence: The Urban Poor in China, 1900–1953* (Princeton, NJ: Princeton University Press, 2012), 63.

13. Chen, *Guilty of Indigence*, 60.

14. *XCHWZ*, 6. 清洁队, 清洁队, 外面干活庙里睡, 冬天喂虱子, 夏天蚊蝇飞, 头枕砖, 麻袋被, 一年季活受罪.

15. *XCHWZ*, 5.

16. *BJHWZ*, 10.

17. BJMA, 2-1-112, 3/1949, Quanshi de qingjie yundong weiyuanhui huiyi jilu [Record of full municipal cleanup movement committee meeting minutes], 1–11.

18. Wang Huiming, "Jingcheng shenghuo laji de youhuan" [The capital city's daily trash concerns], *Beijing wanbao* [Beijing evening news], January 24, 1999.

19. *BJHWZ*, 25–26.

20. *XCHWZ*, 6.

21. "Yufang shiyi qingjie fagui" [Cleaning regulations during epidemic prevention], in *Qing mo Beijing chengshi guanli fagui: 1906–1910* [Late Qing Beijing urban administrative codes: 1906–1910], ed. Tian Tao and Guo Chengwei (Beijing: Beijing Yanjing chubanshe, 1996), 75–79.

22. *BJHWZ*, 30.

23. *BJHWZ*, 71.

24. *BJHWZ*, 24.

25. *BJHWZ*, 25.

26. *BJHWZ*, 105. In hindsight it is hard not to see these extermination campaigns as foreshadowing the Mao era Four Pests (flies, mosquitos, rats, and sparrows) campaigns yet to come, but it also reminds us that the idea of wiping out perceived pests through mass hygiene campaigns was not exclusive to a socialist imaginary of environmental engineering.

27. For more on Beijing planning and construction in the Republican era, Shi Mingzheng (see note 2) and Madeleine Yue Dong, *Republican Beijing, the City and Its Histories* (Berkeley: University of California Press, 2003), provide excellent English-language overviews.

28. Shi, "Beijing Transforms."

29. J. B. R. Whitney, "The Waste Economy and the Dispersed Metropolis in China," in *The Extended Metropolis, Settlement Transition in Asia*, ed. N. Ginsberg, B. Kopple and TG McGee (Honolulu: University of Hawaii Press, 1991), 175.

30. Qiu Zhonglin, "Shuiwozi—Beijing de gongshuiyezhe yu minsheng yongshui, 1368–1937" [Water nests: Beijing's water porters and commoner water use, 1368–1937], in *Zhongguo de chengshi shenghuo* [China's urban life], ed. Li Xiaoti (Beijing: Xin xing chubanshe, 2006), 203–52.

31. Che Hui, "Wo shou: Chuanqi laomo huazhuan, Shi Chuanxiang zhuan" [Handshake: Legendary labor model pictorial biography; Shi Chuanxiang], *Dangdai Laomo* [Contemporary labor model] 27, no. 4 (2010): 73–78.

32. BJMA 136-1-12, 6/1950, Beijing shi renmin zhengfu weisheng gongcheng ju, Beijing shi de fenbian [Beijing Sanitation Engineering Bureau, Beijing's night soil], 17–30.

33. Most were built by shit lords: Du Lihong, "1930 niandai de Beiping chengshi wuwu guanli gaige" [1930s Beiping urban refuse management reform], *Jindaishi yanjiu* [Modern history research] 27, no. 5 (2005): 99–113; rights to their toilets' night soil: Chen Jianting, Li Wanqi, and Mao Dianliang, "Zhen ya Beijing Tianqiao eba" [Suppressing the bullies of Beijing's Tianqiao], *Wenshi jinghua* [Essence of literary history] 19, no. 5: 52–57.

34. Zhao Wanyi, "Pingshi chuli fenbian de yi ge teshu zuzhi" [The peculiar organization handling Beiping city's night soil], *Shizheng pinglun* [Urban administration review] 4, no. 12 (1936): 34–39.

35. Zhao, "Pingshi chuli fenbian de yi ge teshu zuzhi," 35.

36. BJMA 136-1-12, Beijingshi de fenbian, 21.

37. Zhao, "Pingshi chuli fenbian de yi ge teshu zuzhi," 34–39.

38. Herbert Lou, *Beipingshi gongshangye gaikuang* [An overview of Beiping city's business sector] (Beiping: Beipingshi shehuiju, 1932), 660.

39. "Ruhe qudi fenba?" [How can we get rid of shit lords?], *Jingbao* [Beijing news], December 9, 1933, 6.

40. Rogaski, "Hygienic Modernity in Tianjin," 214.

41. The reader will notice that at times the name Beiping is used rather than Beijing. This is because from 1927 to 1949 the Nationalist government moved the national capital from the city of Beijing to Nanjing. Beijing means "Northern Capital," the character "jing" 京 denoting capital, so when the Nationalists ended the city's status as the capital they renamed it Beiping, replacing "jing" with "ping" 平 meaning "peace."

42. Lou, *Beipingshi gongshangye gaikuang*, 663.

43. David Strand, *Rickshaw Beijing: City People and Politics in the 1920s* (Berkeley: University of California Press, 1989), 155.

44. Zhao, "Pingshi chuli fenbian de yi ge teshu zuzhi," 38.

45. Strand, *Rickshaw Beijing*, 155.

46. Du, "1930 niandai de Beiping chengshi wuwu guanli gaige," 107.

47. Xing Guihuan, "20 shiji 30 niandai Beipingshi zhengfu de fenye guanban gouxiang yu huanjing weisheng de gaige" [1930s Beiping municipal government's idea of government sponsored night soil management reform], *Zhongguo shehui lishi pinglun* [Chinese social history review] 3, no. 8 (2007): 163–82.

48. Xing, "20 shiji 30 niandai Beipingshi zhengfu de fenye guanban gouxiang yu huanjing weisheng de gaige," 176–77.

49. Xing, "20 shiji 30 niandai Beipingshi zhengfu de fenye guanban gouxiang yu huanjing weisheng de gaige," 174.

50. *XCHWZ*, 11.

51. Shi Chuanxiang, "Rang wuchan jieji de geming jingshen daidai xiangchuan" [Let the proletarian revolutionary spirit be passed from generation to generation], *RMRB*, January 26, 1965.

52. *XCHWZ*, 9.

53. BJMA 4-2-13, Nongyao, dafenye diaocha baogao [Report on fertilizer and night soil industry survey], 9–24.

54. BJMA 136-1-12, Beijing shi de fenbian, 27–28.

2. FROM IMPERIAL CAPITAL TO SECONDHAND EMPORIUM

1. Madeleine Yue Dong, *Republican Beijing, the City and Its Histories* (Berkeley: University of California Press, 2003), 300.

2. "Shoe soles for the poor": Dong, *Republican Beijing*, 300; insulating shoes and caps: J. S. Burgess, *The Guilds of Peking* (New York: Columbia University Press: 1928), 119.

3. Dong, *Republican Beijing*, 206.

4. Memoir of a BRC manager, Xuanwu district office (unpublished; author's personal collection), 9.

5. Memoir of a BRC manager, 11.

6. Memoir of a BRC manager, 12.

7. Chang Renchun, "Jiu jing dagu er de" [Drum beaters of the old capital], *Beijing Shiji* [Beijing document], no. 12 (1999): 53–56.

8. Memoir of a BRC manager, 12.

9. Lu Qi, "Beijing de xiaoshi" ["Beijing's small markets"], *Luyou* [*Travel*] 1, no. 4 (1994): 6-9.

10. Memoir of a BRC manager, 13–14.

11. BJMA 22-12-2391, 6/14/1956, "Guanyu laji fenlie hou shougou wenti de yijian" [Suggestions to handle problems with the sale of [scrap] after trash sorting].

12. The term *dawn market* could also be used for several other markets that gathered in these hours before dawn, so there were fruit, vegetable, and candy dawn markets as well. The dawn market for scrap was the "the odds and ends market" (零物市).

13. Yao Zhengsheng, "Yeshi manyu" [Musings on night markets], *Beijing gongshang daxue xuebao* [Beijing Business College journal] 2, no. 1 (1982): 71–72. The quote is taken from a late Qing publication, 朝市丛载.

14. Memoir of a BRC manager, 28. One anecdote describes a wastepaper seller who often hid his dog inside the piles of paper in order to weight the scales, a tough trick to pull off in broad daylight.

15. Herbert Lou, *Beipingshi gongshangye gaikuang* [An overview of Beiping city's business sector] (Beiping: Beipingshi shehuiju, 1932), 681.

16. The term 鬼市 is also used at times to refer to dawn markets, and the lines between these markets are not always crystal clear.

17. Lou, *Beipingshi gongshangye gaikuang*, 683.

18. Chen Deguang and Gao Fengshan, "Dong xiaoshi manbi" [Jottings on east dawn market], *Beijing wenshi ziliao jingxuan, Chongwen juan* [Selections from Beijing cultural history materials, Chongwen volume], ed. Beijing shi zhengxie wenshi ziliao weiyuan hui (Beijing: Beijing chubanshe, 1986), 297–303.

19. Liu Enlu, "Cong Dongdan Da Di dao Dongsi Renmin Shichang" [From Dongdan Big Grounds to Dongsi People's Market], *Beijing shi Dongcheng qu wenshi ziliao xuanbian di 1 ji* [Selections from Beijing Dongcheng district cultural history materials, number 1], ed. Beijing shi Dongcheng qu weiyuan hui (Bejing: Beijing chubanshe, 1988), 123–38.

20. Dong, *Republican Beijing*, 205.

21. Dong, *Republican Beijing*, 184.

22. Dong, *Republican Beijing*, 137.

23. Lou, *Beipingshi gongshangye gaikuang*, 582.

24. Chen Zhongyuan, *Guwan shihua yu jianshang* [A history and appreciation of antiques] (Beijing: Guoji wenhua chubanshe, 1990), 101–2.

25. Burgess, *Guilds of Peking*, 121.

26. Liu Peng, "Qingmo minchu Beijingshi de diandangye" [Late Qing early Republic Beijing pawn shops], *Beijing shehui kexue* [*Beijing Social Science*] 11, no. 1 (1996): 84–91.

27. Lou, *Beipingshi gongshangye gaikuang*, 219–20.

28. *Baoding shi zhi di 2 ce* [Baoding gazetteer, book 2], ed. Hebei sheng, Baoding shi defangzhi bianji weiyuanhui (Beijing: Fangzhi chubanshe, 1999), 377.

29. Memoir of a BRC manager, 20–22.

30. Lou, *Beipingshi gongshangye gaikuang*, 431.

31. Burgess, *Guilds of Peking*, 113.

32. Mei Songsong, "Minguo Beijing guwan jiaoyi changsuo shiling" [Tidbits of Beijing antique market (1912–1949)], *Yishu shichang* [Art market], no. 3 (2011): 76–80.

33. Susan Strasser, *Waste and Want: A Social History of Trash* (New York: Henry Holt, 1999).

34. Joshua O. Reno, *Waste Away: Working and Living with a North American Landfill* (Oakland: University of California Press, 2016), 80.

35. To begin looking into repair and maintenance in our current economies, readers might look to: Stephen Graham and Nigel Thrift, "Out of Order: Understanding Repair and Maintenance," *Theory, Culture and Society* 24, no. 3 (2007): 1–25; and Steven J. Jackson, "Rethinking Repair," ed. Tarleton Gillespie, Pablo Boczkowski, and Kirsten Foot,

Media Technologies: Essays on Communication, Materiality and Society (Cambridge, MA: MIT Press, 2014). For thoughts on differentiated ontologies of repair in discarded electronics, see Lara Houston, "The Timeliness of Repair," *Continent* 6, no. 1: 51–55, http://continentcontinent.cc/index/php/continent/article/view/280.

MODERNITY OF A DIFFERENT SORT

1. Wang Shaomin, interview in Sanlitun Beijing, May 18, 2008.

2. Shu Guang Zhang, *Economic Cold War: America's Embargo against China and the Sino-Soviet Alliance, 1949–1963* (Stanford, CA: Stanford University Press, 2001).

3. THE RURAL EXILE OF URBAN WASTES

1. BJMA 2-1-112, 3/1949, Quanshi de qingjie yundong weiyuanhui huiyi jilu [Record of full municipal clean up movement committee meeting minutes], 1–11.

2. "Qingchu jiefang qian jicun laji" [Removal of pre-liberation accumulated trash], *RMRB*, April 3, 1949. See also BJMA 2-1-112, 4.

3. "Qunzhong reqing canjia qingjie yundong" [The masses warmly join the clean-up campaign], *RMRB*, November 28, 1949.

4. *BJHWZ*, 31. The city's name was changed to Beijing on October 1, 1949, with the founding of the People's Republic.

5. Sanitation Engineering Bureau: *XCHWZ*, 16. The name and administrative structure of the Sanitation Bureau changed several times during the Mao years and then in the reform era (see the appendix). 172 jin (about 1.1 pounds) of grain per month: Beijing weisheng gongcheng ju [Beijing Sanitation Engineering Bureau], "Beijing de qingjie gongzuo" [Beijing Sanitation Work], *Beijing dangan shiliao* [Beijing archive material], no. 28 (1992): 25–31.

6. BJMA 2-1-112, 7.

7. "Beiping de qingjiedui bian le yang" [Beiping's clean-up teams have changed], *RMRB* April 29, 1949.

8. "Zhuhu gai xiu shenshui gou keng" [Residents should fix open sewers], *RMRB*, April 4, 1949.

9. "Qunzhong reqing canjia qingjie yundong."

10. *BJHWZ*, 52.

11. Trash trucks reached 75 by 1952: *BJHWZ*, 57.

12. #1QJCZ, 47. The motorized truck fleets (which also took over night soil transport) were managed by the East and West City Sanitation Truck Yards, which coordinated their routes with the Sanitation Engineering Bureau's night soil and garbage collecting teams in each district.

13. "Aiguo weisheng yundong zhong de Longxugou" [Dragon's beard ditch in the Patriotic Hygiene Campaign], *RMRB*, September 7, 1952. Ruth Rogaski, in *Hygienic Modernity: Meanings of Health and Disease in Treaty Port China* (Berkeley: University of California Press, 2004), writes in some detail about this first Patriotic Hygiene Campaign and places it in the context of the claim that the United States was using germ warfare in the Korean War at the time.

14. "Yifengyisu de aiguo weisheng yundong zai Beijing" [The behavior transforming patriotic hygiene campaign in Beijing], *RMRB*, October 7, 1955.

15. "Beijingshi renmin zhengfu fachu zhishi haozhao quan shi renmin canjia xia qiu jijie aiguo weisheng yundong" [Beijing Municipal People's Government issue instructional call for all residents to participate in summer and autumn patriotic sanitation campaign], *RMRB*, July 18, 1953.

16. *BJHWZ*, 77--78.

17. BJMA 4-2-13, 1949, Nongyao dafenye diaocha baogao [Fertilizer and night soil trade survey report], 9-25.

18. BJMA 4-2-13, 1949, 24.

19. For other examples of policies aimed at reforming the behavior of marginalized and impoverished urban groups see Aminda M. Smith, *Thought Reform and China's Dangerous Classes: Reeducation, Resistance and the People* (Lanham, MD: Rowman and Littlefield, 2013).

20. BJMA 101-001-308, 1950, Fenye laozi jiti hetong gongzuo zongjie [Summary of labor-capital collective contract work in night soil industry], 29-32.

21. *XCHWZ*, 16-17.

22. *XCHWZ*, 18.

23. BJMA 2-4-144, 8-12/1952, Weisheng gongcheng ju guanyu Fuwai fenchang gudong bagong shijian chuli de qingkuang baogao [Sanitation Engineering Bureau report regarding the handling of the agitation for labor strike at Fuwai night soil yard], 28-33.

24. Zhong He, "Laodong zui guangrong: Taofen gongren Shi Chuanxiang de chuanqi rensheng [Labor is the most glorious: The amazing life of shit worker Shi Chuanxiang], *Xin Xiang pinglun* [New Xiang review], no. 10 (2010): 22-24. While clearly sanitation managers were delighted by Shi Chuanxiang's innovations, one cannot help wondering how his coworkers felt about the steep increase in their workload.

25. BJMA 2-6-212, 4-6/1954, Shi weisheng gongcheng ju guanyu jieguan cancun he siying fenbianye qu fen diduan fangan [City Sanitation Engineering Bureau, Regarding the program to take over surviving privately owned night soil businesses and eliminating drying yards], 4-15.

26. *BJHWZ*, 62.

27. BJMA 137-1-60, 12/1956, Shangxia shuidao gongcheng ju guanyu nongmin fanying fenfei zhiliang wenti baogao [Above/Below Watercourse Engineering Bureau report regarding peasant response to night soil fertilizer quality problems], 1-2.

28. Throughout the Mao era, in various policies areas one can find a complex mix of at times valorizing popular or local technologies as scientifically valuable and in other cases denigrating them. For sustained and thoughtful analyses of these issues see Sigrid Schmalzer, *Red Revolution, Green Revolution: Scientific Farming in Socialist China* (Chicago: University of Chicago Press, 2016), as well as *The People's Peking Man: Popular Science and Human Identity in Twentieth-Century China* (Chicago: University of Chicago Press, 2008).

29. *BJHWZ*, 63-64.

30. *BJHWZ*, 63-64.

31. *BJHWZ*, 56.

32. BJMA 2-14-269, 3-11/1962, Shi weisheng ju guanyu 1962 nian dawa chengshi huafenchi fei yuan zhiyuan nongye; guanyu zuzhi nongcun jifei renyuan jin taofen de yijian

[Municipal Sanitation Bureau, Suggestions regarding 1962 big excavation of septic tank fertilizer to support agriculture, and regarding organizing peasant fertilizer collectors to enter [the city] and remove night soil], 1–25.

33. BJMA 2-14-269, 3-11/1962, 11.

34. BJMA 22-12-2391, 1956, Shi Shangxia shuidao gongcheng ju, Beijingshi shixing laji fenlei shouji chuli jihua (caoan) [Municipal Above/Below Watercourse Engineering Office, draft of Beijing pilot trash separation collection and handling plan], 60–67.

35. BJMA 47-1-34, 3/1956-5/62, Beijingshi shangxia shuidao gongcheng ju guanyu chengqu tuixing laji fenlei shouji gongzuo de qingkuang he jihua [Beijing Municipal Above/Below Watercourse Engineering Office regarding the conditions and plan for urban districts to carry out trash separation and collection work], 4–6.

36. BJMA 22-12-2391, Draft trash separation plan, 61.

37. BJMA 47-1-34, 12/1956, Guanyu canguan Shijiazhuangshi shixing laji fenlei shouji gongzuo de baogao [Report regarding our inspection of Shijianzhuang city's implementation of trash separation and collection work], 7–9.

38. Andrew Morris, "'Fight for Fertilizer!' Excrement, Public Health, and Mobilization in New China," *Journal of Unconventional History* 6 no. 3, (1995): 62–63.

39. BJMA 2-14-268, 1962, Beijingshi nonglin ju, Beijingshi gonggong wiesheng ju, Guanyu liyong chengshi laji jifei qingkuang ji jinhou yijian de baogao [Beijing agriculture and forestry bureau, Beijing public sanitation bureau, report regarding present and future suggestions for using urban garbage for composting], 10–14.

40. Ms. Wang, interview with author, Beijing, February 2018.

41. *Shanghai huanjing weisheng zhi* [Shanghai environmental sanitation gazetteer], ed. Shi Zhenguo and Cai Dexuan (Shanghai: Shanghai shehui kexue chubanshe, 1996), 109. This remix problem appears again in the source separation campaigns in the 2000s.

42. BJMA 1-21-215, 2/1960, Beijingshi Xicheng qu feijiu wuzi huishou gongsi, Fusuijing wai gouzhan laji san fenlei de shidian jingyan jieshao [Beijing Xicheng District Scrap Recycling Company, explaining our Outer Fusuijing depot "three separates" trash pilot experience], 24–25.

43. BJMA 2-9-40, 12/1957, Beijingshi renmin weiyuanhui bangongting guanyu ge xian nongmin dao Beijing taofen he cun shai fenbian wenti ji dongyuan huan xiang shengchan de gonghan [Official letter from Beijing Municipal People's Committee work office regarding the problem of peasants from various counties coming to Beijing to dig night soil and staying to dry it and compeling them to return home for production].

44. BJMA 2-14-268, 1962, Shirenwei guanyu zhengdun waisheng shi he jiaoqu wu zuzhi nongmin Jincheng taofen shaifen [Municipal People's Committee regarding rectifying unorganized peasants from outside city, province, and suburban districts entering the city, stealing and drying night soil], 5–9.

45. BJMA 2-17-140, 4-10/1965, Beijingshi huanjing weisheng ju: Guanyu chuli san-huanlu yinei shailiang fenbian de qingkuang huibao [Beijing Municipal Environmental Sanitation Bureau: Report regarding handling the situation with night soil open air drying inside the third ring road], 10–11. There were of course many more policies and discourses that worked to build a clear divide between rural and urban spaces, people, and activities in the Mao era. See Jeremy Brown, *City Versus Countryside in Mao's China: Negotiating the Divide* (Cambridge, UK: Cambridge University Press, 2012).

46. *BJHWZ*, 62.

47. BJMA 2-17-140, Guanyu chuli sanhuanlu yi nei.

48. By 1962 the state's *hukou* system of household registration was firmly in place, differentiating urban from rural residents and also placing cities in a hierarchy. In almost every respect Beijing and Shanghai were the most elite and privileged locations, and it was nearly impossible for those from lesser cities or rural areas to attain registration in either city, making the workers' eagerness to renounce that privilege all the more remarkable.

49. BJMA 2-14-266, 6/1961-12/1962, Beijing gonggong weisheng ju guanyu fenbian gong ren huan xiang wenti de qingshi [Request from Beijing public sanitation office regarding the problem of night soil workers returning to the countryside].

50. Shi Chuanxiang, "Rang wuchan jieji de geming jingshen daidai xiangchuan" [Let the proletariat revolutionary spirit pass from generation to generation], *RMRB*, January 26, 1965.

51. Shi, "Rang wuchan jieji de geming jingshen daidai xiangchuan."

52. *BJHWZ*, 11.

53. Che Hui, "Woshou: Chuanqi laomo huazhuan, Shi Chuanxiang zhuan" [Handshake: Legendary labor model pictorial biography; Shi Chuanxiang], *Dangdai Laomo* [Contemporary labor model] 27, no. 4 (2010): 77.

54. *#1QJCZ*, 33–37.

55. BJMA 128-2-281, 8/2/1974, Beijing shi gongyong ju, Beijing shi nonglin ju: Guanyu zuzhi bufen shedui qingtao chengqu huafenzhi de baogao [Beijing Public Works Bureau, Beijing Forestry and Agricultural Bureau: Report on organizing a portion of communes to clean out city septic tanks], 5–6.

56. BJMA 128-2-537, 7/15/1977, Beijing shi gongyong ju geming lingdao xiaozu: Guanyu quxiao chengqu fenku he zai sanhuanlu yiwai jian fenku qingkuang de baogao [Beijing Public Works Bureau Revolutionary Leadership Small Group: Report on eliminating urban shit storage and building shit storage outside the third ring road], 32–33.

57. *BJHWZ*, 58; and BJMA 128-1-186, 7/28/1973, Beijing shi gongyong ju geming lingdao xiaozu: Guanyu shixing laji jizhong fenlei wuhaihua chuli de shiyan yanjiu gongzuo de baogao [Beijing Public Works Bureau Revolutionary Leadership Small Group: Report on research work into trash separation collection and sanitization treatment], 8–10.

58. *#1QJCZ*, 46–47.

59. *#1QJCZ*, 53.

60. Schmalzer, *Red Revolution, Green Revolution*, 12.

61. BJMA 181-16-140, 5/15/1978, Beijing shi geming weiyuanhui, guanyu jiangdi fenxi gongying jiage de tongzhi [Beijing Municipal Revolutionary Committee, notice on lowering the sale price of feces].

62. J. B. R. Whitney, "The Waste Economy and the Dispersed Metropolis in China," in *The Extended Metropolis, Settlement Transition in Asia*, ed. N. Ginsberg, B. Kopple and TG McGee (Honolulu: University of Hawaii Press, 1991), 182.

63. As the reader I am sure understands, there are many versions of this fantasy of an "away" for wastes in modern societies, and the idea and its many resonances and contradictions are a central trope in discard studies. See Reno, *Waste Away*; and Joel Tarr, *Search for the Ultimate Sink: Urban Pollution in Historical Perspective* (Akron: University of Akron Press, 1996). The fantasies of "away" operate on so many levels in the waste-scape, from the

hiding of acts of physical hygiene, to dreams of leak-proof disposability, to the perpetual motion hallucination of "zero waste" idealized in the three-arrow recycling icon; for explorations of this and much more, I commend readers to explore the embarrassment of riches at discardstudies.com

4. STANDARDIZING CHAOS

1. Chen Ji, "Dongdan renmin shangchang" [Dongdan People's Market], *RMRB*, April 2, 1949. The humiliation referred to was the Shen Chong case, the rape of a Peking University student by two US Marines in December 1946, which fueled a surge of anger against the US forces in Beijing.

2. Ibid.

3. Wan Jing, interview with the author, June 20, 2008, Shanghai.

4. Janet Y. Chen, *Guilty of Indigence: The Urban Poor in China, 1900–1953* (Princeton, NJ: Princeton University Press, 2012), 191–93.

5. Chen, *Guilty of Indigence*, 224–25.

6. Bo Yibo, *Ruogan zhongda juece yu shijian de huigu, shang juan* [Recollections of several important decisions and incidents, vol. 1] (Beijing: CCP Central Party School Publisher: 1991), 440–41.

7. Bo, *Ruogan zhongda juece yu shijian de huigu*, 445.

8. Bo, *Ruogan zhongda juece yu shijian de huigu*, 443.

9. "Beijing gongshangye xin bianhua" [New changes in Beijing's business sector], *RMRB*, October 13, 1949.

10. Chen, *Guilty of Indigence*.

11. Wang Shude, interview with author, February 27, 2018, Mentougou.

12. BJMA 22-12-838, 1/1/1951, Beijing shi fei zhi liao ye tong ye gonghui baoqing Beijing shi gongshang ju [A request submitted by the Beijing Municipal Guild of Waste Paper Materials and Related Business to the Beijing Municipal Bureau of Industry and Commerce].

13. Liu Enlu, "Dongdan Dadi dao Dongsi Renmin Shichang," 134.

14. Wang interview, February 27, 2018.

15. Shu Guang Zhang, *Economic Cold War: America's Embargo against China and the Sino-Soviet Alliance, 1949–1963* (Stanford, CA: Stanford University Press, 2001).

16. BJGXSZ, 134. The full name of the Zhongguo tuchan gongsi was Zhongguo tuchan xuchan jin chukou zong gongsi (China National Native Products and Livestock Import Export Company).

17. "Quanguo gongxiao hezuo zongshe guanyu jiaqiang feipin huishou gongzuo fangan" [All-China Federation of Supply and Marketing Cooperatives plan for strengthening scrap recycling work], *ZGGXSXB*, August 1955, 573–76.

18. "Zhongcaiwei guanyu zatong shougou gongzuo gai you quanguo hezuo zongshe fuze shougou de tongzhi" [Central Finance Committee notice regarding assigning responsibility for scrap copper collection work to the Federation of Supply and Marketing Cooperatives], *ZGGXSXB*, August 29, 1952, 573.

19. BJMA, 4-13-26, 5-10/1953, Huabei xinzheng weiyuanhui wei tongzhi Huabei qu feigangtie you hezuoshe shougou [Huabei Administrative Committee notification to Huabei

districts that crap ferrous is to be collected by SMC]. Summarized and paraphrased to simplify.

20. BJMA 88-1-431, 8/2/1954, Zhongyang renmin zhengfu shangye bu, Zhonghua quanguo hezuoshe lianhe zongshe lianhe tongzhi: Wei lianhe xiada yagao ruanguan huishou banfa, xi renzhen guanche zhixing [Central People's Government Commerce Bureau and All-China SMC joint notice: Coordinated issuance of soft toothpaste tube take-back method, hoping for serious and thorough implementation].

21. BJMA 88-1-431, 12/3/1954, Beijing shi gongxiao hezuo zongshe, gongsi heying qiye deng feipin huishou zhanxing guiding (cao'an) [Beijing Municipal SMC, draft of interim regulations on scrap recycling for joint public/private partnership enterprises, etc.].

22. Memoir of a BRC manager, Xuanwu district office (unpublished), 17.

23. BJMA 4-16-424, 9/28/1954, Guanyu zhuyao yuanliao feipin huishou gongzuo jinxing qingkuang baogao [Report on the ongoing conditions of scrap recycling work in key raw materials], 7–13.

24. "Ba fei jinshu chongfen liyong zai jianshe shiye shang" [Fully utilize scrap metal in work of construction], RMRB, March 6, 1955.

25. Guowuyuan zhuanfa Zhonghua gongxiao hezuo zongshe guanyu feizatong, feixi shougou gongzuo zhong cunzai de wenti he jiejue yijian de baogao de tongzhi [State Council forwarded to All-China SMC notice of report on current problems and suggested solutions in scrap copper and tin collection work], November 21, 1956, www.cn8law.com/gwy/news/xzfg/gsqy/19561121/7731.html.

26. BJMA 88-1-431, 12/30/1954, Beijing shi gongxiao hezuo zongshe 1954 nian shougou tong tie gongzuo zongjie baogao [Beijing Municipal SMC 1954 overall summary report of copper and iron collection work].

27. Ding Zhilin, Chai Chengxing, and Li Guiwen, "Weishenme ba daliang wuzi dangcheng laji?" [Why treat huge quantities of materials as garbage?], RMRB, December 19, 1954.

28. "Shanghai quan shi gongye bumen jieyue yuancailiao shiyong daiyongpin" [Production units across all of Shanghai conserve virgin materials and use substitutes], RMRB, November 22, 1954.

29. Ge Xian, "Ji xiao cheng duo" [Many littles makes a lot], RMRB, June 16, 1955.

30. "Shoudu shaonian ertong juxing xiang zuguo xian xiangrikui dahui [At the Sunflower Conference the capital's youth uphold contributing to the motherland], RMRB, November 6, 1955.

31. "Yi dian yi di de jieyue kenengxing ye yinggai haohao liyong" [Every bit and every drop of possible thrift should be well utilized], RMRB, October 30, 1955.

32. Ye Wa, interview with author, January 2018, Berkeley.

33. Lest we see this trope as only appealing to socialists, I point out that this image differs little from the fantasies of foreign corporations regarding accessing the China market. If every Chinese person just bought one bottle of coke . . .

34. BJMA 2-9-110, 3/1957, Guowuyuan di san he di wu bangongshi guanyu wajue dixia zatong ziyuan de tongzhi [State Council #3 and #5 Offices notice on excavating underground scrap copper resources], 10–13.

35. Memoir of a BRC manager, 24. Tianjin and Shanghai did the same.

36. Memoir of a BRC manager, 13.

37. BJMA 22-12-2319, 3/16/1956, Beijing shi shougongye shengchan hezuoshe lianhe zongshe, guanyu gongxiao zongshe feipin jingying chu zhenggou yewu yingxiang wo bu shougou qing [two indecipherable characters] geiyu jiejue [Beijing Municipal Handicraft Production Cooperative Association regarding request for help resolving the SMC Scrap Management Office combative purchasing practices influencing our department's collection and purchasing], 45.

38. BJMA 22-12-2319, 5/22/1956, Zhonghua quanguo gongxiao hezuo zongshe, Beijing shi pifa yewu lianhe banshichu, guanyu Beijing shi feipin shichang cunzai de wenti ji jiejue yijian de baogao [All China SMC and Beijing Wholesale Businesses Association Office, report regarding current problems in Beijing's scrap recycling market and suggestions for its resolution], 46–52.

39. BJMA 22-12-2319, 1956, Beijing shi shangxia shuidao gongcheng ju guanyu qing jiejue ben shi jianzhi mei zhi ren de jiuye wenti de qingshi [Beijing Above/Below Watercourse Engineering Bureau request to please resolve this city's problem of employing coal and paper pickers], 60–68.

40. BJMA 22-12-2319, 4/27/1956, Zhonghua quanguo gongxiao hezuo zongshe Beijing shi pifa yewu lianhe banshichu guanyu laji fenlei shouji chuli ying you wo chu suo shu feipin jingying chu zuzhi peihe [All China SMC Beijing Municipal Wholesale Business Association Office regarding that our scrap management office should organize coordination of trash separation collection], 44.

41. Memoir of a BRC manager, 25.

42. BJMA 22-12-2117, 9/28/1955, Dongsi qu siying shangye yinshiye pucha bangongshi gongzuo jianbao Beijing shi congwen qu shichang guanli chu [Summary report of the work of Dongsi District Private Business and Food and Beverage Business Inspection Office and Beijing Chongwen District Market Management Office].

43. "Zhonggong Beijing shi wei caimao bu guanyu Dongsi Renmin Shichang xuanbu an hangye gongsi heying hou de gaizao xingshi he gonzi wenti de jiejue yijian de baogao (1956 nian 5 yue 22 ri)" [Beijing Central Party Committee Finance and Trade Department, report of recommendation after the announcing [of] the public/private partnership transformation of business organization and wages by sector at Dongsi People's Market (May 22, 1956)], in *Zhongguo zibenzhuyi gongshangye de shehuizhuyi gaizao, Beijing juan* [The socialist transformation of Chinese capitalist businesses, Beijing volume] (Beijing: Zhonggong Dangshi chubanshe, 1991), 411–13.

44. BJMA 88-1-386, 9/1/1956, Zhonghu quanguo gongxiao hezuo zongshe Beijing feipin jingying chu, Feipin hangye xiaoshang xiaofan gaizao fang'an (cao'an) [All-China SMC Beijing Scrap Management Office draft plan for reform of scrap sector small businesses and peddlers], 1–7.

45. Lynn T. White, "Low Power: Small Enterprises in Shanghai, 1949–67," *China Quarterly* 73 (1978): 72.

46. Memoir of a BRC manager, 25.

47. You Chuanxin, "Yi zhi zengchan jieyue de duiwu" [A frugal production increasing team], *RMRB*, March 30, 1957.

48. Memoir of a BRC manager, 27.

49. Zhang Runsheng, Zheng Yu, "Kuochong gongye yuanliao, zengjia renmin shouru, ge di gongxiaoshe shougou le daliang feipin" [Expand production inputs, increase the

people's income, SMCs from everywhere collect large quantities of scrap], *RMRB*, January 7, 1957.

50. Zhang Runsheng, Zheng Yu, "Kuochong gongye yuanliao, zengjia renmin shouru, ge di gongxiaoshe shougou le daliang feipin."

51. Zheng Yu, "Feipin shangdian" [Junk shop], *RMRB*, January 7, 1957, 7

52. *Feipin huishou shouce* [Scrap recycling handbook], ed. Zhonghua quanguo gongxiao hezuo zongshe feipin zong guanli ju (Beijing: Caizheng jingji chubanshe,1956), 11, 37, 54, 56, 64–66.

53. This is not to say that a technique like using resonance to determine a metal alloy's identity is a form of mystification, but such methods were not teachable via handbooks or similar depersonalized training; bureaucratic rationalization could not simply replace the roles of experience and specialization, as was often implied.

54. Wang interview, February 27, 2018.

55. Di Yinlu, "From Trash to Treasure, Salvage Archeology in the Peoples Republic of China, 1951–76." *Modern China* 42, no. 4 (2016): 415–43. Di Yinlu's work is stunningly revelatory regarding how scrap campaigns and CR confiscations helped build the collections of China's museums.

56. Regarding how the shift to state-managed collectives affected the transmission of skill, comparisons with the papermakers in Jiajiang Sichuan described by Jacob Eyferth are instructive. See Jan Jacob Karl Eyferth, *Eating Rice from Bamboo Roots: The Social History of a Community of Handicraft Papermakers in Rural Sichuan, 1920–2000* (Cambridge, MA: Harvard University Asia Center, 2009).

57. Zsuzsa Gille, *From the Cult of Waste to the Trash Heap of History* (Bloomington: Indiana University Press, 2007). Many aspects of analysis here and in other parts of this book owe much to Gille's concept of waste regime; moreover, much in this chapter and chapter 5 echoes Gille's descriptions of Hungary's "cult of waste" under the "metallic waste regime" of the 1950s and 1960s. To summarize Gille, from the advent of socialism in Hungary in 1948 until around 1974, a "metallic waste regime" prevailed under which wastes were characterized as inherently useful by-products, "free" resources to be reused to fulfill the economic plan. This idealization of maximizing reuse gave way, from the mid-1970s to mid-1980s, to one of averting waste generation; by the mid-1980s, Hungary had entered a "chemical waste regime" in which wastes were treated as inherently useless and toxic. There are undeniable parrallels to be drawn here, but I think the differences are distinct and important enough that I have chosen not to borrow the terms *metallic* or *chemical* waste regime.

58. BJMA 258-1-742, 1957, Beijing shi renmin weiyuanhui guanyu jiaqiang guanli feipin shichang de jixiang guiding [Beijing Municipal People's Committee, Several rules regarding strengthening the management of the recycling market].

59. BJMA 20-10-88, 10/31/1957, Guowuyuan zhuanfa Zhonghua quanguo gongxiaoshe guanyu dangqian zatong shouhui qingkuang he jinhou yijian de baogao [State Council forwarding to All-China Federation of Supply and Marketing Cooooperatives report on the current situation of scrap copper collection and suggestions going forward], 63–67.

60. Hunan sheng jihua weiyuanhui [Hunan Province Planning Committee], "Guanyu wo sheng zatong shougou gongzuo cunzai wenti ji jinhou yijian de baogao" [Report on current problems in our province's scrap copper acquisition work and recommendations going forward], August 36, 1957.

61. BJMA 20-1-88, Guanyu dangqian zatong shouhui qingkuang, 66.

62. BJMA 22-12-1230, 11/2/1957, [Beijing shi] gongshang bu guanyu guyi mianbu shichang guanli qingkuang de baogao [(Beijing) Industry and Commerce Bureau report regarding the conditions in used clothes and cotton cloth market].

63. BJMA 90-1-80, 8/11/1958, Jijian: Beijing shi Dongcheng qu baihuo lingshou guanli chu guanyu jiang 58 nian 8 yue 8 ri wujia zuotanhui jilu zhuanfa xiyu guanche zhixing de tongzhi [Urgent dispatch: Beijing Municipal Dongcheng District Department Store Retail Management Office notice regarding August 8, 1958, price meeting minutes for thorough implementation], 60–62.

64. BJMA 90-1-136, 6/5/1959, Beijing shi Dongcheng qu shangye ju guanyu jiuhuo jige guanli de jixiang zhanxing guiding [Beijing Municipal Dongcheng District Commerce Bureau regarding several interim regulations for old goods price management], 12–18.

65, Wu Lutang, "Jiuhou shanghang xin fengqi" [A new attitude in old junk shops] RMRB, January 7, 1957.

66. "Daliang feiwu bian huo bao" [Lots of waste turned to treasure], RMRB, June 8 1959; and "Wei shehui zeng caifu, wei qunzhong zeng shouru, Heilongjiang sheng shangye xitong kuoda feipin shougou de jingyan" [Increase wealth for society, increase income for the masses, the experiences of Heilongjiang province expanding the commerce networks collection of scrap"], RMRB, April 5, 1959.

67. BJMA 2-10-88, 10/3/1958, Beijing shi wuzi gongyingju guanyu shi feijiu wuzi hui-shou gongsi yewu xiafang de qingshi [Beijing Municipal Materials Supply Office request for instruction regarding transferring authority over the BSC].

68. BJMA 86-2-68, 7/30/1958, Beijing shi zhiyuan gongye dayuejin yundong zong ban-gongshi guanyu Xicheng qu kaizhan zhiyuan gongye yundong qingkuang de baogao [Beijing Head Office for Supporting Industry in the GLF Campaign report regarding Xicheng district's support industry campaign], 1–8.

69. BJMA 2-20-826, 12/5/1958, Guowuyuan guanyu diaohui zhiyuan di gangtie shang-chan de da, zhuan, zhong zhi deng xiao zai xiao xuesheng hui xiao xuexi de tongzhi [State Council notice regarding transferring students of universities, middle school, professional schools from supporting various local steel production back to schools to resume study-ing], 27–28.

70. Shanxi sheng renmin weiyuanhui guanyu tigao fei zatong shougou jiage de tongzhi [Shanxi Province People's Committee notice regarding raising the price to purchase scrap copper], April 28, 1959.

71. Ge Jianshui, Wen Tongyuan, and Song Weilian, "Zhongguo zaisheng ziyuan (shangye) hangye dashiji" [Major events in China's recycling resources (business) sector], Zaisheng ziyuan yanjiu [Renewable resources research] 16, no.1 (1995); 15–17.

72. Guwuyuan guanyu jiaqiang fei gangtie zatong shougou gongzuo de zhishi [State Council directive on strengthening the acquisition of scrap ferrous and copper], Septem-ber 27, 1958.

73. BJMA 90-1-136, 10/23/1959, Beijing shi wuzi gongying ju, Beijing shi shangye ju guanyu bofu tangci mianpen huangou jiu tong zhipin de tongzhi [Beijing Materials Allo-cation Bureau and Beijing Commerce Bureau regarding allocations for the exchange of enamel basins for old copper goods].

74. Jiangxi sheng remin weiyuanhui, guanyu jiaqiang zatong shougou, diaoyun gong-zuo de tongzhi [Notice of the Jiangxi Province People's Committee regarding strengthening acquisition and delivery of scrap copper], November 21, 1958.

75. BJMA 90-1-259, 4/8/1961, Dongcheng qu shangye ju guanyu jiuhuo hangye wujia chuxian de wenti ji gaijin yijian de baogao [Dongcheng District Commerce Office report regarding old goods shops' emerging pricing problems and suggestions for improvements], 36–37.

76. BJMA 90-1-259, 7/1/1961, Beijing shi shangye ju guanyu dui jiuhuo jiage de jiancha baogao [Beijing Municipal Commerce Bureau report regarding survey of old goods prices], 31–34.

77. BJMA 90-1-259, 7/1/1961, 33.

78. BJMA 111-1-382, 5/1962, Beijing shi shangyeju guanyu xintuo hangye jingying pin piao pin juan shangpin gongying banfa de tongzhi [Beijing Municipal Commerce Bureau notice regarding consignment shops using scrip and coupons for provision of goods], 37–39.

79. BJMA 5-1-546, 5/1/1961, Shougongye diaocha ziliao di san, Beijing shi tieguo diaocha ziliao [Handicraft sector survey material number 3, Beijing iron pot survey materials], 6–10.

80. BJMA 2-15-165, 11/1963, Zhongguo renmin yinhang Beijing shi fenhang guanyu Beijingshi jinshu gongsi zaishengtie jiaya wenti de baogao [People's Bank of China, Beijing branch report regarding the problem or scrap iron overstock at Beijing municipal metal company], 7–8.

81. Dorothy J. Solinger, *Chinese Business under Socialism: The Politics of Domestic Commerce, 1949–1980* (Berkeley: University of California Press, 1984), 27.

82. Gille, *From the Cult of Waste*, 80–81. Gille's description of these trends closes with a wonderful quote from a Hungarian anthropologist, Akos Domotor, summing up the socialist effort to reuse waste as the "transformation of waste into garbage at a significant expense" (82).

5. EFFORTFUL EQUILIBRIUMS OF THE STATE-MANAGED SCRAP SECTOR, 1960–1980

1. Wang Shude, interview with author, February 2018. The SMC was seen by leftists as harboring pro-market tendencies and was met with suspicion whenever leftist radicalism was in command (disbanded in 1958 at the start of the GLF, reconstituted in 1961, attacked in 1966 at the start of the CR, then subsumed under the ministry of commerce in 1970). Also most BRC workers had been small peddlers before 1949, and though many had been among Beijing's poorer residents, they were still saddled with the class label of small merchants, whom leftists viewed as ideologically suspect.

2. Janos Kornai, *Economics of Shortage* (Amsterdam: North Holland Publishing, 1980).

3. *BJGXSZ*, 164.

4. Ge Jianshui, Wen Tongyuan, and Song Weilian, "Zhongguo zaisheng ziyuan (shangye) hangye dashiji" [Major events in China's recycling resources (business) sector], *Zaisheng ziyuan yanjiu* [Renewable resources research] 16, no. 2 (1995): 13–15.

5. A more literal translation of 回收 would be "return collection." From here on I use BSC for the company before 1966 and BRC for after that date. Adam Liebman has done

fabulous work analyzing the conceptual differences lost in translating these terms; see, for example, "Reconfiguring Chinese Natures: Frugality and Waste Reutilization in Mao Era Urban China," *Critical Asian Studies* 51, no. 4 (2019): 537–57.

6. Chen Tanqiang, "Diudiao 'guanjiazi': Yong zuo renming de haoqin wuyuan—Beijing shi gongxiao hezuo she zhuren Du Jianming zijue de gaizao sixiang gaijin gong-zuo" [Throw away "bureaucratic airs": Forever be a diligent servant of the people—Beijing SMC director Du Jianming self-consciously reformed his thought and improved his work], *RMRB*, March 20, 1966.

7. BJMA 90-1-318, 1/13/1962, Beijingshi gongxiao hezuo she: Guanyu jiqiang suliaodai huishou gongzuo de tongzhi [Beijing SMC: Notice regarding strengthening plastic bag take back work], 122.

8. BJMA 117-1-1599, 6/1965, Beijing shi wuzi guanli ju: Beijing shi mu baozhuang hui-shou fuyong guanli shixing banfa [Beijing Materials Management Office: Beijing wooden crate take back and reuse management trial method], 27–28.

9. BJMA 90-1-693, 2/4/1965, Beijingshi wuzi huishou gongsi guanyu jiangdi jiubaozhi jiage de qingshi [Beijing BRC regarding request to lower the price on old newspaper], 42.

10. BJMA 192-1-28, 5/15/1966, Beijing shi shangye ju, Beijing shi wuzi ju, Beijing shi gongxiao she: Guanyu huifu yi jiu huan xin huishou yagaoguan de lianhe tongzhi [Beijing Commerce Bureau, Beijing Materials Bureau, Beijing SMC: Joint notice regarding resumption of the old for new trade to recycle toothpaste tubes].

11. *BJGXSZ*, 143.

12. BJMA 90-1-318, 6/23/1962, Beijingshi gongxiao hezuo she guanyu tiaozheng jiuxie, bumao, lanzhi deng huishou jiage de qingshi [Beijing SMC regarding price adjustments for old shoes, wool scrap, waste paper, etc.], 69–70.

13. "Quanguo gongxiao hezuo zongshe dangzu guanyu feijiu wuzi gongzuo qingkuang de baogao" [All-China SMC party group report regarding the situation in scrap material work], *ZGGXSXB*, (September 8, 1965), 590–92.

14. "Shangye bu: Guanyu feijiu wuzi huishou liyong qingkuang he yijian de baogao" [Commerce Bureau report of the situation and suggestions regarding scrap material recovery and use], *ZGGXSXB*, May 25, 1973, 592–94.

15. "Qingli cangku, xiujiu lifei, wujin qiyong, Jiaozuo kuangwu ju zhixing Mao zhuxi 'beizhan, beihuang, wei renmin' weida fangzhen" [Clear warehouses, repair the old and use wastes, maximize use of everything: Jiaozuo mining bureau carries out Chairman Mao's "Prepare for war, ready for disaster, for the people" great guiding principle"], *RMRB*, February 13, 1970.

16. Wu Fumin and Feng Yichen, "Bu heli de guiding yinggai gaibian" [Irrational regulations should be changed], *RMRB*, February 21, 1979.

17. BJMA 2-16-110, 9/25/1963, Guwuyuan pizhuan guojia jihua weiyuanhui, guojia jingji weiyuanhui deng bumen: Guanyu gaijin feijinshu huishou guanli gongzuo de baogao [State Council forwarding National Planning Committee, National Economic Council, et al.: Report on improving management of scrap metal recycling].

18. "Zunzhao Mao zhuxi guanyu 'Yao jieyue nao geming' de weida jiaodao, shoudu fadong qunzhong huishou feijiu gangtie" [In accord with Chairman Mao's teaching "make

revolution through economizing," the masses of the capital mobilize to recycle scrap ferrous], *RMRB*, March 21, 1970.

19. "Wei shehui zhuyi jieyue de qingsao gongren—ji Shenyang yelianchang qingsao gongren, gongchangdangyuan Li Zichun tongzhi" [A cleaning worker for socialist economizing—remembering Shenyang smeltery cleaning worker, Communist Party member Comrade Li Zichun], *RMRB*, February 26, 1970.

20, Wang Shude, interview with author, Mentougou, July 10, 2018.

21. "Meiyou juedui de feiwu" [There are no absolute wastes], *RMRB*, June 20, 1964; Huang Jun and Sun Shaoying, "Huishou feijiu peijian yinggai shui guan?" [Who should manage recycling of old scrap machine parts?"], *RMRB*, November 27, 1964; "Daigou daixiao dian shixing na zhong baochou banfa hao?" [What kind of compensation method is best for supply and marketing agents?"], *RMRB*, June 1, 1969.

22. BJMA 192-1-173, 4/ 4/1971, Beijing shi fei gangtie guanli bangong shi: Fei gangtie huishou jianbao #4 [Beijing Scrap Ferrous Management Office: Scrap ferrous recycling brief, no. 4], 22–25. The ditty in Chinese reads: 不拣不知道, 一拣吓一跳, 回收没到顶, 潜力真不小!

23. "Shangye bu: Guanyu feijiu wuzi," *ZGGXSXB*, 594.

24. BJMA 182-14-469, 11/14.1974, Chongwen qu wuzi huishou guanli chu: Guanyu kaizhan jiedao daigou gongzuo yijian de baogao [Chongwen District BRC Management Office: Report regarding suggestions for neighborhood purchasing agent work], 3–4.

25. BJMA 88-3-117, 10/12/1981, Beijing shi gongxiao hezuo she: Guanyu quanguo renda (5.3) di 376 hao ti'an "qing youguan bumen liji caiqu cuoshi zhizhi jizhan che feipin huishou wangdian bing zai xin lou qunzhong zengshe feipin shougoudian naru jijian fenpei jihua" ti'an de chuli jianyi [Beijing SMC: Suggestions for how to handle National People's Congress (5.3) proposal no. 376 to "please have relevant departments implement the removal of crowded recycling nodes and relocate them to new areas of buildings to add new collection points to cover the infrastructure distribution plan"], 8–11.

26. BJMA 88-3-117, 10/12/1981.

27. *ZGGXSXB*, "*Beijing Ribao* she # 2229 *Neibu cankao*, 'Yige bukeshao de hangye, Beijing shi gongzi gongzuo huiyi pangting ji zhi si'" [From the *Beijing Daily's Internal Reference* no. 2229, "An indispensable sector, fourth set of notes on Beijing conference on wage work"], 600–601.

28. Niu Yinguan, "Jiakuai feijiu wuzi huishou liyong gongzuo de bufa" [Hasten the progress in scrap material recycling and reuse work], *ZGGXSXB*, 605–8.

29. In one example of this progression associating industrial waste management with environmental protection, in November 1972 the Three Wastes Management Office was established, in 1975 it was renamed the Environmental Protection Office, and in 1979 the Beijing Environmental Protection Bureau was created.

30. Xu Yijie, "Xin Zhongguo huanjing baohu qu cheng xiezuo chutan: Yi Guanting shuiku shuiyuan baohu gongzuo wei li" [Preliminary research into New China's Environmental Protection District cooperation: Using the Guanting Reservoir water resources protection work as an example], *Dangdai Zhongguo shi yanjiu* [Contemporary Chinese history studies] 22, no. 6 (2015): 69–81.

31. *BJSGSZ*, 138.

32. BJMA 88-3-101, 9/16/1980, Beijing shi wuzi huishou gongsi guanyu jianli feipin chuli zhongxin de baogao [BRC report on building scrap handling centers], 77–82.

33. BJMA 88-3-117, 12/24/1980, Beijingshi wuzi huishou gongsi guanyu banli quanguo renda daibiao ti'an de baogao [BRC report on implementing the National People's Congress proposal], 113–16.

34. BJMA 88-3-101, Guanyu jianli feipin chuli zhongxin.

35. BJMA 88-3-117, Guanli quanguo renda de 376 che feipin huishou wangdian, 8–11.

36. The stereotyping of scrap and waste workers as corrupt and unethical is also deeply intertwined with forms of racism. Carl Zimring's *Clean and White: A History of Environmental Racism in the United States* (New York: New York University Press, 2016) is an excellent history of the racism and anti-Semitism experienced by US scrap and waste workers. Part 3 of this book shows that Beijing's migrant recyclers, many of whom came from Henan province, faced relentless discrimination from Beijing natives based in part on their being Henanese. This ethnic and racial abuse intertwines with the profound biases that arise out of the disruptive place of waste work within our fantasized ideals of hygienic and economic systems. The point is not that scrap/waste sectors are by nature corrupt, but rather that if we wish to analyze how the institutional discrimination and social abuse confronted by recyclers is relentlessly perpetuated across a variety of societies, economies, and regulatory structures, the liminality of waste as an economic sector must be addressed.

37. BJMA 2-16-110, Guanyu gaijin fei jinshu huishou.

38. BJMA 2-16-110.

39. *BJGXSZ*, 160.

40. BJMA 90-1-136, 3/2/1959, Guanyu jiqiang huishou gongye yuanliao de yijian [Suggestions for strengthening recycling of industrial materials], 51–59.

41. BJMA 90-1-318, 11/1/1962, Beijingshi shougongye guanli ju guanyu luntaidi chang shengchan de luntaidi buxie peiqian de baogao [Beijing Municipal Handicraft Management Office report regarding money loss by tire tread factory in producing tire tread bottom cloth shoes], 108.

42. Ge, Wen, and Song, "Zaisheng ziyuan dashiji," 13.

43. Dorothy J. Solinger, *Chinese Business under Socialism: The Politics of Domestic Commerce, 1949–1980* (Berkeley: University of California Press, 1984), 207.

44. Solinger, *Chinese Business under Socialism*, 207–15.

45. BJMA 119-3-106, 1977, Beijing wuzi huishou gongsi: Guanyu bu tongyi Beijing shi yejin ju tongguan quanshi youse jinshu de baogao [Beijing BRC: Report on disagreeing with the Beijing metallurgy bureau's monopolizing the entire municipality's non-ferrous metals], 54–57.

46. "Zhou Enlai tongzhi dui feijiu wuzi huishou liyong gongzuo de qinbi tici" [Comrade Zhou Enlai's calligraphy dedication to waste materials recycling and reuse work], *ZGGXSXB*, 601.

47. *ZGGSXXB*, 601–13.

48. Fu Hongjun, interview with author, Beijing, December 22, 2010.

49. BJMA 5-2-1143, 12/1/1965, Beijing shi jihua weiyuanhui: Wo shi yi kaishi dui feijiu wuzi dazhua huishou henzhua liyong [Beijing Planning Committee: Our city has already begun to tackle large-scale recycling and diligently grasp (re)use], 1–3.

BEIJING'S WASTE-SCAPE ON THE CUSP OF MARKET REFORM

1. Several BJMA documents discuss taking special care regarding toilets and trash during international events like visits from France's president Georges Pompidou. Indeed, some foreign dignitaries came especially to inspect Beijing's trash and night soil achievements; though mud-sealed composting had been a failure in practice, the city still touted a model experimental site in Liangmaqiao that attracted visits from groups of UN scientists. BJMA, 128-2-491, 11/22/1973, Beijing shi gongyong ju geming lingdao xiaozu, guanyu wei choujian laji chuli shiyanchang he huayanshi gouzhi ban gongyong pin de baogao [Beijing Utilities Bureau Revolutionary Small Group, Report on purchasing materials to prepare the model garbage treatment yard and laboratory].

2. BJMA, 90-1-259, 6/1/1961, Beijing shi shangye ju guanyu dui jiuhuo jiage de jiancha baogao [Beijing Commerce Bureau, Report regarding a survey of used goods prices].

3. Jennifer Altehenger, "Maoism by Design: Why Furniture Became a Political Problem in 1950s China" (unpublished manuscript, 2018). Used with permission of the author.

4. Marcia Yudkin, *Making Good, Private Business in Socialist China* (Beijing: Beijing Foreign Language Press, 1986).

5. 1976 surveys discussed in Chen Shoufang and Fu Baoping, "Beijing shi 1984 chengshi laji diaocha baogao" [Beijing municipal 1984 urban garbage survey report], *Chengshi huanjing weisheng tongxun* [Urban Environmental Sanitation communication] 2, no. 3 (1985): 29–35.

6. Wang Weiping, "Zhongguo chengshi shenghuo laji duice yanjiu" [Research on solutions to domestic solid waste in cities in China], *Ziran ziyuan xuebao* [Journal of natural resources], 15, no. 2 (2000): 128–32.

7. *BJGXSZ*, 145–46.

8. BJMA, 5-2-1143, 3/4/1966, Beijing shi jihua weiyuanhui, wuzi huishou liyong jianbao [Beijing Municipal Planning Commission, Materials recycling and reuse brief], 20–21.

9. *BJGXSZ*, 147.

10. *BJGXSZ*, 144–48.

11. *BJGXSZ*, 142 (files for pulping); and Mary Louise O'Callaghan, "China Shops for Overseas Investment in Resources," *Christian Science Monitor*, May 16, 1983 ($188 million).

12. BJMA, 192-1-220, 11/28/1972, Beijing shi di yi shangye ju geming lingdoa xiaozu guanyu gaijin xintuo hangye jingying guanli de baogao [Beijing Number One Commerce Bureau Revolutionary Leading Small Group report on improving management of consignment shops].

FIGHTING OVER THE SCRAPS

1. David Harvey's work on capitalism and the production of space explores the many ways in which creative destruction is embedded in capital circulation itself; among these, processes of urban renewal—destruction and reconstruction—can drive new cycles of wealth accumulation. David Harvey, *The Condition of Postmodernity* (Oxford: Blackwell, 1990). The image of creative destruction is particularly fruitful for analyzing such waves of

demolition and construction from the perspective of waste. See especially Kao Shih-yang, "The City Recycled: The Afterlives of Demolished Buildings in Post-War Beijing" (PhD diss., University of California, Berkeley, 2013).

2. B. Steuer, S. Salhofer, R. Linzner, and F. Part, "Is China's Waste Management Legislation Successful? Evidence from Urban Chinese Waste Management Practices" (paper presented at 4th International Conference on Industrial and Hazardous Waste Management, Crete, Greece, 2014).

3. Kao Shih-yang and George C. S. Lin, "The Political Economy of Debris Dumping in Post-Mao Beijing," *Modern China* 44, no. 3 (2018): 305. Both in this article and in his dissertation, Kao shows how various groups one might consider to be relatively powerless find unexpected ways to use wastes to empower themselves.

4. City residents still had intestinal worms, for which Beijing's children were annually dosed, throughout the Mao era.

5. Chen Shoufang and Fu Baoping, "Beijing shi 1984 chengshi laji diaocha baogao" [Beijing municipal 1984 urban garbage survey report], *Chengshi huanjing weisheng tongxun* [Urban Environmental Sanitation communication] 2, no. 3 (1985): 29–35.

6. Daniel Hoornweg, "What a Waste: Solid Waste Management in Asia," (New York: World Bank Urban Development Sector Unit, East Asia and Pacific Region, 1999) 8.

7. Wang Weiping and Wu Yuping, "Lun chengshi laji duice de yanjin yu laji chanye de chanshen" [On the evolution of urban garbage countermeasures policy and the emergence of a waste industry], *Shengtai Jingji* [Ecological economy] 17, no. 10 (2001): 34–37.

8. Zhong Jing and Sun Lin, "Beijing daliang laji jiujing ruhe xiaona [How can we ultimately dispose of Beijing's huge quantity of garbage?], *RMRB*, January 21, 1981.

9. Shi Yang, "Beijing shi huanjing weisheng shiye gaige qingkuang jianjie" [A brief introduction to environmental sanitation reform in Beijing], *Chengshi huanjing weisheng tongxun* [Urban Environmental Sanitation newsletter] 3, no.2 (1985): 8–12 (contracting out); and Tian Yinlu, "Beijing laji duifang zhuangkuang ji qi weihai" [Beijing's garbage landfill siting situation and its hazards"], *Chengshi huanjing weisheng tongxun* [Urban Environmental Sanitation newslettter] 4, no. 3 (1986): 22–25 ("fields and remote spots"). An aerial photo of Beijing taken in 1989 was said to show more than 4,500 garbage dumps, which together occupied more than 1,150 acres of land between the city's third and fourth ring roads, a ring of dumps that the *People's Daily* dubbed "A Great Wall of Garbage" (*laji changcheng*). See Map 2 in the Introduction.

10. "Beijing shi shirong huanjing weisheng guanli guiding" [Beijing municipality regulations on urban appearance and environmental sanitation management] *Chengshi huanjing weisheng tongxun* [Urban Environmental Sanitation newsletter] 1, no.1 (1984): 2–4.

11. Li Zhenshan, Yang Lei, Qu Xiaoyan, and Sui Yumei, "Municipal Solid Waste Management in Beijing City," *Waste Management* 29 (2009): 2596–99.

12. Zhang Weihua and He Duanchi, "Chengshi huanjing weisheng zijin qian xi' [Analysis of Urban Environmental Sanitation funding], *Chengshi huanjing weisheng tongxun* [Urban Environmental Sanitation newsletter] 3, no. 2 (1986): 2–5 (about .5% of the city budget); and Yu Dianting "Jiejue Beijing shi laji chulu de jishu duice" [Technical countermeasures for solving the way out of Beijing's garbage], *Chengshi huanjing weisheng tongxun* [Urban Environmental Sanitation newsletter] 3, no. 3 (1986): 8–11 (cheapest option).

13. Lu Ying, "Lajichang weihe you xiyinli [Why are garbage dumps so attractive?], *RMRB*, December 9, 1989.

6. A TALE OF TWO CITIES, 1980–2003

1. Liao Yalan, "Polanwang jian hui Jinshan" [Junk Kings pick a gold mountain], *RMRB*, December 20, 1992.

2. Fu Zimei, "Beijing shi Chaoyang qu Zhongxing feijiu wuzi gongsi xingjian kai guanli le 5 ge feijiu wuzi huishou shichang" [Beijing Chaoyang district Zhongxing Recycling Company is building 5 managed waste materials recycling markets], *RMRB*, April 22, 2002. See also Table 2 in the conclusion to part 2.

3. Wang Shude, interview with author, Mentougou, February 2018.

4. Li Yongyun (BRC Haidian district company manager), interview with author, Jinghai, March 14, 2008.

5. "Beijing feipin huishou xi you lu" [The joys and woes of recycling in Beijing], *Youse jinshu zaisheng yu liyong* [Nonferrous metals recycling and utilization], no. 8 (2006).

6. BJMA 88-3-117, Guanyu quanguo renda de 376 che feipin huishou wangdian, 11.

7. BJMA 88-3-101, Guanyu jianli feipin chuli zhongxin.

8. *BJGXSZ*, 165.

9. "Bian bao wei fei de 'feipin huishou' yinggai feizhi—zai Jilin youtian fujin feipin shougou bumen de jianwen" [Change treasure to trash "recycling" should be abolished—Reports about the recycling acquisition division in the neighborhood of a Jilin oil field], *RMRB*, November 17, 1979.

10. Xie Kaihui, "Guonei zaisheng ziyuan lei kanwu de fazhan taishi" [The state of development in domestic resource recycling periodicals], *Ziyuan zai liyong xinxi* [Resource reuse news], no. 6 (1989): 3. Offices that put out new publications included branches of the Materials Bureau, Metallurgy Bureau, and Urban/Rural Construction Bureau, at locations including Beijing, Shanghai, Anshan, Heiliongjiang, and Hunan.

11. Zhang Qingsheng, "Jiaqiang jinshu zaisheng ziyuan guanli zhi wo jian" [My views on strengthening metals renewable resource management], *Ziyuan zai liyong xinxi* [Resource reuse news], no. 3 (1989): 8–12.

12. Guowuyuan guanyu jiaqiang zaishen ziyuan huishou liyong guanli gongzuo de tongzhi [State Council notice on strengthening the management of resource recycling use], December 26, 1991.

13. G. H. Hsin and J. Hou. "Structural Inflation and the 1994 'Monetary' Crisis in China," *Contemporary Economic Policy* 15, no. 3 (1997): 73–81.

14. Li interview, March 14, 2008.

15. Li interview, March 14, 2008.

16. Beijing wuzi huishou gongsi guanyu zhenxing Beijing shi guoying zaisheng ziyuan hangye de jianyi [Beijing Recycling Company suggestion regarding revitalizing the state owned resource recycling industry], 1999, 1–8.

17. "Guangzhou liang 'lajilao' wei zheng kuangquanshui ping yinfa guyi shang ren shijian" [Two Guangzhou "trash hicks" trigger a case of intentional assault over a plastic water bottle], *Nanfang Ribao* [Southern daily], August 14, 2001.

18. The article by Tang and her colleagues is a piece of vivid description and insightful analysis, and I urge anyone who finds this chapter interesting to seek it out. Jean-Philippe Beja, Michel Bonnin, Feng Xiaoshuang, Tang Can, and Philip Liddell, "How Social Strata Come to Be Formed: Social Differentiation among Migrant Peasant of Henan Village in Peking, Parts 1 and 2," *China Perspectives* 23 and 24 (1999).

19. Boss Lu, interview with author, Beijing, August 4, 2000.

20. Li interview, March 14, 2008.

21. Li interview, March 14, 2008.

22. Beja et al., "How Social Strata Come to Be Formed."

23. Beja et al., "How Social Strata Come to Be Formed."

24. Boss Lu interview, August 4, 2000.

25. A huge amount of scholarly work exists on household registration. For some of the best work on the 1980s and 1990s in Beijing see Dorothy Solinger's *Contesting Citizenship in Urban China: Peasant Migrants, the State, and the Logic of the Market* (Berkeley: University of California Press, 1999) and Zhang Li's *Strangers in the City: Reconfigurations of Space, Power and Social Networks within China's Floating Population* (Stanford, Ca: Stanford University Press, 2001).

26. Wang Zhangyi (bike cart collector), interview with author, Beijing, July 20, 2000.

27. Zhang Yongqiang and Lin Hui, "Beijing bianyuan de 'liudong xuexiao,'"[The migrant schools on the edge of Beijing], *RMRB*, August 30, 2000.

28. Jiang Shan, "Yange guanli, yifa baohu, Beijing jiaqiang wailai renkou guanli gong-zuo jian chengxiao" [Strictly control, protect based on the law, the strengthened enforcement work on the migrant population is visibly effective], *RMRB*, March 3, 1998.

29. Wang Feiling, "Reformed migration control and new targeted people: China's hukou system in the 2000s, *China Quarterly* 177 (2004): 115–32.

30. Tang Can and Feng Xiaoshuang analyzed this phenomenon, explaining how Beijing rural natives who chose to "eat roof tiles" (the local idiom for becoming a landlord) often found themselves sharing common interests with the migrants whom they rented to and increasingly becoming accomplices in migrants' informal and illegal activities. Their analysis in some ways ran contrary to the simplistic narrative stereotyping migrants as the source of moral disruption, showing how Beijing locals were equally culpable in defying regulations. Tang Can and Feng Xiaoshuang, "Jinfang shehui shikong: wailai renkou yu chengxiang jihe bu diqu de liyi yitihua guanxi" [Beware losing control of society: Migrants and peri-urban village unity of interests], *Zhongguo guoqing guoli* [China's national conditions of strength] 3 (1998): 26–28.

31. Mr. and Mrs. X, interview with author, Dongxiaokou, December 24, 2010. (I have edited this from a fifteen-minute portion of a two-hour conversation.)

32. Survey conducted by author and volunteers at Beijing Nature University, December 2010. We covered two large markets, Haunjingyuan in Fengtai and a complex of over one hundred stalls in Dongsanqi (thriving 2006–2016), filling out questionnaires with fifty-nine market stall bosses, twenty-nine of whom had been working in recycling in Beijing since before 2002.

33. Mr. C. (Bajia stall boss), interview with author, Haidian, July 28, 2000.

34. Mr. C. (after relocation to Chaoyang District), interview with author, Chaoyang, June 18, 2001.

35. For insights into this aspect of 1980s and 1990s China, see Nick Bartlett, *Recovering Histories: Life and Labor after Heroin in Reform Era China* (Oakland: University of California Press, 2020), chaps. 1 and 2.

36. Wang Weiping, *Guanyu Beijingshi shenghuo laji ziyuan huishou liyong he xiangguan chanye wenti de diaoyan baogao* [Survey report on Beijing postconsumer trash resource recovery and reuse and related problems in the sector] (Beijing Council of China's Zhigongdang, 1999), 3.

37. Wang, *Guanyu Beijingshi shenghuo laji ziyuan huishou liyong he xiangguan chanye wenti de diaoyan baogao*, 7.

38. Hou Yushan, "Tansuo shoudu feijiu wuzi huishou hangye fazhan de youxiao tujing" [Exploring the efficient path of development for the capital's recycling sector], *Zaisheng ziyuan yanjiu* [Renewable resources research] 22, no. 1 (2000): 1–13.

39. Wu Zhenduo, "Zhili huanjing wuran kaifa liyong zaisheng ziyuan" [To control environmental pollution develop the use of renewable materials], *Zaisheng ziyuan yanjiu* [Renewable resources research] 21, no. 6 (1999): 2–6.

40. Hou, "Tansuo shoudu," 4.

41. Mr. and Mrs. X interview, December 24, 2010.

42. Liu Xiaobin, "Laji fenlei chuli ji dai tuiguang" [Waste classification and treatment needs urgent promotion], *Guangming Ribao* [Guangmin daily], October 3, 1997; and Zong Chunqi, "Guoyou huishouye lu zai he fang" [Where is the road leading for the state's recycling sector?], *Beijing Ribao* [Beijing daily], May 11, 1999.

43. Beijing shi Chaoyang qu chengshi huanjing zonghe zhengzhi weiyuanhui bangongshi [Beijing Chaoyang District Urban Renewal Committee Office], "Guanyu qudi geti polanshi shiban guoying feijiu wuzi shichang de qingshi" [Request to eliminate independent markets and launch a pilot of state-run recycling markets], December 5, 1997, 1–3.

44. Beijing shi Chaoyang, "Guanyu qudi geti polanshi shiban," 1.

45. Beijing shi Chaoyang qu zhongxing feijiu wuzi huishou gongsi [Beijing Chaoyang District Zhongxing Waste Materials Recycling Company], "Yi shichang xingshi jiaqiang dui feijiu wuzi huishouye de guanli" [Using a market model to manage the waste materials recycling sector], *Zhongguo ziyuan zonghe liyong xiehui tongxun* [China Comprehensive Resource Use Institute newsletter] 52, February 18, 2000, 5–6.

46. Tian (manager of model market), interview with author, Chaoyang, August 9, 2000.

47. For an incisive theorizing of *suzhi* discourse, see Yan Hairong, *New Masters, New Servants: Migration, Development and Women Workers in China* (Durham, NC: Duke University Press, 2008), 111–38.

48. Zong, "Where Is the Road Leading."

49. Beijing shi Chaoyang, "Yi shichang xingshi," 5.

50. Jun Jing, "Environmental Protests in Rural China," in *Chinese Society, Change, Conflict and Resistance*, ed. E. Perry and M. Selden (New York: Routledge, 2010), 197–214.

51. Ding Renyuan, "Duiyu 'jianshao ziyuan langfei he zhili huanjing wuran xu zhongzhen shichang feipin huishou' de ji dian renshi he jianyi" [Several aspects to understand and suggestions regarding the need to concentrate markets for scrap recycling to reduce resource wasting and control environmental pollution], May 28, 1998.

52. Chaoyang Zhongxin, "Yi shichang xingshi," 6.

53. Beijing shi shangye weiyuanhui deng jiu bumen yinfa guanyu cujinhe guifan Beijing shi shequ zaisheng ziyuan huishou tixi jianshe de shishi fangan de tongzhi [Beijing Commerce Committee, etc., Nine departments notice regarding the implementation plan for promoting and standardizing the construction of a neighborhood resource recycling system in Beijing], June 5, 2001.

54. "Qudi polan wang, buxu zai yaohe" [Banishing the junk kings, they won't shout anymore], *Beijing qingnian bao* [Beijing Youth news], June 12, 2001.

55. Mr. Z (collector for Zhouji), interview with author, Beijing, August 5, 2001.

56. Zhouji Company, "Jiangzheng zhanxing guiding" [Rewards and punishments interim rules"], July 6, 2001, 1–6.

57. Mr. C (Zhouji CEO), interview with author, Beijing, August 5, 2001.

58. Mr. C interview, August 5, 2001.

59. Beijing shi renmin zhengfu guanyu yinfa Beijing shi di san pi quxiao he diaozheng xingzheng shenpi shixiang mulu de tongzhi [Beijing Municipal People's Government notice on printing and distributing the catalog of the third batch of cancellations and adjustments], April 2, 2003, www.beijing.gov.cn/zhengce/zfwj/zfwj/szfwj/201905/t20190523_72430.html .

60. Xin Tong and Dongyan Tao, "The Rise and Fall of a 'Waste City,'" *Resource Conservation and Recycling* 107 (2016): 10–17.

61. Tiantianjie manager, interview with author, Wangfujing, July 7, 2008.

7. TOP OF THE HEAP

1. Chen Jie, "Aoyunhui Beijing yanzhenyidai, jin Jing xu chuju zhengming" [For the Olympics Beijing will be on guard, entering the capital will require presenting permits], *Jinghua shibao* [Beijing times], September 15, 2006.

2. Tan Lingzhi and Lu Mingzhong, "Dui feijiu wuzi huishou de guanli zhengce fenxi" [Analysis of waste material recycling sector management policies], *Zaisheng ziyuan yanjiu* [Renewable resources research] 27, no. 4 (2005): 9 (re: studies confirmed that Beijing's landfills had almost nothing worth recycling in them).

3. "Dalian: Dianfu chuantong de xin 'Polanr wang'" [Dalian: New junk kings overturn tradition"], CRRA, June 27, 2008. The word 差 might also be translated as "backward" here, as the implication is that what is "deficient" is sufficiently modern equipment and so forth. www.crra.org.cn/index.php?m=content&c=index&a=show1&catid=24&INAR_ID=12892.

4. R. Linzner and S. Salhofer, 896. Ralph Linzner and Stefan Salhofer, "Municipal Solid Waste Recycling and the Significance of [the] Informal Sector in Urban China," *Waste Management & Research* 32, no. 9 (2014).

5. Survey conducted by author and volunteers at Beijing Nature University, December 2010.

6. Benjamin Steuer, "Is China's Regulatory System of Urban Household Waste Collection Effective? An Evidence-Based Analysis of the Evolution of Formal Rules and Contravening Informal Practices," *Journal of Chinese Governance* 2, no.4 (2017): 411–36.

7. Xin Tong and Dongyan Tao, "The Rise and Fall of a 'Waste City,'" *Resource Conservation and Recycling* 107 (2016): 10–17. I have written a response quibbling with some

aspects of this article, but it was a groundbreaking piece, and I credit the authors for flagging this regulatory change as pivotal in the evolution of Beijing's recycling geography.

8. Wang Tongcai, interview with author, Tongzhou, March 23, 2008. Also confirmed by Kao Shi-yang, "The City Recycled: The Afterlives of Demolished Buildings in Post-War Beijing" (PhD diss., University of California, Berkeley, 2013).

9. Li Bin, interview with author, Dongxiaokou, Apr 2008.

10. There were about twenty-five to forty large (fifty-plus stall) independent scrap markets in Beijing, but I only ever heard of two that were owned by migrant recyclers, one in Dongxiaokou, the other in Tongzhou, owned by Wang Tongcai, a Gushi native who joined the CCP and had a high profile back at home as a pioneer investor and philanthropist.

11. Liu Jinsong, "Beijiing's Biggest Recycling Market to Be Demolished, an Environmentalist Raises Questions," *Economic Observer*, December 2, 2011.

12. For a rich, in-depth sociological analysis of the Dongxiaokou recycling community, see Feng Jia, "Migrant Livelihood and Business in Urban China: The Case of Henancun and Recycling in Beijing" (PhD diss., Michigan State University, 2016).

13. Hongbu Township Party secretary, interview with author, Hongbu, February 2008.

14. Gushi xian zhengfu, "Cong shuchu laodong li dao yinhui shengchan li: Gushi xian laodong jingji, huigui jingji fazhan qingkuang" [From sending out labor power to attracting production power: Gushi county's labor economy and the economic development returns], 2005.

15. Jean-Philippe Beja, Michel Bonnin, Feng Xiaoshuang, Tang Can, and Philip Liddell, "How Social Strata Come to Be Formed: Social Differentiation among Migrant Peasant of Henan Village in Peking, Part 2," *China Perspectives* 24 (1999): 47.

16. Hao Wang and Chunmei Wang, "Municipal Solid Waste Management in Beijing, Characteristics and Challenges," *Waste Management and Research* 31, no.1 (2013): 68–72 (MSW more than doubled); and Linzner and Salhofer (double to quadruple 1990s estimates).

17. Site visit, Norske Skog paper baling company, Daxing, May 28, 2008.

18. Li Ping and Du Xing, "Beijing Wu Jian Gongsi Wenan quan di 3,700 mu lajicheng zao zhiyi" [Beijing No. 5 Construction Company's acquisition of 3,700 mu for a garbage city raises questions], *Jingji guancha bao* [Economic observer], November 20, 2006.

19. *Wenan xian zhi* [Wenan county gazetteer], ed. Hebei sheng Wenan xian difangzhi bianji weiyuanhui (Beijing: Zhongguo shehui chubanshe, 1994), 228–35, 244.

20. Li Wanxin and Paul Higgins, "Controlling Local Environmental Performance: An Analysis of Three National Environmental Management Programs in the Context of Regional Disparities in China," *Journal of Contemporary China* 22, no. 81 (2013): 409–27.

21. Yang Shaohong, "'Feisuliao zhi du' shache" ["Waste plastic capital" halted], *Nanfang dushi bao* [Southern metropolis daily], July 7, 2011.

22. For more on the plastic recycling process and conditions in Wenan see Joshua Goldstein, "A Phyrric Victory," *Modern China* 43, no. 1 (2016): 3–35.

23. Plastic shredder mechanic, interview with author, Wenan, June 20, 2009.

24. Caizheng bu, guojia shuiwu zongju guanyu feijiu wuzi huishou jingying yewu youguan zengzhishui zhengce de tongzhi, caishui [2001] 78 hao [Ministry of Finance, National

Tax Bureau, notice regarding policy implementing VAT on recycling enterprises, finance tax (2001) no. 78], April 29, 2001.

25. Jin Yu and Wang Kala, "Hebei Wenan zhili jiusuliao jiagong, Beijing feisuliao huishou shou yingxiang" [Hebei's Wenan manages used-plastics processing, Beijing's waste plastic recyclers feel effects], *Xin jing bao* [Beijing news] August 15, 2011.

26. Zhou He, "Yiliao laji zhicheng shiyong qimin, zhiming shashou cheng yaoqianshu" [Medical waste made into food containers, turning a killer into a cash cow], *Jinghua shibao* [Beijing times], July 28, 2003.

27. "Hebei Wenan deng di you du shipindai liuxiang Jiang Zhe" [Poisoned food bags from Hebei's Wenan area flow to Jiangsu and Zhejiang], *Xinwen chen bao* [Shanghai observer], February 20, 2004.

28. Liu Juhua and Ge Subiao, "Yicixing canju zhiliang wenti jiexi feisuliao guanli ling ren you" [Analysis of disposable food container quality problems indicates management of waste plastics is worrisome], Xinhua wang [Xinhua net], November 5, 2005, http://news .xinhuanet.com/food/2005-11/05/content_3735758.htm.

29. Plastic stall boss, interview with author, Fengtai, June 2007; and Zhang Ying "Shenmi Hebei deng di feisuliao chanyelian; cunmin: 'ni dei wen shui mei de bing'" [The Hebei region's secret waste plastic processing chain; Villager: "You need to ask who isn't sick."], *Zhongguo qingnian bao* [China youth daily], June 24, 2015.

30. Clinic doctor in Wenan, interview with author, Wenan County, June 21, 2009.

31. Mr. Pang, (Wenan resident, former plastic processor, and area cab driver), interview with author, Wenan, March 14, 2008; Mr. Duan (recycled pellet shop owner), interview with author, Wenan, June 20, 2009; and Mr. He (shredder supply dealer), interview with author, Wenan, June 22, 2009.

32. "Wo xian zhaokai zaisheng suliao hangye zhili zhengdun xianchang hui" [Our county holds a plastic recycling industry rectification meeting], *Qingnian Wenan* [Wenan youth], June 15, 2005, www.youth-wa.com/news/view.asp?id=523.

33. Zhang Yongliang, "Rang nongcun wushui jin chang tuowu: Wenan jian nongcun wushui chulichang jishi" [Rural polluted water enters plant for decontamination: Report on the building of a rural water treatment plant in Wenan], Hebei wang [Hebei net], December 17, 2007, www.heb.chinanews.com/news/shfz/2007-12-13/19781.shtml.2007.

34. Hebei sheng huanjing baohu ting [Hebei Provincial Environmental Protection Office], "Wenan xian kaizhan nongcun huanjing zonghe zhengli, quanmian qidong zaisheng suliao hangye zhili zhuanxiang xingdong" [Wenan county initiates comprehensive rural environmental control, complete mobilization targeting recycled plastics enterprises], August 25, 2009.

35. Mr. Zhang, interview with author, June 20, 2009.

36. "Facts and Figures about Materials, Waste and Recycling," United States Environmental Protection Agency, www.epa.gov/facts-and-figures-about-materials-waste-and -recycling/national-overview-facts-and-figures-materials.

37. Evan Osnos, "Wastepaper Queen," *New Yorker*, March 30, 2009, www.newyorker .com/magazine/2009/03/30/wastepaper-queen.

38. Unless otherwise noted, trade volume statistics are based on the United Nations Commodity Trade Statistics Database at http://comtrade.un.org/db/.

39. Fan (ZEPIP manager), interview with author, Ziya, August 7, 2006.

40. Mr. Pang, interview with author, Wenan, June 28, 2008; and Duan interview, June 20, 2009.

41. Basel Action Network and Silicon Valley Toxics Coalition, "Exporting Harm: The High-Tech Trashing of Asia," 2002, http://svtc.org/wp-content/uploads/technotrash.pdf; and "Anfang Taizhou 'yanglaji' shichang dianluban jing neng lian jinzi" [Secret visit to Taizhou's "foreign trash" market, circuit boards can be turned to gold], *Beijing qingnian bao* [Beijing youth news], March 20, 2002.

42. Yvan Schulz, "Modern Waste: The Political Ecology of E-Scrap Recycling in China" (PhD diss., University of Neuchatel, 2018), 132–35.

43. See, for instance, the following import regulation that changed how imported electronics scrap was to be registered but made no mention of banning it. National Environmental Protection Bureau, "Guanyu jinkou di qi lei feiwu youguan wenti de tongzhi" [Notice on problems pertaining to import of no. 7 category wastes], January 26, 2000, http://210.73.66.144:4601/law?fn=chl324s820.txt.

44. "Xin Zhongguo 60 nian zaisheng jinshu gongye fazhan zhuangkuang ji tese jingyan zongjie" [Summing up 60 years of development and special characteristics of New China's metal recycling industry], *Zhong lü wang* [Aluminum net], February 12, 2011, http://news .cnal.com/industry/2011/02-12/1297476647213950.shtml.

45. Wang (ZEPIP manager), interview with author, Ziya, August 8, 2006.

46. Wang interview, August 8, 2006.

47. "Tianjinshi Ziya huanbao chanye yuan cheng guojia xunhuan jingji shidian yuanqu" [Tianjin's Ziya Environmental Protection Industry Park becomes a national circular economy pilot park], Tianjin gang wuliu xinxi wang [Tianjin port shipping news net], July 9, 2008.

48. Ziya enterprise manager, interview with author, March 14, 2008. If one was to ask what alternative there might have been to the ZEPIP as a way to handle this problem more equitably, rather than turning small recyclers into wage laborer, one possible solution would have been for the district to invest in a single enterprise to buy and process superfines from area processors. The dozens of shredders in ZEPIP were a huge waste of capacity.

49. Wang Jiwei, "Development Prospects of Non-ferrous Metal Scrap Recycling and Utilization," *China International Metal Recycling Forum* (2003): 341–43.

50. Zhang Xizhong, "Development Trend of China's Regenerated Copper Industry," *China International Metal Recycling Forum* (2003): 364–76.

51. "Suliaodai 4 tian hou jiang gaobie mianfei shidai" [In four days say goodbye to the time of free plastic bags], CRRA, May 27, 2008, www.crra.org.cn/index.php?m=content&c =index&a=show1&catid=24&INAR_ID=12602.

52. Sun Xiuyan, "Lüse Aoyun: Fa yu xin jian yu xing (Beijng jian hang chengnuo)" [Green Olympics: From heart to practice (Beijing fulfills promises)], *RMRB*, July 14, 2008.

53. UNEP, *Independent Environmental Assessment, Beijing 2008 Olympic Games*, 2009, 83, www.uncclearn.org/sites/default/files/inventory/unep36.pdf.

54. "Beijing zhong xiao xuexiao yao naru laji fenlei danwei" [Beijing elementary and middle schools want to be on the list of waste sorting work units], Beijing Yule Xinbao [Beijing entertainment news], October 23, 2007.

55. "Beijing Mentougou: Laji fenlei gai diao cufang shi xiguan" [Beijing Mentougou: Garbage sorting reforms rough habits], CRRA, December 11, 2007.

56. Chen Liwen, "Beijing tuidong laji fenlei shi duo nian, wei sha feili bu xiao xiaoguo bu hao?" [After over 10 years of Beijing pushing garbage sorting, why has the effort been so great and the results so small?], Zhongguo Huanjing Bao [China environment news], March 27, 2015.

57. "Beijng 1200 ge xiaoqu shidian qidong laji fenlei huodong" [An additional 1,200 Beijing communities launch trash sorting activities], Fazhi wanbao [Evening legal news], March 24, 2011, http://news.sina.com.cn/c/2011-03-24/125322173755.shtml.

58. Jingji ban xiaoshi [Economy half hour], "Beijing: 'Fen bu dong' de laji fenlei" [Beijing: "Inseparable" trash separation], CCTV, July 26, 2013, http://tv.cctv.com/2013/07/26/VIDE1374851158812695.shtml.

59. Ziran zhi you [Friends of Nature], 2012 nian Beijing laji fenlei shidian xiaoqu diaoyan baogao [Report on 2012 investigation of Beijing residential community trash separation pilot], 2013; and "Duo ge laji zhongzhuanzhan laji bei tongyi yasuo" [Most trash transfer stations compact all trash together], Xin Jing Bao [Beijing news], July 23, 2017.

60. Zhu Han, Zhao Renwei, Sun Renbin, and Tian Jianchuan, "Cong 'liuliang' dao 'huijia'—ting daibiao weiyuan shuoshou laji fenlei xianlutu" [From "aimless wandering" to "coming home"—listening to delegates describe the road map to garbage sorting], Xinhuawang [Xinhua net], March 8, 2017, www.xinhuanet.com/politics/2017lh/2017-03/08/c_1120593076.htm.

61. Liu Taiyuan, interview with author, Fengtai, July 26, 2009.

62. "Beijing shi Fushizhang Zhao Fengtong jiancha Aoyun changguan shenghuo laji ke huishou wu ziyuan liyong gongzuo luoshi qingkuang" [Beijing vice-mayor Zhao Fengtong inspects the garbage and recycling implementation at Olympic sports arenas], CRRA, July 28, 2008.

63. "Aoyun dui lüse chengruo, changguan laji ke huishou wu liyong gongzuo qidong" [A green Olympic promise fulfilled, venue trash recycling gets underway], Beijing Wanbao [Beijing evening news], July 24, 2008.

64. "Beijing shi Haidian qu shougou feipin dangtian yun zou"] [Same day removal of recycling in Beijing's Haidian District], Beijing Yule Xinbao [Beijing entertainment news], July 29, 2008.

65. "Beijing feipin huishou dui zhoumo jin shequ" [Beijing recycling teams will enter residential communities over the weekend], Beijing Wanbao [Beijing evening news], July 9, 2008.

66. "Beijing feipin huishou jin shequ caoyue 'jin men fei'" [Beijing recyclers entering communities are harassed for "entry fees"], Beijing Wanbao [Beijing evening news], July 15, 2008.

67. Beijing shi shangwu ju guanyu jin yi bu jia da feifa zaisheng ziyuan huishou zhandian (jisan shichang) qudi gongzuo lidu de tongzhi, Jingshang jiaozi [2007] di 80 hao [Beijing Commerce Bureau notice to further increase efforts to eliminate illegal recycling stands and markets, municipal commerce notice, no. 80], August 31, 2007.

68. Fu Zimei "Zhende fei guan bu ke ma?" [Is there really nothing to do but shut it down?], RMRB, June 28, 2004.

69. "Beijing shi zaisheng ziyuan huishou jiang she zhuanmen jisan changdi" [Beijing municipal plan for specialized resource recycling collection/processing centers], *Chengshi guanli yu keji* [City planning and technology] 8, no. 4 (2006): 183.

70. Beijing shi shangwu ju guanyu tuijin Beijing shi zaisheng ziyuan huishou tixi chanyehua fazhan shidian fangan de shishi yijian [Beijing Municipal Commerce Bureau recommendations on developing a model plan for the industrialization of Beijing's municipal recycling system], October 13, 2006.

71. Photos of these events and many others can be found at the Scaler website for this book. https://scalar.usc.edu/works/remains-of-the-everyday-kipple-yard/index.

72. Kao Shi-yang learned a great deal more than I about Li Bin's past and the murder case in his fieldwork; see "The City Recycled," chap. 3. Ironically, that Nanqijia site at one point made it onto the city's ever-changing list of permanent recycling sites, and though the township that controls the land is presently (as of fall 2019) trying to force it to close, Li Bin's wife holds an unprecedented fifty-year business license from the Municipal Commerce Bureau for the Nanqijia site.

73. Osnos, "Wastepaper Queen."

74. "Zhuangjia wuran juechan, baixing shangxin, zhengfu buguanbuwen" [Crops polluted to death, heartbroken people, government turns a blind eye], Tengsun shipin [Tencent video], September 1, 2011, https://v.qq.com/x/page/Zoo8oZD8ydi.html.

75. And possibly the easiest one to target. No study ever proved what kind of pollution was involved, and Wenan had many other large polluting industries, including metal plating factories.

76. Zhonggong Wenan xian wei, Wenan xian renmin zhengfu [Wenan Communist Party Committee, Wenan County People's Government], "Zhonggong Wenan xian wei wenjian, 22 hao" [Wenan Communist Party Committee document, no. 22], June 28, 2011.

77. Ran Ran, "Perverse incentive structures and policy implementation gap in China's local environmental politics," *Journal of Environmental Policy and Planning* 15, no. 1 (2013): 17–39; and Alex L. Wang "The Search for Sustainable Legitimacy: Environmental Law and Bureaucracy in China," *Harvard Environmental Law Review* 37, no. 2 (2013): 365–440.

78. Zhonggong Daliuzhen zhen weiyuanhui, Daliuzhen zhen renmin zhengfu [Daliuzhen Town Communist Party Committee, Daliuzhen Town People's Government], "Gao zhi shu" [Notification], July 7, 2011.

79. Xiao Mei and Shen Yuanyuan, "Lüse chanye de shengmingli, Wenan Dongdu Zaisheng Ziyuan Huanbao Chanye Yuan fazhan xunli" [The vitality of green industry: A tour of Wenan Dongdu Recycling Resources Environmental Protection Industrial Park], *Zhongguo jianshe bao* [China construction news], June 3, 2011.

80. Li and Du, "Beijing Wu Jian Gongsi Wenan quan di 3,700 mu lajicheng zao zhiyi."

81. "Wenan suliao shichang zhengdun" [Rectification of Wenan's plastic market], Baidu, posted July 10, 2011, http://zhidao.baidu.com/question/289322759.html.

82. Jin and Wang, "Hebei Wenan zhili jiusuliao jiagong.".

83. Mr. X, interview with author, Beijing, June 8, 2013.

84. Zhang Ying, "'You Need to Ask Who Isn't Sick.'"

85. "Baoding feisuliaodui qihuo, yangzhichang 500 duo zhi ji bei huohuo xunsi" [Baoding: Waste plastics catch fire, over 500 birds at one chicken farm killed by smoke], *Baoding*

wanbao [Baoding evening news], June 11, 2014, http://hebei.sina.com.cn/news/s/2014-06-11 /101497330.html.

86. "Feijiu suliao zaisheng wangguo" [The kingdom of waste plastic recycling], November 3, 2009, http://info.plas.hc360.com/2009/11/03151281426-3.shtml.

87. Yvan Schulz, "Towards a New Waste Regime? Critical Reflections on China's Shifting Market for High-Tech Discards," *China Perspectives* 3 (2015): 43–50.

88. In addition to works already mentioned (Benjamin Van Rooij, Ran Ran, Alex Wang), see also Genia Kostka, "Environmental Protection Bureau Leadership at the Provincial Level in China: Examining Diverging Career Backgrounds and Appointment Patterns," *Journal of Environmental Policy and Planning* 15, no. 1 (2013): 41–63; and Maria Edin, "State Capacity and Local Agent Control in China: CCP Cadre Management from a Township Perspective," *China Quarterly* 173 (2003): 33–52.

89. WASTE and Skat, "Economic Aspects of Informal Sector Activities in Solid Waste Management," 2007.

8. NO LONGER THE WORLD'S GARBAGE DUMP!

1. Livia Albeck-Ripka, "Your Recycling Gets Recycled, Right? Maybe, or Maybe Not," *New York Times*, May 29, 2018, www.nytimes.com/2018/05/29/climate/recycling-landfills -plastic-papers.html.

2. In the summer of 2019 Indonesia returned 148 containers of plastic waste to the United States; Cambodia declared it would return 83 containers to Canada and the United States; and Malaysia worked throughout 2019 to return hundreds of containers to their ports of origin. A. Ananthalakshmi, "Malaysia Works to Clear Hundreds of Plastic Waste Shipments at Ports," Reuters, October 17, 2019, www.reuters.com/article/us-malaysia -waste-plastic/malaysia-working-to-clear-hundreds-of-plastic-waste-shipments-at-ports -officials-idUSKBN1WW19C#:~:text=KUALA%20LUMPUR%20(Reuters)%20%2D %20Malaysia,country%20for%20months%2C%20officials%20say.

3. ISRI and the US delegation to the WTO have both raised the complaint that China's ban does not distinguish between waste and resource. Colin Staub, "China Reiterates Total Ban and Tries to Define 'Solid Waste,'" *RR*, April 12, 2019.

4. Muyu Xu and David Stanway, "China Plans to Cut Waste Imports to Zero by Next Year," Reuters, March 27, 2019, www.businessinsider.com/china-plans-to-cut-waste -imports-to-zero-by-next-year-official-2019-3.

5. Colin Staub, "China Continues to Decrease Permits for Imported Paper," *RR*, January 7, 2020.

6. "Xi Jinping guanxin de zhe liu jian shi" [Six things Xi Jinping cares about], Xinhuawang [Xinhua net], March 8, 2017, www.xinhuanet.com//video/2017-03/08/c_129504253.htm.

7. Liu Jianguo, "Laji fenlei yu jinzhi yang laji ru jing" [Garbage sorting and the ban on "foreign trash" entering our country], *Zhongguo jingji baogao* [China economy report], June 29, 2018, www.chinacace.org/news/view?id=9420.

8. Beijing shi renmin zhengfu bangongting, Beijing shi xinzeng chanye de jingzhi he Xianzhi mulu (yi) [Beijing People's Government Office, Beijing municipal catalog of enterprises prohibited and limited from expansion], 2015.

9. See Sigrid Schmalzer, "The Global Comrades of Mr. Science and Mr. Democracy," forthcoming in *East Asian Science, Technology, and Society*.

10. Heidi Wang-Kaeding, "What Does Xi Jinping's New Phrase 'Ecological Civilization' Mean?," *Diplomat*, March 6, 2018, https://thediplomat.com/2018/03/what-does-xi-jinpings-new-phrase-ecological-civilization-mean/.

11. Kiki Zhao, "China's Environmental Woes, in Films That Go Viral, Then Vanish," *New York Times*, April 28 2017.

12. "Duihua: 'Yang suliao' laji rang bufen heliu zhongdu wuran" [Dialogue: "Foreign plastic" garbage seriously pollutes some rivers], *Xin Jing Bao* [Beijing news], December 22, 2014.

13. Steve Toloken, "China Getting Tough on Recycling Imports," *Plastic News*, November 19, 2012.

14. Steve Toloken, "China's Green Fence Makes Unprecedented Cuts in Recycled Plastic Imports," *Plastic News*, May 19, 2013.

15. Patty Moore and Sally Houghton, "An Inside Look at Operation Green Fence," *RR*, October 18, 2013.

16. "Two-Month Crackdown Relating to China's Plastic Scrap Imports," Bureau of International Recycling, November 5, 2015, www.bir.org/news-press/latest-news/two-month-crackdown-relating-to-chinas-plastic-scrap-imports/.

17. "Xi Demands Enhanced Supervision over Reform Efforts," CCTV.com English, April 18, 2017, http://english.cctv.com/2017/04/18/ARTINHuQg6O5QNBAvLXALW8P170418.shtml (emphasis added).

18. Colin Staub, "Chinese Reform Committee Considers Restricting Imports," *RR*, April 25, 2017.

19. Colin Staub, "China Continues to Constrain Plastic Imports," *RR*, February 7, 2018.

20. "Exit the Dragon: A Chinese Ban on Rubbish Imports Is Shaking Up the Global Junk Trade," *Economist*, September 29, 2018.

21. "What Chinese Import Policies Mean for All 50 States," Waste Dive, www.wastedive.com/news/what-chinese-import-policies-mean-for-all-50-states/510751/. This website was still being updated as of November 2019 and aggregates news from every state using hyperlinks.

22. Adam Liebman, "No More of Your Junk," *New Internationalist*, December 5, 2018.

23. Steve Toloken, "Execs Say Plastic Recycling Is at a 'Tipping Point,'" *Plastic News*, November 21, 2018.

24. Most recently China has stated that it will begin to impose strict inspections on imported recycled resin pellet. Colin Staub, "Another Potential Export Disruption on the Horizon," *RR*, January 8, 2020.

25. Colin Staub, "Where Exports Displaced from China Are Finding a Home," *RR*, January 18, 2018.

26. Colin Staub, "Why Vietnam Is Shutting Out Scrap Plastic," *RR*, May 31, 2018. It has not, in fact, become permanent, and many Southeast Asian countries are trying to figure out precisely how to configure their policies around scrap imports because, of course, not all scrap plastic and paper scrap processing is necessarily horribly polluting and exploitative.

27. Colin Staub, "Exports to Thailand Collapse after Ban," *RR*, September 6, 2018.

28. "Jingji bange xiaoshi: Yang laji jieduan le yihou [The economy half-hour: After foreign garbage is cut off], CCTV, January 22, 2018, http://tv.cntv.cn/video/C16624/c8eb5734644040268a6a491bc5111a7b.

29. "Jingji bange xiaoshi: Hebei Wenan; Chengse yujing li de weigui shengchan" [The economy half-hour: Hebei Wenan; orange alert from illegal production], CCTV, January 23, 2018, https://v.qq.com/x/page/x05385in4op.html.

30. Author's field notes, February 2018.

31. "Duterte zongtong shuo: Lai Feilubin chuli fei suliao ba, daliang de ziyuan dengdai zhe Zhongguo qiyejia" [President Duterte says, "Come to the Philippines to process your plastic scrap, a huge quantity of materials awaits Chinese entrepreneurs!"], November 18, 2017, www.sohu.com/a/205097949_270404 (italicized text is in red typeface in original).

32. Fan Fan, "Fei suliao ye jie qing zilu, zhe shi Dongnanya fazhan de changyuan zhi ji" [Waste plastic sector, please be self-disciplined, this is the long-term development plan for SE Asia!], December 7, 2017, https://freewechat.com/a/MjM5MTM5NjM4NA==/2662315321/1.

33. "Malaixiya fei suliao gongchang bei chafeng, yejie zhiqing renshi gei chu zhe 3 dian shouming" [Malaysia waste plastic factories seized; industry insider provides three clarifications], Fei suliao xin guancha [Waste plastic observer], October 10, 2018, https://m.huanbao-world.com/view.php?aid=48329.

34. GAIA, Discarded: Communities on the Frontlines of the Global Plastic Crisis, April 2019, https://wastetradestories.org/wp-content/uploads/2019/04/Discarded-Report-April-22.pdf.

35. Charlotte Middlehurst, "Q&A: China's Waste Ban Debate Is 'Misinformed' and 'One-Dimensional,'" China Dialogue, August 24, 2018, https://chinadialogue.net/article/show/single/en/10789-Q-A-China-s-waste-ban-debate-is-misinformed-and-one-dimensional-.

36. Frank Esposito, "North American Prices for PE, PP Tumble" Plastic News, November 29, 2018.

37. European Commission, "Proposal for a Directive of the European Parliament and the Council on the Reduction of the Impact of Certain Plastic Products on the Environment," May 28, 2018.

38. NDRC and MEE, "Guanyu jinyibu jiaqiang suliao wuran zhili de yijian" [Suggestions for further strengthening the control of plastic pollution], January 16, 2020.

39. Liu Jianguo, "Laji fenlei yu jingzhi 'yang laji' ru jing" [Trash sorting and banning "foreign garbage"], Zhongguo xunhuan jingji xiehui [China Association of Circular Economy], June 29, 2018, www.chinacace.org/news/view?id=9420.

40. Liu, "Laji fenlei yu jingzhi 'yang laji' ru jing."

41. Street recycling collectors, interviews with author, Beijing, February 2018.

42. Guojia fazhan gaige wei [National Development and Reform Commission], "Shisan wu quanguo chengzhen shenghuo laji wuhaihua chuli sheshi jianshe guihua" [Thirteenth Five-year plan national urban residential solid harmless waste treatment facilities construction plan], December 2016.

43. Liu Zhe, "Laji fenshao: Shisan wu hangye zhizhu" [Trash incineration: A pillar industry of the Thirteenth Five-Year Plan], Zhongguo Jianshe bao [China construction news], May 29, 2015.

44. Liu Jianguo, "'Jifen jiangli' guanyong ma? 'Xian fen hou hun' zenme po? Fenlei ji neng jian liang? Shimin ruhe canyu?" ['Reward points' management? Breaking through the 'First sort, then mixed' problem? Will sorting really reduce trash? How can urbanites contribute?], *Huanjing Pinglun* [Environmental commentary], August 3, 2018, https://mp.weixin.qq.com/s/onQ7FtfI5wQgb7uSDEb5gQ (emphasis in original).

45. Guowuyuan bangongting [State Council Office], "Guanyu zhuanfa guojia fazhan gaige wei zhufang chengxiang jianshe bu shenghuo laji fenlei shidu shishi fang'an de tongzhi" [Notice forwarded to NDRC regarding domestic waste classification system implementaiton by the Ministry of Housing and Urban-Rural Development], March 18, 2017.

46. "Jiu yue 1 zhou quanguo gong fabu 62 ge laji fenlei fuwu caigou gonggao" [First week of September sees 62 waste sorting service procurement announcements], *Huanjing Sinan* [Environmental compass], September 9, 2018, https://huanbao.bjx.com.cn/news/20180909/926628.shtml.

47. Xu Xiao, "Laji chuli qiye ying lai xin jiyu" [New opportunities for waste treatment companies], *Gongren Ribao* [Workers' daily], January 14, 2020.

48. I urge readers interested in these issues to seek out these authors and their writings or blogs. Most recently, Adam Minter's *Secondhand* (New York: Bloomsbury, 2019) presents a compelling argument about the distorted representations of e-waste workers in Ghana and Nigeria.

49. Xin Tong, Reid Leifset, and Thomas Lindhquist, "Extended Producer Responsibility in China: Where Is 'Best Practice?,'" *Journal of Industrial Ecology* 8, no. 4 (2005): 6–9; and Chen Liwen, "E-Waste Recycling in Beijing and the Impact of China's WEEE Directive: Competition or Collaboration Between Informal Recyclers and Authorized Recycling Enterprises" (master's thesis, Memorial University of Newfoundland, 2019).

50. Basel Action Network and Silicon Valley Toxics Coalition, *Exporting Harm: The High-Tech Trashing of Asia*, 2002, http://svtc.org/wp-content/uploads/technotrash.pdf. A thoughtful reader of this quote might immediately wonder, on seeing the claim that a so-called waste computer has a negative value, "To what country is the author referring?" Surely such valuations differ in different markets. Such simplistic universalizing claims about the value of "wastes" are common in writings on plastic recycling also. One would surely be skeptical of any analysis that claimed that a good/commodity, say a tomato, had a universal price that was the same everywhere in the world under all market conditions all the time, yet such claims about so-called wastes are often accepted without question.

51. Lepawsky, *Reassembling Rubbish: Worlding Electronic Waste* (Cambridge, MA: MIT Press, 2018). 30–35; and Josh Lepawsky, "E-Waste: Mapping a Controversy," *Reassembling Rubbish* (blog), https://scalar.usc.edu/works/reassembling-rubbish/e-waste-mapping-a-controversy?path=the-rubbish-bin.

52. Estimates comes from Chen, *E-Waste Recycling in Beijing*. In addition, many items that cannot be repaired can be harvested for components that have resale value and can be used to repair other devices.

53. J. Huisman et al., *Countering WEEE Illegal Trade (CWIT) Summary Report, Market Assessment, Legal Analysis, Crime Analysis and Recommendations Roadmap* (Lyon: Interpol, WEEEForum, UNICRI, UNU-IAS, 2015), 61.

54. I am not arguing that the destruction of the health and environment of poorer nations and communities caused by the informal waste trades is a minor problem to be tolerated, but that the Basel Convention's approach, specifically in relation to DEEE, is misguided. I believe working with stakeholders in developing countries to provided targeted waste management funded in part or whole by OEMs would be a better approach. Nor do I wish to impugn the environmental NGOs and activists that have worked so hard exposing the toxic damage caused by the IT sector and seeking to find a just solution; I simply believe the dominant analysis and policy approach has been problematic.

55. Chen, *E-Waste Recycling in Beijing*.

56. Yvan Schulz, "Towards a New Waste Regime? Critical Reflections on China's Shifting Market for High-Tech Discards," *China Perspectives* 3 (2015): 45.

57. Chen, *E-Waste Recycling in Beijing*; and "Feijiu dianqi chuli jijin chi 'duanchui' quekou kuoda jidai xinfangxiang"[E-waste treatment fund pool is dried up and urgently needs new direction], June 1, 2018, https://tech.huanqiu.com/article/9CaKrnK8VOA.

58. Wang Feng, "Keji + gongyi: Shenzhen tansuo 'hulianwang + laji fenlei' quanmin canyu xin lujing" [Science and technology + public welfare: Shenzhen explores new path for national participation in "internet + waste classification"], March 29, 2018, www.xinhuanet.com/2018-03/29/c_1122610280.htm.

59. In popular media the phrase *liang wang ronghe* (merging two networks—the policy about merging garbage and recycling bureaucracies) has frequently been mixed up with O2O (using apps to facilitate recycling) to such an extent that most people think *liang wang ronghe* is O2O.

60. An Ye, "Xiao Huang Gou jin shequ, zhineng laji fenlei de linglie tansuo" [Small Yellow Dog enters neihgborhoods, an alternative exploration of smart waste sorting], Huanbao wang [Environmental protection network], August 24, 2018, https://ecep.ofweek.com/2018-08/ART-93011-8420-30259965.html.

61. "INCOM Group signs plastic waste commitment," *China Daily*, November 12, 2018, www.chinadaily.com.cn/regional/bda/2018-11/12/content_37244273.htm.

62. Contrast this arrangement with the typical one made with informal collectors, who pay residential communities around 1,000 yuan monthly for the right to collect scrap on their grounds.

63. Chen, *E-Waste Recycling in Beijing*, 131–42.

64. Ni Yunqing, "Zhineng laji fenlei huishou shoufeng, Xiao Huang Gou huo 10.5 yi yuan touzi" [Smart trash sorting rakes it in; Little Yellow Dog wins 1.05 billion yuan investment], *21 shiji jingji bao* [21st century economic news], June 21, 2018, www.21jingji.com/2018/6-21/yOMDEzODFfMTQzNjgyOQ.html.

65. Liu Jing, "Fenlei huishou zaisheng ziyuan 'Xiao Huang Gou' jin shequ saoma shou laji" [Recycling sorting renews resources, Little Yellow Dog enters communities scan and collect trash], *Beijing qingnian bao* [Beijiing youth daily], November 28, 2018, http://bj.people.com.cn/n2/2018/1128/c82840-32339235.html.

66. Chen Yongle, "Laji fenlei huishou ji Xiao Huang Gou gongsi binlin pochan yidu rongzi chao 10 yi" [Garbage sorting machine company Little Yellow Dog that once raised 1 billion on verge of bankruptcy], *Sina Finance*, August 21, 2019.

67. In fact there is as yet no national policy on what the categories should be or even if four is the magic number, but almost every large city engaged in the merge has chosen to create more or less the same four categories, though whether to use the term *wet* or *organic* waste has been hotly debated.

68. Zhang Hengxing, "Laji fenlie bankuai zhang ting chao: laji fenlei gainian na jia qiang? [The trash sorting sector at peak tide: Whose approach to trash sorting is the strongest?], *Sina Finance*, June 20, 2019, https://finance.sina.com.cn/stock/t/2019-06-20/doc -ihytcerk8232481.shtml.

69. Zhang Xueqing, "Beijing jinnian chaungjian 84 ge laji fenlei shifan qu" [This year Beijing created 84 model garbage sorting communities], *Zhongguo huanjing bao* [China environment news], November 1, 2018, http://env.people.com.cn/n1/2018/1101/c1010 -30375610.html.

70, Zhang Rui, "Laji fenlei you duoshao wuqu he kunnan?" [Trash sorting faces how many mistakes and difficulties?], Renmin wang [People's net], November 1, 2018, http:// env.people.com. cn/n1/2018/1101/c1010-30375630.html.

71. "Shanghai begins enforcing 'Strictest trash separation': Max fine 200 yuan for sorting incorrectly," China News web, July 1, 2019, http://www.xinhuanet.com/politics/2019 -07/01/c_1124691464.htm.

72. Liu Lin, Shi Yue, Zhang Xue, and Wang Shufei, "Laji fenei shuang cheng ji: Beijing Shanghai" [Trash sorting diary of two cities, Beijing, Shanghai], *Beijing wanbao* [Beijing evening news], July 23, 2019, www.chinanews.com/sh/2019/07-23/8904220.shtml.

73. Tian Hong, "Da Jiangdong: Zan Shanghai, laji fenlei da biao jiu cheng! Ruhe 'fen' de geng hao?" [Da Jiangdong: Praise Shanghai, 90 percent of garbage sorting meets standards! How to "sort" even better?], Renmin wang [People.cn], January 19, 2020.

74. Wu Di, "2021 nian Shanghai laji fenlei zhiyuanzhe lizheng dadao 100 wan ren" [Shanghai will strive to reach 1 million garbage sorting volunteers by 2021], *Shangguan xinwen* [Shanghai observer], December 5, 2019.

75. Xu, "Laji chuli qiye ying lai xin jiyu."

76. Jia Yuankun, "Laji fenjian gong de xinnian yuanwang: Qing bu yao zai ba sui boli he putong laji fang zai yiqi" [Trash sorting workers' New Year's wish: Please stop putting broken glass in together with regular garbage], Xinhua wang, January 1, 2020, www.xinhuanet .com/fortune/2020-01/10/c_1125447533.htm.

77. Elizabeth Balkan, "The Dirty Truth about China's Incinerators," *China Dialogue*, April 7, 2012, www.chinadialogue.net/article/5024-Dirty-truth-about-China-s-incinerators; and Andreea Leonte, "China Is Burning Away Its Ecological Future," *Foreign Policy*, March 26, 2019. Some put the number at closer to 590,000 than 440,000 because in fact a vast number of incinerators in China are operating over capacity—which also means that they are not operating within design-based safety standards.

78. Mao Da, "Quxiao laji fenshao cuowu butie, beihou de daoli xiaoxuesheng dou dong" [End the misguided subsidy for trash incineration; even elementary school children can all understand the logic], *Dongxi gushi* [East/west (stuff) stories], October 29, 2019, https://mp.weixin.qq.com/s/GHCa7-iTqaaslN7TwZH68w.

79. Fieldwork with informants who must remain anonymous.

80. Amy Zhang, "Rational Resistance: Homeowner Contention against Waste Incineration in Guangzhou," *China Perspectives* 2 (2014): 52.

81. Nature University, "Waste Incineration, a Cruel Act to the Environment in China: Report of Investigating 10 Incinerators under Everbright International" (unpublished manuscript, 2015).

82. Qie Jianrong, "Huanbao zuzhi diaocha: 27 zuo laji fenshaochang 25 tian chao pai 2533 ci" [Environmental protection organizations survey: 27 incinerators over 25 days exceed regulatory limits 2,533 times"], *Fazhi Ribao* [Legal system daily], January 11, 2017. Researchers tried to get data on ninety-nine plants that had made a transparency pledge, but only twenty-seven cooperated by providing data.

83. Michael Standaert, "As China Pushes Waste to Energy Incinerators, Protests Are Mounting," *Yale Environment 360*, April 20, 2017, https://e360.yale.edu/features/as-china -pushes-waste-to-energy-incinerators-protests-are-mounting.

84. Rob Schmitz, "The Burning Problem of China's Garbage," National Public Radio, February 2, 2017, www.npr.org/sections/parallels/2017/02/20/515814016/the-burning -problem-of-chinas-garbage#:~:text=According%20to%20a%20World%20Bank,in %20profits%20than%20clean%20air.

85. Mao, "Quxiao laji fenshao cuowu butie."

86. Wang Chen, "Can China's Waste Incinerators Appease Local Opposition?," *China Dialogue*, January 13, 2020, https://chinadialogue.net/article/show/single/en/11777-Can -China-s-waste-incinerators-appease-local-opposition-.

87. Chen Xihan, "Shui lai qudai 'Xiao huang gou' [Who will replace "Little Yellow Dog"], *Shangguan xinwen* [Shanghai observer], October 15, 2019.

88. Tang Liwei, "Shanghai zaisheng ziyuan huishou qudao xitong guifan polan wang zhuanbian wei zhenggui jun" [Shanghai renewable resource recycling collection system regulates junk kings transforming them into regular army], *Sina Shanghai*, July 5, 2019, http://sh.sina.com.cn/news/m/2019-07-05/detail-ihytcerm1436781.shtml.

89. Adam Liebman and Goeun Lee, "Garbage as Value and Sorting as Labor in China's New Waste Policy," *Made in China Journal*, December 12, 2019; and Yu Qin and Xiang Huilian, "Shihuang jianghu xingshuai shi: Beijing ceng zuiduo you 17 wan shihuangzhe" [The history of the rise and fall of a wasteland: Beijing at its peak once had over 170,000 scavengers], *Caijing zazhi* [Finance], September 13, 2019.

90. "Rang laji fenlei chengwei xin shishang" [Setting a new fashion for trash sorting], *RMRB*, March 27 2019. Nanqijia market, run by Li Bin's wife, is also still operating, though its situation is extremely complex; for a more detailed look at this and developments as the merge progresses, see Scalar https://scalar.usc.edu/works/remains-of-the-everyday-kipple -yard/.

91. Ministry of Commerce, Beijing shi xinzeng chanye de jinzhi he Xianzhi mulu [Catalog of enterprises banned and restricted from new construction in Beijing], 2013.

92. Yu and Xiang, "Shihuang jianghu xingshuai shi." Old-hand migrant recyclers claim there are still a few very well-hidden, illegal recycling stalls right in the center of the city, under the government's nose, but I never saw these sites.

93. For example, Beijing gaosuqiao xia laji chuli hei wodian bei duan, 8 ren bei xingju [An illegal nest of garbage sorting under a Beijing freeway overpass is wiped out, 8 persons

arrested], *Fazhi ribao* [Legal daily], June 20, 2019. The report makes no claim any of the goods were stolen and does not specify what laws the suspects involved allegedly broke, aside from not registering as a business and conducting their scrap sorting under an overpass.

94. Yu and Xiang, "Shihuang jianghu xingshuai shi."

95. Yvan Schulz and Anna Lora-Wainwright, "In the Name of Circularity: Environmental Improvement and Business Slowdown in a Chinese Recycling Hub," *Worldwide Waste: Journal of Interdisciplinary Studies* 2, no. 1 (2019): 1–13.

INDEX

administrative structures *(tiaokuai)*, policy failures and, 220–22. *See also* specific organization names.

agriculture: chemical fertilizers, increased use of, 87–88; collectivization of, Socialist High Tide, 103; loss of farm fields to trash dumps, 87, 144, 193, 194, 195; proximity of farms to urban areas, 36, 43, 89; seasonal changes, night soil and, 73, 80; standardization, Mao era (1949–80), 111; suburban farming, Reform era (1980–present), 157–58; waste collection reforms, increase in rural dumps and, 87–88; wet (kitchen) waste, uses of, 250. *See also* night soil collection.

All-China Federation of Supply and Marketing Cooperatives (SMC), 15, 93; night soil reform (Mao era 1949–80), 73; recycling company reorganization, Reform era (1980–present), 185–86; scrap collection, BRC regulation of (Mao era, 1960–80), 134–39; scrap collection, BSC standardization of, 108–12; scrap collection, Reform era (1980–present), 163–64; state control of scrap trade (Mao era 1949–80), 96–101, 103–7; timeline of events, 265–67

Altehenger, Jennifer, 144–49, 146*tab*, 147*tab*

America Chung Nam, 202

Animal Products Company, 114

antique shops *(guwan pu)*, 53, 57

archival documents, 55

ash: cinder bricks, problems with, 80; cinder disposal, Mao era (1949–80) reforms, 73, 78–82, 88, 89, 105; coal balls and beehive coal briquettes, 78; copper scrap in, 103; decline in waste stream, 146, 156; management of, Republican era (1911–49), 26, 30, 31, 34, 43, 271n1; from waste-to-energy (WtE) incinerators, 252

Association of Southeast Asian Nations (ASEAN): scrap imports relocated to member countries, 231, 233–34

Asuwei, 251

"away," fantasy of, 89, 279–80n63

backhaul, 202–3

Backyard Steel Furnace, 115–16

Baizhifang (White Paper Workshop), 56

Bajia, 171

Bajia recycling enclave, 190*map*

Banana Peel, 244, 245–46

Ban + Merge policies: Ban, 228–36; e-waste and, 240–44; incineration, 250–53; informal recycling, future direction for, 260*fig*, 262–63; mandatory trash sorting 246–50, 248*fig*; Merge, 234–57; online-to-offline (O$_2$O) systems, 244–46; overview of, 224–26, 256–57; recycling recriminalized, 253–56

309